Dietrich Icon

GERD GEMÜNDEN
and MARY R. DESJARDINS, *editors*

Duke University Press Durham and London 2007

Printed in the United States of America
on acid-free paper ∞
Designed by C. H. Westmoreland
Typeset in Adobe Minion with Musee display
by Tseng Information Systems, Inc.
Library of Congress Cataloging-in-Publication Data
appear on the last printed page of this book.
Duke University Press gratefully acknowledges
the support of Dartmouth College, which provided
funds toward the production of this book.

CONTENTS

ACKNOWLEDGMENTS

The international conference "Marlene at 100," out of which this book developed, was made possible by the financial support of the Departments of German Studies and Film and Television Studies at Dartmouth, the John Sloan Dickey Center for International Understanding, the Leslie Center for the Humanities, and the German Academic Exchange Service (DAAD), as well as the support of Provost Barry Scherr, chief administrator for collaborative projects, and Jamshed J. Bharucha, then dean of the faculty.

Special thanks go to the German Studies Department administrators: Stephanie Taylor expertly handled the budget, while Karen Petek helped prepare many of the illustrations for print. Victoria (Vicky) Hoelzer-Maddox efficiently copyedited the complete first draft of the volume. Werner Sudendorf and Silke Ronneburg, at the Marlene Dietrich Collection of the Filmmuseum Berlin, assisted with locating stills and other materials and were a tremendous resource for all kinds of questions on the life and career of Marlene Dietrich. Peter Riva, Marlene Dietrich's grandson, generously gave us permission to use images. Barbara Hall and Jenny Romero of the Special Collections Department of the Margaret Herrick Library, Academy of Motion Picture Arts and Sciences, once again pulled off some last minute miracles, and we are grateful for their efforts. At Duke University Press, our editor Ken Wissoker supported the project from the beginning, while Courtney Berger, Pam Morrison, and Maura High smoothly guided the copyediting process. We are grateful to Duke's two anonymous readers for their criticism and suggestions.

We like to dedicate this book to the memory of our close friend and colleague Susanne Zantop, who was involved in the planning stages of the conference and whom a cruel death prevented from enjoying the fruits of her labor.

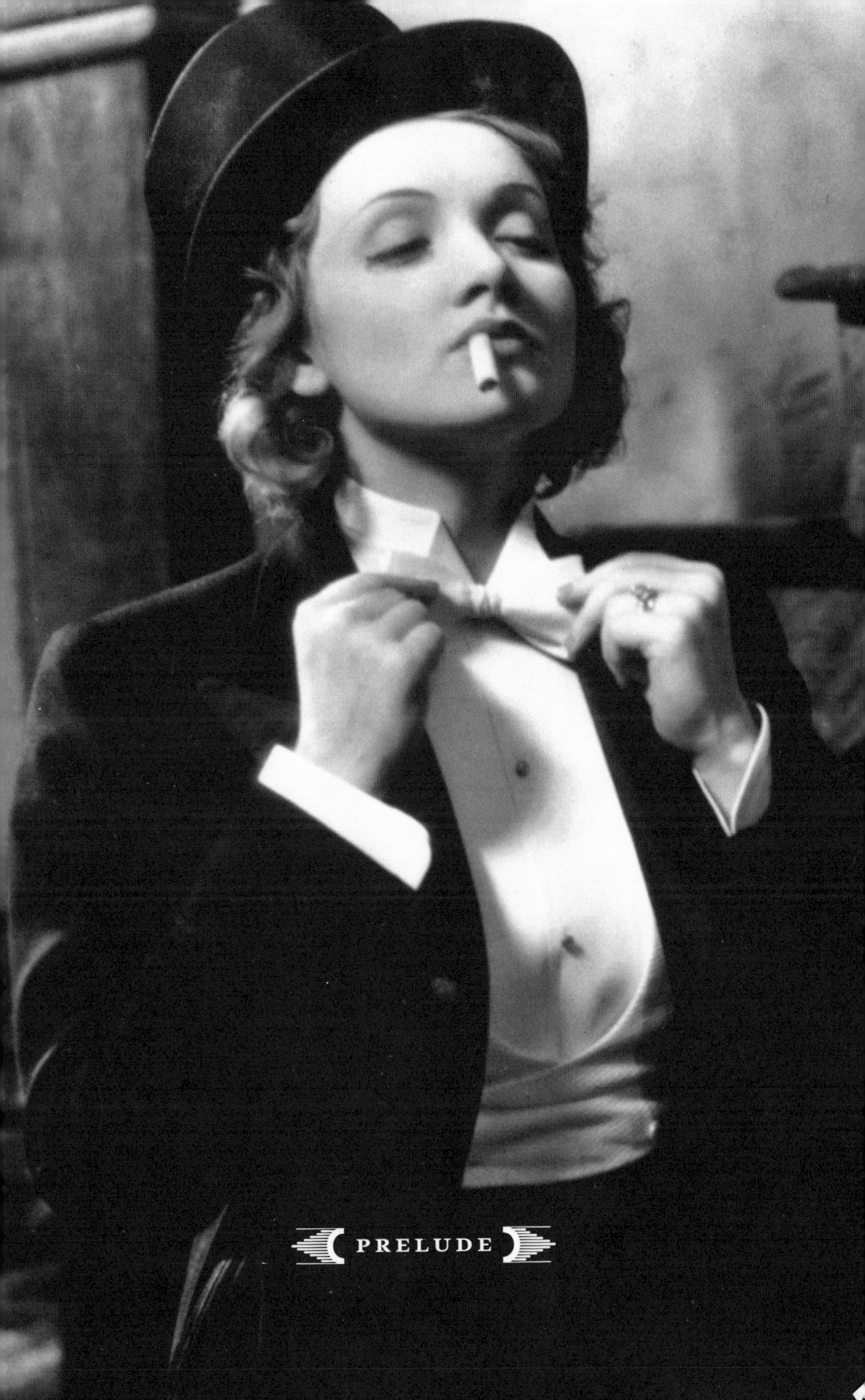

PRELUDE

Filmmuseum Berlin—Marlene Dietrich Collection Berlin.

MARY R. DESJARDINS *and* GERD GEMÜNDEN

Introduction

Marlene Dietrich's Appropriations

ON 16 MAY 2002, Marlene Dietrich was named an honorary citizen of Berlin in a celebration held in City Hall. Her grandson, Peter Riva, received a certificate of honor from Walter Momper, president of the Berlin Parliament, and in his laudatio the city mayor Klaus Wowereit expressed his pride about the achievements of Berlin's most famous native daughter. But the mayor also reminded his audience of the difficult relationship between Berliners and Dietrich, who had faced suspicion and hatred in this city and elsewhere in Germany after World War II, most visibly when her 1960 concert tour was picketed. As many in the audience knew, the efforts to make her an honorary citizen of Berlin dated as far back as 1991, and for a good part of the 1990s the city was involved in an unsuccessful and ultimately publicly embarrassing struggle to name a street after her in her native district of Schöneberg. Even her funeral in Berlin, ten years prior to the event in City Hall, was an occasion for controversy, when what had been planned as a celebration of homecoming became once again the target of some Berliners' long-standing resentments toward "the traitor" (see Koch, "Exorcised"). Honoring Dietrich in 2002 was thus for Berlin's politicians a much belated act of restitution, the final stage of a slow process of rapprochement that was, in Wowereit's words, "not without pain and embarrassment."[1]

The process of reconciliation between Dietrich and "her" Berlin(ers) is part of a long and drawn-out love-hate relationship between the diva and the Germans that began with her rise to fame in 1930 and extends into the present. Yet the struggle over claiming and disclaiming Dietrich as part of Berlin and Germany's cultural heritage partakes in strategies of appropriation in which Dietrich has to be seen not only as the object of cultural capital but also as an agent. For the appropriation of most diverse styles, fashions, and personas was, in fact, a trademark of Dietrich's career, and central to the on-screen and offscreen image that she and others designed for her. These styles of dress, behavior, and artistic performance might be best described in terms of the transformations, masquerading, and perhaps most of all, mobility, they suggested—mobility among high and low cultures; among heterosexual, bisexual, and homosexual identities; among masculine and feminine gender identities; among European and American cultures. Although many others in the 1920s, especially those in the arts and entertainment fields, also embraced a playful attitude toward identity construction, Dietrich's masquerades and transformations were enacted with discipline and wit and were conceptualized as part of a plan to further her ambitions. As Joseph Garncarz shows in his essay in this volume, Dietrich had carefully modeled her Weimar screen roles on the Swedish Greta Garbo's Hollywood image long before Josef von Sternberg's "discovery" of her, as part of a carefully planned strategy to attract the attention of American film studios. She would later discard the Garbo imitation (although many, from studio promotion men to lesbian fans, continued to link the two stars in a variety of ways) and, in a collaboration with film director von Sternberg, created a persona seemingly defined by a cool, witty self-reflexive knowledge of the masquerades that constitute identity.

The result of Dietrich's talent for creative appropriation, invention, and reinvention is an international professional career of some seventy years, one that included not only classic Hollywood cinema, Weimar silent film, and the concert hall, but also classical theater, modern theater, musical comedies, vaudeville, army camp shows, radio, recordings, television, even circus and the ballet. It has made her one of the most multivalent icons of the twentieth century. *Dietrich Icon* explores this multivalency. While it joins other recent critical works focused on one film star, this volume attests the degree to which Dietrich—like no other star image—has been central to discourses of both the polis (e.g., the projects of nationalization) and the academy (e,g., the projects of film theory).[2]

Nationalizing Dietrich

Today's debate about (dis)claiming Dietrich for Germany had its beginnings even prior to her 1930 departure to Hollywood. For many Berliners, Dietrich's penchant for the femme fatale, her refusal of traditional roles of womanhood in favor of sexual independence and androgyny was profoundly un-German. Conservative cultural critics perceived these tendencies to be symptomatic of the destabilizing, if not degenerate, effects of modernity, often blaming them on an "Americanization" that invaded all spheres of public and private life (see Stefan Zweig). *The Blue Angel* (1930) underscores the ambivalence of belonging of its female protagonist by foregrounding the problematic of arrival, departure, and ill-fated homecomings. As Elisabeth Bronfen explores in her essay in this volume, in her role as Lola Lola, Dietrich anticipates her actual departure from home and her relocation in Hollywood, performing the story of the birth of the female star as a radical negotiation of displacement and loss of home. The liminality of the film was also dictated by the fact that it was shot in two languages and produced by two studios. Patrice Petro's essay in this volume reassesses the film's hybrid nature and position between sound and silent film, Ufa (Universum Film AG) and Paramount, and the film's contested status in German and American national film history by taking a closer look at what exact role Dietrich's famous legs played in this. What both essays underscore is that from the beginning Dietrich's fame was accompanied by the question whether she really was a "German" star.

After 1930, Dietrich returned to her native country only for short visits, resisting Joseph Goebbels's many offers to join the film industry of the Third Reich. Erica Carter's contribution to this volume shows how the efforts of the Nazi film industry to promote a popular cinema revolved around creating a star system for which the absent Dietrich became a most important model. Attacked in the Nazi press for her "Dirnenrollen" (roles as prostitutes; qtd. in Knopp 369) and her collaboration with "the Jew Sternberg," Hitler secretly admired and courted her throughout the 1930s. A U.S. citizen as of 1939, she actively supported the war effort by performing for U.S. troops stationed abroad and was awarded the Medal of Freedom in 1947, the first woman to receive this distinction.

In many ways, the flip side of the difficult relationship between the émigré Dietrich and her homeland is her political attitude toward the United States. A typical first-generation immigrant, she firmly believed in the host country's founding principles, developing a strong sense of political loyalty, and a willingness to support and uphold these principles.[3] That Dietrich did so much beyond the call of duty we can credit to her Prussian sense of duty, to her astute insight into the real dimension of Nazi Germany's military threat, and to a true commitment to American democracy. Dietrich's first return to Germany after the war was in the company of U.S. combat troops. Postwar Germany treated her with the resentment and ostracism typical for the returning émigré. When her 1960 concert at the Titania Palast was picketed, the signs read "Marlene, hau ab!" *and* "Marlene go home," just to make it absolutely clear that she no longer belonged in Berlin. It is no accident that the first Berlin politician to officially reach out to Dietrich was himself a returning émigré—Willy Brandt, mayor of Berlin from 1957 to 1966, and later German chancellor. By virtue of the fact of how easy it had been for Dietrich and others to decide which side to fight on, they challenged the notion of Germans as victims of Hitler's machinery of manipulation. Dietrich, the seducer, had no difficulty in resisting the Nazis' power of seduction, and in upholding fundamental notions of human judgment. Dietrich's own family provides the best example of the glaring contrast of political choices—her sister, Elisabeth Will, followed her husband Georg to Bergen-Belsen to operate a movie theater for concentration camp guards, assuming in essence the same function of entertaining the troops as Dietrich would on the other side.[4]

A decisive step toward reconciliation was taken by Dietrich herself, who, moved by the fall of the Berlin Wall in 1989, willed to be buried in her home city, next to her mother, despite not having visited Germany for many years. This step was followed up in 1993, when the city bought Dietrich's extensive estate from her daughter, Maria Riva, and made the Marlene Dietrich Collection a central part of the new Filmmuseum Berlin. Werner Sudendorf, head curator of the Dietrich Collection, describes in his contribution to this volume the history of the acquisition of the collection and its impact on Dietrich scholarship, and he lists in detail what the collection comprises.[5] Five years later, the Marlene-Dietrich-Platz was inaugurated in the midst of the reconstructed Potsdamer Platz, the new capital's showcase for entertainment and commercialism.[6] A postage stamp issued in 1997 now celebrates Dietrich as an important woman in German history, alongside such figures as philosopher Hannah

Dietrich's grave, Berlin. *Photo by Gerd Gemünden.*

Arendt, artist Käthe Kollwitz, and resistance fighter Sophie Scholl. In 2001, numerous events in Berlin and all over Germany commemorated the hundredth birthday of Dietrich, and President Johannes Rau praised Dietrich.

Most recently, on 12 June 2003, the city of Paris inaugurated *its* Place Marlène Dietrich, in recognition of her loyalty to France and her longstanding love of French culture (she was also made a member of the French Legion of Honor in 1951). Like so many German émigrés, Dietrich returned to Europe, but not to Germany. Instead, she made Paris her home for the last, reclusive years of her life, a choice for which the city showed its appreciation when for a while it paid rent for the apartment of the bankrupt diva. For her burial in Berlin, Dietrich's coffin was draped with the Tricolore, then the Star-Spangled Banner, and finally the German flag—the diva's parting gesture to the Germans that her homecoming was still a conflicted one.

Theorizing Dietrich

The past and ongoing contemporary debates about national identity in relation to Marlene Dietrich suggest a placement of her biographical and performative personas in specific historical, cultural, and even geographic contexts. Dietrich's star image has also been central to film theory, from the auteurist analyses of von Sternberg, to some of the most important debates on how film functions as an ideological and psychic apparatus. But these film theories have not always contextualized her star image in very specific historical terms, except as it serves to exemplify the character, strategies, and effects of the classic cinema tradition that dominated Hollywood film production—its narrative, visual, and soundtrack practices—from the late 1920s to the 1960s.

Cahiers du Cinema's collectively written ideological critique, "Josef von Sternberg's *Morocco*," analyzes how the erotic mythology of the woman in classic Hollywood film functions to mask social determinations. In the essay's reading of *Morocco*, Dietrich may represent the epitome of the fetishistic eroticization that defines a star as star, but von Sternberg's need to appropriate to himself the value of the star (exemplified by such statements as "Marlene is not Marlene, Marlene is me, and she knows that better than anyone") results in filmic patterns in which male characters both devalue Dietrich's character as an object of desire and fantasize and mourn her abandonment of or inaccessibility to them (Cahiers du Cinema Collective, 180–81). The Cahiers editors employ auteurist, psychoanalytic, and ideological (Marxist) theories to conclude that the film's use of Dietrich within its "plastic effects" of masks, veils, and plays with light constitutes the image itself as gauze or screen, determines its fetishistic appeal, and ultimately exposes it as one of the preeminent examples of classic Hollywood cinema's implication within the bourgeois, patriarchal capitalist system of production and erotic expression.

The Cahiers essay, with its focus on the figure of woman/Dietrich as object of exchange in a patriarchal system, presaged not only the feminist film theory that followed in the 1970s and 1980s, but that theory's preoccupation with Dietrich's image in particular. Claire Johnston, whose 1974 essay "Women's Cinema as Counter-Cinema" serves as a mediating link between the Cahiers essay and Laura Mulvey's highly influential "Visual Pleasure and Narrative Cinema," argues that the implications of the Cahiers analysis is that classical Hollywood cinema constructs a binary not of male and female, but male and nonmale. The fetishization of the female functions as a phallic replacement, and, argues Johnston, the popularity of stars such as Dietrich and Mae West (at one time Dietrich's dressing-room neighbor at Paramount) suggests the degree to which such phallocentrism is a collective fantasy.

Mulvey's famous argument, published in 1975, basically agrees with much of these earlier assessments, but deepens and complicates the place of Dietrich's image within classical cinema's practices. As is well known, Mulvey links the camera, the filmic character, and the (masculine) spectator of classical cinema as constructed within positions of looking that control the female image. While Mulvey suggests that the "look" in the films of Hitchcock submits the female character and image to sadistic control as a way to assuage the anxiety of castration the character or image provokes, she uses von Sternberg's imaging of Dietrich to exemplify the fetishization of the female image. Although she argues that such fetishization allows for the threat of woman to be disavowed through her overvaluation, her use of close textual analysis, with its special attention to the way von Sternberg uses screen depth, light, costume, and mise-en-scène (elements given less attention in the previous theoretical analyses of Johnston and Cahiers) to create an image of woman through Dietrich, makes her conclude that the Dietrich character is not mediated for the spectator by the controlling gaze of the male protagonist. Instead, Mulvey argues provocatively, the spectator has access to "direct erotic rapport" with Dietrich.

Mulvey's essay has, by some accounts, elicited more commentary—both assenting and dissenting—than any other piece of film theory. While it is impossible to account for all responses, several have a particular place within the theorization of Dietrich's star image and its relation to patriarchal filmic constructions of femininity. Peter Baxter's 1978 essay, "On the Naked Thighs of Miss Dietrich," is in many ways compatible with Mulvey's argument—the image of Dietrich (here, the circulation of Dietrich's image as Lola Lola in *The Blue Angel*) is an invitation to reexperience the dread and pleasure of past infantile experience in which the mother has a central role. But Baxter departs from Mulvey when he proposes that this association of Dietrich with the maternal is not necessarily misogynist. He argues that Dietrich's image as Lola Lola is so compelling in the film and in its continued circulation in print because it speaks to the libidinal experiences that a capitalist, patriarchal culture tries to repress. In other words, for this Marxist-psychoanalytic critique from the 1970s, the ongoing circulation of Dietrich's image is a potentially liberating return of the repressed.

In the 1982 essay "Spectacle and Narrative Theory" by Lea Jacobs and Richard de Cordova, the authors analyze *The Scarlet Empress* (the von

Sternberg film in which Dietrich plays Catherine the Great) in light of Mulvey's insight that the insertion of woman in the system of narrative and spectacle of classical Hollywood film has ideological implications. However, in their attempt to better delineate the specific filmic nature of spectacle, they argue that this mode of expression in some scenes of *Scarlet Empress* is one of direct address, a fact that suggests the performer—here, Dietrich—participates in the enunciation, or at least its performance. In other words, they broach the possibility of a politics and expression of performance associated with Dietrich in which the star has some power of authoring meaning.

In her 1988 book *In the Realm of Pleasure: Von Sternberg, Dietrich, and the Masochistic Aesthetic*, Gaylyn Studlar provides one of the most thorough critiques of Mulvey's model even though she continues the dialogue about the power and meaning of Dietrich's image within a psychoanalytic context. While Studlar agrees with Mulvey that the von Sternberg films expose the projection of male fantasy onto the female/Dietrich, she argues that the pleasures of looking in these films are structured around masochistic, rather than sadistic or sadomasochistic conflicts and pleasures. The male character-spectator submits to the gaze of the female/Dietrich in longing for a pre-Oedipal relation to the mother, before scenarios of maternal castration and lack dominate the formation of subjectivity. This argument is a direct intervention in the debates Mulvey initiated about the images of woman and the positions offered to both male and female spectators of the classical Hollywood film, suggesting that there are films and forms of spectatorship that subvert a patriarchal, heteronormative power agenda. In subsequent developments of her theory, Studlar argues that Mulvey does not explore the implications of her own point that von Sternberg's films with Dietrich allow for "direct erotic rapport" between the female image and spectators. Here, Studlar emphasizes the role of Dietrich, both as performer-enunciator and star image, in this subversion. Dietrich—the performer, not just Dietrich as von Sternberg character—"possesses an aloofness that suggests a distanciation from her constructed image, a refusal to invest in her 'femininity'" and its presumed aim of attracting men (Studlar, "Masochism, Masquerade" 243). It is through this quality that Dietrich, as well as her characters, gain power and appeal to women as well as men.

Around the same historical moment Studlar is developing a more complex theory for the Dietrich image and performance in relation to a "masochistic aesthetic" and the "direct erotic rapport" that she seems to achieve with the spectator of the von Sternberg films, Judith Mayne refutes the notion that the transgressive aspects of Dietrich's star persona lie in her "returning" the gaze of the male in such diverse films as *The Blue Angel* and *Witness for the Prosecution*. Mayne argues that if "resistance" is the appropriate term to define the Dietrich image it is because "resistance is fully part of the narrative and visual imagery that comprise the Dietrich persona" (Mayne, "Marlene Dietrich" 42). For Mayne, this resistance is most clearly evident in Dietrich's enactment of characters who move among multiple modes of performance. In other words, resistance is an effect of the self-consciousness of performance itself, especially in the ironic imitations of the conventions of femininity enacted by Lola Lola of *The Blue Angel* and Christine of *Witness for the Prosecution*.

Taken together, the analyses of Dietrich from the late 1970s to the late 1980s suggest a movement away from understanding her star persona as an inert, passive image entirely constituted by a collective phallocentrism, toward an understanding of the Dietrich star persona as performed, contributing to the enunciation of the films' meanings and multiple positions available for spectators. Mayne's essay also gestures toward a historiographic understanding of the Dietrich star persona as developed and replayed over time, across different genres, national contexts, and historical moments. This is not to say that Dietrich had never been considered in historical context before by film scholars—both Marjorie Rosen's *Popcorn Venus* (1973) and Molly Haskell's *From Reverance to Rape: The Treatment of Women in the Movies* (1974) placed Dietrich alongside other "sex goddesses" and "femme fatales" of the 1930s in their survey treatments of filmic representations of women—but theoretical works about Dietrich in and since the 1990s most frequently intervene as *historiographic* studies, self-reflexive about the implications of historical work for theoretical insights. This is to say, while Haskell and (especially) Rosen, for all their valuable insights, often present overgeneralized views of Dietrich in Hollywood film history, the more recent works, including the essays in this volume, carefully delineate circumscribed industrial, national, and historical contexts for examining Dietrich, and in doing so, actually end up enlarging the perspectives of and places for Dietrich's star persona in film history and theory.

Several of the main contexts for examining the Dietrich persona in recent work have been in terms of queer politics and lesbian history, film genre studies, the female body, and technology, race, and biographical representational forms.[7] While Dietrich is discussed in some early film scholarship on homosexuality and Hollywood cinema, it is characteristic of these works to acknowledge her lesbian allure (often through mention of the "kissing scene" between Dietrich and another female character in *Morocco*), while dismissing it as an "exotic" touch likely meant to arouse the male spectator (Tyler; Russo) or as abandoned in the films' overwhelming advancement of the "male plot" (Arbuthnot and Seneca). However, Andrea Weiss, in her 1992 study of lesbians in film, *Vampires and Violets*, argues for the power of what are often "isolated moments" in Dietrich's films to pose a threat to the "male plot" and heterosexual renderings of homosexuality as exotica. One of the most significant aspects of her study is the emphasis on what Dietrich's performative queering of gender and sexuality might have meant for an underground, but growing, lesbian subculture in 1930s America. She contextualizes Dietrich's expression of queerness within what the available understandings of lesbianism at the time were for (often closeted) spectators (30–50). Patricia White's examination of the Greta Garbo–Mercedes de Acosta–Marlene Dietrich romantic triangle in 1930s Hollywood is also interested in historicizing what constitutes the signs of lesbian identity and style, what we now call lesbian "chic." The two female stars shared a female lover (de Acosta), but also a love for wearing trousers, and contributed to the historical construction of what can be encoded and decoded as lesbian (White, "Black and White"). So much of the early theory featuring Dietrich is focused on her films from the 1930s, but these works give us one of the best indications of how a particular group of spectators in that era might have actually understood and desired the Dietrich they saw both in films and in extratextual materials circulating at the time. White and Mary Desjardins have also analyzed representations of the queer Dietrich (White, *Uninvited*; Desjardins), again paired with Garbo, in the experimental video maker Cecelia Barriga's *Meeting Two Queens*. This 1991 video works by editing together not only the "isolated moments" of queerness in films starring Dietrich and Garbo, but also by creating new queer associations by juxtaposing shots of the two stars so that they appear to be in a movie together, longing for each other. White emphasizes the place of the video in acknowledging and creating a lesbian archive, while Desjardins suggests that the video both acknowledges a historical lesbian community of the past and the present, and offers a melodramatic fantasy scenario that also solicits and queers female heterosexual desire (White, *Uninvited*; Desjardins). In this volume, Alice Kuzniar argues that the compilation of "isolated moments" of lesbianism and queerness in Dietrich's films can be a dissatisfying enterprise, especially as it encourages a spectatorial position wedded to fetishistic practices. As an alternative, she asks that we consider the narratives of Dietrich's films as queer, with Dietrich's excess display of femininity suggesting she is "passing" for straight. Kuzniar then finds a continuum in Dietrich's star persona by examining the narratives of a number of von Sternberg's films alongside *A Foreign Affair*, the post-war film directed by Billy Wilder, as films suggesting the secrecy of "the closet," and affording extended and contextualized queer moments in the spectator's construction of Dietrich.

Among the scholars centralizing the importance of Dietrich's star persona in Hollywood film industry history, at a time in the early 1990s when the psychoanalytic paradigm guiding textual analysis and spectator studies was being decentralized, were those focusing on the production histories of the fallen woman film, the genre that best characterizes the majority of films Dietrich made with von Sternberg. Lea Jacobs's examination of the Hollywood Production Code Administration (PCA) and of its negotiations with studios over their production of the "fallen woman" genre contributes to a more historically contextualized understanding of Dietrich's persona—in fact, Dietrich was not the only female star whose persona was partially constructed in terms of the sexually transgressive characters she played on screen in the 1930s. What is significant about Dietrich in *Blonde Venus*, one production in this genre that posed special problems for the PCA, is that her star persona is called on in the film to suggest something about sexuality that would be taboo in the maternal character she plays. Jacobs argues that the film exploits a division between star and character (for instance, constructing scenes of Dietrich as Helen performing domestic duties juxtaposed to Dietrich as star performing her familiar "deviant" songstress femininity in the "Hot Voodoo" number) to introduce aspects of transgressive femininity not acceptable in the nonspectacle moments of the film (Jacobs, 101–2).

Peter Baxter's chronicle of von Sternberg's relation to Paramount

Studios and to American culture in the 1930s similarly relies on detailing the production of this same film, and he reveals numerous pieces of evidence about Dietrich's collaborative role with von Sternberg in constructing the narrative and her character in terms of the pair's understanding of maternal melodramatic fantasies (Baxter, *Just Watch*). Janet Staiger, in *Perverse Spectators*, follows the various script versions of the film as it went through the PCA process to argue that despite the PCA-mandated changes evident in the final film, the extratextual material published in fan magazines about not only the studio-PCA negotiations, but most especially about Dietrich's own unconventional relationships with her husband and von Sternberg (resulting in von Sternberg's wife very publicly suing for divorce), suggests that audiences of the time might have still read the film in terms of an unsanctioned transgressive female sexuality. Patrice Petro has critiqued the exclusion (or simplification) of feminist theory's discussion of the film's representation of race, arguing that the meaning of Dietrich's filmic character and her star persona are inflected by Weimar Germany's fascination with an imaginary African American primitivism and the influence of Josephine Baker on Dietrich's performance style. Dietrich's "Hot Voodoo" number and her German character's relationships with American black women in the film suggest to Petro a complex discourse on race and national otherness that exemplifies why *Blonde Venus* and Dietrich need to be considered in terms of hybridity and ambivalence (Petro).

A number of essays in this volume continue and expand on this earlier work focusing on genre, censorship, extratextual materials, and the female sexuality represented by Dietrich's star persona. Mary Beth Haralovich's essay explores how Dietrich's persona contributed to the available meanings of *Blonde Venus* in relation to the film's advertising campaigns in several locales. She argues that while the advertising campaigns for Hollywood films typically conjoin ideologies of courtship, sexual attraction, and love, the campaign strategies for this fallen-woman film were compatible with other extratextual contexts that made room for the film's erotic possibilities. Key to this strategy was a focus on Dietrich's face, inviting contemplation rather than revelation of the narrative's character. Film advertising is an underexplored context in film studies for historicizing meanings of films and star personas, and Haralovich's essay attests again to how Dietrich's persona and films can be used to exemplify the practices of Hollywood film narratives, their audiences, and the industrial practices that produce the former and position the latter. Gaylyn Studlar's essay closely details the contexts of the transformation of Dietrich's star persona in the 1930s, as the filmic characters that were one element of that construction became problematic in shifting social, generic, and industrial environments. One of the central features of the industrial environment that changed from Dietrich's arrival in Hollywood in 1930 to the mid-1930s were the strategies of censorship. Studlar is attentive to the details of how the studios tried to make Dietrich's persona more acceptable to a changed production code and presumedly changed audience by redefining it generically (from the fallen women of *Dishonored* and *Blonde Venus* to the heroines of romantic comedy in *Desire* and *Angel*) and then by the end of the decade by Americanizing her in westerns, such as *Destry Rides Again*, the role that brought her back to box office and critical popularity. The aspects of the Dietrich persona that most attract audiences today, such as her aloofness from her objectified female subjectivity, had to be negotiated, perhaps even threatened with "elimination" by the late 1930s. Mark Williams's essay confirms aspects of Studlar's research, as he traces Dietrich's performances in a series of popular westerns, including *Destry Rides Again*, from 1939 to 1952. Like those in the von Sternberg cycle of texts, these characters are not containable by the generic contexts of marriage. Williams argues that the erotic and social dynamics of the western and its masculine scopic regime require the Dietrich character to submit to generic and male-defined demands of the "law." Like Studlar's essay, Williams's piece examines the construction of Dietrich's star persona outside the usual auteurist contexts, and considers how different generic, historical, and industrial environments contribute to the transformation of the star over time.

Although previous critical work has centralized aspects of Dietrich's physicality—her legs, for instance—in explaining the power of her star persona, several essays in this volume examine her body and voice in terms of their performative manifestation in specific historical moments, media practices, technologies, and acting traditions. Nora Alter's essay on Dietrich's legs examines how this body part most associated with the star's persona and most frequently discussed in ahistorical terms as a fetish might have had particular meanings for audiences in different historical moments. She argues that the typical psychoanalytic understanding of the fetish replacing the absent phallus in a drama of individual subject formation is inadequate to explain the fascination with Dietrich's legs, which were prominently on display in her live cabaret days in post–World War I Weimar Germany and conspicuously covered by military fatigues in her World War II performances. For Alter, Dietrich's legs have had a "legacy" because of the way they summon a historical referent of dismembered male bodies in wartime. Lutz Koepnick's essay focuses on Dietrich's face as a constituent element in her star persona since the 1930s, when she actively intervened in its transformation and maintenance to increase her market value, but argues that it not so much possesses a content as reveals "the material reality and excessive circulation of signs in modern mass culture." As many critics have done, Koepnick productively places Dietrich's emergence as star in the late 1920s and 1930s in relation to Greta Garbo, the other major European female performer to become a major focus for the energies of the Hollywood studio system and its anciliary industry of fan magazines and glamour portrait photography. However, he argues that Garbo's face suggests the residual place of the silent film aesthetic in the new sound film visual economy, inviting a depth reading. Dietrich's face, on the other hand, resisted reading and thus anticipates the new technologies and economies of circulation of images characteristic of not just the sound film era, but the digital age of the late twentieth and early twenty-first centuries.

Key to Koepnick's argument about Dietrich's persona (as revealed by the face) is its refusal of authenticity. Amy Lawrence's essay in this volume characterizes Dietrich's voice as rejecting the alleged authenticity of emotion, distinguishing her from emotionally expressive singers such as Judy Garland. The effect of this style is often a self-conscious doubleness, a self-awareness of her status as disciplined performer. Lawrence's argument about Dietrich's persona (as constituted by voice) departs from Koepnick's definition of Dietrich's persona (as constituted by face) in that she demonstrates that the star's emotionally restrained, multilingual persona, suggesting cosmopolitan world-weariness, is "an impenetrable surface" against which her audience speculates, projects, and fantasizes. Lawrence's essay is an especially valuable addition to the scholarship on Dietrich because not only does she analyze an undertheorized component of star performance—voice—but she also examines its performative valence as Dietrich moved into media (stage cabaret in Las Vegas and radio) rarely considered to be important in the ongoing construction of film star personas. Steven Bach, in his personal reminiscence about "listening in" on Dietrich's stage rehearsals for a Los Angeles performance in the 1970s, confirms many of Lawrence's conclusions about the effects of Dietrich's voice on radio and recording listeners and their use of it as a "screen" of fantasy projection.

Judith Mayne's essay in this volume is also concerned with the relation of Dietrich's stage performance style to what is almost unanimously considered by scholars (both in and outside this volume) to be Dietrich's ironic, distanced perspective on the conventions of gendered identity construction. Mayne, however, also focuses on some of the very last public performances of Dietrich, in which she also seems to be presenting "her archive," a loose narrative rendering of her past career. Dietrich's aging body is central to her star persona, and Mayne questions the degree to which other archivists have displaced Dietrich's agency by their particular evocation of this body.

Agency in archiving is also a central theme in Lucy Fischer's "Marlene: Modernity, Mortality, and the Biopic," and in the essays in this volume by Amelie Hastie and Mary Desjardins. Fischer discusses *Marlene*, Maximilian Schell's 1983 documentary film of Dietrich in relation to the star's resistance to a voyeuristic gaze on her aged body and her active (although somewhat coerced) participation in analyzing her own image. Hastie, like Fischer and Mayne, is invested in examining to what degree Dietrich's knowledge based on memory and lived experience becomes a central aspect of her star persona in the last half of her life and career. In this regard, Hastie provides the first scholarly analysis of Dietrich's "dictionary" of life, *Marlene Dietrich's ABC*, published in 1960. Like other kinds of star texts (films, biographies, fan magazine articles, and other kinds of promotional materials), *ABC* interpellates a subject desiring to know more, and thus like those other texts, participates in producing the star herself. But Hastie suggests that the singularity of Dietrich's authorial agency lies not in its production of just another star text, but in its relation to subjectivity in modernity, in its similarity to women's advice literature, Roland Barthes *A Lover's Discourse*, and Benjamin's *Arcades Project*, as both testament to and hedge against ephemerality. Desjardins examines the continuous posthumous construction of the Dietrich star persona through biographical and autobiographical forms that compete with, confirm, or contradict other media manifestations of her image. Looking specifically at Maria Riva's memoir of her mother, Desjardins suggests that the author is torn between her own longing for a mother-daughter relationship of mutual recognition and an admiration for her mother's disciplined crafting of her own self-mythologization. Since Riva's memoir makes Dietrich accessible through the "family romance" in which the mother, like the star, is a figure inviting an ambivalent affective identification, Desjardins concludes that the form offers a particularly powerful exploration of how star images "haunt" our fantasies.

Creating Dietrichs

Many of the essays in this volume were first presented at a conference held at Dartmouth College in October 2001. As the above outline of these essays indicates, the purpose of this academic event was the critical reviewing of Dietrich from an interdisciplinary vantage point and across numerous fields of inquiry. Yet the Dartmouth event was of course just one of many commemorating the hundredth anniversary of the diva all over the world. Apart from retrospectives, public events, speeches, and celebrations it also occasioned the publication of numerous books on Dietrich, ranging from biographies, homages, and portraits (Bemman, Bosquet, Jacob, Kreuzer and Runge, Salber, Sanders-Brahms, Skaerved, Sudendorf, Wiebrecht, Wood) to books of photography (Nauder and Peter Riva), her correspondence with writer Erich Maria Remarque (Fuld and Schneider) and even a Dietrich cookbook (Weth). The year 2001 clearly underscored that the Dietrich legacy is alive and well, still cherished by her aging fans and ready to be discovered by a younger generation.

These celebrations also made it clear that Dietrich's relationship to Germany and Berlin, which we mapped in some detail earlier, is symptomatic for the larger debate about how Germany ought to remember and confront its postwar legacy. As Werner Sudendorf has said, Dietrich is "a litmus test for how Germans deal with their history" (qtd. in *Vernissage* 7). The shift of sentiment toward Dietrich reflects the complex and contradictory discourses of the last decade on how to evaluate the significance of the past for the present. The example of Dietrich shows signs of genuine reconciliation, but it also indicates that efforts at rehabilitation can easily turn the past into a museum. Politicians and cultural representatives have not been the only ones involved in this effort, nor have they been the most hagiographic or conciliatory, as Wowereit's cautious speech exemplifies. Indeed, some of the ideologically most problematic forms of reclaiming Dietrich have come from fellow artists.

Among these efforts, three plays and one film from the last decade stand out. Pam Gems's play *Marlene* is set in the Paris of the early 1970s, featuring Marlene Dietrich, her tour manager Vivian, and the mute dresser Mutti, apparently a concentration camp survivor, as we witness how the star readies backstage for a concert. Premiered at the Oldham Coliseum Theatre in the United Kingdom in 1996, the play had a short and disappointing run in New York in April 1999. "A moving celebration of the woman behind the myth," as the cover text tells us, *Marlene* focuses on the personal agony behind the ecstatically glossy image. But if the play analyzes the construction of the star, it does so only to laud the sustained discipline and creative efforts that went into it. Featuring many of Dietrich's songs, it offers fans the chance to revisit, or experience for the first time, a glorious moment in the star's career. A far more complex and intriguing look behind the curtains is provided in the personal account of Dietrich's acclaimed biographer Steven Bach, which serves as an overture to this volume.

Interestingly, in Berlin the play has been a tremendous success, with over 250 performances since its 1998 premiere at the Renaissance Theater. In Volker Kühn's German adaptation of Gems's text, the play now revolves around Dietrich's infamous 1960 Berlin concert, climaxing with the performance of several songs, heavily applauded by the audience (in contrast to Gems's version, in which songs pepper the play throughout). Rewriting trauma as triumph, Kühn's *Marlene* has thereby become one of the most startling examples of the effort to normalize the city's relation to the star, providing her with an imaginary homecoming she never received during her lifetime.

Nothing could be further from such a reconciliatory stance than Thea Dorn's play *Marleni: Preussische Diven blond wie Stahl* (Marleni: Prussian Divas Blonde as Steel, 2000). Events are set in the Paris apartment of the diva on the evening prior to her death in May 1992. The play begins with Leni Riefenstahl entering the apartment of the reclusive star through the balcony, to which she had to climb up—as in a mountain film—because the concierge denies entry to anyone wanting to see Dietrich. Riefenstahl has come to cast Dietrich as the heroine in a Penthesilea film, intended to be a comeback for both, the long-blacklisted director and the star who has sunk into oblivion. The bizarre confrontation between the alcoholic Dietrich, severely marked by her advanced age, and the uncannily vigorous Riefenstahl, only one year her junior, is an encounter between colleagues whose political choices drove them apart after 1933, but whose respective afterlives have remarkable similarities, as the title of the play suggests. Dorn's Dietrich insists that "everything in life depends on which war front you spread your legs" (17), but her Riefenstahl counters that the only legs she ever spread at a front were those of her camera tripod. In Dorn's imagined dialogue, Dietrich and Riefenstahl emerge as sisters under the mink, or anorak, whose very different embodiments of the New Woman of Weimar were curtailed by similar concessions to a male-dominated world. If Dietrich was the controlling, manipulative femme fatale, a personality cultivated both on-screen and offscreen, Riefenstahl was the athletic, asexual, and independent actress-director. But both artists, the play insists, had to make heavy sacrifices in order to advance their careers, and the similarity of the sacrifices ultimately outweigh the political differences that lie between them. Further similarity is found in postwar Germany's disavowal of Dietrich as U.S. army slut amd Riefenstahl as mistress of the Führer. The parallelism of *Marleni* calls for a rewriting of both artists' biographies, but with more radical implications for Riefenstahl's. Her postwar blacklisting and continued dismissal as protofascist artist is seen by Dorn as a form of sexism that denies women artistic independence, while Dietrich's fame, the play makes clear, can outlive the star only as long as its true price tag is withheld from the public. (On the similarities between Dietrich and Riefenstahl see also Bronfen 2000, who does not consider Dorn's play.)[8]

Moritz Rinke, *Der graue Engel: Ein Monolog zu zweit* (The Gray Angel: A Monologue for Two, 1995) is a performance piece about "Marlene D" that deconstructs the fetish into which the aging diva has been turned—and turns herself. Set amid the star's arsenal of suitcases that spill the props, dresses, and jewelry accumulated during a lifelong career, we are witness to a monologue in which an angel figure (a human? a mythical figure? the Blue Angel?) talks to her mute *intimus* Konstantin (who is he?) to defy her fear of death and the boredom of a long day ahead. Chal-

Marlene Dietrich and Leni Riefenstahl with the American actress Anna May Wong. *Photo by Alfred Eisenstadt/Time Life Pictures/Getty Images.*

lenged to assemble the collage of verbal and gestural quotes that make up the play, the spectator realizes the impossibility of that task, an impossibility that ultimately points to the implosion of the speaking subject and all she stands for. Analytic rather than performative, Judith Mayne's essay in this volume focuses on very similar concerns, namely how the specter of aging—of denying it and negotiating with it, of examining it and running away from it—is dramatically foregrounded during Dietrich's career. Considering not only her film career (most notably her last film, *Just a Gigolo*), but also her career as a chanteuse, as well as Maximilian Schell's famous documentary, Mayne shows how Dietrich's eagerness to control the preservation of her image also bespeaks a passion for storing memories.

The most high-profiled effort to reclaim Dietrich for Germany by streamlining her biography has been Joseph Vilsmaier's big budget biopic *Marlene* (2000), which is dicussed in detail in this volume by Eric Rentschler. As Rentschler shows, Vilsmaier's film suppresses the ambiguities that are the hallmark of Dietrich's stardom, in order to make her into a figure that can heal the open wounds of German history. According to Vilsmaier's version of her life, Marlene's fame precedes her Hollywood career, where she undergoes an Americanization from which she suffers but which never undoes her loyalty to Germany. Her true love is Carl, an entirely fictitious character serving as an officer in the Wehrmacht, whose life Marlene saves by helping him escape from the Americans—betraying the Americans, *not* the Germans. After the war, we find out that Carl was actually in the resistance—as so many Germans would later claim. That the film bombed at the box office indicates that the public upholds certain standards regarding the truthfulness of a celebrity's biography and the rewriting of history, but it also shows that in the relationship between Dietrich and Germany, there's always room for one more embarrassment.

These multiple reworkings of Dietrich are rounded out by two documentaries. Guido Knopp's portrait *Marlene Dietrich: Die Gegnerin* (Marlene Dietrich, the Adversary, 2001) focuses on the star's resistance to Hitler's efforts to lure her back to Germany. As one segment of his five-part television series *Hitlers Frauen und Marlene* (Hitler's Women and Marlene), it contrasts political clear-headedness with those women (some of them artists as well) who actively supported the National Socialists. (See also Knopp's accompanying book.) The portrait *In Her Own Song* (2001) by Dietrich's grandson David Riva provides yet another overview of Dietrich's career, but, like Knopp, with a strong political emphasis. A significant portion of this film deals with the star's support of the U.S. war effort and her strong opposition to Hitler.

This emphasis on the World War II period of Dietrich's life and career is perhaps not surprising considering the documentary's distribution and funding status. It was cofunded and first aired in America by Turner Classic Movies (TCM), a commercial-free television channel offered to cable and satellite subscribers. Television currently rivals the publishing industry as the medium most invested in and profiting from the recirculation of images from World War II and the classical, studio era of Hollywood stardom. In December 2001 TCM capitalized on presumed audience interest in both war and stardom by naming Dietrich its "star of the month" and airing *Dietrich: In Her Own Song* and over a dozen of her films.

This volume of essays contributes to the ongoing dialogue on the Dietrich star persona that has spanned a variety of discursive genres and artistic modes across continents in two different centuries. As our introductory discussion and the volume's essays suggest, one would be hard pressed to point to any other film star whose meaning has had such high stakes for so many cultural projects. Diverse social and cultural agents have and continue to participate in debates around Dietrich, not like the helpless and besotted "moths around the flame" of her most famous song, but as the beneficiaries of the flame's power to illuminate the place of national identity, gender and sexuality, and mass media in modern culture.

Notes

1. Portions of Wowereit's speech are reprinted in Newsletter 40 (31 May 2002) of the Marlene Dietrich Collection Berlin. The newsletters can be found at http://www.mdcb@filmmuseum-berlin.de.

2. Scholarly books focused on a single star include Andrew Britton, *Katharine Hepburn: Star as Feminist*; Paul Smith, *Clint Eastwood: A Cultural Production*; S. Paige Baty, *American Monroe: The Making of a Body Politic*; Ramona Curry, *Too Much of a Good Thing: Mae West as Cultural Icon*; Rachel Moseley, *Growing Up with Audrey Hepburn*; Murray Pomerance, ed., *Enfant Terrible! Jerry Lewis in American Film*; Adrienne L. McLean, *Being Rita Hayworth: Labor, Identity, and Hollywood Stardom*.

3. In *Marlene Dietrich's ABC*, she writes under the entry "Nationality": "Changing your nationality is not an easy step to take, even when you despise the beliefs and actions your country has adopted. Whatever you may tell yourself to the contrary, denying what you were brought up to cherish makes you feel disloyal. The love and respect for the country that is taking you in has nothing to do with it" (120). For a detailed discussions of this book, see Amelie Hastie's essay in this volume.

4. In later years, Dietrich would deny the existence of her sister Elisabeth, although it remains uncertain if this was for political reasons. In his biography, Werner Sudendorf surmises that Marlene kept silent about her older sister to conceal her own age. From 1945 until Elisabeth's death in 1957, Marlene did support her financially (137).

5. See also the documentary *Das Zweite Leben der Marlene* (Christian Bauer, 1995), which narrates the story of the Dietrich Archive and its journey to Berlin.

6. At the Potsdamer Platz, one can find Dietrich's Bistro and the Marlene-Bar in the Hotel Inter-Continentel. Elsewhere in Berlin, the restaurant Der Blaue Engel serves dishes made after Dietrich's own recipes and at the Babelsberg Filmstudio the largest studio has been named Marlene-Dietrich-Halle. In Postdam we also find a Marlene-Dietrich-Allee.

7. Some scholars continued into the 1990s using the Dietrich image to exemplify the theoretical implications of Hollywood classical cinema outside particularized historical, industrial, and social contexts. For example, in *Femmes Fatales*, Mary Ann Doane analyzes the use of veils in von Sternberg's imaging of Dietrich to suggest that classical cinema shares with modern philosophy a tendency to project the instabilities of its own discourse onto the figure of the woman (74).

8. In real life, Dietrich and Riefenstahl did not meet after the star's 1930 departure for Hollywood. In a 1987 interview with *Bunte*, a German yellow press journal, Riefenstahl claims to have suggested Dietrich to Sternberg for the part of Lola Lola. Dietrich reacted by cabling *Bunte*: "The Riefenstahl story is so ridiculous that Sternberg and Remarque would have laughed themselves to death if they weren't dead already." In a 1991 letter, Dietrich was asked to meet with Riefenstahl "to clear up a few things, which to the great regret of Leni Riefenstahl might be standing between you and her." Dietrich's sole response was to write "Nazi" on the letter. Dietrich's relation to divas of the Third Reich is also the subject of Elfriede Jelinek's insightful obituary, "Das zweite Gesicht."

Falling in Love Again

"SOMEBODY MOVED THE MICROPHONE," she said.

She said it in that voice Hemingway wrote "could break your heart," but that was not its aim at the moment. There was an insistence in it now that sounded not from emphasis, but from reserve—a hush almost overridden by the scrape of adjusting chairs and the snap of instrument cases clicking open and shut somewhere on the stage behind her. There was the faintest break in this rustle of busy background as another voice, this one male, said "Sorry?"

"Somebody moved the microphone," she repeated, as calmly as before, as quietly.

"Fellas, *please*," said the man. Scraps of sound on the stage scudded into silence. "I didn't get it, Marlene," he said.

"Somebody moved the microphone while we were at lunch." She colored the words with the faintest hue of authority—not with volume, but with shading, modulation, a veil. "Moving the microphone is nightclubs. This is not nightclubs. This is *theater*. This is *concerts*."

Her final word resonated in silence.

Then, "Right, Marlene," the man said, and dutifully turned to the others, his voice flat: "No touching the mike, okay, fellas?" just as if they had not been there to hear it for themselves.

"Thank you, Burt," said the break-your-heart voice at the precise instant a squeal ran through the sound system, as if some gremlin in the circuitry were confirming her point.

Silence. Then the slash of a downbeat.

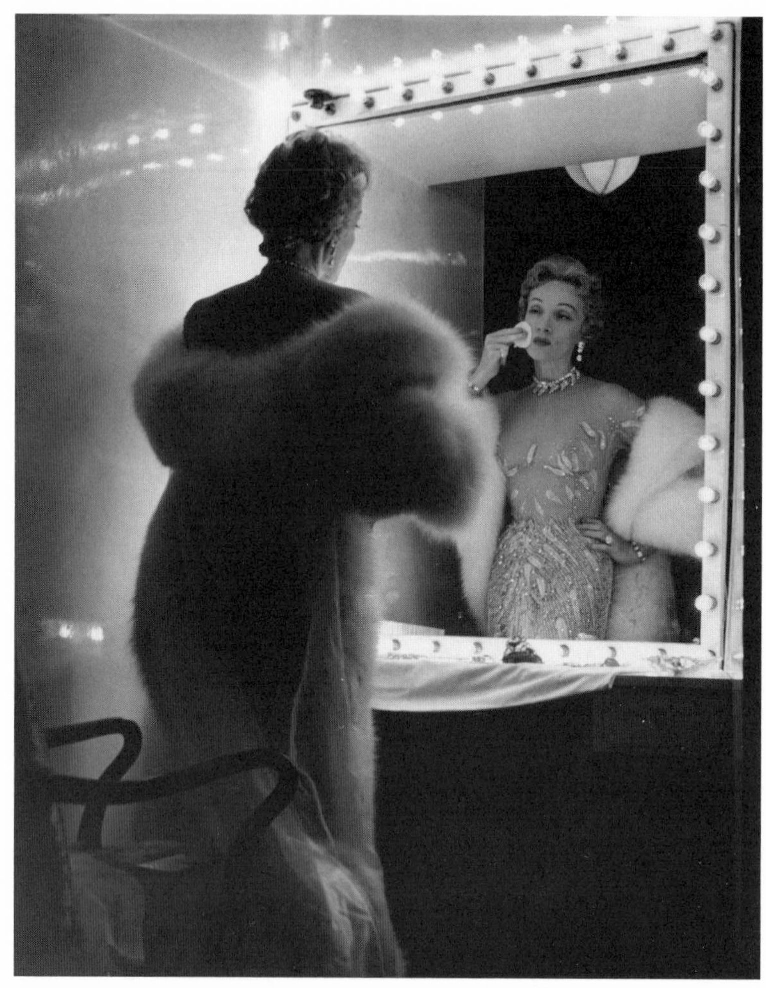

Dietrich in the dressing room. *Filmmuseum Berlin—Marlene Dietrich Collection Berlin.*

A song began to play.

"I can't give you anything. . . ."

The screech of the speaker pierced the offices on the third floor of the Ahmanson Theater in Los Angeles, on the stage of which the microphone had been moved, far below and far from anyone's view. Through one of those design oversights that prompted architects' suicides-of-honor in the age of the Habsburgs, the Ahmanson, part of the giant Music Center complex in downtown Los Angeles (whose patrons were mostly emperors of savings-and-loans), had been built without offices for the organization that mounted productions in the large 2,071-seat Ahmanson and the more modest, mostly more adventurous Mark Taper Forum just steps away, which turned out to have neither offices nor even a proper backstage in which to stow away the stuff of artifice.

Although such standard necessities had been overlooked, the architects responsible (or their patrons) had shrewdly enough decreed bars for each of the Ahmanson's three levels of theater seating, and each bar was equipped with a sound system leading directly from the stage to alert patrons and bartenders that something was about to begin or end.

When it was pointed out that no offices existed in the bankers' multimillion dollar edifices, the Ahmanson's third floor bar was quickly and neatly converted to windowless cubicles for the two theaters' staffs. Work supplies were stored in cabinets designed to hold champagne and crystal behind doors with locks, from which dangled tiny keys. They sometimes swayed, giving theater workers visible evidence that somewhere in the windowed world a seismic event was occurring. Were the entire City of the Angels to be leveled by an earthquake, they joked, not one theater employee would know, were it not for those swinging little keys.

Seismic events of moment to theater people are often of minor geologic magnitude, like the moving of a microphone. It was to track such occurrences that the speaker system from the stage to the converted bar had been switched on, allowing theater staffs to eavesdrop on the rehearsal below in windowless, clandestine privacy.

It was, in fact, the first time in anyone's memory that this speaker system had ever been turned on. While most theater people are notoriously curious and excitable, they are also blasé to the bone and, in this case, had work to do. Activation of the sound system was less a tribute to anything on stage—at the beginning, anyway—than due to the persistence of the staff's most recent arrival, the newly hired assistant to the creative director. This newcomer worked at a script-laden table next to the drone of the duplicating machine, which happened to be located directly beneath the speakers and the switches that controlled them. The switches that controlled *him* were mostly out of sight.

There were a dozen or so staff members, preparing productions, rejecting scripts, conducting auditions, planning publicity, signing up subscribers. They ran the theatrical gamut: experience-toughened pros from New York who had Seen It All, to frighteningly dedicated (and ambitious) newcomers right out of drama school. Some were twenty-five-going-on-fifty; some were fifty going on nerves and little else. But they shared a common and ageless affliction: their veins, whether hardened with disillusion or flexibly free to experience Everything, were chock full of greasepaint. They were (or wanted to be) Theater People, and every ear, dimmed by time or still wet-behind with innocence, was being firmly bent by a sixty-six-year-old woman who was assuring them in a cognac voice that there was nothing she could give them "but love, Baby," and was making greasepaint bubble and flow, quickening half-remembered dreams of the pros and half-formed fantasies of the tyros.

Everybody knew the words and tune of the old chestnut purring now through the speakers from the stage, but to their slowly growing surprise twenty-six musicians and a German grandmother were making it sound freshly minted. She was slurring it and nudging it in its durable ribs and grinning through the words. There was smoke in that voice, faint echoes of decades: Berlin in the twenties, Hollywood in the thirties, locales exotic and tragic—not just the Riviera and Morocco and Shanghai, but El Alamein, too, and battlefields in a dozen countries in the forties. But these echoes were muted now, hidden behind humor, and she was making them forget all that, so the Now could pierce—or displace—the Then; promising "diamond bracelets Woolworth doesn't sell," every facet flawless, glinting in swing.

And then—suddenly—she wasn't promising anything anymore. She had stopped abruptly in mid-phrase, and it took conductor and orchestra several moments to realize this and wind down in a discordant blare, like a carousel whose gears have slipped and was grinding to a crazy, whimpering halt.

Faces around the office speaker exchanged glances as silence loomed and broadened.

"Don't tell me she's going to do 'the microphone bit,' again," said the publicity lady, Peg, an off- and on-Broadway wizened soul, rolling cynical eyes that knew every nook of every cranny on, off, or near 42nd Street. Still, even she cocked an ear to the speaker's crackle.

"What is it, Marlene?" asked the man—Burt Bacharach, to be sure—her arranger, conductor, and accompanist from 1955 to 1964, who had agreed to return for just this one concert in 1968, four years after a decade that had ended in Edinburgh.

"The electric guitars," she replied.

"What about them?" Bacharach didn't sound alarmed or even very interested.

"One of them is too loud," she said, with the quiet confidence of a radar technician.

"They're not too loud, Marlene. Let's keep going."

"*One* of them is too loud," she repeated, the decibels diminishing as if in deference, but calibrated with hairline exactness to control.

There was a pause before Bacharach yielded. "Okay, fellas. *Readings*." Then another pause. "Fred?"

"She's right, Burt," said Fred, faint but clear. "Must've accidentally kicked it up."

"Well, kick it down," ordered Bacharach tightly. Then a beat. "Okay, Marlene?"

"Thank you, Burt," she said, and within a rhythmic blink was again promising—and delivering—"the only thing I've plenty of, Baby" . . .

"She must have ears like a *bat*," said publicity Peg to the group clustered around the speakers. "I don't know if that old broad can even sing, but *something* sure as hell is going on down there!"

It was Theater, performed for an audience of twenty-six local musicians to whom she had her back on that stage. They were mostly studio musicians, among the best in the world (she had reason to know), but often casual by conditioning, by "cool." Expert technicians, flawlessly but perhaps indifferently doing a gig. They would accompany her for two weeks, following four days of eight-hour rehearsals, of which this was the first for them, the thousandth for her.

"This is not nightclubs," she had said. "This is *theater*. This is *concerts*," and with a minor *coup de théâtre*, standards had been posted. Twenty-six adult professionals—and even a famous composer—had been informed this was no *gig*. They were to give her, as she was to give her audience, "all those things you've always pined for," bar by bar, beat by beat, purr by purr.

Maybe those twenty-six union men sensed something special about this concert. Maybe the reason Bacharach had consented to come back briefly from his composing and his films. Maybe there was a heightened tension there, an awareness that this was, as Berlin had been in 1960—and Bacharach had been there, too—a kind of homecoming where there was no longer any home; a return to the past designed to convey only the present.

They all knew that just across the concrete plaza from this theater and the smaller Mark Taper Forum, past the ponds and fountains and the contorted Jacques Lipchitz sculpture staring blindly at the Department of Water and Power across the way, there was an even grander ostentation, the Pavilion. It was there, focused in the cameras of the world, that Hollywood bestowed golden statuettes upon its annual elect, though Dietrich—like Chaplin, like Garbo, like Astaire—had never been elected.

Maybe this theater, this concert, this town and audience, then, would be different from London or Paris or Rio or Warsaw or Moscow or even Broadway. This stage on which she stood was in the heart of a company town that could be cruel and callous or—even worse—indifferent. It was capital to an industry whose current managers would be there Friday night, "suits" for whom she was mostly a memory or a scrapbook of irrelevant stills, but of whose history she was an immutable part, a legendary icon; and they were people who respected no history older than yesterday's grosses.

Maybe that was why on this first day of rehearsal, as the voice insinuated itself again and again around rhythms already perfect, that through the elegance of the phrasings, the shimmer of the orchestrations, shone something else: the glint not of glamour but of honed steel; a legend's determination to endure.

Neither Dietrich, nor Bacharach, nor the orchestra was aware of the surreptitious surveillance of their rehearsals going on far above their heads and behind their backs. But by the second morning of run-throughs, the theater's administration *was* and clamped down fast. The obvious slowing in workaday activity was not the point: it was as if Babe Ruth had stopped off for a little batting practice and the home team was allowed to climb the fence for a look. This much seemed harmless, maybe even instructive, good for morale.

Lost time could be made up, *would* be, but a breached contract was not so easily repaired, and Miss Dietrich's producer (herself) had strictly forbidden observation of her rehearsals, and the auditorium had been placed under contractual quarantine. Technically, perhaps, nothing was being breached but faith. The theater itself was merely being booked for her engagement, and she herself was responsible for every aspect of its presentation, from posters and lighting to liability insurance and costs of the musicians and their union dues. She therefore had the right to demand and to get what she demanded. However pleasurable or even edifying electronic eavesdropping might be, it was at the expense of a guaranteed privacy, and somehow deemed not quite "professional." Various grumbles from the new assistant and others that nothing could be more professional than studying a work-in-progress did not stay the edict: "Over and out with the squawk-box and back to work!"

This did not sit well with most of the staff, old or new. Small rumbles of resentment began to hum through the offices like the drone of the duplicating machine, as if the normal daily routine were some new and unheard-of imposition or outrage, and there was some confusion as to whether Dietrich herself were to blame, or the theater's "suits."

The only member of the staff inconvenienced in any real way didn't even work on the third floor, and thus escaped the grumble following the speaker system ban. This was the Ahmanson's stage manager, whose office was located (another architectural mystery) below the orchestra floor, reachable only by trekking through the auditorium.

This grizzled and unflappable professional solved his problem simply by arriving before Dietrich and her entourage started work around ten o'clock each morning, and leaving after they had finished, about six. What he did between ten and six was anybody's guess and nobody's business, for with Dietrich in temporary charge of his theater, he had no current responsibilities beyond keeping the lights on and himself out of sight.

On the third floor, however, things began to simmer with a sense of deprivation. Publicity Peg tried to assuage these feelings by promising to get press passes for those who were least well paid or whose noses were most out of joint. Even this normally routine accommodation was problematic, however, for press tickets were all but gone and "paper"—free tickets to fill empty seats—was forbidden by the Dietrich contract.

Gloom deepened and Miss Dietrich's privacy increased.

That might have been the end of it, were it not for the gloating a member of the technical staff did at the resumption of routine. The Taper's stage manager had groused from the first about being "up to my ass in glamour," which he poisonously pronounced as if his personal stores of props were under personal threat from the foreign temptress. He was mostly tolerated by the creative staff because his technical skills were varied and many, though he liked to display contempt for the theatrical arts his skills were meant to support or conceal. "Make-or-break is my job," he often announced, and sometimes it was true.

Because he was suspected of being responsible for the thunder and lightning of the eavesdropping ban, the creative staff was not displeased to hear him announce his departure for "where the *real* work gets done." He left for wherever that might have been and, as he exited, the open door briefly admitted muted orchestral strains spilling into the corridors from the third-floor balcony.

"Five'll get you ten he's going where he always goes," Peg murmured cynically. "When there's 'work' to do."

"Where's that?" asked Bob, her trainee.

"Stage manager's office, where else?" she said, her index finger tracing a path across an expanse of imaginary auditorium and downward again. She began humming "I Can't Give You Anything but Love, Baby," with something like melody, eyes twinkling with malice.

The office newcomer turned away from the photocopier, put down whatever he was duplicating, and made for the corridor.

"Let it happen," Peg called after him.

"You can bet on it," he replied, and slipped through the door into the warm, floating rhythms of "Honeysuckle Rose." He threw caution to impulsive, even dangerous winds by slipping through into the top row of the final balcony.He was relieved to find the theater dark except for work lights on stage, but he hunched down in the first seat of the last row to avoid the remote possibility of being seen from the stage.

"Honeysuckle Rose" was snapping and slinking down there, with a swagger that suggested Lola Lola from *The Blue Angel* had lightened up her act and linked arms with Fats Waller to saunter down Broadway. What riveted his attention was not the elegant swing, nor the silk of the orchestrations, but the pale blonde figure, barely swaying before the microphone. Somehow he had expected feathers and spangles and lighting that enhanced and concealed. Instead of plumes, she wore a simple daytime suit in the glare of naked bulbs, and the image was so contemporary, so workaday, that questions of age and the past became irrelevant.

The almost imperceptible sway was accompanied by the occasional flick of a finger or the turn of a wrist suggesting pleasure at toying with the swing. It seemed to him the most elegant economy of effect he had ever seen. The low voice flowed through the theater like liquid amber, bubbling with amusement at the improbability of turning a Harlem evergreen into blonde velvet. He wasn't close enough to see the grin or the wink, but they were there to hear in the voice which, for the second time in as many days, abruptly stopped.

Far below, at about the tenth row of orchestra seats, the husky, squat figure of the Taper's stage manager was clanking his nuts and bolts across the forbidden auditorium just as Peg's finger had predicted, on the only path to the stage manager's office below. Even he did not fail to hear an entire orchestra grind to a halt, and his stride faltered. He turned to the stage, to the pale blonde figure who stood there straight and silent and shining sharp. He began hoarsely to explain himself. His voice echoed in the empty theater and his self-assurance withered as he found himself addressing twenty-six musicians and a conductor, for the lady, no grins or winks now, had vanished.

This should have been a clear cue for the crouching witness to depart the top balcony while the departing was good, but he had a streak of pettiness and remained, relishing the discomfort into which the intruder had fallen a couple of thousand seats below. His words were having no effect, for Burt Bacharach stood at his piano not even listening. He was looking into the wings where Dietrich had disappeared. The stage technician's voice seemed to dribble away, and he backed down the aisle, clanking much less than before, and did his own vanishing act.

As soon as he was gone Dietrich marched back on stage, regarded Bacharach in silence for a moment as if they shared unspeakable burdens.

Even from the last row of the top balcony it was possible to see that not a muscle moved anywhere on stage. Then Dietrich turned to her conductor and in that silken voice, that satin scabbard for the steel within, said, "Let's do some lights."

She pivoted back to face the auditorium, and her observer in the balcony had the impression she was staring directly at him as he crouched there guiltily. Instead, the voice called out—projecting strongly now—to someone unseen, somewhere in the theater. "Joe?"

"Ready," said Joe, from somewhere.

"Try to hit me here," she said, positioning herself again squarely before the microphone, "for the end of 'Honeysuckle.' Full up."

She stood there unmoving as lights began to play. She waited patiently, then, "There, there, that's it," though no one on stage—or in the last row of the balcony—could tell how she knew.

"At the end I do the two steps. . . ." She paused and frowned. "This stage is too deep . . . *three*. I'll do three steps back—applause, applause, then three to my right for the bow . . . no, *two*," she said, adjusting her movements to the shape and dimensions of the stage. "Gold, please. Not the pink."

She moved briskly as she talked, going through her moves, pausing for light adjustments in the daytime suit and low-heeled shoes. She raised her chin slightly, as if acknowledging applause in the empty theater, paused, called out, "Too hot. *Here*." Her palm pressed against her temple. An adjustment was made in the light, her skin tested it again, and she pronounced it "fine," moving into another pattern of movements, pausing for settings of lights her pale skin could seemingly measure, not unaware that an orchestra was watching this display of sensitivity not merely to light, but to the minutest details of stagecraft.

"Now 'Where Have All The Flowers Gone?' " she said to Joe, and resumed her position before the microphone, crossing her arms behind her back. The pinks and blues and golds disappeared, and she stood there in street makeup, her face haloed by pale hair pulled back sharply from her forehead and held in place by a ribbon across the crown, a candle flame, steady, unwavering.

"More," she told Joe. "A little higher," and even from the top balcony drama formed, dependent on nothing more than a light and facial planes that softened and glowed against the immense, dark stage. She stood there like an exclamation point against the darkness.

It was not a question of beauty. Not "mere" beauty, anyway, the assistant thought, not of any conventional kind. It was that, all right, but something beyond that. It was what she had said it was: theater, but of no kind he had seen or experienced before.

Just then, another light appeared, a slice of it to his left. Bob, the publicity trainee peered into the balcony and whispered, "Are you crazy or what? Get the hell out of there."

The assistant glanced back one more time as the silent show of lights continued. He stepped reluctantly into the corridor. The publicity assistant looked exhilarated by the gossip he passed on as they reentered the offices.

"Guess who just got fired?" he asked grinning.

"By whom?" asked the newcomer, that candle flame still burning.

"The Great White Bureaucrat," Bob said. "On the telephone from New York. That Kraut lady don't fool around. And you're next, if there's any more of *that*."

"New York? If the Beloved Leader isn't here, we can turn the sound system back on," said the newcomer.

"Are you impossible, or what?" groaned Bob.

The speakers went back on.

The third day of rehearsals began with more stage directions, more light settings, more polishing and honing of movement and music in a drive to perfection.

"Then I'll say, 'And here's a song from *The Blue Angel*,'" the voice murmured through the speakers, "and someone will begin to applaud, and I'll say 'No, no, it's not *that* one,' and then someone will call out 'Lola....'"

"She must have goddam 'plants' in the audience," said Peg knowingly.

"Or, if no one *does*—this is Hollywood, after all, where memories are short," came the voice with an edge and a smile, exactly as if she had heard Peg, "I'll tell them myself—'Lola'—and then move *here*...."

Peg cocked an eyebrow and smiled to herself as the corner of her eye caught the new employee abandoning his copy machine and scripts and scurrying down the corridor toward the door. "Oh, to be so green, so very, very green," Peg thought, and maybe wished she was.

The musical repertoire had broadened over the hours of rehearsal, though they were still pieces of a mosaic, rather than a finished product. French and German rubbed shoulders with Tin Pan Alley and Hollywood, and there was a relentless repetition as each number in whatever language or mood was polished to a perfection that perhaps no ear but their singer's could detect.

No violin or strum of bass viol's strings, no grace note of piano or clarinet, no shadow or beam of light was exempt from her attention, her correction. She drove the lights and shadows and sounds as she drove herself, tirelessly, without complaint or drama. She exhausted every opportunity for improvement, every musician on that stage, everything but her apparently inexhaustible self.

As the newcomer, alone or with others, watched this force of nature disguised in smart but simple street clothes as just a person, he began to sense the pattern of the mosaic she was constructing.

He, like the rest, had expected a parade of "Dietrich's Greatest Hits": Lola Lola from *The Blue Angel*, segueing to Frenchy from *Destry Rides Again*, or Shanghai Lily alighting from her *Express* in veils and black feathers. Instead, he was getting none of them, or *all* of them, but subtly altered, matured, crossed and mixed, simplified and deepened. They were there, but something more was, too. She dared to strive for the perfection that conceals art while revealing her mastery of every trick of artifice at her disposal, and though she did so with the energy of a tank corps, was making it look easy.

And still the mosaic was incomplete. The drive for perfection concealed the final pattern. It was like observing the most perfect of precision watchworks without knowing the time.

At the end of the third day of rehearsals Bob asked, "What happens when she puts on the famous dress and they turn on all the lights and she switches on the *real* magic?"

"The earthquake?" joked the other.

"You haven't been paying attention," crackled Peg's dry voice from her office. "That's been happening all week. And," she added tartly, "the week ain't over."

The fourth and final day of rehearsals the theater "suit" returned from New York. There were no more stealthy trips to the upper balcony, no crowding around the speakers; just an impatient suspense as to how and if she were pulling the pieces together. It wasn't just "I Can't Give You Anything but Love, Baby" and "Honeysuckle Rose," with their bright impertinence, but "La Vie en Rose" and its melancholy, and "Frag nicht warum ich gehe," with its fatalistic farewell to lost love. Or the one they had never heard before, the one from Israel that she sang like a lioness in some wilderness. And "Lili Marlene," cloudy with the smoke of battlefields, and "Where Have All the Flowers Gone?" hurled at the rows of empty seats like an accusation from an angry goddess.

Finally, late in the fourth day, the coast cleared. The speakers were switched back on in time to hear Bacharach thank his musicians and announce that rehearsals were over. The expected snap and click of instrument cases and the hubbub of small talk didn't happen. There was silence on the speakers that lingered, becoming ominous, until broken by a voice that was hushed, but heavy as the world.

"All right," she said. "All right. Burt says rehearsals are over, it's time to stop, time to go, and Burt knows. He knows your union rules and your own rules; he knows your freeways and your lawn sprinklers and your swimming pools and your televisions, your standards and your aspirations." The voice grew even quieter, more somber than it had ever sounded in any film, on any recording. "And so you must go home to your little wives in your little houses in the hills or the San Fernando Valley. I am prepared and willing to stay here all night. All night and all tomorrow, too. To get it right. To justify this thing we are doing, this act of theater. But no. Your pools and martinis and television sets and wives are waiting, so never mind. Never mind that we open tomorrow night before the most cynical audience in the world. And we are not ready for them. But go. Go home to Burbank or Encino or Covina . . . and relax. And as you do, think that we open tomorrow night, and that tomorrow night will be . . . ," her voice hushed to near inaudibility, "a disaster."

Footsteps carried her off the stage.

Finally Bacharach said, "That's it," and gathered his music. The stage cleared without another word.

The day of predicted disaster began in calm and quiet, as there was no stage rehearsal on which to eavesdrop. There was another calm, lingering from Dietrich's final words to her orchestra. No earthquake, no tantrum: just a glacial flow, a quiet avalanche of reproach.

Tasks neglected since Monday were resumed or completed. There were no leftover press passes, as it turned out, nor unsold tickets at the box office, so none of the staff would be attending the premiere performance. At day's end the pros and the tyros extended weekend wishes to each other and joined the crush on the crowded freeways home.

The Taper's new creative assistant did so in a subdued silence, unbroken by the usual chatter of his car radio. When he arrived at his tiny apartment, he showered, shaved, brushed, and donned his one suit and best tie, got back into his third-hand car to drive to the corner market, where he bought a bottle of California champagne, and then guided himself back to the freeway, back to the Music Center.

He parked in the underground cavern, took the escalator to the plaza as he did each day, and with work keys let himself into the offices, now deserted.

He set the champagne on the table next to the duplicating machine, retrieved a coffee cup from an overhead shelf, and stepped into the windowed third-floor lobby to watch the traffic patterns around the complex, just as the fountains of the Department of Water and Power began to play, and lights came on across the dusky, endless sprawl. City of the Angels.

The off-ramps of the freeways were clogging now, and limousines crawled around the block, pausing to permit gowns and black-ties to exit and stroll across the plaza to the theater. Who were they? he wondered. What were they coming to see? He returned to the office.

He switched on the speakers to the stage and listened to the babble of that elite: voyeurs with no investment in this opening but the price of a ticket. He wondered at his own investment and, oddly, could not calculate it. Or reason why he had one.

He pushed the plastic cork from the bottle of champagne and filled his coffee cup. As the audience grew silent and the music began on the speaker system, he sipped and listened. The orchestra blared a few bars of "Falling in Love Again" as if it were an anthem, and applause drowned out the music before that blonde velvet began to croon, "I can't give you anything but love, Baby. . . ."

He had heard it a hundred times that week and suddenly knew he had not heard it at all. There was a melting warmth to the voice, an intimate, ingratiating shrug that said "See how easy this is?" and the orchestra was a seamless, gliding thing that followed the voice as if on a leash.

He put down his cup, drawn out of the office and down the corridor by the voice, into the narrow standing space just inside the balcony. It was all working now, he saw. Theater in progress. Far below, the candle flame was glowing, making magic. She was wearing what looked like liquid stars poured over a perfect body, and her hair swayed and swirled like a golden curtain when she flung her head in delight or lowered it in the deep bow with which she received homage the audience hadn't known it was going to give.

It wasn't a legend down there, some waxworks figure of nostalgia, but a Presence, an actress leading her audience through a range of moods and personality they hadn't guessed were there. She was giving them the legend, of course, but playing with it and on it, ringing changes, letting them know she had gone beyond it, had been, perhaps, always more than that streamlined icon of erotic sophistication they had come to remember. It was a display of majesty and variety, custom so elegant it could not stale, and the seeming ease conveyed to those thousands of eyes in whose glow she basked, that all of it was inevitable and, maybe, indestructible.

The assistant had heard each word, each note, each prediction of movement and lighting and audience response. He knew nothing had been left to chance or accident, but still felt caught up in the web of some sorcery, some enchantment, and he realized at last what made it work. It wasn't "Lola Lola" he watched, or "Frenchy," or any of the other images he knew: this was Dietrich's Dietrich, the *Ding an sich*, the essence of whatever she was or wanted them to believe she was, or maybe what *she* wanted to believe she was. With that she overwhelmed and obliterated the past. There was only Now, diamond-dusted and glowing like a moon. Ageless and fleeting and forever, in that place that time can't reach.

The "disaster" was widely reviewed, of course. The following Monday, now that the auditorium was no longer rehearsal ground, the assistant crossed the rows of empty seats on his way to the Ahmanson stage manager's office, scripts for technical breakdown under his arm. As he walked he read the town's most important review, the one in the *Los Angeles Times*. "This timeless sorceress," he read, "sang, or performed, or did whatever it was she did and gave you gooseflesh. . . ."

He interrupted his reading to descend the stairs to the stage manager's office. The old pro sat feet crossed at the ankles on his desk, a steaming cup of coffee at his lips.

"Yeah?" he said.

"Scripts," said the younger man, handing them to him.

"These are for the Taper," the stage manager said, handing them back after the briefest glance.

"Yes, but—"

"He'll be back. It was only a fake firing. Just to make a point, just for effect, just for the week." The gray-haired man tugged at his coffee cup and let his eyes wander to the tape recorder on his desk. He heaved his feet from the desktop, grunted, and punched a button on the machine. The reels began to turn and the basement office filled with the voice Hemingway said could break your heart.

"And then I'll say, 'And here's a song from *The Blue Angel*,' and someone will begin to applaud and then I'll say 'no, no, it's not *that* one. . . .' "

The stage manager switched the machine off and leaned heavily on the desktop. "The speaker system feeds down here, too, you know," he said. "All four days of it is there on tape. Every word. All the sweat. You ever want to hear it, come on down."

"But why?" asked the assistant.

"Because," said the older man. "*Because*."

He sipped at his coffee, then nodded to the newspaper open to the review in the assistant's hand. "Because it'll be proof of what happened Friday night," the stage manager said, his voice mellow and firm. "It'll prove what happened and how you get to be a star and how you get to *stay* a star."

I understood. Or thought I did. And went back to work.

I. THE ICON

Filmmuseum Berlin—Marlene Dietrich Collection Berlin.

LUTZ KOEPNICK

Dietrich's Face

IN 1934, A *Film Pictorial* article entitled "Composite Beauty—Hollywood Standard" surveyed the bodies and physiognomies of several leading female film stars in order to compile an image of physical perfection.[1] Norma Shearer ranked first in the category of hair, Loretta Young was seen as having the most desirable eyes, and Irene Dunne and Claudette Colbert surpassed the looks of all other film stars when it came to the shape of noses and mouths. No other star, however, had as many perfect body parts to offer than Marlene Dietrich, the highest grossing screen actress of the time. After Paramount had marketed Dietrich two years earlier as "the women all *women* want to see" (John Baxter 75), the *Film Pictorial* essay now instructed the fans exactly what to look at when admiring their star on screen. Dietrich featured with no less than four body parts in the essay's normative vision of female beauty, three of them located in her body's lower regions and all of them, in Dietrich's early Hollywood films, often involved in a calculated aesthetic of display and concealment: her hands, legs, ankles, and feet.

Sarah Berry (*Screen Style*) has recently examined the extent to which Hollywood star images of the early 1930s encouraged fantasies of personal self-transformation and social mobility that, to some degree, challenged received notions of individual sovereignty, identity, and authority. Accordingly, star images were designed to empower individual spectators to flirt with temporary losses and mimetic transgressions of their ordinary selves; they promoted an ethos of individual self-formation that invited the viewer to adopt the star's features and translate them into a multiplicity of vernacular uses and meanings. In some sense, the 1934 article in *Film Pictorial* was the culmination of this trend. It not only presented the stars' bodies as prototypes for acts of personal self-redress, but literally dismembered the stars' corporeal appearances in order to fuel desire and capture the imagination. The notion of perfect beauty here bordered the monstrous. Far from recalling classical ideals of physical integrity, balance, and symmetry, the article's vision of composite beauty in fact reached Frankensteinian proportions. In its efforts to exploit the Hollywood cult of stardom at its fullest, *Film Pictorial* surreptitiously spoke the truth about the reifying logic of Fordist consumer culture. Instead of circulating star images as signs of authenticity and wholeness, *Film Pictorial* endorsed visions of the human body as marked by atomization and aggregation, by syncretism and montage. Instead of defining beauty as humanity's most captivating attraction, the article invited the fan to enter and exalt in nothing other than the realm of the posthuman, of prosthetic identities.

Given Dietrich's star status in Hollywood in the early 1930s, as well as the continual realignment of her persona with the tastes of Depression-ridden America, Dietrich's prominent position in the *Film Pictorial* ranking should hardly come as a surprise. What may astonish, however, is the fact that in its search for ideal body parts the article completely bypassed any mention of Dietrich's facial features: her sharp, elongated eyebrows, her dramatically elevated cheekbones, the enigmatic smile of her mouth, the canvas-like composition of her forehead and skin. In the perspective of the judges of *Film Pictorial*, Dietrich's body and its beauty seemed to begin somewhere below the star's neck. They had no eyes for how Dietrich tended to exhibit her face to her director's camera, nor did they encourage fans to mimic what has marked the circulation of the Dietrich image ever since, namely to emulate how Dietrich staged her countenance as a fetish, one that involved the viewer in a dazzling game of hide and seek, of lure and endless deferral, of multivalent attraction and theatrical artifice.

Film Pictorial's silence about Dietrich's face is particularly surprising if we consider the extent to which Dietrich, in her initial efforts to secure and increase her market value in 1930s Hollywood, subjected her face to a scrupulous process of remodeling and transformation. A good number of production stills and publicity materials, rejected by Dietrich for publication, and gathered at the Marlene Dietrich Collection in Berlin, docu-

Dietrich's markings for photo touch-ups. *Filmmuseum Berlin—Marlene Dietrich Collection Berlin.*

ment in a highly instructive manner Dietrich's quest for facial makeover during the 1930s. Time and again, we can see the trace of Dietrich's pen in these images, pointing out or even correcting certain unwanted aspects of her facial appearance: unwelcome shadows under her eyes; tiny wrinkles around her mouth; stray hairs, which by stubbornly sticking up seem to spoil a balanced framing of her face; and—of course—the much talked-about unsightliness of her nose, when seen in full or semiprofile. What is interesting to note is that almost all of Dietrich's interventions seek to remake her face by changing the distribution and collision of shadow and light in her countenance. Rather than dissecting the materiality of her face itself, Dietrich's ink pen literally sought to cast new light onto and thereby recompose her facial makeup. Like a fill light, it aspired to erase irritating shadows and harsh outlines; like a key light, this pen wanted to shift the viewer's attention to different areas of the face as captured in the respective image. Facial beautification, in these rejected publicity stills, was an effect, not of surgical intrusion or makeup modification, but of Dietrich's proficient rearrangement of lighting, its sources as much as its directions. Dietrich's pen here, to modify Alexandre Astruc's famous term, aspired to the status of a *light-stylo*. As it reworked given reproductions, it hoped to ensure that Dietrich's face could be seen as a direct expression of her own intentions, as a self-contained design actively authored by the star, as a form of language and writing effectively communicating a subject's interior visions.

Or so it seems at least. "Neither a realist nor a comic," writes James Naremore about the acting style of Marlene Dietrich, "she inhabits a realm where visible artifice becomes the sign of authenticity. She also challenges our ability to judge her acting skill, because her image is unusually dependent on a controlled, artful *mise-en-scène*" (Naremore 131). It is the task of the following pages to argue that Naremore's account of Dietrich's self-imaging does not even go far enough. Focusing on the production and circulation of Dietrich's face around 1933, I suggest that Dietrich's facial appearance not only urges the viewer to question conventional notions of acting and thespian skill. More important, this face asks us to unravel the very trope of authenticity that, in so many ways, informed the Hollywood cult of stardom at the time as much as the avant-garde's emphasis on authorship and aesthetic self-realization. Rather than merely synthesizing the artificial and the authentic, Dietrich's face provided something qualitatively different, something that questioned these terms' very validity and dialectic. Dietrich's face was a face without qualities; a site at which human and apparatical aspects, the corporeal and the technical, entertained symbiotic relationships. To read her face either as a sign of subjective expressiveness or as an auteur's text and language misses the point. For Dietrich's face invited her viewers to brush aside the whole conceptual matrix according to which critics and scholars had come and continue to evaluate the appearance of actors and images on screen, concepts such as authorship, expressiveness, authenticity, and intentional meaning. Instead of emphasizing the notion of the artist and star as a charismatic demiurge, as the sole creator and proprietor of works, Dietrich's face reveals the material reality and excessive circulation of signs in modern mass culture. Though often compared to the mask-like expression of Greta Garbo, Dietrich's face was of a completely different order from that of her Swedish competitor. Unlike Garbo's, Dietrich's face resisted reading and unsettled semiotic interpretation. In fact, Dietrich's relation to Garbo, as I will argue in what follows, equals that of digital to photographic images, of the morph to the classical performer. And it is precisely this cyborgian economy of Dietrich's face that might explain why *Film Pictorial*, in its 1934 issue, ignored the face of the woman all women were supposed to see. The beauty of Dietrich's face was so post-human, so much affected by and assimilated to modern technology, so much steeped in the ecstasy of image circulation, that it out-reified the essay's own strategies of reification and dismemberment. That Dietrich's face remained unnamed simply reflected the fact that, in the perspective of *Film Pictorial*, this face did not really exist.

Beyond Art and the Aesthetic

In 1933, a year before the publication of the mentioned issue of *Film Pictorial*, we find Dietrich on the Paramount sets for her first Hollywood production not directed by Josef von Sternberg—Rouben Mamoulian's quite provocative *Song of Songs*. "Solomon," Stephen Bach has written mockingly about this film and its challenges to contemporary production codes, "would not have objected: Marlene standing on her tip-toes, shoulders thrust back, breasts thrust forward, nipples at attention, pudenda smooth as a baby's bottom at a time when even a baby's bottom was a no-no at the Hays Office. It is not merely nude; it is naked" (Bach 167). *Song of Songs* tells the story of Lily Czepanek (Marlene Dietrich), an innocent country girl propelled into the hands of a Berlin-based Bohemian sculptor, Richard Waldow (Brian Aherne), after the death of her parents. Waldow molds Lily's body into a sleek sculpture only to cause Lily's social and his own emotional downfall. A direct product of male desire and fetishistic transferral, art in this film simultaneously intensifies and displaces life; it causes both ecstasy and trauma. Though Mamoulian's camera frequently lingers on Dietrich's face itself in order to open intimate windows on her ever shifting appearances, it spends almost equal time to offer us images of her statue in scenarios of what Gaylyn Studlar would call "iconic tex-

Dietrich and Josef von Sternberg. *Filmmuseum Berlin—Marlene Dietrich Collection Berlin*

tuality," that is, highly choreographed scenarios emphasizing the sign as a creation independent of its referent (Studlar, *Realm of Pleasure* 85–107). In what is the film's perhaps most uncanny and excessive sequence, we see Waldow despairing in his studio over his aborted affair with Lily while the camera captures a number of quasi-photographic shots of the statue's face. Throughout this sequence, the editing increasingly separates the image of the statue's face from Waldow's own point of view. Close-ups of Waldow's own face alternate with close-ups of the sculpture as seen from a variety of ideal viewing angles. Meanwhile, the soundtrack carries us back to earlier times, in particular the time of the sculpture's making. Waldow's statue thus seems to gain a fantasmatic life of its own. As we explore the artist's tormented mindscape, the film's images fetishistically divorce the sign from its referent. The statue's face, in Waldow's inner perspective, seems to hold the absent referent in what Studlar calls an "I-know-but nevertheless" suspension (92). Although Waldow as much as the audience of course knows better, the sculptured face here becomes more real than the real, Mamoulian's camera engages our fantasy with a substitute of desire that sustains painful illusions of autonomy.

Song of Songs, in my view, is one of Dietrich's most important films, not because of its high degree of self-referentiality, but because it—as her first post–von Sternberg production—invites us to examine dominant narratives about the making of the Dietrich persona and its dependence on von Sternberg's authorship. In the early 1930s, the Armenian-Russian immigrant Mamoulian was known in Hollywood as a competent engineer of dramatic images and innovative sounds. A former student of Eugene Vakhtangov, who himself was a disciple of Stanislavsky, Mamoulian had entered the film industry as an experienced stage director. His pictures prior to 1933 had privileged expressive stylization over naturalistic restraint; both *Applause* (1929) and *City Streets* (1931) had been praised widely for their innovative camera work and intelligent sound editing, their way of translating relatively unassuming stories into compelling aesthetic surfaces. Paramount, therefore, had good reasons to endorse Mamoulian as a proficient substitute for von Sternberg, as a director capable of showcasing Dietrich as an exotic and enigmatic presence. Dietrich herself, however, initially disagreed with the studio's decision. As she was for many years to come, Dietrich at the time of the making of *Song of Songs* was far from ready to renounce the myth of von Sternberg's aesthetic genius and demiurgic power over her appearance, a myth best summarized by Otto Tolischus in a 1931 feature of *Photoplay Magazine*: "Like an artist working in clay, von Sternberg has molded and modeled her to his own design, and Marlene, plastic and willing to be material in the director's hands, has responded to his creative moods" (28). By severing her image from the ingenious talent of von Sternberg, *Song of Songs* in the eyes of Dietrich seemed to thwart her status as a singular art work, an extraordinary creation, a fantasmatic masterpiece in which surface became essence and artifice the sign of overwhelming authenticity.

The von Sternberg myth continues to hover over most discussions of *Song of Songs*, including the ones by Maria Riva in her 1993 portrayal of her mother's career and by Helma Sanders-Brahms in her 2000 book, *Marlene and Jo*. Riva recalls the making of *Song of Songs* as a story of her mother's artistic emancipation and self-constitution. It was while working on this film, Riva argues, that Dietrich took control over her own star image, learning some of the basic principles of cinematic lighting and recording in order to stage her face and body most effectively (without von Sternberg's aid). Not only did Dietrich, during the shooting, watch some of her earlier features in a private screening room (with her daughter in attendance) so as to better understand how to stage her corporeal features in front of the camera. On the set, she also made extensive use of a special mirror helping her to manage her own looks and prepare for the recording process. This mirror was a full-length contraption, bolted on a trolley, with three high-wattage light bulbs on either side. As Riva narrates: "The electricians plugged it in, the grips, under my mother's directions, positioned it until she, standing on her marks within the shooting set, could see herself exactly as the camera would. Mamoulian and Victor Milner, the cameraman, watched with dawning respect, fascinated. It had taken her only a few seconds to know the exact angle and position of the first shot" (175). Once she was used to this mirror, Dietrich—in Riva's memory—took command over the technicians behind the camera as well. She asked the lighting crew to change the angle and position of key and fill lights while looking at her reflection, to the utter admiration of the film's production staff and director. Looking at this mirror, Dietrich finally learned how to create and administer her own image on film and cast her face into an alluring work of art, a step into independence enthusiastically welcomed by her daughter: "She had done it! All by herself, she had achieved what she had set out to do! I was so proud of her—I could have kissed her! Of course I couldn't because of the makeup, but I felt like it anyway" (179).

Sanders-Brahms largely follows Riva's account, yet carries the argument into a slightly different direction. What in the eyes of Riva constitutes a story of self-empowerment and emancipation, in the perspective of Sanders-Brahms represents a narrative in whose course Dietrich learns how to recreate the ideal model designed for her by von Sternberg. According to Sanders-Brahms, what von Sternberg tried to teach Dietrich was to stage her face in front of different light sources in such a way that smallest physical movements could produce dramatic changes in appearance: "She realizes that, whenever she raises or lowers her chin a little, whenever she moves a millimeter to the left or the right, she can produce different shadows and illuminations on her face. And that she can thus change her face—yes, even more, that her face can change its inner expression. The flatter and more expressionless her face, the higher the intensity by which light will transform it and even signify emotions" (117). In Sanders-Brahms's understanding, the intelligent, albeit unimaginative, Mamoulian was in no position to achieve comparable effects in

Shanghai Express (1932). *Filmmuseum Berlin—Marlene Dietrich Collection Berlin.*

his films. Forced by legal threats to show up on the set, Dietrich's principle concern thus became to save her face both literally and metaphorically. Removed from von Sternberg's molding hands, Dietrich had to actualize the master's teaching on her own, that is to say, to counter or infuse Mamoulian's murky craftsmanship with von Sternberg's awe-inspiring aesthetics of light. Hence her request to have the mirror placed right next to the camera. Hence her attempt to take command over the film's lighting crew, her determination to tell the film's gaffer and his assistants where to place key, fill, and spot lights, and how to shape and emphasize the features of her countenance. Hence also, according to Sanders-Brahms, the film's ultimate failure, caused by the unresolved clash between two different cinematic styles, that is, Mamoulian's inability to elevate his own work to the level of Dietrich's diegetic self-creation as a transcendent work of art, a phenomenon of a distance however close it may be.

In Sanders-Brahms's understanding, the Dietrich of *Song of Songs* became her own director, gaffer, and best boy in order to mold her appearance into a mesmerizing object of to-be-looked-at-ness. Separated from the master's creative authority, the post–von Sternberg Dietrich had to take things into her own hands in order to warrant her status as an aesthetic attraction—even at the cost of undermining a film's narrative coherence and stylistic unity. While Sanders-Brahms's version of the von Sternberg myth might be intriguing, it—like Riva's—fails to address the full significance of Dietrich's skillful and reciprocal relationship to the recording apparatus. For Dietrich's performance in front of the camera, her management of immaterial light rays in order to modify material facial properties, invalidated the very notions both Riva and Sanders-Brahms used in order to celebrate Dietrich's face as a stunning work of art. Dietrich's face might be beautiful, but it no longer belongs to the sphere of "beautiful semblance" traditionally reserved for works of art. Dietrich's face, in particular in the post–von Sternberg period, might be the product of her own work, but it also emancipates the notion of "work" from aesthetic ideologies of authorship and authenticity.

Two years after Dietrich's appearance in *Song of Songs*, Walter Benjamin wrote about the relation between camera and film actor, recording and performance: "The camera that presents the performance of the film actor to the public need not respect the performance as an integral whole. Guided by the cameraman, the camera continually changes its position with respect to the performance. The sequence of positional views which the editor composes from the material supplied him constitutes the completed film. It comprises certain factors of movement which are in reality those of the camera, not to mention special camera angles, close-ups, etc. Hence, the performance of the actor is subjected to a series of optical tests" (*Illuminations* 228). Had Benjamin watched more films and read more about contemporary cinema than he—I suspect—actually did, he could have found in Dietrich a welcome subject to radicalize his theoretical model. Whether directed by von Sternberg or not, Dietrich's performance was one in which the film actor, rather than simply being tested by camera, editor, and public, subjects herself to a ruthless process of optical self-examinations. Far from merely encouraging the audience to identify with the work of the apparatus, Dietrich's performance itself already relied on a highly experimental negotiation of machine and body, of the ephemeral and the transitory, of camera, light, and human flesh. What makes Dietrich's face so fascinating, then, is the fact that it provided a screen for apparatical inscriptions. It was at once object and subject of technical recording. Being its own camera, this face came into being only in deliberate adaptation to, by testing and managing, the various machines of cinematic fantasy production. As it mimetically bridged the gulf between the human and the apparatus, Dietrich's face thus displayed the extent to which in Benjamin's age of mechanical reproduction "art has left the realm of the 'beautiful semblance' which, so far, had been taken to be the only sphere where art could thrive" (*Illuminations* 230). The art of Die trich's face was postaesthetic, whether it was staged in front of von Sternberg's or Mamoulian's camera, whether it was filmed by inspired directors or put on display by Dietrich herself. Dietrich's face was a copy without original, a sign without a referent, pure surface without depth. In this face, technical effects became attractive essences, purely graphical presentation prevailed over the logic of realism and representation. Dietrich's face urged its viewer to reject the hierarchy of content and form, product and process, meaning and production, so central to bourgeois aesthetics as well as to dominant film language. Instead, her face was all about the process by which we make meaning and put on identities. In its fluidity and technological hybridity, Dietrich's face encourages us to deface dominant notions of work and ownership. Contrary to both Sanders-Brahms's and Riva's assumptions, this face denied the very concepts according to which modern bourgeois culture has hailed works of art as expressions of aesthetic genius, individual creativity, and authentic expressiveness. And in doing so, it also denied the very gesture by which scholars and critics—as well as Dietrich herself—have elevated von Sternberg (or Dietrich) to the status of godlike artists, creating Dietrich's image from scratch like sculptors working in clay.

It is interesting to note in this context that Mamoulian's *Song of Songs*, perhaps more than any other film, is quite aware of the postaesthetic beauty of Dietrich's face. In many respects, *Song of Songs* was designed to allow Dietrich to do "her thing." Like any star vehicle, the film frequently interrupts its own narrative progress in order to exhibit the star's peculiar features to the viewers' consuming perception. We see Dietrich in poses of mystery and ambiguity, of irony and multiple entendre, of fetishistic masquerade, seduction, and cold rejection. Many close-ups of her face foreground the act of appearance and performance itself, playing on the theme of veiling and revelation, the visible and the hidden. As in her roles in most of von Sternberg's films, Dietrich's star presence in *Song of Songs* crucially depends on her talent to signify that—in Bill Nichols's words—"she seems to be something she is not, and that she is in control of the difference" (125). The fetish of her face thus remains triumphant, situating the viewer in a position of waiting without ever exposing or fulfilling what it seems to promise. "Everything is in the face," we hear Dietrich say in her role as innocent country beauty Lily Czepanek, while Waldow prepares himself to knead his clay and mold his model's face and breasts as if they were the real thing. And yet, even though *Song of Songs* clearly capitalizes on the display of its star as fetish, in the end the film is eager to denounce its own ideological implications, namely the aesthetic fetishism of both bourgeois art and, by implication, middle-brow cinema. When Lily, in the last sequence, finally rebels against her own reification, her life as artwork and iconic representation, Dietrich's first blow is directed at nothing other than the statue's head. Dismantling her own statue, Lily dismantles the romantic myth of art as being superior to life, the myth that transfigures art as an expression of aesthetic genius and authorial control whose sublime values demand from us to—in Rilke's famous words—change our life.[2] *Song of Songs* ends with emblematic images of mutilation and defacement, and these images—in however hypocritical form—indicate the extent to which traditional discourses of art, creativity, and aesthetic beauty are of no use to understand why Dietrich's face fascinates.

Dietrich as Morph

Song of Songs opened to mixed reviews in July 1933. Critics largely disparaged the film's dull narrative and lack of inner drama, but they were eager to isolate Dietrich's performance from the rest of the film and celebrate the star's appearance as a sign of coming attractions: "No one," wrote the *Los Angeles Examiner*, "will dare call Marlene Dietrich the Trilby to Josef von Sternberg's Svengali again!" (4 August 1933). *Motion Pictures* did not hesitate to add that in the role of Lily Czepanek Dietrich even "out-Garbos the Great Garbo" (29 July 1933), who—according to some reporters—had left her mythical seclusion to see *Song of Songs* at a local theater not only once but twice.[3] While Dietrich's next two pictures for Paramount, *The Scarlet Empress* (1934) and *The Devil Is a Woman* (1935), returned her once more into the hands of Josef von Sternberg, Rouben Mamoulian moved over to the lot of MGM in order to direct an extravagant melodrama starring none other than that Great Garbo. Mamoulian's *Queen Christina* became perhaps Greta Garbo's greatest film, but did she manage to strike back here and in her regal role out-Dietrich Dietrich? Did Mamoulian succeed in rebuilding the Swede's slipping popularity and have Garbo win the gripping face-off with her German rival?

Nothing, I believe, is more misleading than to see Dietrich and Garbo, these two Hollywood icons of European alterity and exoticness, in direct conversation and competition with each other. To be sure, both of them, at roughly the same time, struggled with each other over box office returns and the public's recognition; and both of them, in and after 1933, experienced the impact of New Deal politics—increasing isolationism and growing xenophobia—as a threat to the definition of their stardom. But none of this should ever make us think that Garbo could have out-Dietriched Dietrich or Dietrich out-Garboed Garbo. For even when framed by the same director, their screen personas were of different ontological orders, their bodies on screen occupied dissimilar possible worlds, and their faces displayed incommensurable regimes of representation and value.

"I want your face," Mamoulian instructed Garbo during the shooting of *Queen Christina*, "to be a blank sheet of paper. I want the writing to be done by everyone in the audience. I'd like it if you could avoid even blinking your eyes, so that you're nothing but a musical mask" (Milne 74–75). Mamoulian's hope was to present Garbo in such a way that the audience would have to project thought and affect onto her face; Garbo's face was to serve as the viewer's vortex drawing them into the enigmatic depths of human passion and desire. There is no doubt that Mamoulian got what he wanted. Garbo's mask-like expressions in *Queen Christina* provide signature shots for her entire career. Her facial tableaux of outward disaffection continue to mystify the viewer, stimulating our desire for affect and meaning. But how does Greta Garbo's mask-like appearance in her 1933 film compare to the mask that was Marlene Dietrich? How does Mamoulian's orchestration of facial signs and expressions in *Queen Christina* differ from the play of shadow and light that was Dietrich's face?

Time to consult an author whose famous discussion of Garbo's face inspired the whole enterprise of this essay. The face of Garbo in *Queen Christina*, Roland Barthes wrote famously in 1957, is "not a painted face, but one set in plaster, protected by the surface of the colour, not by its lineaments. Amid all this snow at once fragile and compact, the eyes alone, black like strange soft flesh, but not in the least expressive, are two faintly tremulous wounds. In spite of its extreme beauty, this face, not drawn but sculpted in something smooth and friable, that is, at once perfect and ephemeral, comes to resemble the flour-white complexion of Charlie Chaplin, the dark vegetation of his eyes, his totem-like countenance" ("Face of Garbo" 536). Barthes agrees with Mamoulian that Garbo's face, at its best, was a palimpsest of audience projections. Yet, according to Barthes, the true drama of Garbo's countenance in *Queen Christina* resulted from the interplay of what was mask—defined as a sum of lines—and what was face—understood as the thematic harmony of the mask's graphic lines. In *Queen Christina*, Garbo's face simultaneously represents and transcends classical, archetypical beauty. It displays a singular embodiment of an idea, reconciling the abstract and the concrete, the material and the transcendental, the ephemeral and the timeless. The beauty of Garbo's face here points to the stylized world of silent cinema, but it becomes recognizable only in the moment of this world's evanescence, that is, after the advent of synchronized sound and the new kind of realism it brought with it: "Garbo's face represents this fragile moment when the cinema is about to draw an existential from an essential beauty, when the archetype leans towards the fascination of mortal faces, when the clarity of the flesh as essence yields its place to a lyricism of Woman" (537–538).

The beauty of Garbo's face, in the eyes of Roland Barthes, resulted from the way in which it articulated a sense of timelessness and eternity, not by fleeing from, but by fleeing into the transitory textures of modern temporality. Garbo's face fascinates because its appearance momentarily suspended the gravity of time. Synthesis of mask and face, her countenance converted time into space and thus extended a sudden shock of immortality to an ever changing present. It is in how Garbo's face negotiated the temporal and the spatial, I suggest, that its categorical difference from Dietrich's face becomes the clearest. Garbo's face, in its playful refusal to signify, appealed to the viewer's desire for meaning: Garbo promised depth, immortal essence, and essential truth precisely by hiding something behind the mask-like surface of her face. Dietrich's face, by contrast, hid things at the surface itself; it mystified the viewer by juxtaposing seemingly incompatible exhibition values, by involving us in a bewildering play of empty signs. In its relentless testing of and assimilation to the cinematic apparatus, Dietrich's face appears to the viewer as a face of radical exteriorization. Everything was indeed in this face, even though we often fail to see it because we look for it in the wrong places. Garbo's face was a semiotician's dream; it was designed to be read and deciphered, to be endowed with significant meaning and transcendent value. Dietrich's face, by way of contrast, resists our desire for reading and meaning as it evacuated the viewer into a realm of pure figuration. Space here became time and thereby revoked the dialectics of surface and depth, the existential and the essential, the mortal and the immortal, so central not only to Garbo's face but modernist aesthetics in general.

If the beauty of Garbo's face secretly pointed to the photographic stillness of silent cinema, then Dietrich's face—let me suggest in closing—in its ceaseless apparatical forming and reforming, anticipated what in our own experience today seems to supersede former cinematic pleasures. Dietrich's face fascinates because it denies hierarchical meaning and reflects an extraordinary ability to transform matter, quickly and easily, in time and space. Mimesis of woman and machine, this face is essentially protean. It visibly represents substantial transformations as a consequence, not of physical labor and material intervention, but of technological will and skill. In this, Dietrich's face foreshadows contemporary cinema's digital morphs, whose visual designs and narrative figurations—according to Vivian Sobchack—take all the bildung out of the bildungsroman. The morph privileges becoming over being; its very fluidity destabilizes dominant metaphysics of identity; its spatial shiftiness and temporal reversibility, its emphasis on playful quick-change and effortless transformation, deflates the gravity of photographic representation and cinematic realism. "As our physical double, the morph interrogates the dominant philosophies and fantasies that fix our embodied human being and constitute our identities as discrete and thus reminds us of our true instability: our physical flux, our lack of self-confidence, our subatomic as well as subcutaneous existence that is always in motion and ever changing. As our cultural double, the morph enacts our own greedy and effortless consumerism—at the same time as it terrifies us with reflected images of our own consumption" (xii).

Like the digital morph, Dietrich's face appeals to that part in us that wants to escape the gravity of time and space so as to partake in the flux and endless becoming of Being. The beauty of Dietrich's face is therefore of a different order from that of Garbo's, whose dialectics of depth and surface, mask and flesh seemed to open temporary windows onto the timeless and eternal. Due to its mimetic assimilation to the cinematic apparatus, Dietrich's face—like that of the digital morph and cyborg in contemporary science fiction—displays a sense of effortlessness and malleability terminating the grounds of Garbo's humanism: Garbo's pathos of bodily coherence and immortality. Garbo's face was immortal because it—like Baudelaire—embraced the fleetingness of modern time as the condition for touching the eternal, essential, and absolute. Dietrich's immortality, by contrast, derives from the fact that it is simply impossible for us to think and speak of a morph's death, to think of its finality in substantial, not narrative terms. Garbo's beauty was that of classical aesthetic modernism; Dietrich's was prosthetic, seamlessly incorporating technology into a new kind of posthuman organism.

It should therefore also come as no real surprise that, in our own contemporary media landscape, Garbo's face serves Turner Movie Classics as an icon to promote the pleasures of watching "the greatest movies of all time. All the time," whereas Dietrich's face in the late 1990s became the trademark of Virtual Celebrity Productions, Jeff Lotman's Los Angeles–based company seeking to reincarnate the dead, trade star images in digitized form, and in the long run revolutionize the possibilities of cinematic representation (Bun). I am not sure how many more years of technological refinement it will take in order to fulfill Lotman's dream, namely to produce a partial remake of *Casablanca* starring Humphrey Bogart and the digital Dietrich. One might also have legitimate doubts about the desirability of such a remake. What strikes me as quite appropriate, however, is the use of Dietrich's face as an emblem of Lotman's operations, of a discourse privileging skill over genius expressiveness, becoming over being, reversibility over teleology. For Dietrich's face went digital long before the advent of the computer. Its beauty emerged from the fact that it transcended the grounds of human mortality and cinematic temporality, that it reconfigured our sense of what it means to be human vis-à-vis modern machines of quick-change. And looking at the current state of digital rendering and morphing, we can safely assume that, for many years to come, the peculiar beauty of Dietrich's face will still be able to out-digitize our own repertoires of digital reproduction.

Notes

Many thanks to Silke Ronneburg and Werner Sudendorf for their help in conducting research at the Marlene Dietrich Collection Berlin, and to Mary Desjardins and Gerd Gemünden for their helpful comments on earlier drafts of this article.

1. Article in 1934 clipping file, Marlene Dietrich Collection, Filmmuseum Berlin.

2. "Du mußt dein Leben ändern" (from Rainer Maria Rilke's poem "Archaischer Torso Apollos," in *Ausgewählte Gedichte* [Frankfurt am Main: Insel Verlag, 1932], 47).

3. "Garbo Likes Dietrich": "Perhaps the most striking thing in connection with the picture is that Greta Garbo came out of her seclusion and saw the film not once, but twice!"

NORA M. ALTER

The Legs of Marlene Dietrich

THE DEVELOPMENT OF innovative editing devices in the second decade of cinema greatly contributed to the production of female stars such as Asta Nielsen, Henny Porten, and Mary Pickford.[1] "Star" status could only be achieved if the camera literally fell in love with the actor. The concept of "photogenie" owes its essence to this love.[2] Each star had to have that something, a unique quality, that became a personal identifying mark. What Clara Bow's mouth, Louise Brooks's "bob," Bette Davis's eyes, and Greta Garbo's face all had in common was that each of these features functioned as a signature for their respective star (Wollen, "Brooks and the Bob" 24). These exaggerated traits, fragmented from the whole and functioning like the "fetish" described by Sigmund Freud (in an essay written precisely when these actresses were attaining stardom), lost none of their auratic power to fascinate twentieth-century audiences.[3] However, audiences were also attracted to features that were baser, located further down, below the waist. Indeed, in 1934, a *Film Pictorial* article, "Composite Beauty—Hollywood Standard," noted that Paramount's Marlene Dietrich was judged to have more perfect body parts than any other actress of that period, and that most of these parts—for example, her legs, ankles, and feet—were from her body's lower regions.[4] Of course, the myth that Dietrich's legs were insured by Lloyd's of London only furthered their allure. This is a lesson many subsequent stars (and especially their producers) obviously took to heart, culminating in popular myths about Betty Grable's insured legs, Britney Spears's abdomen, and Jennifer Lopez's derrière. In his study on stardom, Richard Dyer suggests that stars become associated with particular genres. While Dyer explicitly cites "Monroe's 'dumb blonde' roles," and "Garbo's 'melancholic romantic' roles," it would not be an overstatement to say that the role Dietrich came to be known for was that of the femme fatale (Dyer 70). The latter became a stock character of the Hollywood film noir genre, featuring a dangerous, alluring female—at once attractive and repellent—whose power and agency is determined by a barely concealed sexuality and a worldly knowledge. The very presence of the femme fatale threatens to subvert traditional patriarchal order; hence her character often includes self-destructive traits that prevent her from complete domination.[5] Moreover, Dyer shows how the particular physical trait that served as the star's signature is linked to a genre: hair for the dumb blond, blank facial expressions for the melancholic romantic, and legs for the femme fatale.[6] Dyer situates Dietrich not incorrectly within this filmic genre; however, as I shall argue, what makes the persona of Dietrich all the more intriguing is that her status as femme fatale, both in origin and scope, transcends the cinematic medium.

Before the face, the legs. Indeed, when Marlene Dietrich was first gaining notoriety and was introduced to American audiences in the early 1930s, it was not her face that was discussed in the popular press. Rather, if a body part was to be singled out, functioning as a synecdoche for this sultriest of movie stars, it was her legs. These notorious, scandalous, incendiary legs had already developed a successful career of display long before director Josef von Sternberg molded, sculpted, fashioned, and enhanced Dietrich's face through careful makeup, lighting, and camera angles. Prior to the extreme artifice and the regime of diets (at 5′5″ she weighed 145 pounds during the filming of *The Blue Angel* in 1929, made it down to 130 for *Morocco* the following year, and at Sternberg's insistence shed a few more pounds before starring in subsequent films)—in other words prior to von Sternberg's meticulous construction of the film star's image—Dietrich relied on her extraordinary legs for her allure and survival. Though weight may have affected their appearance, Dietrich's legs constitute the part of her body that changed the least in the five decades of her career. Indeed, it was surely the awe-inspiring stability of Dietrich's legs that led General Patton during World War II to make "LEGS" her official military password. Thus in a persona marked, one could even say defined, by artificiality, there stands what is a surprisingly natural feature that exists most dramatically in the luminosity of its very nakedness. But it was not just as an elongated spectacle of well-toned flesh that Dietrich's legs drew attention and arrested the gaze of so many spectators, for these limbs were also provocative when they were not visible, clothed in tuxedo pant legs. Revealed or concealed, Dietrich's legs continue to intrigue viewers today, and give us pause to reflect on the relationship between this singular body part or unit and the social construction of her stardom.

The legs of Dietrich make their first public appearance in Berlin of the early 1920s when the actress worked as a model for shoes, stockings, and records, to support her ambition to become a stage and celluloid figure. The remarkable success of Dietrich's legs as an advertising gimmick led to a number of other gigs that highlighted them, including her performance as a member of the Thielscher Girls Chorus line. The latter was a variant of the better-known "Tiller Girls," whose regimented and synchronized bodies and movements Siegfried Kracauer described in "The Mass Ornament" (1927) as "products of American distraction factories" (75).[7] Until 1929, when Dietrich starred in von Sternberg's *The Blue Angel*, her career consisted primarily of stage and cabaret performances. She did have a few roles in 1920s films, such as *Man by the Wayside* (1923), *Tragedy of Love*

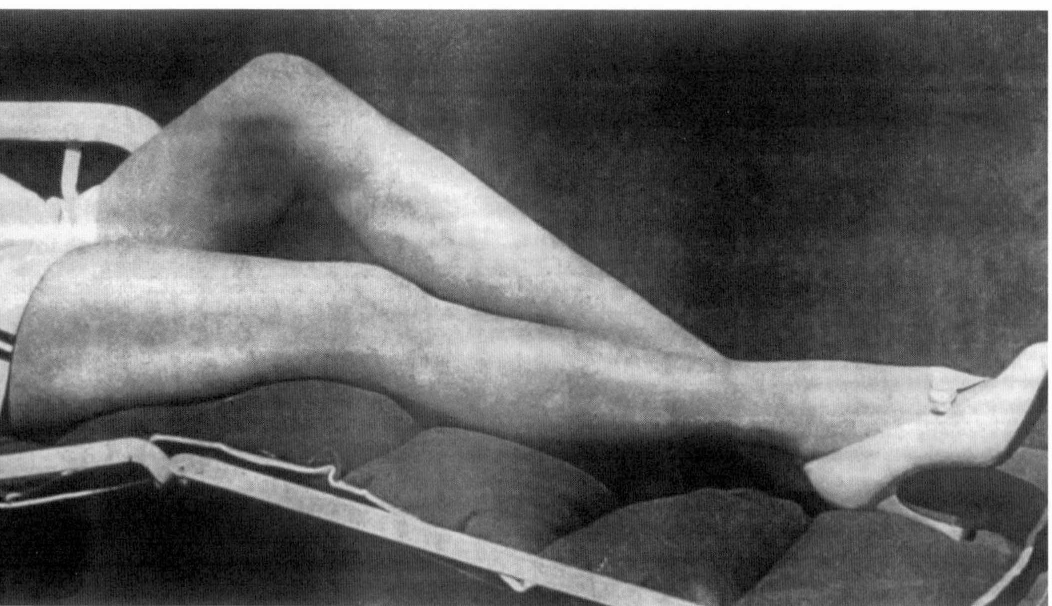

Dietrich's legs. *Filmmuseum Berlin—Marlene Dietrich Collection Berlin.*

(1926), and *Café Electric* (1927), but for the most part during this decade her acting took place in front of a live audience. Indeed, it was in one of these theaters that von Sternberg first saw Dietrich in the musical comedy *Two Bow Ties*. Sternberg was at the time searching for an actress to star in his upcoming film based on Heinrich Mann's novel *Professor Unrat*, which the director had decided to call *The Blue Angel*; Dietrich had been recommended to him by several professionals as an undiscovered "Ingenue: Naive" (Bach 8). In *Two Bow Ties* she played a leading role in a cast of approximately fifty other singers and dancers. Despite his reported disparaging response when asked by two female acquaintances to give an assessment of her performance: "What? That untalented cow?!" she clearly made an impression on Sternberg (Bach 10). Of course, by downplaying Dietrich's talent and stage presence in the 1920s, von Sternberg inflates his subsequent role in fashioning her stardom. Yet, it is worth recalling that theatrical performances differ fundamentally from filmed ones, in that the audience's gaze in a theater is not mediated or ultimately controlled by a camera. By contrast, in film there are a multitude of technical devices that frame and help to delineate the image, the most obvious being the zoom and close-up. A face, enlarged to fill a whole screen and held by the camera for several seconds, creates a very different relation to the star than does a figure on a distant stage whose facial features are all but indecipherable. And certainly von Sternberg's role in highlighting Dietrich's face and establishing it as a photographic icon cannot be underestimated. However, what makes an impression, on stage, is the human body—especially in its movements and its limbs. This, after all, is the essence of the attraction that cabarets and female revues featuring such acts as the Tiller Girls or Thielscher Girls—in which the choreography of the legs produced the ultimate spectacle—had on its initial audiences. The oscillation of limbs, bodies, and the choreographed group on stage moving together in unison contributed in no small part to the fascination of such chorus girl performances in the twenties. But even within the context of limbs there was a hierarchy. As Kracauer noted about these "ornamental" visual spectacles: "arms, thighs, and other segments are the smallest component parts of the composition" (78). The legs were the central attraction. And legs made Dietrich stand out on stage.

Sternberg obviously realized the potential of Dietrich's legs on-screen. *The Blue Angel* was filmed in both English and German simultaneously,

Young Dietrich modeling a record. *Filmmuseum Berlin—Marlene Dietrich Collection Berlin.*

with Universum Film AG (Ufa) in charge of distribution in Germany and Paramount in the United States. The German-language version premiered in Berlin in April 1930 and the U.S. English-language print was released nearly eight months later, at the end of that year. The reason for the delay was strategic, and was related to Dietrich's success in *Morocco*. (For a detailed history and analysis of the two language versions of the film, see Patrice Petro's essay in this volume.) *The Blue Angel* was Dietrich's first acting role in English. Sternberg quickly noticed that he could more than sufficiently make up for the star's linguistic deficiencies by accentuating and highlighting her body. Of course, this was in tandem with Sternberg's strategic emphasis on the mise-en-scène of the screen image over the character involvement and narrative, leading to his oft-quoted comment that he would "welcome his films being projected upside down so the story and character involvement would not interfere with the spectator's undiluted appreciation of the screen image" (Mulvey, "Visual Pleasure" 14).

The abundance of publicity stills from *The Blue Angel* and subsequent films attest to the fact that Dietrich's legs become the master signifier for the actress. They take on the status of supreme visual fetish as they arrest our eyes and imagination. Sternberg's camera makes Dietrich's legs glow, regardless of whether they are in motion during a narrative scene or frozen in a provocative pose. In this sense, the actress and the screen figure are collapsed into one, recalling Bertolt Brecht's contemporary critique of film's inability to maintain the crucial gap between actor and role that exists in theater. Dietrich's legs, whether filmed, photographed, or in performance, become subjects, complete with their own identity and purposiveness. This, it is worth recalling, is the essence of Freud's "fetish," fragmented from the whole and taking on its own raison d'être.[8] The erotic interplay between revealing Dietrich's legs in their naked state or concealing them in male trousers only heightens the displacement. Hence, one must inevitably ask what it is about Dietrich's legs that results in their fragmentation and isolation from the rest of her body? And why do they fascinate viewers as much as they do, commanding so much attention? In Dietrich's perhaps overly modest view, her "legs are not that beautiful." Yet she was quick to add that she was always well aware of "what I should do with them." Thus she was not content to rely solely on the attractiveness of her legs, but incorporated them fully into her overall performative program by endlessly training and conditioning them. What she did, in essence, was to keep her legs perpetually on center stage. Knowing that they attracted attention and granted her power, she made her legs work for her. And it is precisely this—Dietrich's conscious manipulation of her most alluring asset—that constructs her status as a femme fatale.

The figure of Dietrich has lent itself superbly to psychoanalytic discourses of fetishism in film studies. Indeed, it is Dietrich whom Laura Mulvey in her seminal essay of 1975, "Visual Pleasure and Narrative Cinema," cites as an example of the complexities of visual identification and pleasure. As Mulvey notes, "Sternberg produces the ultimate fetish, taking it to the point where the powerful look of the male protagonist (characteristic of traditional narrative film) is broken in favor of the image in direct erotic rapport with the spectator. The beauty of the woman as object and the screen space coalesce: she is no longer the bearer of guilt but a perfect product, whose body, stylized and fragmented by close-ups, is the content of the film" (22). Following on Mulvey's analysis, Gaylyn Studlar devoted *In the Realm of Pleasure: Von Sternberg, Dietrich, and the Masochistic Aesthetic* (1988) to the interplay between spectatorial masochistic desire and Dietrich's screen image. Part of Studlar's thesis hinges on the role of "performance as a way of foregrounding the meaning of the gaze" and of serving "as the focal point for uniting the depiction of female sexuality in a patriarchal society" (69). A few essential points of her argument apply quite directly to Dietrich's legs. Studlar, also adapting theories of female masquerade introduced by Mary Anne Doane (*Femmes Fatales*) and others, interprets Dietrich's trousered legs as a defense strategy within a patriarchal society. She concludes that Dietrich's "cross-dressing is not indicative of a flattering emulation of the 'superior' male. Instead it serves to demonstrate the fluidity of sexual identity even as it parodies male phallic narcissism.... In donning male attire, Dietrich transforms the spectacle of female representation into a ritualized acting out of bisexual identification" (73). Film historian James Naremore has also read Dietrich's legs as fetish objects, arguing that they simultaneously displace the anxiety of castration and reinforce the actress's persona as "cruel woman."[9] Thus Dietrich's legs clearly have a fetishistic nature, although this is a nature that is constantly changing and transmogrifying as a result of shifting historical conditions.

One definition of the Freudian fetish is that it plays with "unacknowledged truth," a line of argumentation that when pursued in the context of Dietrich has led some to focus on the actress's ambiguous sexuality. Andrea Weiss, for instance, suggests that Dietrich introduced the theme of lesbianism in her style of performance by eroticizing her approach to other women while devising fetishistic strategies to reassure the movie audience of her heterosexuality. In her discussion of the celebrated "kiss" scene with another woman in *Morocco*, Weiss argues that Dietrich momentarily steps "out of her role as femme fatale" and acts out that "rumored sexuality on the screen" ("Queer Feeling" 287). In this context the fetish serves both as a defense and as a subversive device. However, I would argue that Dietrich's sexual proclivities were hardly unacknowledged in their original historical context. Both her real-life reputation as a "garçonne" in Berlin with her numerous sexual liaisons with women, as well as her on-screen characters that indulged in a series of same-sex flirtations, were well known to German audiences. As one eyewitness of the premiere gala of the *Blue Angel* at the Gloria Palast recalls, Dietrich "had pinned a bunch of violets in a place where no woman ever wears flowers—just where the legs part" (Spoto 64). And the actress was known to sleep with anyone she found attractive, male or female. If, then, the fetish of the legs hides a *secret* truth, it is not, I want to maintain, centered purely on Dietrich's staged bisexuality, for that was no secret. Rather, I would like to follow another path and examine a few important moments when the camera gives Dietrich's legs an exaggerated stress. As I noted earlier, her legs were prominently featured throughout the Weimar period, culminating in her performance as Lola Lola. As she began her Hollywood career, though, the focus on her legs was uneven. For example, although legs are highlighted in both *Morocco* (1930) and *Dishonored* (1931), there are virtually no leg shots in either *Shanghai Express* (1932), *The Scarlet Empress* (1934), or *The Devil Is a Woman* (1935). Yet the legs return in *Destry Rides Again* (1939) and reach a level of unprecedented spectacle in their golden incarnation in *Kismet* (1944).

Dishonored and *Morocco* were both made during Dietrich's early years in Hollywood. In *Dishonored*, Magda is a prostitute in World War I Vienna. As secret agent X 27, she sacrifices herself to a firing squad from her own country rather than allow her lover, a Russian army officer, to be executed. *Dishonored* begins with a close-up of Dietrich's legs as she adjusts her stockings. At the end of the film, before a military firing squad, she once again reveals her legs as she fixes her hosiery in preparation for death. Her character in this film is a military one. She uses unconventional weapons, but is highly effective as a soldier nonetheless.

Morocco takes place in a port town on the coast of southern Morocco. The film opens with a shot of an obstinate donkey that firmly plants its legs and will not move. As the animal blocks the path, immobilized, the soundtrack plays marching music, and the very mobile legs of the Foreign Legion as they return to Mogador after one of their military forays appear on screen. Amongst the soldiers, Tom Brown (Gary Cooper) is immediately singled out as a ladies' man. The scene cuts to a ferry entering the harbor, and a close-up shot of Dietrich in the role of performer Amy Jolly. As the actress is introduced, the promiscuous camera immediately pans down to her legs and lingers on them briefly. Thus, both Cooper and Dietrich enter the Moroccan city at the same time, albeit from different venues, and together set up a parallelism that is in part determined through the linking of their legs—a parallelism that continues throughout the film. On the evening of Dietrich's first performance in a Mogador nightclub, the camera tracks Cooper's legs as he searches for a seat in the audience. Dietrich, in turn, emerges on stage in a tuxedo that conceals her legs, leading to hoots and hollers from the predominantly male audience. Throughout *Morocco*, Cooper and Dietrich exchange positions with each other a number of times, with the transitions often effected through the mirrored placement and posing of their legs. As Naremore has noted, the overall effect is one of Dietrich seemingly taking on the role of a soldier. The leading metaphor of *Morocco* voiced by Dietrich is that "there is a foreign legion of women, too," which Naremore correctly interprets as allowing the actress, "often wearing pants, to adopt postures of men, standing or sitting with legs spread, arms akimbo" (137). Indeed, the final scene of the film features a barefoot Dietrich joining the "rear guard" of the Foreign Legion and following them off into the desert. Like Agent X 27 in *Dishonored*, Amy Jolly too is a soldier, and in both roles Dietrich's legs are highlighted. The "soldiering" of the female body recalls the military glamour and whips-and-bondage display of the Kurfurstendamm and the old-world military code on which Dietrich played throughout her life. But she carried this military persona one step further in the early 1940s, when she joined the ranks as an officer, going on tour entertaining troops for the United Service Organizations (USO) in 1944.

Dietrich entered a third phase of her career during World War II. Yet this phase was very much a continuation of her early Weimar days, prior to her sojourn to the United States. During the war Dietrich returned to performing in front of a live audience. Indeed, she resumed her stage career in 1942 when she joined the war effort and set out on a nationwide tour of Kurt Weill's and Cheryl Crawford's *One Touch of Venus*. The center of focus in this production was once again Dietrich's legs, which was appropriate insofar as she had resumed her cabaret acts. Here it is worth summoning a contemporary Hollywood film, *Follow the Boys* (1944), featuring Dietrich. An updated, filmic version of the Tiller Girls performing for the troops to raise their spirits, *Follow the Boys* was made in the genre of the Hollywood revue. Karsten Witte has convincingly shown how in the Weimar context the revue served as an anticipation of war in the realm of entertainment, with the deindividualized bodies of the female performers functioning similarly to those of the soldiers. Witte also argues that once the link is established between the choreographed legs in motion and the soldiers, still legs will also semiologically perform the same function. Here it is worth recalling the extraordinary lengths to which Dietrich went in the 1944 film *Kismet* to create a spectacular attraction with which to market the film. The publicity poster for the film displayed a still of Dietrich's legs painted gold, contributing to the box office success of this production. As Bach notes, "It was Dietrich's legs that sold the picture. They stretched from 44th Street to 45th Street, languorous and golden, on a Broadway billboard as big as a B-52" (Bach 283). Since her career was by this time clearly established, and since she was now known as much for her face and voice as for her legs, her willingness to reemphasize the latter is significant, and, I want to suggest, is not unrelated to the film's release during World War II.[10] Whether still or in action, Dietrich's legs kicked up during wartime or when there were military themes in her films. Needless to say, the appeal of her legs was always to a large extent erotic. But following Witte's analysis of female revue performers, there was something more about her naked legs that fascinated, especially in their excess. Perhaps the character Dietrich plays in *Morocco* can provide a glimpse of what that might be.

When Amy Jolly announces that "there is a Foreign Legion of women too," she immediately adds that "we don't wear wound stripes." In other words, the female soldier's body is not officially marked by medals and honors, nor privately by actual scars or disfigurement. Her scars and dismemberment remain symbolic. Such wounds are carried out to a macabre conclusion in the Weimar paintings of Otto Dix, George Grosz, and Ludwig Kirchner, made during the early days of Dietrich's career. What Dix, Grosz, Kirchner and others at the time sought to represent with their ghastly images of amputees, automatons, and prostitutes was a society rendered grotesque by war. Indeed, as is well known, the First World War devastated German society, as it did European culture at large. Two million German soldiers lost their lives, and another four million returned home physically and/or psychologically maimed. In his discussion of Kirchner's *Self-portrait as Soldier* (1915), Richard Cork observes that the painter's "macabre amputation fantasy serves as a brutal symbol of his impotence now that illness has brought his military service to an end. Unable either to paint or fight, he brandishes the raw and useless limb like an accusation" (267). Cork goes on to argue that "Kirchner's growing awareness of sexual ambivalence brought him closer, in his own feverish mind, to the condition of the whores he had painted with such strident assurance in the pre-war period" (267). Therefore, amputation metonymically signifies impotence, which in turn leads to the identification of the mutilated male soldier's body with that of the female (sometimes diseased) body of the prostitute. Maria Tatar has argued that the war experience was subsequently imbricated with threatening female sexuality, dominated by femmes fatales—coupled in the social imaginary with prostitutes—such as Lola Lola, whose power in large part was located in the fact that she was whole with no war wounds or stripes.[11] Indeed, women's wholeness at the time inspired male misogynist fantasies, which all too often culminated in brutal sex crimes and the disfigurement and dismemberment of the victims. Whereas Tatar maintains that the anxiety of the war was played out in the carnage of the woman's body, Cork argues that this violence was in fact self-mutilation and self-inflicted punishment. But I want to suggest another scenario—one that is less consciously violent but perhaps more powerful than those that have to date been offered.

If the amputees testified to the brutality of war through their lack, how do we read the opposite phenomenon: an overabundance of fully toned legs? For the vibrant, fleshy, and mobile legs of revue girls and performers were in stark contrast to the silent, absent signifier—namely the phantom limb(s) of the amputee. This was surely an important aspect of the contemporary allure of the dancing girls, a phenomenon that also begins to explain the attraction generated by the excess of Dietrich's legs. Just as Dietrich's feminine image was always doubly encoded as excessively and marginally feminine, her legs also pointed to their opposite. This is not to imply that this process of encoding the absent signifier took place solely at an unconscious level. A still from the *Blue Angel*, for example, at once features the legs of Dietrich and a graffiti image of an amputated leg. The placement of the dismembered leg in the context of the cabaret performer is significant. As Freud observes in "The Uncanny" (1919), "dismembered limbs, a severed head, a hand cut off at the wrist . . . feet which dance by themselves, . . . all these have something peculiarly uncanny about them. . . . As we already know this kind of uncanniness springs from its association with the castration complex" (244). From this perspective, Dietrich's legs as fetish functioned to arrest the trauma not only of symbolic castration but of actual amputation. The fear of death aside, one of the greatest anxieties of those engaged in war is the possible return home minus a limb, and especially a leg.[12] The actualities of the First World War, therefore, brought to the surface the uncanny return of a repressed castration anxiety. (That Freud wrote this essay immediately following The Great War is significant in and of itself.)

But there is more. A number of publicity photographs of Dietrich prominently featuring her legs explicitly represent the female threat of disempowerment after the war. A case in point is an early image of Dietrich performing in 1927, during which she plays a musical saw between her naked calves. The history of the musical saw is located in the conventions of vaudeville. The saw is usually held between the knees while seated, with the blade extending to the side, projecting slightly upward. The player bends the blade into an "S" shape, and then creates a vibration at the junction of the two opposite curves of the S with the aid of a stringed bow. The director Robert Klein recalls that he came upon the idea of contacting Dietrich when in the middle of preparing an intimate musical revue he decided that "there wasn't sufficient sex appeal on the stage": "We called [Marlene] and I asked her whether she had any special talents which might be used in a revue. She said she could play the violin and the saw. I had never heard anyone play the saw and I asked her to display this art for us [the] next day. . . . She took her legs apart, put the saw in between and played" (Bach 83). Here it is as interesting as it is revealing to note the immediate sex appeal of the saw, which goes beyond the level of imagery.[13] For there is also a linguistic pun at play—in German the word to play a violin or a saw (*eingeigen*) is also vulgar slang for sexual intercourse. The first stage performances employing the musical saw took place sometime around the turn of the century, with probable origins in Germany.[14] Significantly, the saw was conventionally played by men. Dietrich was trained in playing the violin, yet her appropriation of the saw is striking. Surely she was not unaware of the provocative image she struck with the sharp, serrated blade between her fleshy, naked legs. Furthermore, the sound of the bowed saw is an eerie and alluring one, referred to in vaudeville culture as a siren's song, or a banshee's wail.

The image of a siren was frequently employed in nineteenth-century representations of the femme fatale, which proliferated in European

Otto Dix, "War Cripple," 1920. © 2006 *Artists Rights Society* (ARS), *New York/ VG Bild-Kunst, Bonn.*

Otto Dix, "Match Seller," 1920. © 2006 *Artists Rights Society* (ARS), *New York/VG Bild-Kunst, Bonn.*

opposite: *The Blue Angel* (1930).
Filmmuseum Berlin—Marlene Dietrich Collection Berlin.

Dietrich playing the "singende Säge." *Filmmuseum Berlin —Marlene Dietrich Collection Berlin.*

art and literature in the second half of the nineteenth century. Patrick Bade has traced the evolution of the femme fatale in painting, literature and theater of that century, relating painterly representations of Gustav Moreau, Franz von Stuck, and others to the theatrical persona of Sarah Bernhardt, the dances of Loie Fuller, and the many stagings of the opera *Salomé* at the turn of the century. Bade's study reveals that although the image of the femme fatale almost entirely disappears from painting around 1900, it returns first in the figure of the living, performing woman (modeled on previous artistic renderings) at the turn of the century, and then is picked up by the film medium. Dietrich, playing the saw on stage in the decade following the First World War, assumes the figure of the femme fatale as she evokes the threat of amputation and castration. Hence, in the following years she was pivotal to the introduction of this figure to the medium of film, serving as a direct link between the femme fatale on stage and its full-fledged adoption by cinema. Put more strongly, Dietrich is key to understanding the metamorphosis of the femme fatale character as it transitions from the nineteenth century into the twentieth, from stage onto film. Yet, the femme fatale, as a type, is taken up for different reasons in the new century, mobilized in response to changing anxieties. If, as Bade shows, the proliferation of the image of the femme fatale in the nineteenth century corresponded to an "increase in male anxiety about women" and the beginnings of a "change in the status of women" (23), then in the Weimar period the figure reemerges in the context of a newfound, albeit powerful male anxiety and fear of castration brought about by the traumas of the First World War. Yet, the question of what happens to this figure twenty years later remains to be addressed.

Dietrich left the saw behind when she moved to the United States to continue her career. But when she joined the war effort in 1942, she took a saw along with her on trips overseas to perform for the troops. As an eyewitness recalls about one of Dietrich's visits to a makeshift hospital near the front: "[Dietrich] could scarcely suppress her horror at the sight of so many boys wounded, limbless and blind. Trying to hide her emotion she

Dietrich plays the singing saw in World War II USO Show.
Filmmuseum Berlin—Marlene Dietrich Collection Berlin.

visited each bedside, and when one ward would not stop cheering her, she pulled out her musical saw and improvised" (Leonard and Graebner 191). "Legs" indeed, to summon General Patton's military code name for Dietrich; there is clearly a lot to unpack in this anecdote about the battlefield hospital, not least of which is the fact that this was an Allied convalescent ward and Dietrich was German.[15]

In a celebrated publicity photograph of 1944, the musical saw is placed between Dietrich's legs, now clad in military fatigues. Once again, the presentation of her legs in men's trousers disavows sexual difference, making them androgynous. Here, in a soldier's uniform, she takes on the identity—even if only momentarily—of one of the guys. Coded as male, this image of Dietrich points more clearly to the anxieties of dismemberment encountered by soldiers. As if it was not enough that the saw directly referenced the tool used to perform the gruesome task of amputation, its transformation into a musical instrument that in the popular imagination wailed the song of the sirens (and hence led men to destruction) made the appearance of this object in World War II pictures of Dietrich even more problematic.[16]

Whereas in 1927 the musical saw, coupled with Dietrich's bare legs, produced the double image of a castrating femme fatale siren, the fetish could at that time still be located in the tension of legs and saw. This all changed during the Second World War, however, when Dietrich was encouraged to drape her legs in military fatigues. The U.S. authorities felt that it would be too obscene to allow the actress to perform with bare legs in a convalescent ward—especially given that she was German in the context of maimed Allied troops. With the legs concealed, not only was Dietrich's femme fatale persona blunted as she assumed the more blatantly virile identity of the conquering military troops, but the fetish, in turn, was now fully displaced onto the saw. No more fleshiness and wholeness: the arresting object was now the sharp, toothy blade. But while it unconsciously triggered traumatic memories of the First World War and its millions of dead and wounded, within the context of World War II the saw's significance became even more complex, at once indexically pointing to real amputees and summoning the psychic impotence, dismemberment, and castration of the German nation as the outcome of the war became increasingly clear.

Notes

1. Richard deCordova, in *Picture Personalities: The Emergence of the Star System in America*, makes the important distinction between the "film personality" and the "star." Whereas the former designates the professional life of someone who worked in film, the "star" discourse emerges as public knowledge about an actor's personality which extends to their public life.

2. Jean Epstein declared "photogenie" as "the purest expression of cinema" (qtd. in Abel 138–39, 243, 315).

3. Roland Barthes said as much in his famous essay of 1957 celebrating Garbo's face: "Garbo still belongs to that moment in cinema when capturing the human face still plunged audiences into the deepest ecstasy, when one literally lost oneself in a human image as one would in a philtre, when the face represented a kind of absolute state of the flesh, which could neither be reached nor renounced" (536).

4. As quoted in Lutz Koepnick, "Dietrich's Face," in this volume.

5. For a formulation and detailed discussion of the role of the femme fatale in film noir, see Kaplan, *Women in Film Noir*.

6. As Janey Place observes, "The femme fatale is characterized by her long legs" (45).

7. As Peter Wollen has pointed out, Kracauer was wrong in identifying the Tiller Girls as American: they were in fact British. See Wollen, "Modern Times," 54.

8. Or in popular advertising jargon, these images "have legs"; that is, they seem to have a surprising capacity to generate new directions and surprising twists in an ad campaign, as if they had an intelligence and purposiveness of their own.

9. "Dietrich's persona clearly derives from the cruel women imagined by Victorian aesthetes—Swinburne's Dolores, Pater's Mono Lisa, Wilde's Salome, and Sacher-Masoch's Venus. At this level, psychoanalysis has an important explanatory value, even suggesting that a strong social prohibition against homosexuality gives rise to certain types of fetishistic imagination" (Naremore 135).

10. "MGM and *Kismet* wanted their poetry to have oomph. That meant Marlene. That meant legs. Marlene gave them gold ones" (Bach 282).

11. Tatar limits her discussion to visual arts and does not treat film.

12. Johan Ulrich Bilguer already indicated this as early as 1761, when he wrote: "Nichts kan natürlicher als die allgemein herschende Neigen seyn, lieber zu sterben, als das Abschneiden großer Glieder geren und willig ausstehen zu

wollen" (Nothing can be more natural than to prefer to die than to have a limb amputated). Qtd. in Engelstein 225.

13. Thomas Elsaesser briefly mentions the saw, interpreting it psychoanalytically as a "vagina dentata." See Elsaesser, "Falling in Love," 347–355.

14. For a history of the musical saw, see Leonard and Graebner.

15. Although she had become an American citizen at the outset of the war, she was still perceived to be German because of her accent.

16. The 1940 film *Seven Sinners*, set in the South Pacific with Dietrich performing in the navy, includes a number in which she plays the saw.

AMY LAWRENCE

Marlene Dietrich

The Voice as Mask

DIETRICH'S VOICE is as instantly recognizable and as widely parodied as is her image. Just as her face can be easily caricatured, conveyed with a minimum of lines because it is so abstract, our understanding of her "voice as instrument" is equally simplified, condensed into an instantly recognizable product, unvarying in quality, always meeting expectations. Just as Dietrich was arguably more an icon than an actress, her voice at first seems more iconic than expressive, the vocal equivalent of an acting style characterized by emotional distance, limited range, discipline, and a marked lack of sentimentality.

How then to account for descriptions like the following? Someone who worked with her in the early 1950s reported, "Her voice alone is enough to drive you crazy."[1] In a tribute to Dietrich in *Life* magazine in 1952, Ernest Hemingway wrote, "If she had nothing more than her voice, she could break your heart with it."[2]

Both accounts were written in the early 1950s, when Dietrich's film career had slowed to a halt and her concert career had not yet begun. The late 1940s and early 1950s also marked the period where age became an insistent presence in public references to Dietrich (see Mayne's essay on old age and the archive in this volume). It is exactly in the period when the marketability of her image was in question that the importance to fans—and to Dietrich—of her voice as an alternative performance medium increased substantially. In this essay I would like to explore the way critics and fans negotiated the tensions between their emotional re-

Dietrich performing for *Café Istanbul*, 1952. *Author's collection*

actions to Dietrich's voice and their intellectual awareness of her work as stylized, iconic performance.

In order to explore the way critics and fans characterized Dietrich's voice in this period, it is important to maintain a clear distinction between her voice as a singer and her speaking voice. A third element that comes into play regarding Dietrich's voice is her relation to language, including both the ease with which she moves between German, English, and French and her lifelong retention of a German accent when speaking English.

Dietrich Sings

For those particularly moved by Dietrich's singing voice, the primal scene centers on a phonograph. A "Mr. Harper" in *Harper's Magazine* in May 1955 recalls, "We remember her first from the soft spring evenings, two or three decades back. . . . There would be someone who had a phonograph in an attic room . . . , someone too who owned the imported Telefunken records, worn by a hundred adolescent reveries—'Jonny,' 'Peter,' 'Wo ist der Mann?' 'Moi, je m'ennuie. . . .' The husky voice of Marlene Dietrich was part of the temperamental environment of that generation of Americans. . . . We absorbed, from this endlessly replenished source, the promise of unexplored sophistications to come" (82, 83).

The novelist John O'Hara, in March 1954, recounts a strikingly similar memory: "It started when I first heard her sing 'Blond Women' ('Blonden Frauen') on a phonograph record. The record was not played on one of those phonographs with the megaphone-type sound apparatus, but let's just say that there were still a few of them around." He adds, "She has, in fact, been on my mind for more years than either of us would care to admit" (6).

Harper and O'Hara both emphasize the pastness at the heart of their obsessions with Dietrich—that it was long ago, they were merely boys, the records are now lost, the technology obsolete. But what is notable is how these remembrances focus exclusively on Dietrich's vocal persona. What moved Hemingway, Harper, and O'Hara was Dietrich's singing.

As one commentator on Dietrich's vocal range suggests, you could not describe it in octaves. "The voice was a warm, rich mezzo-bass-baritone, spanning little more than one octave, . . . [with] no overt straining to reach an upper register" (Bret 150). In fact, there is an outright refusal of pyrotechnics of any kind. There is no bravura display of high notes, or low notes, or sustained notes. There is no Garlandesque outpouring of emotion or illusion of spontaneity. When Dietrich sings "See What the Boys in the Back Room Will Have" in *Destry Rides Again* (1939), her character mocks the effect of crying by exposing how it is produced (using her hands to jiggle her throat on the line "tell them I cried"). In doing so, Dietrich explicitly rejects the alleged authenticity of emotion and the consequent display of vulnerability this kind of vibrato enacts.

Rather than undermining her effectiveness as a singer, such restraint intensifies the effects Dietrich achieves. The main effect is often a self-consciousness or doubleness, as if she were outside watching herself sing. In his book *Acting in the Cinema*, James Naremore finds her singing in films to be the perfect embodiment of her acting style overall. "Her typical 'act' was to play a spectacular woman of the world working in some low dive, singing half-heartedly, almost contemptuously. The laziest gal in town, she was sexy precisely because of the way she threatened to expose the illusion of her performance" (143). It often seems in Dietrich's films that she is not so much a singer as an actress who *plays* a singer—self-aware, self-contained, aware of her effects (as Naremore says), contemptuous of or indifferent to response, whether it be the lusty catcalls in *Blue Angel* and *Blonde Venus*, the stunned surprise and laughter of *Morocco*, the wry appreciation in *Foreign Affair*, or the raucous cheers in *Destry*.[3]

When Dietrich sings in films, her face does not change. The kind of lighting Dietrich demanded made her face a mask, a blank surface, a screen available for projection. Unlike more animated performers (again Garland comes to mind, or operatic singers), Dietrich does not contort her face to produce sound any more than she would to produce emotion. The voice "within" may animate the mask but it does not change the nature of the mask as a mask.

David Bret writes, "because there was no overt straining to reach an upper register, her diction was impeccable. The words, and not the melodies of the Dietrich repertoire, were what counted."[4] However, according to the accounts of mid-century American fans, the opacity of the untranslated is central to Dietrich's appeal as a singer. American listeners such as O'Hara and Harper had an investment in *not* knowing the words. They wanted an inexhaustable "otherness," closed off but available for projection. In a brief essay entitled "The Kraut Woman" (evidently a term of endearment from Hemingway), Harper describes an "American Dietrich" as being inherently "less mysterious, almost wholesome" (82–83). Harper and O'Hara each list German titles as the key texts in their adolescent reveries ("Wo ist der Mann" and "Blonden Frauen" respectively). Harper exclaims, "[To say we] even understood the lyrics would be an exaggeration; we merely accepted" (83). And if you learned German to "understand" the songs, Dietrich could just as easily switch to French. (See the unsubtitled "Elle est jolie" in *Morocco*.) Her cosmopolitan, multilingual persona becomes another means of presenting herself as an impenetrable surface against which we can only speculate and fantasize.[5]

Dietrich and Language

Dietrich's linguistic skills were as essential to her persona as her looks and her voice. The screen test for *Blue Angel* is a perfect example.[6] Standing beside a piano, Dietrich sings the English song "You're the Cream in My Coffee." The tempo is too quick, and as Dietrich sings the opening verse three times running, she rolls her eyes, simultaneously bored at the repetition and emotionally disconnected from the insipid lyric.

> You're the cream in my coffee.
> You're the salt in my stew.
> You will always be my necessity.
> I'd be lost without you.

As the words threaten to become meaningless, it is not surprising to find that the song is merely a pretext. Having proven she can sing in English, the scene then focuses on her acting ability, demonstrated in her growing irritation with the piano player. Distracting her with the wrong tempo and missed notes, he ruffles her cool until she lashes out. Banging on the keys, she berates him (in German) and climbs onto the piano, straightening her stocking with the casual insolence of a dominatrix.

As Patrice Petro discusses elsewhere in this volume, what has become Dietrich's best-known German-language film was also conceived as an English-language film, not dubbed into English but refilmed. Ironically it is the subtitled German version that has come to be considered "the authentic" version of the film, despite the English-language version's wide release in the United States in the 1930s. Because this version has not been discussed frequently, I would like to explore how the perception of Dietrich's character changes when the language in which she sings *and* speaks changes.

For an American audience, Dietrich's English in *The Blue Angel* makes her stand out from the rest of the cast. Dietrich's Lola Lola not only speaks English, she is supposed to *be* English. Despite her accent, Lola Lola supposedly does not even understand German. When people speak to her in German she is put in the position of having to ask what they said. This happens more than once, as much of the dialogue in the English version is still in German. As in a silent film where titles are not given for every line, it is assumed that the audience will understand the gist of the conversation from other cues (for instance when an argument breaks out between the club owner and the other singers, or when the police raid the club). The English Lola Lola's exclusion from those around her provides a natural link between her and Professor Rath; as a professor of English, he is presumably the one character who can really understand her. When he first meets her, he is also immediately in the wrong: he apologizes for having addressed her in German and repeats what he said in English.

Her language position at times makes Lola Lola appear vulnerable, for instance when hecklers in the audience yell out comments in German during the song "I Want a Real Man." In the German film, Lola seems disdainful during this scene, just ignoring the men. In the English version—to an English-speaking film audience—she seems isolated because she (and we) do not understand whether the male voices are hostile, suggestive, rude, or not. On the other hand, where it is often hard to understand the other actors when they attempt English, Dietrich's English is fine. This makes her character more accessible to an English-speaking audience. It also marks Dietrich (as well as her character) as being more flexible, a survivor where other actors struggle and fail. (Emil Jannings, who plays Rath, is a case in point, having left Hollywood at the height of his career purportedly because of his difficulties with English and his pronounced accent.)

Even more striking in the English-language version is that all of the songs are also in English. It is rare in pre-1970s prints of foreign-language films for lyrics even to be translated in the subtitles, let alone for the songs to be rerecorded. In her Hollywood films (as with "Elle est jolie" in *Morocco*) it would become common for Dietrich to sing in an untranslated, unsubtitled foreign language. Ironically, it was one of the translated songs that became the most famous number from the film and essential to Dietrich's image. Bret calls Jimmy Connelly's "English adaptations" of the four songs in *The Blue Angel* ("by Friedrich Hollaender, Walter Rillo and Robert Liebmann") "excellent" (32). Harper deems it nothing less than "a triumph of translation [that] brought "Falling in Love Again" out of "Ich bin von Kopf bis Fuss auf Liebe eingestellt" and gave [Dietrich] a theme song" (83).

Dietrich's German accent when speaking in the English *Blue Angel* is presented as "not-to-be-read," but it will become essential in her American films, where her accent functions as a marker of difference, a guarantee of her "otherness." (She never loses her accent. Once formed, the icon "Dietrich" never varies.) Nevertheless, her accent must be accounted for, never more so than when she speaks rather than sings. Rarely identified as German, more often than not Dietrich's accent serves as a (not altogether serious) sign of an all-purpose "foreignness." She is French in *Morocco* (1930) and *Destry Rides Again* (1939), Russian in *Knight without Armour* (1937), a gypsy in *Golden Earrings* (1947), Mexican in *Touch of Evil* (1958), and so on.

On radio in the late 1930s, with war looming, Dietrich's accent is more carefully negotiated. In December 1937, Cecil B. DeMille himself certifies her patriotism to the United States when he introduces a *Lux Radio Theater* adaptation of the film *Song of Songs*. After telling us about her recent trip to Europe, he notes, "Marlene expects to visit London again next summer. But then her passport will read 'Marlene Dietrich, Citizen of the United States.'"[7] Her American patriotism eventually becomes a matter of negotiating language, accent, and song.

Dietrich Sings for Freedom

In a persona distinctive for its doubleness, it is striking how consistently Dietrich's support for the war effort is described as a sincere and genuine expression of her "real" self. From Tallulah Bankhead to General Omar Bradley, Dietrich's acquaintances at the time say pretty much the same thing. Bankhead stated: "During the war, many people entertained the troops briefly and then came home to make movies. Dietrich went with the troops and stayed with them. She loved it." And Bradley reported (a little more officially): "Many of us came to admire her spirit and to appreciate her contribution because she was so much interested in entertaining our soldiers over a long period of time and because she quite often visited very close to the front lines" (both qtd. in *Colliers*, "Dietrich" 27).

Dietrich's war work as a singer was memorialized in record albums, including what Harper calls "one of the most perennially satisfying [records] I know—the ten-inch Columbia LP called *Marlene Dietrich Overseas*" (83). Surprisingly, the album Harper recalls with such affection was not made for an American audience; the songs are all in German. "A remake of the songs she sang for the OSS to broadcast to German soldiers,"[8] in this album Dietrich sings *in* German *to* German soldiers *for* Americans. In other words she becomes professionally German, a native who speaks German on behalf of and at the behest of the Americans. This is not to imply any colonialism or victimization. Just as her political commitment to fighting fascism was a personal choice, Dietrich's English was a professional attainment, sought out, learned, and deployed in a way that would enable her professional advancement in Hollywood—and did. However, given the crucial role the war plays in Dietrich's star persona, the clash of national and linguistic identity in these vocal performances makes them especially intriguing. It is the release of albums like this one in the early 1950s that seems to have provoked the nostalgia of long-time fans such as O'Hara and Harper. The latter brings national identity to the forefront as he describes the songs on the album this way: "Mostly they are American pop tunes, with the words revised to make them morbid and Teutonic, twisting the knife of nostalgia" (Harper 83).

Translated into German, Dietrich's songs on *Marlene Dietrich Overseas* are *echt* American. The most surprising, perhaps, is a version of Rodgers and Hammerstein's "The Surrey with the Fringe on Top" from *Oklahoma*, with lyrics written in German by Lothar Metzl.[9] In its original incarnation, the song describes the consumer nirvana of having the latest model vehicle with a customized options package: "The wheels are yella, the upholstery's brown, the dashboard's genu-ine leather." When the singer is asked, "Would you say the fringe is made of silk?" he answers, "Wouldn't have no other kind than silk."

Dietrich's version tells a different story. Gone are the detailed description of the surrey, the slang, and the regionalisms ("Ain't no finer rig, I'm a-thinking. You can keep yer rig if you're thinkin' that I'd keer to swap"). In their place we find a winter scene and a fragile romance.

Der Bach singt unter dem Eise
ich schmieg mich an dich
und ich fühle dass du
das Ziel bist am Ende der Reise.
Weisse Flocken weben den Schleier
kalte Winde wehen vom Weiher
doch in Herzen brennt mir ein Feuer
weil ich dich nur sehe
in dem Schlitten mit den Schellen
und dem Tal tief in Schnee.
[The brook sings under the ice
and I lean on you

and I feel that you
are the goal at the end of the trip.
White flakes weave a veil
cold winds blow from the pond
but in my heart there's a fire
because I see only you
in the sleigh with the bells
in the valley deep in snow.]

Instead of a surrey there is a sleigh, complete with the "dream-like ringing" of sleigh bells. In the American song, it is the surrey that is the fantasy; in German it is the relationship, as we see in the last verse.

Du bist mir nah
und du lächelst mir zu
doch ich, ich weine ganze leise.
Ich halte dich nicht
denn ich fühle dass du
schon denkst ans Ende der Reise.
Traurig schreien im Dunkel die Raben.
Lass den Schimmel langsamer traben.
Lass die Illusion mich doch haben
dass ich dich noch sehe
in dem Schlitten mit den Schellen
und im Tal, tief im Schnee.
[You're close
and you smile to me
but I, I cry softly.
I don't hold you
for I feel that you
are already thinking of the end of the trip.
Sadly the ravens cry in the dark.
Let the white horse go slower.
Let me still have the illusion
that I still see you
in the sleigh with the bells
in the valley, deep in snow.][10]

As the "ravens cry" and ("aching already") the singer pleads to keep her illusions, we can see what Harper meant by "twisting the knife of nostalgia." Despite his highly caricatured view of German as "morbid" and "Teutonic," Harper's 1955 reading of the emotional tone of these songs corresponds to accounts by Dietrich's wartime contemporaries. In the documentary *Marlene Dietrich: Her Own Song* (2001), a former member of the OSS recounts that the songs were recorded for the purpose of demoralizing German troops and making them not want to fight anymore. German soldiers who heard her Allied radio broadcasts testify to the emotional power of her singing, especially when she sang in German.

The war has become a privileged location of authenticity in accounts of Dietrich's life and career, put forward time and again as the place where one can find the real Dietrich—what she really thought, what she stood for, where her own genuine emotions are finally spontaneously expressed. Nothing exemplifies this better than a moment in *Marlene Dietrich: Her Own Song*, where Dietrich's voice is recorded in what is clearly a spontaneous, unrehearsed outburst.

After supporting the Allied war effort (including the bombing of Berlin, where her mother still lived), performing for U.S. troops across Europe, and risking her life at the front, there came a moment at the end of the war when Dietrich was finally allowed to speak briefly by telephone with her mother. They were required to speak in English so that the Allied censors (who presumably recorded the conversation) could listen in. Despite the language obstacle (English being noticeably more difficult for Dietrich's mother) and the awareness that people were listening, Dietrich's words, voice, and delivery seem a direct expression of her deepest feelings. She hurries to tell a mother she has not spoken to in years how much she loves her. Her voice choking with emotion, rushing her words because there is not much time, she repeatedly asks for forgiveness, telling her mother that she knows she has suffered on Dietrich's account—"for me, for me. Forgive me."

While Dietrich's family (*Marlene Dietrich: Her Own Song* was coproduced by David Riva, one of Dietrich's grandsons) has an investment in promising us a unique, "never-before-available," glimpse into Dietrich's otherwise inaccessible private life, the pain we hear is so direct, her emotions so unguarded that listeners might feel embarrassed for having wanted such knowledge in the first place. (Despite the fact that insights

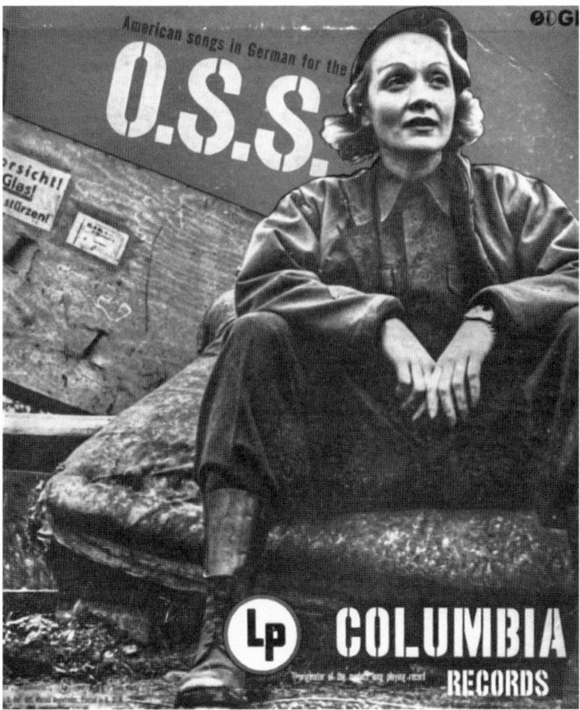

Marlene Dietrich Overseas, Columbia Records, 1951.
Author's collection.

into the deepest private feelings of a performer are often exactly what audiences most hope for [see deCordova].)

After the war, Dietrich's film offers began to slow down, hitting a nadir in the 1950s. (After *Rancho Notorious* in 1952 she did not have another leading role until 1957 [*Witness for the Prosecution*].) Dietrich had to orient her career in a new direction.[11] Unlike other aging stars of the period, Dietrich was quite insistent about *not* doing television. "She has turned down a fortune in TV. She feels—so far, at least—that it's not right for her" (*Colliers*, "Dietrich" 28). Dietrich said, "If I do television it will have to be something special. People expect something special of me" (28). Instead she turned to a medium she was more comfortable in—radio.

Dietrich's Speaking Voice: Radio

Naremore argues that as a performer Dietrich maintains her elusiveness and ambiguity by balancing every gesture with a countergesture: being first feminine then masculine, romantic then cynical, the "lazy, half-hearted, contemptuous" performer who is at the same time a disciplined perfectionist (148). Attempts to describe the physical qualities of Dietrich's voice return again and again to its contradictory nature. Time and again, this is a doubleness that blurs boundaries between human and animal, male and female. A coworker on her radio show recounted, "Once she called me to give me her phone number so I could call back about something, and that voice, just speaking a telephone number, was . . . well, it was . . . it was like another woman talking of love. You know? And still though she's the absolute female, she has a completely masculine mind" (Paul Rose, qtd. in *Colliers*, "Dietrich" 26).

Twenty years after having seen *The Blue Angel*, one 1950s critic described the "mythic" figure of Lola Lola in audio terms: "This myth spoke with a low, caressing voice that had the evocative power of an animal mating call" (Sargeant 86). When Dietrich sang, another noted, "the words were doubly feline in so low a voice, the poses more suggestive in male clothing" (Harper 83). Her voice even transgresses the boundary between pleasure and pain: Kenneth Tynan called her "The Venus in furs, with black leather in her voice." Jean Cocteau said that her very name "Marlene" was "at first the sound of a caress" but with "Dietrich" it became "the crack of a whip" (Harper 83). Perhaps the most striking example of the unsettling effect of this protean shifting between categories can be found in a comic routine from a March 1949 episode of the radio program *Duffy's Tavern*, where the streetwise Archie gives some "fatherly advice" to the slow-witted Finnegan.[12]

Archie. I'd like to talk to you as a father to a son. You see, you're not a little boy anymore, Finnegan. You're a grown man now and I feel that the time has come for you to meet Marlene Dietrich.

Finnegan. Is this anything like the birds and the bees, Arch?

Archie. This *is* the birds and the bees. [laughter] Now say hello to Marlene.

Finnegan. Duh, hello.

Marlene. (in her lowest, most drawn-out voice) Helloo.
Finnegan. Oh boy, now I can have a baby! [laughter]
Archie. You'll have to excuse him, Marlene. He ain't read the Kinsey Report.

(If the Kinsey Report falls short of explaining the full perversity of Finnegan's response, perhaps Freud's Dr. Schreber would be more to the point. Both men yearn to be impregnated by a hyperphallic god—played here by the voice of Marlene Dietrich.)

After countless guest appearances on programs ranging from *Lux Radio Theater* to *The Burns and Allen Show*, Dietrich starred in her own radio series, *Café Istanbul*. In his *Encyclopedia of Old-Time Radio*, John Dunning describes Dietrich's 1952 radio series as "another of the adventure shows peopled by high-profile Hollywood film stars that dotted the network schedules in the medium's last decade" (130–31). Whether it had a familiar formula or not, Dietrich took an active role in the production.

A radio executive told *Colliers*: "The radio show is her package. She got the idea for it—based on the role she played in *The Blue Angel*—and she hires the actors and writers with her own money" (*Colliers*, "Dietrich" 28). *Time* magazine reiterated: "Marlene worries about plot so much that she stayed up with her typewriter until three o'clock one morning, pecking out 17 pages of script revisions for the first show. 'She's a worker, a hard worker,' says Producer Leonard Blair admiringly. 'She really rolls up her sleeves. Her suggestions are very good'" (*Time*, "Still Champion" 40).

Dietrich's ideas were more than suggestions. A brief essay called "Marlene's Joint," published in *The New Yorker* in November 1952, gives a contemporary account of a rehearsal of *Café Istanbul*.

> Miss Dietrich read on until she came to "All that evening the smoke had swirled and eddied about the Cafe Istanbul in nervous circles, as if looking for escape."
> "This 'eddied' is English?" she inquired.
> "Sure it's English," said [director] Burnett.
> "Take it out," said Miss Dietrich. "If I don't know it, they won't know it in Idaho." (33)

Time called the show's plots "chaotic," but still opined that radio audiences would be "content just to listen to the clinging, faintly accented voice of Marlene Dietrich" (40). "As she has countless times since the classic *Blue Angel*, Marlene played the same romantic, weltschmerz role and whispered snatches of French and German songs. Some listeners may have felt cheated because Marlene was limited to a few choruses of "La Vie en Rose" and four bars of a song in German. 'It's a hell of a job to do a dramatic show in half an hour,' she explains with a shrug. 'There isn't time for singing because you have to worry about character and plot.'"

Café Istanbul first aired on ABC in January 1952 and ran through December.[13] A revamped version of the show (retitled *Time for Love*) which ran on CBS from January 1953 to May 1954, had even less time for singing, though there was still plenty of intrigue, spies, and the familiar *Casablanca* ambience.[14]

An episode of *Time for Love*, "The Foreign Agent," carries the comparison with *Casablanca* to an extreme, including being set in a nightclub in North Africa where there is an avid French police lieutenant and a romance interrupted at the airport. After the announcer introduces the show by changing the title into a double-entendre ("It's 'Time for Love' with Marlene Dietrich"), Dietrich's character meets the police lieutenant at the airport, where she has gone to meet her boyfriend's plane. As they watch the passengers exit she purrs, "You're not offended about last night?"

Lieutenant. I created a picture in my mind, having supper with you, and you shattered my picture. . . . You seem to be interested in someone.

Dionne. Yes, the gentleman in the white suit. A very old friend of mine. . . . [Calls out] Karl! Karl, don't you know me? Is it so long ago?

Karl. Dionne, my dear. Forgive me my rudeness. I—

Dionne. Karl? Is something wrong?

Karl. No, no, nothing—[EXPLOSION]

Dionne. What happened?

Karl. Some maniac threw a bomb! This way! [Crowd noises . . .] There, that's better—

Lieutenant. Mademoiselle. You will please come with me.

Dionne. Go with you? Where?

Lieutenant. Police headquarters. You are under arrest.

Dionne. Arrest? For what?

Lieutenant. As if you do not know. [Music swells.]

Dietrich's vocal performance is engagingly varied in this scene. In the beginning, she murmurs flirtatiously, pouting and mocking the lieutenant's disappointment at not being able to have dinner with her the night before. When she sees her old friend, her diction sharpens and her voice rises as she recognizes him. When she greets him and reintroduces herself, her voice is warm and musical ("Don't you know me? Is it so long ago?") The exaggerated presence of her German accent here can only be described as *heimlich*. When she is arrested, she immediately assumes a lower range, sounding dismissive and sharp as she bites off her words. "Go with you? Where?"

Despite the star's engaging performance, *Café Istanbul* and *Time for Love* struggle with the overfamiliarity of the genre. After the chaotic flurry of events in the scene described above, the rest of the episode focuses on Dietrich's attempts to reform her German friend, who is working as a spy for what she refers to with great contempt as "that regime." This episode, with its explosions, arrests, and espionage (all in one scene!), shows the program's emphasis on "action and intrigue" as does the episode "In Darkest Africa," where Dietrich's character, Dionne la Volta, confronts German gunrunners while on safari in Kenya during the Mau-Mau uprising. Her globe-trotting journalist-boyfriend Michael saves her from a lion while telling her that *she* is the most dangerous animal in the jungle.

With Dietrich involved, there is not only adventure, there is the ever present question of whether she is an adventuress, with that term's connotations of exoticism, travel, possible criminal tendencies, and independent sexuality (more reminiscent of her characters in *Morocco* and *Shanghai Express* than Lola Lola in *The Blue Angel*). In a mostly comic episode set in Scotland ("Stolen Love"), Dionne's boyfriend Michael instructs her in how to behave when he leaves town. "Don't accept any packages from strangers, don't get mixed up with the police and don't look twice at any other man"—in other words, he forbids her to adhere to the requirements of the genre and of her character's place within it. Of course Dietrich/Dionne just can't help it and does all three. Even worse, she shows up at Michael's hotel room, uninvited. He reacts badly.

Michael. I was gonna shut you out of my mind and suddenly a door opens and like witchcraft, there you are.

Dionne. Is that bad?

Michael. Well, right now it's not good. Dionne, do you know what it's like being in love with you? It's like chasing a rainbow. . . . I know you're there but I can't get hold of you. Then even if I did catch you, I'd only have a bull by the tail.

Dionne. That's a pretty picture. . . .

When she volunteers to leave, he accuses her of running out on him. Trying to control her temper, she turns on him with a succinct feminist deconstruction of his model of romance.

Dionne. Do you know what it is to love *you*, Michael? . . . It's like being in love with a broken record. The melody is sweet and haunting and filled with passion, and the harmonies are subtle and tempting enough to melt a woman's last defenses. And then suddenly the needle sticks and the spell is broken while it whines and whines again, "I must possess you completely, I must possess you completely, I must possess you." No one person can ever possess anyone completely.

Despite this rousing and passionately delivered statement of sexual and emotional independence, Dionne and Michael are eventually reunited (in the back of a cab) and, as the music swells, they finally find "time for love."

Café Istanbul and *Time for Love* bring together all the elements Dietrich is known for—glamour, singing (honored in the breach in the second series), international travel, foreign intrigue, elements from the mystery and adventure genres (including the character of the sexual adventuress), even the connection with her sponsors—the U.S. Armed Forces Radio Service—while giving her control in the production of her own (vocal) image.

Because Dietrich's voice was so central to her persona, it seemed reasonable to expect that her voice alone could convey the full complexity of her star persona in this exclusively aural medium. So why did the program fail? Perhaps her timing was off. The genre *was* overly familiar and *Café Istanbul* and *Time for Love* offered listeners nothing new. Paradoxically, this is exactly what Dietrich would capitalize on for the rest of her career.

Unchanging

In 1970, star chronicler David Shipman wrote of Marlene Dietrich: "Age does not wither her, nor custom stale her infinite sameness" (156). What Dietrich did in the 1950s was to find a way to transform the drawback of being "the same" into a source of wonder. That she was unchanged year after year became a constant source of pleasurable surprise, so that each time the audience saw her they could feel the thrill of discovering anew that she was—to their amazement—still "the same."

Writers began describing Dietrich as a "legendary" beauty, an icon of timelessness, around 1948 when the cover of *Life* magazine announced that "the Blue Angel" was a grandmother. Needless to say, "grandmotherliness" seemed to be at odds with nearly every aspect of her image—erotic, cold, indifferent, sexy, glamorous, and above all unsusceptible to time. However Dietrich managed to take the well-publicized fact of her age and combine it with the erotic, exotic, mocking "Dietrich." The radio program *The Burns and Allen Show* (17 March 1949), provides a prime example. Gracie does not want to leave George home alone, sick with a cold, when she goes out with friends. At the same time, she is afraid that he will use her absence as an excuse to bring in some young thing as his "babysitter," so she insists he hire a grandmother. He outsmarts her by hiring Dietrich. The joke(s) depend on the audience's awareness of Dietrich as being simultaneously a grandmother and irresistibly sexy. How this combination is achieved is left to the imagination on radio, depending not only on memories but on intertextual knowledge of contemporary publicity images of "today's Dietrich," such as "Grandmother Dietrich" on the cover of *Life*.[15]

But it was through her resumption of concert tours that Dietrich would find her greatest extracinematic success in the last decades of her career, and her first appearance in Las Vegas illustrates exactly how Dietrich created a balance between the audience's visual and auditory expectations.

John O'Hara put it bluntly: "Let's face it: Marlene Dietrich is not Irene Dunne, and the way things are now constituted in the entertainment world, the Dietrich product is not most advantageously displayed on TV or the cinema. When you see Marlene on either screen you are not getting the full treatment, and you know it. Anyway, I know it" (6). The "full treatment" would require something extra.

When she played the Sahara Hotel in Las Vegas in December 1953, the focus of the publicity (besides how much she was paid) was not on her singing but on how she looked, specifically when wearing what Harper calls simply "the Las Vegas dress" (83). "A $6,000 dress made of a material that has been described as rhinestones-and-nothing" (a British writer called it "a glacier glinting in the sunlight" [Milton Shulman, qtd. in Harper 83]), the dress became a symbol of Dietrich's own allure. Despite the fact that, according to *Colliers*, one of Dietrich's grandsons told her, "You look just like a Christmas tree," most critics saw more when they saw less (Leo Lerman, qtd. in *Colliers*, "Dietrich" 29). "That extraordinary dress," one wrote, "apparently transparent, actually opaque, mesmerizes" (Derek Monsey, qtd. in Harper 83). Like the best magicians, she did it with mirrors, blinding the audience with its own desire to look.

Dietrich protested that "the news pictures of my Las Vegas dress were misleading. It was not transparent; those flash-bulb shots, they shoot right through the dress." But she didn't protest too much. "What do they expect?" she said. "I should come out here for $30,000 a week and just say 'allo,' and not be beautiful?" (*Colliers*, "Dietrich" 29). *Colliers* wryly noted, that despite "Miss Dietrich's" "sincere dislike for publicity," by wearing that dress she managed to get "her picture on page one of an astonishing number of newspapers" (25).

The Voice as Mask: Performance or Emotional Authenticity?

In this period Dietrich made sure that the *labor* that went into maintaining the "Dietrich" image—face and voice—would be visible. If her return to the concert stage was a return to her legacy as a chanteuse, it was also a way to reintegrate her physical image into her contemporary persona. Even as a singer, Dietrich had always been keen to use her appearance to publicize her voice. Her image had always been on the covers of her LPs. A famous series of photographs by photojournalist Eve Arnold appeared at this time, documenting Dietrich, music in hand, during a recording session.[16] (Legendary photographer Robert Capa quipped to Arnold, "Your work, metaphorically of course, falls between Marlene Dietrich's legs and the bitter lives of migratory potato pickers.") By making an *image* of herself as a singer, Dietrich perpetuated her status as a visual icon even when working in a strictly audio medium.

Her publicity also made the public continually aware of her mastery of her self, of the discipline and professionalism she brought to bear on the body that provided the basic materials with which she worked. In 1952 *Life* reported: "Glamour is, to Marlene, not only a matter of natural talent, it is a triumph of technique" (Sargeant 88). It was around this time that Hitchcock was quoted as calling Dietrich "a professional—a professional cameraman, a professional dress designer . . ." (*Colliers*, "Dietrich" 28). In the same article, fellow émigré William Dieterle described her, more sympathetically, as "one of the most self-controlled, self-disciplined people I know" (29). Describing her concert career, Burt Bacharach once said admiringly that in the dozen years she worked with him on the concert stage, she never changed a single note.

Dietrich's performances, whether in film or radio, on record or on stage, visual or aural, could consequently be read as performances of control—her iron-clad refusal to be overcome by emotion, to age, to gain weight, to not get into the sparkly dress. For some, this display of discipline—the very unchangingness for which she was celebrated—proved that her voice was no more inherently genuine, no less a tightly controlled performance, than the visual aspects of her star image. For some fans, the "truth" about Dietrich's star image could thus be seen as the willful denial of emotion, a sardonic juggling with "real" feeling, leaving nothing finally but the fundamental blankness of a mask. "Of course, it is the same old Dietrich, the same old songs" ("Mr. Harper" wrote in *Harper's*). "Practice has made her perfect at the full-time job of being Marlene Dietrich, but it has cumulatively revealed her secret—which was never to be what she seemed, or seem what she was" (83). By dividing Dietrich in two—the "real" Dietrich and the mask—fans such as Harper negotiated the tensions between their emotional reactions to Dietrich's voice and their awareness of her work as stylized, iconic performance. Such arguments overlook the way performance itself can function as the product and site of the performer's desire.

In Dietrich's work there is no contradiction between performance (discipline, artifice, repetition) and passion. Dietrich does not don a mask to hide a "real" self because her deepest desire is openly displayed all the while. That desire, revealed throughout her career, was to embody "Dietrich, the icon" (in face, figure, and voice), to openly perform—and perfect—the mask she created.

Dietrich's unvarying sameness can be read as a tribute to her fans, her defiance of time as her pledge to remain loyal. Her heroic demonstration of survival becomes her assertion that what she and her audience share (the past) will never change—she will not allow it. By making visible the artifice of "Dietrich, the icon," Dietrich makes visible the lengths to which she will go to give her audience what they expect—the passionately distant, sincerely ironic, constant and constantly changeable masculine woman, the deeply German American patriot, the aging and ageless "Marlene Dietrich."

Notes

I would like to thank the editors: Mary Desjardins for her invaluable assistance with research on 1950s radio, and Gerd Gemünden for his lovely translation of Dietrich's German songs.

1. Rose, qtd. in *Colliers*, "Dietrich" 26.

2. Hemingway 92. The ever competitive John O'Hara has some quibbles with the famed author: Dietrich "has been described by Ernest Hemingway as the woman who knows more about love than anyone else in the world. Ernest's remark must have caused a little debate over at the Hemingways.' . . . Also, if I were doing research on Love, I think I might use other authorities before consulting E.H. But the remark stands as his opinion, and his opinion on anything at all is important, if not necessarily definitive" (6).

3. James Naremore describes her in *Morocco* as "ironically amused and uninterested," with a "slightly crooked smile that acknowledges that everything is a charade" (142, 143). He quotes Raymond Durgnat, who describes Dietrich's "musicianly control, not of gestures merely, but of an emotional façade" (143).

4. Bret continues, "She did not sing her songs so much as speak them, very much in the *Sprechsinger* style of Marianne Oswald, but without that singer's harshness" (150). Naremore calls her "essentially a *diseuse*, as she herself called it, [who] specialized in *Sprechstimme*" (143).

5. Of course, German-speaking fans would have their own Dietrich. There is a different kind of intimacy in listening to a recording in one's own language. Patrice Petro and others have noted that Dietrich's German songs of the early 1930s for many fans epitomize the Weimar era and thus have a strong emotional effect.

6. This screen test is described in great detail by Dietrich in Maximilian Schell's 1984 documentary *Marlene*. He tells her his team cannot locate a print of it. A substantial fragment of it is incorporated in the last episode of Kevin Brownlow and David Gill's series on silent film, *Cinema Europe: End of an Era* (1991), and again in *Marlene Dietrich: Her Own Song* (2001). Dietrich's account of it in the Schell film is extremely accurate.

7. Dietrich is identified in the *New Century Cyclopedia of Names* in 1954 as "American Actress" ("b. at Berlin, Dec. 27, 1904—American Actress"), qtd. in *Colliers*, "Dietrich" 26.

8. The photograph on the album cover seems to illustrate Hemingway's opinion that Dietrich was "as lovely looking in the morning in a GI shirt, pants and combat boots as she is at night or on the screen" (Hemingway 92). Like Hemingway, Harper cannot get over the cover: "Ever the artist in effects, on the jacket-photo she appears in GI clothes and combat boots, an echo of her mannish suits from the Twenties" (83).

9. Lyrics by Oscar Hammerstein II. *Oklahoma* debuted in the middle of the war in 1943, although the film, directed by German émigré Fred Zinnemann, was made in 1955.

10. Translation by Gerd Gemünden.

11. In this she was like Gloria Swanson, who began her own TV talk show in New York in 1948. Dietrich had a great respect for the silent film star, fashion maven, and businesswoman. Columnist Herbert Stein recounts in 1954 how once, "before Gloria Swanson made her comeback [in 1950s *Sunset Boulevard*], while she was still looking for work, a night-club photographer asked Dietrich if she'd mind having Swanson come to her table to pose for a picture together. Dietrich got to her feet and said, 'For Swanson, I'll go to *her* table'" (*Colliers*, "Dietrich" 27).

12. *Duffy's Tavern*, in an episode entitled "Archie Writes a TV Play" from 9 March 1949.

13. Dunning 130. Descriptions of the show are currently all that is available.

14. Although I have not been able to hear any episodes of *Café Istanbul*, the episodes I will be describing from *Time for Love* are "The Foreign Agent," "In Darkest Africa," and "Stolen Love." These are available from the Radio Historical Association of Colorado.

15. While Dietrich-as-icon may have always possessed a self-conscious doubleness, standing outside herself, commenting on her image and her effect on others, the "new" Dietrich seems to have been best expressed in comedy (beginning with *Destry Rides Again* in 1939 and continuing throughout her radio work).

16. For a similar series of photographs, see Blees 123.

II. ESTABLISHING THE STAR PERSONA

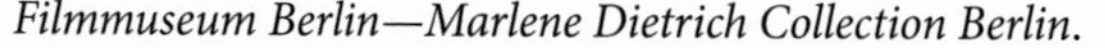

Filmmuseum Berlin—Marlene Dietrich Collection Berlin.

JOSEPH GARNCARZ

Playing Garbo

How Marlene Dietrich Conquered Hollywood

HOW AND WHY DID Hollywood become interested in Marlene Dietrich? In March 1933, *Photoplay*'s answer was a rhetorical question: "Wasn't it Von [Sternberg] who found her as a struggling nobody in Germany and with his genius' eye perceived her possibilities?" ("Is it Goodbye?" 16). It is commonly believed that Dietrich's career began with the overnight success of the German film *The Blue Angel* and the image that von Sternberg created for her with it, that von Sternberg discovered Dietrich as a nobody in Germany, and that he brought her to Hollywood and made her an international star. This story is echoed not only by many biographers but by von Sternberg and Dietrich themselves. Von Sternberg claimed: "I then put her into the crucible of my conception, blended her image to correspond with mine, pouring lights on her until the alchemy was complete" (qtd. in Dietrich, *Marlene* 70). Dietrich agreed: "He created me" (Dietrich, *Marlene* 79).

In what follows I argue that this story is a legend, by confronting it with facts from contemporary sources and by interpreting these facts within film industry contexts of the late 1920s and early 1930s in Germany and in the United States. Unfortunately, no documents that would be of help in this task can be found in the Marlene Dietrich Collection in Berlin or in the Paramount Collection at the Academy of Motion Pictures Arts and Sciences in Los Angeles. Marlene Dietrich collected a huge number of things, but she destroyed everything that did not fit the legend she cultivated all her life.[1] However, the films Dietrich made before she met von Sternberg, as well as published primary sources such as newspaper and fan magazine articles, film reviews, and popularity polls on films and stars, give enough evidence to suggest a different story.

I would like to show that prior to *The Blue Angel*, Dietrich modeled her image on Greta Garbo, using Garbo's high status with American and international audiences to attract Hollywood's attention. Since Paramount had already been searching for a competitor for MGM's Swedish star, they saw their "new Garbo" in Dietrich. Paramount was then able to create a unique image for Dietrich by distinguishing Dietrich's Garbo-like image from Garbo's own image. This unique image became an icon for decades. Thus, neither von Sternberg nor his film *The Blue Angel* were directly responsible for Hollywood's interest in Marlene Dietrich.

The film industry cannot make stars; it can only nominate the candidates for election by its audience (as Francesco Alberoni has put it ["The Powerless 'Elite'" 84]). Film stars are unique actors who arouse a special interest in their audience.[2] "Uniqueness" means that stars are readily distinguishable from one another, and a "special interest" simply means that some actors are preferred over others. My primary focus here is not the question of how Dietrich became a star, that is, how and why she became popular with audiences, but how she became a "candidate" for stardom.

My analysis of Dietrich is relevant for a topic that is central to star studies, namely the question of cultural agency in the creation of popular icons. I will show that the account of von Sternberg as the single creator of Dietrich is only a myth that accords with common ideologies, but that in reality, different individuals and institutions of a specific culture and historical period (in this case, the German and U.S. star systems of the 1920s) interacted in a complex manner. As a rule, if the audience itself does not single out an actor or actress, for example, by writing fan letters in response to a new face, then a studio will nominate a new actor or actress for election by the audience. For this purpose, a studio may initially adopt the strategy of imitation, that is, it will adapt the well-established image of a top star from one of its competitors. Later on, when the studio's new star is successful, it will aim to distinguish the new star from the original.

When a film studio initiates an international search for a candidate with star potential, actors or actresses aiming for stardom may attract attention to themselves by imitating an established star. This is possible and especially likely under production conditions in which actors and actresses themselves are responsible for creating and promoting their images, as was the case in the German film industry of the 1920s.

Thus, a candidate for stardom may be offered to audiences either through the initiative of a film company or the agency of candidates themselves. In Dietrich's case both interests interacted in the process of nomination, that is, her own ambition to become a great international star, as well as Paramount's aim to compete with MGM.

Playing Garbo: How Dietrich Planned to Conquer Hollywood

In her German films of the 1920s, Dietrich imitated Garbo, who was under contract to MGM, in order to attract the attention of the U.S. film industry, and Paramount responded, because it was looking for a competitor. To fully understand this process, one needs to have a basic understanding of the German cinema of the time. The German film industry of the 1920s produced a very successful national cinema. The film market was economically determined by a large number of small production companies, which competed fiercely. Star actors and actresses were usually independent, that is, they were employed on a film-by-film basis and had personal control of their images (see Garncarz, "Art and Industry").

Contrary to Dietrich's own claims, her film career began in 1922; she had already appeared in sixteen German silent films before *The Blue Angel*. Most of the roles were only bit parts, but in 1929 she played leading roles in four feature films. These films are, in chronological order of their release, *Ich küsse Ihre Hand, Madame* (I Kiss Your Hand, Ma'am, released 17 January 1929), *Die Frau, nach der man sich sehnt* (The Woman You Long For, released 29 April 1929), *Das Schiff der verlorenen Menschen* (The Ship of Lost Souls, released 17 September 1929), and *Gefahren der Brautzeit* (The Dangers of Engagement, released 21 February 1930).

The production companies of the first two of these films, Super Film and Terra-Film respectively, had not wanted Dietrich as a leading lady at all. In both cases the directors, not the companies, had proposed her for these roles. The director Robert Land insisted on Marlene Dietrich for *Ich küsse Ihre Hand, Madame* "in spite of the producer's and the distributor's warnings and protests" (Aros, *Marlene Dietrich*). Kurt (later "Curtis") Bernhardt, the director of *Die Frau, nach der man sich sehnt*, remembered: "She was breathtakingly beautiful. But it was a hell of a lot of trouble to sell her to the executives at Terra-Film. They said, 'Who is Marlene Dietrich? Nobody knows her.' But I succeeded in the end."[3]

Marlene Dietrich was not yet a star in Germany prior to *The Blue Angel*. Since stars are actors who are singled out from the mass of actors by the audience, the best evidence for judging who may be considered a star are popularity polls. Unfortunately, such audience surveys do not exist for 1929. However, the publicity was just beginning to mention Dietrich, and she was always considered "a movie debutante" (Hans G. Lustig, qtd. in Gandert 306) in these early years.

Dietrich's first performances in leading roles convinced the vast majority of film critics of her potential for stardom. Typical are the following two comments from contemporary German film reviews: "Rarely does a beginner show such charming prospects" (Hans G. Lustig, qtd. in Gandert 306) and "Only Marlene Dietrich is worth mentioning; her cool, ladylike poise offers proof of an unusual talent for motion pictures" (Hans Sahl, qtd. in Gandert 306).[4]

As many critics noticed, Marlene Dietrich was already imitating Greta Garbo in *Ich küsse Ihre Hand, Madame* and *Die Frau, nach der man sich sehnt*. Garbo was considered a goddess, a beautiful temptress, unattainable and mysterious. In accordance with this image Dietrich's acting was heavily stylized, and she refused to reveal information about her private life. As early as May 1929, one of the many German critics who immediately noticed the similarity between Dietrich and Garbo wrote: "Let women speak! 'She's sooooo sweet'—their lips pucker up when they stand in front of Marlene Dietrich's pictures in the lobby. And the men agree to this plain and simple, but nonetheless aptly formulated judgment. They eagerly absorb any traces of Greta Garbo wherever they can be found: in the gliding, almost somnambulant manner of movement; in the heavy, slow raising of the eyelids and their staying half-closed; in the dreamlike, tired falling into a gesture; and the relaxed, playful lethargy that seems to reverently combine innocence and vice. Minor innocence, minor vice in Marlene Dietrich, though. But Garbo administers such a strong feminine narcotic that it is intoxicating even in small doses. And yet Marlene Dietrich does not imitate; she even carefully avoids doing so" (Frank Maraun, qtd. in Gandert 217).

In one important respect, however, this review is an exception: most of the German critics who remarked that Dietrich's performance was an imitation of Garbo's style did not approve of this "copycat" practice. For example, one critic reviewing *Ich küsse Ihre Hand, Madame* wrote: "Marlene Dietrich is a valuable new discovery and she is a promising talent; if only the directors would release her from that strained Garbo-pose as soon as possible" (Burger 23). Similar remarks were made about Dietrich's second film of 1929, *Die Frau, nach der man sich sehnt*: "Here she is supposed to play Garbo, for whom German film longs. Styled to intoxicating magic. A pity. Otherwise perfectly suited for motion pictures" (Ernst Blaß, qtd. in Gandert 218).[5] The German critics disapproved of Dietrich's assuming "another's persona," and they asked: "Why do they paste the Swedish actress' hairdo onto the German Marlene Dietrich, and why do they put her into Garbo's outfits? Why don't they bring out this woman's own personality instead of forcing another's on her?" (Hans G. Lustig, qtd. in Gandert 306).

The German critics who strongly disliked Dietrich's imitation of Garbo did not discuss her reasons for adopting this strategy. By adopting Garbo's image, however, Dietrich wasn't trying to convince the critics of her acting abilities, but to become as successful as the established star. As early as October 1929, the *Berliner Illustrirte Zeitung* presented the German actresses Marlene Dietrich and Brigitte Helm together with Greta Garbo on its cover and claimed in the caption of the related article: "Doppelgängerinnen—Angleichung an die Erfolgreichste" (Doppelgangers—Copying the Biggest Hit).

But to whom did Dietrich direct her borrowed image? Dietrich may have targeted the sophisticated Berlin audience, but it is unlikely that she aimed to please the German audience at large. Berlin liked Dietrich as a new Garbo. (In early 1930, there was even a private school in Berlin, directed by Eris D. Monisch, that wanted to teach young women how to dress and behave like Garbo.) The average German moviegoer, however, disliked lascivious actresses, as is evidenced by the lists of top stars. Even Garbo herself was not a major star in Germany during this period: she was not among the top ten of the most popular female stars in Germany, and of her sixteen films released in Germany between 1926 and 1932, only

"Doppelgangers: Copying the Biggest Hit." Greta Garbo, the great Swedish-American film star, and two German actresses who adopted the same type of role, Marlene Dietrich (top) and Brigitte Helm (bottom right). Front page of the *Berliner Illustrirte Zeitung*, October 27, 1929.

"Sex appeal" as a school subject. In Eris D. Monisch's school in Berlin, students are taught how to resemble their great idol, Greta Garbo, in expression and manner. *Berliner Illustrirte Zeitung*. March 30, 1930.

two, *Love* and *Mysterious Lady*, were successful in commercial terms.[6] This is not surprising, because in those years there still existed a great cultural gap between German tastes in the capital and in the provinces. Consequently, it is likely that the films in which Dietrich was the leading lady found favor with their audience in Berlin but not in Germany at large. Judging by the annual lists of the fifty top-grossing films in Germany, Dietrich's films from 1929 did not meet the general audience's tastes.[7] Only *Ich küsse Ihre Hand, Madame* was successful; the reason for this, however, was probably not Marlene Dietrich but Harry Liedtke, who was the darling of Germany's young female audience at the time (see Garncarz, "Top Ten Stars" 228).

But if Dietrich's Garbo-like image could hope to find favor with only a small segment of the German audience, who, then, was its primary addressee? I argue that Dietrich's image was, from the outset, actually addressed to Hollywood and its international audiences. Indeed, Germany's film intelligentsia of the period believed that Garbo, in contrast to Germany's top stars of the period, was truly international: "Through the extraordinary prominence of Hollywood films, the Garbo-type has become a big international fashion"; "The world loves Greta Garbo,"[8] was the German critics' credo. Since Germany's film audiences did not like lascivious actresses, the critics said that the German actress Dietrich was "not typically German" at all (Lustig, qtd. in Gandert 306). They even speculated that "Dietrich would be a delightful actress in America, full of unaffected charm" (Ernst Blaß, qtd. in Gandert 218). I cannot prove that Dietrich knew that MGM's American competitors were searching for a new Garbo, nor do I know if Germany's papers picked up this fact. But since contemporary magazines clearly stressed that it was Hollywood that made Garbo an international star, it would definitely have made sense for someone who wanted to become as successful as Garbo to try to attract Hollywood's attention.[9]

When we ask who motivated Dietrich to play Garbo and thus to address Hollywood, we find several possible candidates, namely, the directors of her films of 1929 and the actress herself. As noted above, in the German film industry of the 1920s, the actresses and actors themselves were responsible for the creation and promotion of their images. Dietrich was able to control her image because she worked as a freelancer and the production companies contracted her on a film-by-film basis. As Géza von Cziffra reports in his autobiography, it was initially very difficult for Dietrich to get a role: "At that time there were hardly any managers in the film industry, and so I persuaded a young man, who knew everyone who was anyone in the business, to manage Marlene. The young man's name was Max Pick" (147). Von Cziffra relates how they got Marlene cast with much effort in *Sein größter Bluff* (*His Greatest Bluff*; released 12 May 1927) and *Ich küsse Ihre Hand, Madame*. However, it is unlikely that von Cziffra or Pick significantly influenced Dietrich's image, because otherwise von Cziffra, who was never modest about his achievements, would surely have mentioned the fact.

Dietrich's status as an actress in 1920s Germany, then, was not at all unusual. Furthermore, Dietrich's image is basically the same in the two films to which the German critics refer when comparing Dietrich to Garbo, and these films had different directors and different production companies. Thus, it must have been Dietrich herself who was mainly responsible for creating her image of a young Garbo.

Of course Dietrich's directors may also have contributed to her Garbo image. For instance, it is possible that the director of *Ich küsse Ihre Hand, Madame*, Robert Land, originally came up with the idea, but there is no evidence of this. We do know, however, that Dietrich often resisted taking direction. She wanted to do more than just play the roles given to her: She did her best to present herself in the most favorable way. As Kurt Bernhardt, the director of *Die Frau, nach der man sich sehnt*, remembered: "I wanted her to simply turn to her partner. But there was nothing to be done. From the start, she knew exactly how important lighting was and how her snub nose must be lit. . . . Charles Higham [who published a biography of Dietrich in 1977] told me that she still has that habit (which is no fun for a director) of turning her face to the spotlight. She speaks to her partner indirectly and stays in that position if she believes that the lighting demands it."[10]

Combating the Real Garbo: Why Dietrich Won a Paramount Contract

It is clear from the sources quoted above that Dietrich imitated Garbo to attract Hollywood's attention. But how did Hollywood react to this? My argument is that Paramount awarded a contract to Dietrich because the studio saw in her the type needed to compete with MGM's star Garbo.

In the course of a few years, Garbo had become a major star at MGM; by 1929, she had starred in eleven movies for that studio. Due to a lack of audience surveys for this period, we cannot determine exactly how popular Garbo was as a star.[11] However, there can hardly be any doubt that Garbo must have been well known and popular, otherwise it would not make sense that Garbo's weekly salary was raised to ten times its original amount during this period. As *The Saturday Evening Post* put it in May 1931: "When the talking pictures came crashing in and Greta first turned vocal, large billboards of the land bore simply and almost chastely two words, which might be read afar: Greta Talks. There was no detail in small type, no addenda; just simply and majestically, Greta Talks; or maybe it was Garbo Talks: the advertisers assuming quietly that the information conveyed was the same as 'Hoover elected,' 'Mars inhabited,' 'death inevitable,' or any other fundamental two-word fact in Nature" (Condon 29).

Despite this evident popularity, Garbo's films were, between 1932 and 1937, much less popular with American than with foreign audiences, with Germany probably being an exception (as noted above). Garbo's films *Camille*, *Queen Christina*, *Grand Hotel*, *Anna Karenina*, *Mata Hari*, *Conquest*, and *Painted Veil* generated greater box office overseas than in the U.S. domestic market (Sedgwick 148, table 1).

Nevertheless, because MGM was, by and large, very successful in promoting Garbo, Paramount tried to get a foothold in the market by looking for a new Garbo. As the American magazine *Pictorial Review* explained retrospectively in 1933: "Strangely enough, without Garbo there would be no Dietrich in the American movies today. Miss Dietrich was the answer to a rival company's long, exhaustive search for a personality that might combat the Swedish star's appeal."[12] Since Garbo's MGM films were more popular in foreign countries than in the United States, Paramount may have wanted to use its new Garbo specifically to expand its appeal on export markets.

How was the search for a personality that might compete with Garbo undertaken, and how was Dietrich discovered in the process? The Berlin correspondent of *Variety*, C. Hooper Trask, must have attended the premiere of Dietrich's film *Die Frau, nach der man sich sehnt* on 29 April

1929, since he reported a few days later, on 12 May 1929: "A discovery of a female star is something for a German film to accomplish. Here Marlene Dietrich shows herself as a strong contender for international honors" (Trask, "Woman Longed For" 24).[13] And he accurately anticipated how Dietrich would come to be presented in her first American movies: "At the moment she is imitating Greta Garbo's half closed eyes and languorous eroticism, but there is enough individuality in her work to show that the girl is there. She has the right face and figure and she can troupe" ("Woman Longed For" 24). In addition, Donald Spoto, one of Dietrich's biographers, claims (without giving any evidence for his statement, unfortunately), that "the Berlin representatives of at least two Hollywood studios—Paramount and Universal—cabled home to report on a new international star" (50).

A few months later, in early September 1929, *Die Frau, nach der man sich sehnt* was released as *Three Loves* in the United States. It was the first film with Marlene Dietrich in a leading role ever to be shown in America. *The New York Times*, underlining Hollywood's special interest, wrote: "*Three Loves* possesses the kind of direction that makes American film magnates cable contracts abroad, and pictorial solidarity that comes only once in a while from foreign studios. In addition it boasts of a noteworthy performer in the person of Fritz Kortner and a rare Garboesque beauty in Marlene Dietrich" ("*Three Loves*").

Dietrich claimed on 13 February 1930 that after "long-pending negotiations" Paramount had at last given her a contract: "Paramount had *heard* [*sic*] my English version of *The Blue Angel* and consequently engaged me" (*Film-Kurier*, 14 February 1930). As far as I can determine, the Paramount executives could not have seen more than a few scenes of *The Blue Angel*, since a rough cut of the English version was not finished before 7 April 1930, and after this screening parts of it had to be redubbed and some scenes even had to be reshot (Sudendorf, "*Blue Angel*"). (As Patrice Petro claims in her contribution in this volume, this was probably done because Paramount executives wanted the English version to be sexually less explicit, in accordance with American censors and audiences.) This did not matter much, however, since the talent scouts were not interested in the film itself, but simply wanted to hear Dietrich speak English. A new Garbo without adequate proficiency in the English language would not have been an acceptable candidate, because by this time the industry was already completing its transition to sound. The Paramount executives were apparently satisfied, since they signed Dietrich on 20 February 1930 in Berlin.[14] According to Sudendorf it was Sydney R. Kent himself, Paramount's president, who closed the deal.[15]

The studio planned to pick up Dietrich's image as a young Garbo created in the German films she made prior to *The Blue Angel*, especially *Three Loves*. *Morocco*, her first American film, even tells a story very similar to that of *Three Loves* about a woman between two men, and in it Dietrich is as mysterious and seductive as she is in *Three Loves*. Marlene Dietrich explained retrospectively, "*The Blue Angel* was something completely different, the role of an ordinary, brazen, sexy and impetuous floozie, the very opposite of the 'mysterious woman' that von Sternberg wanted me to play in *Morocco*" (Dietrich, *Marlene* 77). Consequently, the Paramount executives bought *The Blue Angel* but did not release it before *Morocco* had been shown, since they were afraid that Dietrich's image of the "ordinary, brazen, sexy and impetuous floozie" might damage her career (Dietrich, *Marlene* 69). (*Morocco* was released on 14 November 1930 and *The Blue Angel* on 5 December 1930.) Paramount's marketing strategy proved to be well founded, since *Morocco* can be found on the U.S. list of top-grossing movies of 1930–31, but not *The Blue Angel* (Steinberg 339).

Creating a Unique Image for Dietrich: Departing from Playing Garbo

After having contracted her, Paramount further cultivated Dietrich's Garbo-like image. Thus, the Dietrich-as-a-young-Garbo-ploy that was at first addressed primarily to the producers now became the cornerstone of Dietrich's publicity. Regardless of whether it was Paramount or Dietrich herself who was mainly responsible for this publicity campaign, this strategy was very successful. *Photoplay* reported in February 1931: "The battle of Greta Garbo and Marlene Dietrich—one of the most ferocious in the history of the screen—is now raging" (Leonhard Hall, qtd. in Griffith 14). But the discourse not only changed its addressee, it also changed its function: Dietrich no longer needed to content herself with proving that she was just as good as Garbo; she now tried to "threaten Garbo's throne," as *Photoplay* announced as early as December 1930, just a few days after *Morocco* was released (Albert 60).

This media battle started the moment Dietrich arrived in the States. Dietrich left Berlin for Hollywood on 1 April 1930, the day *The Blue Angel* premiered in Berlin. She arrived in New York on 9 April (according to the *New York Times* she was one of the "well-known passengers" on the *Bremen*, an express liner belonging to the north German shipping company Lloyd's ["Eight Liners Due" 23]). On her arrival she was asked by a reporter whether she admired Garbo.[16] Dietrich answered that she had loved Garbo's pictures when she was young (which is probably not true).[17] With this remark she wanted to give the impression that Garbo was much older (which is definitely not true).[18] Since Garbo was well known from silent movies, Dietrich wanted to give the impression that she had never made any silent films herself (which, again, is not true).

After it nominates a new actor or actress for stardom by adapting the well-established image of an existing, successful star, the studio has to differentiate the new star's image from the old one to make it unique. Dietrich would not have had the chance to become a major star by simply being Garbo's "copycat" (Leonhard Hall, qtd. in Griffith 16). In July 1930—neither *Morocco* nor *The Blue Angel* had yet been released in the United States—Dietrich was still being presented as Garboesque: "Two portraits of quite a batch of young ladies. The girl on the left is a lot like the late lamented Jeanne Eagels, about the nose and brow, and there's a hint of Phyllis Haver. The lady on the right is very much Garbo. Both are Marlene Dietrich, new Paramount player from Germany" (*Photoplay*, qtd. in Griffith 13). After *Morocco* had been released, *Vanity Fair* wrote: "Now that Marlene Dietrich, the German star who is Garbo's serious rival, has come along and started doing exactly the same thing, those who saw Miss Garbo in *Romance* and Miss Dietrich in *Morocco* . . . are beginning to feel a little plaintive about it" ("Both Members"). Consequently, the publicity began to change significantly by painstakingly differentiating Dietrich from Garbo. *Photoplay* wrote in February 1931: "And here's the unwitting, or innocent, cause of the great Garbo-Dietrich war now raging—the beautiful Marlene herself. Do you think she looks like Garbo—that she's *trying* to resemble Garbo the Great? True, she's blonde, beautiful, mysterious and alluring. But so are several others. We vote that Marlene Dietrich is Marlene Dietrich, and no copy of anyone!" (Leonhard Hall, qtd. in Grif-

"... very much Garbo."
Photoplay, July 1930.

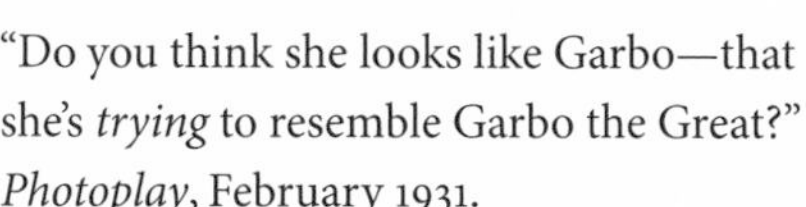

"Do you think she looks like Garbo—that she's *trying* to resemble Garbo the Great?"
Photoplay, February 1931.

fith 15). Thus, by denying that Dietrich wanted to be like Garbo, even if she still resembled her, the discourse began to differentiate Dietrich from Garbo and to create a unique image. This strategy, playing Garbo and then departing from it, was obviously successful, since two of Dietrich's first three American-made films were very popular with American audiences, namely, *Morocco* in 1930–31 and *Shanghai Express* in 1932 (Steinberg 339).

Thus the account that Dietrich's career began with the overnight success of *The Blue Angel* and the image that von Sternberg created for her with this film seems to have little basis in fact. In contrast, as I have argued, Dietrich herself had already created a specific star image (that of a young Garbo) through her leading roles prior to *The Blue Angel*, and the main purpose of this strategy was attracting Hollywood's attention. Paramount became interested in Dietrich because the studio was looking for a star who could compete with Garbo's success at MGM.

The story of von Sternberg who discovered the unknown Dietrich for *The Blue Angel*, brought her to Hollywood and made her famous, is just a legend. But why has the legend about Dietrich's rise to stardom become so popular and durable? When a public figure aims to win the adulation of a majority of people within a given society at a given time, it is necessary to conform to that society's dominant ideology. First, the Dietrich legend refers to patriarchal ideology; the story of Pygmalion, as told in Ovid's *Metamorphoses*, provides the mythical model for Sternberg's relationship to Dietrich. Second, the legend refers to the American dream; it is a version of the rags-to-riches story: Marlene, a nobody from Germany, came to America and found fame and wealth. And last but not least, it is a story about Hollywood itself: Hollywood as the sole creator of true international stars. Thus the legend offered what Marlene Dietrich's eager fans, as well as many of her critics, wanted to believe.

Notes

Translation by Annemone Ligansa. The translations from German into English are original to this essay, unless otherwise indicated.

I would like to thank Werner Sudendorf (Marlene Dietrich Collection Berlin), Barbara Hall (Paramount Collection, Margaret Herrick Library, Academy of Motion Picture Arts and Sciences, Los Angeles), and Christiane Rhefus, who provided me with valuable sources.

1. Werner Sudendorf, director of the Marlene Dietrich Collection Berlin, personal communication to author.

2. See my theory on stardom, in Garncarz, "Die Schauspielerin" 368–93, esp. 368–75.

3. Belach, Gandert, and Prinzler, eds., *Aufruhr der Gefühle* 95. For a contemporary confirmation that Bernhardt cast Dietrich, see *Berliner Tageblatt und Handels-Zeitung* 23.

4. See also "Ich küsse Ihre Hand, Madame," *Der Kinematograph* 3; Fritz Walter, qtd. in Gandert 218.

5. See also Sahl, qtd. in Gandert 218.

6. Garbo reached rank 13 in 1925 and a rank lower than 15 in 1926 (no ranks lower than 15 were given); one year later she vanished from the lists. *Love* reached rank 5 of Germany's top-grossing films in 1928–29, and *Mysterious Lady* rank 26 in 1929–30.

7. *Film-Kurier* 1929, *Film-Kurier* 1930, *Film-Kurier* 1931; *Ich küsse Ihre Hand, Madame* reached rank 23 on the 1929 list.

8. *Berliner Illustrirte Zeitung*, "Sex-Appeal" 566 (first quotation); Lustig, qtd. in Gandert 306 (second quotation); see also Aros, *Greta Garbo*, first page (n.p.).

9. See, for example, *Berliner Illustrirte Zeitung*, "Sex-Appeal" 566.

10. Belach, Gandert, and Prinzler, eds., *Aufruhr der Gefühle* 95. The quotation dates from 1977.

11 I have checked Finler; and Koszarski.

12. Qtd. in Shawell 16. Unfortunately, we do not have a document from the Paramount Collection to prove that this was the case. The earliest extant document is a summary of Dietrich's early contracts with Paramount. From this document we definitely know that her first contract with Paramount was signed in Berlin, 20 February 1930, but we get no idea of how and why Dietrich had been given a contract.

13. C. Hooper Trask reviewed German films not only for *Variety* but also for the *New York Times*; see, for example, "German Film News." In addition, he played a role, Charles J. Merryman, in the German film *Ein blonder Traum* (1932, dir. Paul Martin).

14. *Dietrich, Marlene (Married name Sieber)—Actress.* A summary of Dietrich's early contracts with Paramount. Paramount Contract Files collection, Margaret Herrick Library, Academy of Motion Picture Arts and Sciences, Los Angeles.

15. Sudendorf, *Marlene Dietrich* 61. Sudendorf gives the wrong date.

16. Werner Sudendorf, personal communication to author, 12 July 2001.

17. As far as we know from her diaries, she loved the top female German star, Henny Porten, a German ideal of womanhood, and not Greta Garbo (Sudendorf 24–25).

18. Dietrich was nearly four years older than Garbo; Garbo was born 18 September 1905, and Dietrich 27 December 1901. In her American passport Dietrich made herself younger, by giving her birth date as three years later, 27 December 1904.

ELISABETH BRONFEN

Seductive Departures of Marlene Dietrich

Exile and Stardom in *The Blue Angel*

MUCH HAS BEEN WRITTEN about the manner in which Marlene Dietrich, Hollywood's glamour star par excellence, appeared from the start to be nothing other than a creation of Josef von Sternberg, or, as Richard Dyer notes "a pure vehicle for the latter's fantasies and formalist concerns."[1] Yet one must not forget that von Sternberg was himself responsible for the idea that the icon of female seduction he had artificially constructed was fundamentally uncanny—a refiguration of his masculine self in a feminine body. Casting himself in the role of Svengali Joe, he enjoyed proclaiming, "In my films Marlene is not herself. Remember that, Marlene is not Marlene. I am Marlene, she knows that better than anyone."[2] At the same time, von Sternberg was also the first to admit that, although he was the creator of the starbody "Dietrich," he had not imposed a foreign personality upon her. He had merely known how to emphasize those attributes that he required for the cinematic persona he wanted her to embody, while his makeover of her appearance involved suppressing all the other aspects of his favorite actress that fit neither his fantasy of feminine seduction nor his formal concerns.[3]

The following deals with *The Blue Angel*, even though it was released only after Marlene Dietrich had already been introduced to an American audience with *Morocco*, because von Sternberg's only German film performs the story of the birth of the female star as an even more radical negotiation of questions of displacement and loss of home than does their second collaborative effort. *The Blue Angel* presents Marlene's seemingly irreversible crossing of a concrete geopolitical boundary, that is, her resolute departure from Germany, for which there would be a poignantly ambivalent homecoming after her death. Dietrich, who always stressed her German origins, while being vocal about her opposition to Nazi Germany, had asked to be buried in a Berlin cemetery next to her mother. Yet, although her death did not occur until 1992, she was still not welcome by many older Germans, who continued to see her as a traitor to her country. The official funeral ceremony had to be canceled, because the organizers were worried that there might be a violent outcry among the Berlin population, a repetition of the angry protests that had greeted the former Berlin star during her first tour through Germany after the war.

What is uncanny about *The Blue Angel*, filmed entirely in Berlin with a lead actress who was, as of yet, internationally unknown, is, then, the fact that the story it tells about the birth of the female star anticipates Dietrich's actual departure from home and her relocation in Hollywood—a move that was only made possible because her first collaboration with Sternberg proved to be so successful. What is poignant about the manner in which *The Blue Angel* anticipates Dietrich's exile is, however, the fact that its story distinguishes between homecoming and arrival, reserving the former for the former silent film star Emil Jannings (who acts the part of the teacher), and allocating the latter to the actress about to emerge as an international sound film star. For one of the film's plot lines represents the tragic story of a teacher at a high school in a small German town, Professor Immanuel Rath. Overwhelmed by an outburst of repressed sexual drives, Rath follows his students into the Blue Angel, a local cabaret, and from the moment the young singer Lola Lola catches him with her gaze, he is caught in a trap of female seduction. After their marriage, he leaves his prestigious job and the comfort of his hometown, to accompany the troupe of cabaret performers. When, many years later, he finally returns home, he is now himself part of the spectacle. Dressed as a clown, he finds himself sitting on the stage of the Blue Angel, and, as though he were enacting an obscene counterimage of the humiliation and punishment he used to inflict on his pupils, he allows the director of the troupe to use him as a prop. As the magician breaks an egg over his head, he imitates a rooster's cry. If, in his function as a high school teacher, he had initially believed himself to be in possession of a symbolic mandate that empowered him to punish his students' transgressions, he now finds himself utterly subjugated by the man who had encouraged his own transgression. Von Sternberg thus appropriates the liminality dictated by the fact that his film was shot in two languages and produced by two studios for his thematic concerns. For liminality emerges as the core trope in this story of a man's tragic downfall. Falling in love and leaving home prove to be analogous insofar as the fatality of love serves to disclose the sadistic kernel of any notion of a sustainable sexual romance, while exile serves to disclose the hidden uncanniness written into any home romance. Thus, his protagonist's departure from home can be read as an enactment of Freud's dictum that the ego is forced to acknowledge it is not master of its house. After all, Professor Rath's journey directly results from the fact that the unexpected reemergence of his sexual drives suddenly rendered strange everything he had held to be familiar. Yet von Sternberg's cinematic refiguration of the fundamental dislocation and alienation Freud attributes to the psychic apparatus contains a significant twist, highlighting not only the masochistic aspect of sexual subjugation but, perhaps more significantly, the lethal aspect of a nostalgic desire to return home. The only possible homecoming open to the man who chose exile out of love for a woman is death; the homeland and mother earth proving mutually reflected in the traditional notion of the tomb as womb.

Enmeshed with this story about the price of dislocation one pays for leaving home—both in the sense of a concrete living space as well as in the figural sense of a familiar cultural community—is the story of Lola Lola's rise to fame. Particularly when *The Blue Angel* is read in the context of the historical events that accompanied the success of the actress performing this role, this second version of departure and arrival can also be read as a cypher, albeit less for the way the unconscious necessarily produces psychic uncanniness, than for the cultural displacement experienced by those Germans who, having gone into exile at the onset of National Socialism, were never able to return home. Called upon to fashion a hybrid identity based on the experience of cultural liminality, they found themselves separated forever from a familiar culture and relocated in a foreign world they had chosen as their new home but which would never be fully familiar. After the bewildered Professor Rath, who has returned home only to bear with tragic dignity his public humiliation, silently leaves the stage, it is the young singer Lola Lola who takes his place. Sitting alone on the stage, staring out into space at an invisible audience, poised and suavely in control of her seductive charms, she fully embraces the dislocation that is the price of her celebrity. While Professor Rath turns his back on the audience, she confronts it defiantly with a gaze that seductively combines the gesture of vulnerability with that of empowerment. Von Sternberg concludes *The Blue Angel* (as though he, who had always obscured his European origins—including the aristocratic mark of the "von" before his surname—wanted to insist that once one departs from home a happy return is impossible) with a double image of induration: a female star, depleted of her historic specificity yet having arrived on the international stage, and a male representative of symbolic authority finally arrived home but as a corpse. This narrative resolution proves to be an uncanny forecast when read in the light of the biography of the two German film actors. As Andrew Sarris notes, "The ultimately tragic irony of *The Blue Angel* is double-edged in a way Sternberg could not have anticipated when he undertook the project. The rise of Lola Lola and the fall of Professor Immanuel Rath in reel life is paralleled in real life by the rise of Marlene Dietrich and the fall of Emil Jannings" (*Films of Sternberg* 25).

As master of anticipation—at least in reel life—von Sternberg actually heralds the double alienation that will find its culmination at the end of *The Blue Angel* with the help of several details in the very exposition of his tale. The film begins with a signpost indicating the name of a small German town. After the camera has moved along the rooftops of its quaint rural houses, it stops at a market scene, where a peasant woman is throwing a goose into a large pen. Although von Sternberg thus obliquely anticipates his male protagonist at the end of the film, unwilling to be the gander to this goose, he quite explicitly plays with the visual analogy to the commodification of his female star, immediately cutting to another scene of display. A cleaning woman is pulling up the shutters of a shop window, behind which we find the painted poster of a seductive woman with arms akimbo, her legs spread apart, her lower abdomen pushed slightly forward, her skirt held high above her knees. Her face is framed with curls, and on top of her head sits a huge feathered hat. A small cherub is clasping her right leg, and the name "Lola Lola" is written over

The Blue Angel (1930). *Filmmuseum Berlin—Marlene Dietrich Collection Berlin.*

her left leg. The cleaning lady, clad in a drab apron, briefly examines the poster, then throws a bucket of water against the pane of glass and begins to clean it. Then she suddenly interrupts her work, turns her back to the shop window and imitates the pose of the cabaret singer, spreading her own legs and placing both hands on her hips, while looking back over her shoulder to check whether she has captured the seductive pose correctly. From this grotesque mimicry, von Sternberg cuts to his third expository detail: a close-up of a name plate on a door, which reads "Prof. Dr. Immanuel Rath." It's significant that the heroine is introduced as an image, some twenty minutes before her body will actually be shown, even while she is contained from the start by two signifiers—one pointing to the economic gain to be had from the display of valuable merchandise, the other pointing to the symbolic value attached to a name. Furthermore, in von Sternberg's mise-en-scène the fatally seductive woman is introduced as an object of identification, which can be imitated, though only imperfectly, so that the unique, if dangerous quality of her sexual appeal is also foregrounded from the start. At the same time, she is introduced as a fetish, locked into a showcase behind glass, and as such comparable to the goose placed in the pen. Her provocative pose emphasizes her seductive legs, as does the cherub who clings to them.[4] These legs, and not her face, are visually foregrounded by the poster, as they are also a body part the cleaning lady takes note of and seeks to imitate.

Because von Sternberg immediately cuts from the poster of the cabaret singer "Lola Lola"—who is clearly represented here as an allegory for female seduction and not as a concrete woman with a real family name—to the nameplate on the male protagonist's door, he doesn't just obliquely establish a connection between his two protagonists. He also foregrounds the cultural emplacement of these two figures so as to signal that this positioning will prove seminal in the trajectory of his story. The seductive woman is clearly located within the imaginary realm, given the absence of a symbolic name, while the representative of education and discipline is introduced by virtue of the symbolic title he carries: "Prof. Dr." At the same time, von Sternberg inaugurates the family romance at stake in the film's story. The poster of Lola Lola functions as a perversion of the maternal gaze. The world she represents, and which the poster advertises, is the seductive, pleasurable realm of the cabaret, serving as a heterotopia of transgression and self-expenditure. Clearly opposed to this realm of the imaginary, yet at the same time connected with it, owing to the splicing together of the poster and the nameplate on the door, is the realm of symbolic law, represented by the professor. Significantly, here representation does not involve any body part, but only a plate that signals his symbolic mandate, as though his function as figure of paternal authority requires neither body nor face. If the heroine is introduced by virtue of an image of her seductive body that empties her of any historical reality, so, too, the hero is introduced by virtue of an empty sign that reduces him to his symbolic function. Both characters are to be understood from the start not as individuals, but as allegorical players in a family romance–home romance, in which they represent two psychic registers. As Professor Rath comes to desire Lola Lola as a repetition of the seductive yet also castrating maternal body, while she sees in him a representation of paternal authority she can subvert, they will negotiate the exchange between sadism and masochism within a parable that revolves around the flooding of the symbolic by the imaginary and its harsh restitution. In the course of this narrative, the singer ultimately emerges from the imaginary realm by ultimately accepting her symbolic mandate as an international star, while the representative of the institution of learning and discipline will have come to accept the consequences of his sexual drives, yet at the same time countering his sad humiliation by ultimately returning to the site representing the symbolic mandate he relinquished in favor of love, his classroom desk.

If von Sternberg uses the exchange of one body (the clown who will not cry) for another (the star who will sing) at the end of *The Blue Angel* so as to celebrate the birth of Dietrich as an international star, the success of this transformation is contingent on a reassertion of symbolic authority over and against the transgressive powers of the imaginary. Professor Rath's return is not only introduced with the same poster that bears the image of the woman responsible for his departure from home, but, more important, his name is literally written over the representation of her body. If in the initial expository scene Sternberg uses the cut between the shop window and the professor's door to splice together the image on the poster and the name of the privileged lover of the woman displayed there, in this later scene, the two form a palimpsest, with the latter occluding the full view of the former. The poster again advertised the presence of Lola Lola and her troupe at the Blue Angel, only now a banner is pasted over it, both to cover the image of the seductive female body and to announce the "appearance in person of Professor Immanuel Rath." Yet, even while the public display of the paternal figure of authority is clearly privileged, the maternal seductress is not fully effaced. Her face continues to look down from the left upper corner of the poster, over her left shoulder. On the upper righthand corner of the poster we find her name, "Lola Lola," marking her supremacy as performer, towering over his name. The transition from the first to the second poster marks a significant displacement. By crossing out the painted body of the cabaret singer, and replacing it with the name of her costar, while at the same time preserving her name, what is privileged is precisely her symbolic value as a star. Indeed, one might speculate that the poster not only advertises the double bill about to take place at the Blue Angel but, for the film viewers, also heralds the translation of the fetishized figure of the film's diegesis, Lola Lola, into the star Marlene Dietrich, singing on a stage that is no longer exclusively that of the small-town cabaret, but rather refers extradiegetically to the international stage Hollywood will afford her. An uncanny doubleness inscribes the appearance of Marlene Dietrich as Lola Lola, singing one last time on the stage of the Blue Angel. She is a hybrid figure, on the one hand the cabaret singer who has clearly outgrown the tragic confine-

The Blue Angel (1930). *Filmmuseum Berlin—Marlene Dietrich Collection Berlin.*

ment of her marriage, and, on the other hand, the actress about to leave the limitations imposed upon her by the Berlin film world. Though as an international star she, too, only obliquely refers to the concrete woman Maria Magdalene Dietrich-Sieber, the woman in the penultimate scene of *The Blue Angel* does have a fixed position within the symbolic realm of the international film world, and thus serves as a resilient counterimage to the petrified corpse of Professor Rath/Jannings, which represents both the return home of the reel figure and the descent into oblivion of the real silent actor.

This rupturing of the diegesis in the final scenes of *The Blue Angel* is so salient precisely because the final scene not only refers to the home Professor Rath left behind for a woman. It also serves to illustrate that the paternal figure of this allegorical family romance–home romance has now fully become a mirror inversion of the maternal figure. Recalling the place of the seductive woman on the poster in the shop window, it is now the masculine body that is fetishized, in a final fantasy scenario, in which the imaginary (attributed to the body, its desires, its drives) fully overshadows the symbolic (the code of laws and prohibitions). In the case of Professor Rath's clandestine departure from the cabaret, the difference between these two registers has come to be extinguished, because his home romance has now irrevocably taken precedence over any erotic fantasies. He returns one last time to his old familiar place of work. This fatal homecoming, however, works on the basis of a substitution, in the course of which a symbolic designation of his authority—the nameplate on his door—is replaced by a somatic one, his dead body. To emphasize the intimacy of this return, von Sternberg takes on the position of the witness, coming belatedly to the fatal scene. His camera follows the night porter, who, armed with a flashlight, goes after the strange nocturnal visitor, only to find him at his desk, his hands petrified in death, clasping the top of the table as if in a fatal embrace of the symbolic mandate he had foolishly relinquished in favor of a woman's charms. After all, it was while sitting at this desk that he first held one of Lola Lola's photographs in his hands before placing it in his coat pocket. If the temptation emerging from the image of a seductive woman had rendered visible the professor's liability to transgress the very codes of morality he had tried to impose on his students, then this stain can only successfully be covered over when the body perfectly coalesces with the symbolic law he represents. While the night porter quickly exits from this ghastly scene, leaving behind the flashlight directed at the dead Professor Rath, the camera slowly pulls back into a final long shot of the corpse, illuminated only by a circle of light. If Lola Lola initially caught him in the bright circle of the stage light she had directed at him, isolating him from the crowd after he had entered the Blue Angel, and in so doing allegedly selecting him as her privileged lover, he is now, once more, the privileged object of a gaze. Thus to the end, von Sternberg works with a visual analogy between the singer and her fated lover. Like Lola Lola, who in the previous scene was left sitting on the stage of the Blue Angel, responding to the gaze of an invisible audience, Professor Rath is the object of a disembodied gaze. His is the fetishized body, sacrificed on the double altar of sexual desire and the law of humiliation this entails. He has erected for himself a monument that, in one and the same gesture renders visible the fallibility of his symbolic mandate as representative of a disciplining law, as well as his radical subjugation under the authority of this symbolic law.

Von Sternberg's narrative pits two figurations of dislocation against each other; on the one hand, the paternal figure of authority, disempowered by his sexual fantasies, who can only return to the symbolic position he relinquished, by transforming himself totally into the deanimated object of the gaze of a projected Other, and, on the other hand, the female star, who accepts the fact that, as a subject, she is an image for her audience, yet does so precisely by responding to the gaze of the projected Other. Returning to the beginning of the film with the final images of its two protagonists in mind, the fact that the seductress Lola Lola is initially introduced as a visual representation is further proof of Sternberg's mastery of anticipation. This image of the female seductress actually circulates between the two sites inhabited by the professor, before it finds a material embodiment in Lola Lola/Dietrich, resurfacing in the hands of one of Professor Rath's students. While his peers stand around him, the young man gently blows on the feather skirt on the postcard he is holding in his hand, even though we can't see it. Another postcard passes from one student to the next, only to be confiscated by Professor Rath, who hides it inside his briefcase. Again the image remains unseen. Finally, the students, seeking to play a trick on their teacher, smuggle two postcards into the school bag of his only obedient pupil. They trip their comrade as he is leaving the school building, so that his bag opens and the incriminating photographs fall to the ground. It is only then that the camera finally shows the actual images—a full-body representation of the singer as well as a close-up of her face.

Professor Rath takes the pupil to his private rooms and forces him to confess to the nocturnal escapades of his peers, and, once the latter has left him, he continues to sit alone in his living room. Then he, too, begins to blow on the three confiscated photographs he is holding like a fan in his hands. Fully aware of the transgressive nature of this act, Professor Rath keeps looking furtively over his shoulders so as to make sure that no one is watching him, and in so doing, signifies his own guilt at the perversion inherent to his lustful gaze. Sternberg immediately cuts from the close-up of the photographs in his hand to Lola Lola, who, imitating her own poster image, is standing on the stage of the Blue Angel, as she begins to sing, "I am the stylish Lola, the one adored by all." The triad of photographs functions as a forbidden feminine interpellation, calling upon the professor to enter the cabaret, nominally to punish his students, but actually because, by breathing life into the clandestine image of Lola Lola on the postcard, he has animated his own sexual fantasies. Once he has responded to this seductive call, defamiliarity of the symbolic sets in. The students have covered both blackboards with caricatures of his passionate love for Lola Lola, and, as he enters, chant, "Professor, it smells

The Blue Angel (1930). *Filmmuseum Berlin—Marlene Dietrich Collection Berlin.*

The Blue Angel (1930). *Filmmuseum Berlin—Marlene Dietrich Collection Berlin.*

of filth [*Unrat*]." Professor Rath is no longer master of his house. On the one hand, the desire that has taken hold of him has made him foreign to himself, while on the other hand, the students' public rendition of his sexual drives cannot be erased from the blackboard. The price he pays for having been chosen by Lola Lola as the privileged player in the imaginary domain shared by the audience of the Blue Angel is the loss of his symbolic authority. The dissolution of the boundary between a seductive image and its material referent allows him to assume a clear position within his erotic fantasy scenario, hitherto unfamiliar to him, even while it has brought about his discharge from the school, and the beginning of his life as a homeless clown.

Given the catalytic function of the postcards, it is only logical that the first marital dispute between Professor Rath and Lola Lola should revolve around these scandalous images. During their wedding night, Lola Lola asks her husband to fetch her nightgown from one of the suitcases. As he opens it, a stack of postcards falls to the ground. While he stares at her reproachfully, declaring that, as long as he still owns a penny, these incriminating photographs will not be sold, she mildly laughs at the man kneeling at her feet and replies: "Well, one never knows. Better pick 'em up anyway." Her gaze signifies the double figuration she has come to assume in her husband's fantasy life. Standing between the living room and the bedroom, with the curtain separating these two spaces seductively wrapped around her so as to disclose the contours of her body even while veiling them, she is at the same time the desired maternal body, promising the fulfillment of all pleasures imaginable, and the punishing maternal body, disciplining the child by curtailing its wishes. In this particular erotic scenario, the man is everything but the agent of sadistic power. Rather, he submits masochistically to the seductive ploys of the very woman whom his imagination seemingly gave life to, enjoying his own disempowerment. It is only logical that von Sternberg should introduce the final humiliation of his protagonist with a scene in which the careworn Professor Rath sells precisely the photographs that had once inflamed his own erotic fantasies. The fact that he has been forced to give up his exclusive right to these images is an oblique indication of his wife's actual infidelity, and as such his lack of ownership as a husband.

Thus, from the start, the encounter between the high school professor and the cabaret singer is based not only on a highly duplicitous relay of gazes but, more important, on a theft of power, in the course of which both the spectator and the woman as eroticized object of display oscillate uncannily between sadistic empowerment and masochistic disempowerment. Indeed, from the moment Professor Rath enters the Blue Angel for the first time he is no longer master of his fantasies or his actions. As long as his desire was directed at an image, the boundary between the voyeur and the body erotically displayed for his pleasure was clearly demarcated. In the cabaret, however, this distinction has become uncannily blurred. While the singer is clearly as much an empowered spectator as she is a body on display, the voyeur who seeks her out has equally clearly become an object of both her playful seduction. Furthermore, in contrast to the mise-en-scène of her last song at the end of the film, where Lola Lola performs alone on stage, we find her at this early stage of the narrative as part of a group of women, drinking from beer mugs. Here the distance between the performers and their audience has been reduced to a minimum. Throughout her song they call out comments, as though they were part of the spectacle. This inclusion of the audience in the spectacle is further emphasized as Lola Lola allows the beam of her spotlight to wander across the faces of her spectators, as though to indicate to them that they could literally partake in the scene she is invoking with her song. Her choice will fall on one of them, she declares, before she actually captures the "right man" with her spotlight. As the audience becomes unruly, in part in response to her provocative offer, in part in response to Professor Rath's disturbing entrance, she remains poised on the stage, fully in command of the mayhem she has instigated. The professor, however, finds himself irrevocably caught, though as of yet unaware that he has seamlessly turned into a figure in Lola Lola's performance. Still believing in his own authority, he waves his walking stick, his phallic surrogate to her seductive spotlight, at the crowd, calling out to his students that they cannot escape his punishment. The audience of the Blue Angel is, however, fully in on the joke, and signals its support of the unexpected change in Lola Lola's performance by singing along with the "stylish Lola, the woman all adore."

As Professor Rath enters the singer's dressing room, he finds himself utterly disempowered by her erotic charm. While this unconditional defeat is clearly the culmination of Lola Lola's theft of power, rendering her the sadistic voyeur and him helplessly at her disposal, von Sternberg interpolates into this exchange a third gaze, namely that of the clown. Continually entering and leaving the dressing room, this third figure silently comments on the relay of gazes that takes place between a student, who has hidden himself behind a paravent; Lola Lola, who, aware of his presence, draws the professor's attention to herself; the professor, who is unsure whether his presence in the dressing room compromises him or the singer; and the various members of the troupe who keep entering. The significance of this explicitly silent gaze is that it lays bare the tacit premises of the intrigue, whose guileless victim Professor Rath has become. The clown not only mirrors all the spectatorial positions but, more important, shows that all the players in this complex exchange of gazes have taken on a double position—they are all the bearers of a gaze directed at a foreign body, the professor, while also the privileged object of his unfamiliar gaze. If Lola Lola is an exotic creature for Professor Rath, he, too, is strange to her, while both have not only been chosen as the object of curiosity by others but themselves look back at those looking at them. All the players are self-consciously aware of the relay of gazes they are part of, watching themselves looking at others, but also implicitly watching themselves being looked at. The clown's silent gaze, however, has a different self-reflexive function. It signals the possibility of a spectatorial position outside any opposition between active subject and passive object, and as such exceeds this exchange of gazes. As the one who insists on a distance between viewer and displayed object, he embodies a spectatorial position diametrically opposed to that of Professor Rath, who is about to give himself up completely to the libidinally charged imaginary realm of the cabaret, and in so doing, obliterate all difference between himself and his fetishized object of desire. Yet, while the clown maintains an ironic gaze, he, too, is complicitous with the intrigue unfolding before his eyes. While it is possible to have a privileged spectator, there can be no spectator position outside the circulation of visual desire.

Exile and the Birth of the Feminine Star

Siegfried Kracauer's devastating criticism of *The Blue Angel* focuses on two major aspects of the film, the first of which was Marlene Dietrich's new incarnation of sex: "This petty bourgeois Berlin tart, with her provocative legs and easy manners showed an impassivity which incited one to grope for the secret behind her callous egoism and cool insolence. . . . Of course, the impassivity never subsided, and perhaps there was no secret at all." The other reason for the film's international success, according to Kracauer, could be found in "its outright sadism. The masses are irresistibly attracted by the spectacle of torture and humiliation, and Sternberg deepened this sadistic tendency by making Lola Lola destroy not only Jannings himself but his entire environment." As he explains, two voices can be heard throughout the film, on the one hand the old church-clock chimes, whose tune praises Jannings's inherited beliefs of loyalty and honesty, and, on the other hand, Lola's cabaret songs about the fatality of love. Because the German folk tune is heard in the concluding passage of the film, just after Lola Lola's "Falling in Love Again" has faded, serving as the acoustic accompaniment to the visual depiction of Professor Rath's corpse, Kracauer conjectures that "Lola Lola has killed him, and in addition her song has defeated the chimes" (Kracauer, *Caligari* 217–18). With this pointed if oversimplified criticism of von Sternberg's only German movie, Kracauer seeks to address a political dimension inherent to the relation between star and spectators. Though the political concerns are rather different, feminist film theory has also focused on von Sternberg's ambivalent deployment of Dietrich's seductive powers as a star to emphasize the sadistic element of narrative cinema. As Laura Mulvey has noted: "Sadism demands a story, depends on making something happen, forcing a change in another person, a battle of will and strength, victory/defeat, all occurring in a linear time with a beginning and an end." In the case of classic Hollywood stars, such as Dietrich, Mulvey explains, "the power to subject another person to the will sadistically or to the gaze voyeuristically is turned on to the woman as the object of both," while the spectator can only be complicitous with the sadistic gaze of the implied masculine voyeur ("Visual Pleasure" 14–15).

If one recalls that, according to Freud, the daydreamer can take on various positions in his or her fantasy scenario, then cinematic characters, caught in a relay of explicitly performed gazes, as well as the audience, asked to identify with these characters, are never reduced to one, exclusive spectatorial position. The scene in which Lola Lola sings "Falling in Love Again" for the first time draws its fascination in part from the fact that von Sternberg self-consciously provides identifications that uncannily blur the traditional distinction between feminine performer and masculine spectator, with the woman the bearer of a sadistic gaze, the man the bearer of a masochistic one. Because both the masculine and the feminine positions are multiply encoded, dissolving the distinction between voyeur and exhibitionist, empowered and disempowered subject, privileging only one spectatorial position would reduce the ambivalence and heterogeneity von Sternberg self-consciously enacts. After the director of the troupe has interrupted Lola Lola's song, so as to make Professor Rath's presence in the box known both to her as well as the rest of the audience, a highly ambivalent seduction commences. Lola Lola applauds the presence of the professor, clapping her hands at him as though he were the attraction of the evening. In the ensuing song sequence, von Sternberg opens up the possibility of identifying with Lola Lola, apparently singing only to the privileged guest. One can also identify with Professor Rath, flattered that he has been chosen as the privileged viewer of this spectacle, believing himself to stand apart from the rest of the audience. At the same time, however, Professor Rath is clearly staged by von Sternberg as the object of the gaze of an anonymous audience, of the other singers on stage, as well as the director, standing in the aisle, so that his narcissistic belief in the omnipotence of his spectatorship is undermined even as Lola Lola's attention seems to confirm it. Finally, one could also identify with the silent clown, whose gaze travels from the stage and Lola Lola, up to the box in which her privileged spectator sits, ironically commenting on the relay of seductive gazes being performed.

Equally seminal to Mulvey's discussion of the sadism inherent in narrative cinema is the multiple encoding of the maternal body proposed by psychoanalysis, because the subject initially learns to explore fantasy in its narcissistic identification with figures of maternal authority. While the maternal figure is the source of imaginary plenitude, promising satisfaction of all demands and desires, she is also an object of horror in a twofold sense. Lacking a penis, she comes to represent fallibility, even while she also appears to be endowed with phallic qualities. By insisting on the need for a separation from the child, she introduces the very law of forbiddance and curtailments against which narcissistic fantasies are pitted. Referring to this double encoding of the maternal body as source for all fantasy, Mulvey suggests that the visual pleasure narrative cinema affords is structured around two modalities of the gaze. The first entails a voyeuristic spectator, who believes himself to be in a privileged relation to a feminine star, performing exclusively for his pleasure, and, in so doing, articulating his fantasy, not hers. This is indeed the position embraced by Professor Rath, as he sits in his box seat and enjoys Lola Lola's performance, which is seemingly directed only at him—although Sternberg clearly stages this as a deluded sense of omnipotence. The second modality entails a spectator, who identifies with the hero, and thus, by proxy, believes he, too, is in possession of the feminine star, and one could read the audience of the Blue Angel, enjoying Lola Lola through the eyes of Professor Rath, in this manner. However, Gaylyn Studlar, who also proposes an analogy between feminine star and maternal body, suggests that it might be equally fruitful to privilege the masochism written into the relation between the maternal body and the subject's formation of fantasy. In so doing, she suggests reading the feminine star as empowered, regardless whether she offers voyeuristic pleasure to a privileged spectator, or whether she sadistically entraps him with her charms.[5] What is significant about such a shift in the encoding of the feminine star, which locates Dietrich's fascinating allure in an uncanny oscillation between object and perpetrator of the gaze, is that the allegedly masculine spectator enjoys his subjugation and impotence as much as any imaginary possession of the adored feminine star. Furthermore, while von Sternberg may be seen to reiterate a traditional economy of the gaze, within which, as John Berger noted, "men act and woman appear. Men look at women. Women watch themselves being looked at,"[6] it should not be overlooked that he does so self-consciously. In tandem with the manner in which he stages the passive elements of the masculine position, seemingly in control when actually fully subjected to the object of his fantasy, he also emphasizes the active aspect of the female gaze eliciting male desire, responding to it by playing with it.

Far from unequivocally identified with an empowered sadistic voyeur, the extradiegetic spectator is equally displaced from any neat viewing position, in part believing to possess the star, yet also submitting to the spectacle. One could claim that the spectator can choose between an identification with Professor Rath, masochistically enjoying the murky interface between pleasure and vulnerability, or Lola Lola, willfully playing with his desire, while at the same time, like the silent clown, able to maintain a protective distance to the spectacle.[7] The collaboration between von Sternberg and Dietrich leaves the decision open whether the star is deprived of all agency, whether the privileged masculine spectator is exclusively the sadistic bearer of a gaze that appropriates the star for his fantasy, or whether, in the act of viewing, such rigid positions are dissolved. Furthermore, one could also maintain that von Sternberg's performance of the relay of gazes revolving around his feminine star anticipates Jacques Lacan's description of voyeurism as a sign of excess, as the surplus of pure seeing, which, like all other drives, is aimed at the recognition of a lack. Lacan argues that, while the gaze constitutes the subject, as well as the uncanny split, the *méconnaisance*, upon which all psychic processes depend, this gaze also lies outside the subject, comparable to a partial object (*objet a*) that forces the recognition of "beings who are looked at, in the spectacle of the world." Given the exteriority of the gaze so fundamental to subjectivity, Lacan asks wherein the satisfaction might lie for the subject in "being under that gaze that circumscribes us, and which in the first instance makes us beings who are looked at, but without showing this?" (Lacan, *Four Concepts* 75). For Lacan, the subject is defined by virtue of the fact that it can be gazed at by an invisible Other, and insists that the possibility of being gazed at is more primary than the act of gazing. Significant here is the fact that Lacan implicitly aligns the subject's position with that of the feminine star. One could thus read von Sternberg's staging of his star at the end of *The Blue Angel* as a cinematic visualization of this definition of the subject.

Once more Lola Lola sings "Falling in Love Again," and in so doing implicitly declares to her deranged husband that she cannot be held responsible if her seductive powers prove fatal for her lovers. As von Sternberg cuts from her to Professor Rath, fleeing the cabaret, he indicates to what degree masochistic madness is the precondition for Lola Lola's sadistic triumph as an unparalleled star. While in the earlier scenes she had been placed on the stage in the midst of other women, she is now alone, sitting on a wooden chair, the back of which she straddles between her two legs. She is now isolated from all the other performers of the troupe. No musician and no other singers stand next to her on the stage. Furthermore, although an audience is implied, it is not directly shown to us, as though it were a disembodied force written into her performance. As the camera closes in, the legs that had been the focus of the poster as well as the focus of the camera while she was singing the song during the earlier scene,

The Blue Angel (1930). *Filmmuseum Berlin—Marlene Dietrich Collection Berlin.*

now fall out of the frame. Once Lola Lola has reached the end of her song, she responds to her applause by looking around at the empty space before her in a composed manner. As Sarris notes, this second rendition is "harsher, colder, and relentlessly remorseless," illustrating "a psychological development in Dietrich's Lola Lola from mere sensual passivity to a more forceful fatalism about the nature of her desires," affirming these "not as coquettish expedients, but as the very terms by which she expresses her existence" (*Films of Sternberg*, 25). She seems to enjoy herself as the object of this gaze, while at the same time she seems to know that this gaze firmly places her on a stage, separated from her audience, vulnerable to the view of a disembodied Other, constituting her subject status. What was originally a heterogeneous space, in which the boundary between performers and audience had been fluid, has been exchanged for a homogeneously structured theatrical stage, marking the shift from her ambivalent role in the production of mutually shared fantasy to the acceptance of her symbolic mandate as an international star, with her in charge of the fantasy. This radical restructuring also finalizes her embrace of dislocation as the condition of subjectivity.

If Hollywood stars in general fascinate because of their uncanny oscillation between reanimation as a starbody and deanimation into a mythic sign, Marie Magdalene Dietrich-Sieber's particular charismatic power was to be attributed to Sternberg's iconic drive, which sought to fix her as static, pale, and highly stylized creature, focused almost entirely on her erotic desires. As her stage name "Marlene Dietrich" became ever more entwined with this reel image, the real actress was seemingly consumed by the star body designed for her, albeit a body she also chose to perform. Yet, what is significant about the ending of *The Blue Angel* is that, even if it heralds the transformation of a German actress into a Hollywood star, and in so doing depletes her, she is represented explicitly as the figure of survival in this fatal family/home romance. As bearer of the gaze of the Other—the invisible audience, the director, Hollywood, and implicitly the spectators—she performs the uncanny subjugation before the external gaze that, according to Lacan, constitutes the subject. In other words, she articulates the fact that the only agency available to the subject, once it has entered into the symbolic realm of codes and prohibitions, lies in the conscious recognition that one is always already the object of an interpellation by a symbolic authority which has no material figuration. As a hybrid figure, oscillating incessantly between voyeurism and exhibitionism, Dietrich not only deconstructs the traditional equation between woman and erotically displayed object, by articulating how empowered a woman, who draws the gaze of others onto her self, can be. She also renders visible in what threatening manner the empowered woman as sadistic seductress can come to be fantasized by men, even while she seems to satisfy the spectator's sadistic desire to take scopic possession of her. At the same time, what von Sternberg demonstrates, in his staging of the birth of the glamorous starbody "Marlene Dietrich," is that the one position that can guarantee a survival in the realm of symbolic laws of Hollywood's cinematic language is that of the subject willing to subjugate herself before the gaze of the Other. For it is precisely from this disempowering gaze that Professor Rath flees. Leaving the world of the cabaret behind, he returns to his home romance, with the grave serving as a protective womb. In contrast to her husband, Lola Lola, who as a cabaret singer was from the start more aware of her uncanny inhabitation of her world, can bear being gazed at, and in so doing proves that her real power lies in accepting this inevitable displacement. To rephrase Berger's claim that men act, while woman appear, one could say that the collaboration between von Sternberg and Dietrich means that the female star appears and thus she acts.

As Steven Bach notes in his biography, von Sternberg always claimed that he had submitted Dietrich completely to his artistic project, interweaving her figure with his cinematic images and flooding her with his light until the alchemy was perfect and she materialized in her body his concepts of feminine style and seduction. In turn, Dietrich claimed that the role of the cabaret singer Lola Lola had been foreign to her, given that she had been a rather shy, though well-educated young woman from a typical Berlin bourgeois home. Precisely because in real life she was so different from her reel persona, she felt she had achieved something in *The Blue Angel* she was never to duplicate. As Bach explains, it is seldom noticed "that it is also the end of something. Lola Lola was the last role Marlene Dietrich would ever play in her life that was not created *for* her, or tailored to her measure. There was challenge and aspiration to Lola Lola that would never be there again, the stretch she had to make *as an actress* to fit a role. The roles would now have to fit *her*" (120). If one is also willing to read the final rendition of "Falling in Love again" as a cypher for the ambition of Marie Magdalene Dietrich-Sieber to make it in Hollywood, after a decade of degrading battles for artistic recognition in the Berlin film world, this last image of the feminine seductress calls forth yet another reading. In the archive of Dietrich's films, the Berlin starlet Lola Lola stands as a reminder of the loss inscribed in gain, of how appropriating the reel life of Lola Lola utterly foreign to her was the precondition of her stardom, only to be discarded along with the UFA Studios as she embarked on her journey to Hollywood; an umbilical cord of sorts, jettisoned after this artistic birth, yet reminding one of the cut—psychic, geographic, and cultural—constitutive of all subject formation. Only as a foreigner—as an American living the last years of her life in Paris—would Marlene Dietrich finally return to the place of her natural birth and her birth as a star, in a coffin that had been wrapped in the American flag during the flight from Paris to Berlin, to be covered with a German flag before it was finally lowered into the grave next to her mother.

Notes

1. Dyer offers a useful overview of the debate, focusing on the manner in which Dietrich was seen either as "an empty vehicle for Sternberg's erotic formalism" or as "resisting the construction of her as a goddess for male dreams"

(179). Seeking to arbitrate the various positions, he concludes that "the films can be seen as the traces of the complexities of their relationship rather than just the combination of two voices" (180).

2. Quoted in Flinn 17. In her autobiography *Marlene Dietrich's ABC*, Dietrich in turn called von Sternberg "the man I wanted to please most" (151).

3. See Bach for a discussion of the strange mixture between appropriation and dispossession that was written into the relation between von Sternberg and his star, Marlene Dietrich.

4. For a discussion of the fetishization of Dietrich's legs, see Peter Baxter ("Naked Thighs") as well as Alter's and Petro's essays in this volume.

5. Studlar privileges the position of the masochist in the manner in which von Sternberg stages Dietrich. She argues that Dietrich's performance refigures the position of the maternal body, conceived as highly empowered, both as dangerous and pleasurable, depending on the child's degree of proximity to it. (See Studlar, *Realm of Pleasure*.)

6. Berger 47. Indeed, E. Ann Kaplan correctly questions whether one is justified in declaring the gaze performed in narrative cinema, as it is supported by both the protagonist and the camera, and as it elicits an identification from the viewer a masculine gaze. In her reading of the collaboration between Dietrich and von Sternberg, she insists on Dietrich's agency, which is to say her self-empowered deployment of her body as an object of display. The self-consciousness she attributes to Dietrich calls forth an uncanny disturbance in the stage's fantasy scenario, given that Dietrich plays the part of the passive, appropriated woman even while she gives voice to the fact that she is both fully cognizant and in control of this appropriation. (See Kaplan, *Women's Pictures*.)

7. De Lauretis questions the validity of any overgeneral theorization of cinematic spectatorship, shifting her focus instead to how individuals view a film, how they identify with a fantasy scenario, and the manner in which public phantasy scenarios satisfy private desires in a multifarious manner. Given the fluid boundary between the fantasy scenario performed by a film and the intimate fantasies of the individual spectator, she insists that one cannot postulate a single mode of identification between spectator and star, but rather only a heterogenous, multiple, and often ambivalent one, dependent on particular structurations of desire. See also Walters, as well as Stacey ("Feminine Fascinations"), who argues that as viewers and critics of films, we must oscillate between an embrace of the pleasures called forth by narrative cinema and an ideological critique.

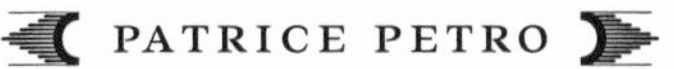

PATRICE PETRO

The Blue Angel in Multiple-Language Versions

The Inner Thighs of Miss Dietrich

IT IS WITH SOME trepidation that I undertake an analysis of a film that has been the subject of such an extensive secondary literature and the topic of so much discussion over so many years. But given my focus on multiple-language versions—a topic that has hardly received the attention it deserves—I hope to mitigate this initial hesitation by suggesting a fresh way to think about the transnational components of *The Blue Angel* and its historical status as a copy without an original.

I would like to begin by addressing the allusive subtitle to this essay, deliberately and provocatively titled "The Inner Thighs of Miss Dietrich." The reference to Miss Dietrich's "naked thighs," of course, recalls Peter Baxter's 1978 essay of the same name. Baxter's concern to trace the circulation and censorship of perhaps the most famous Dietrich image, her "casual pose on the stage with one leg upraised," in her performance as Lola Lola in *The Blue Angel*, is not, as I will suggest, entirely dissimilar from my own. However, it was the German author Heinrich Mann, upon whose 1905 book the film was based, who made the initial observation about "Miss Dietrich's naked thighs."[1] As the story goes, Mann not only agreed to the massive changes to his novella when it was adapted for the screen, but also said that he wished that he had thought of them himself. He nevertheless had problems with the finished film. As one critic reports

The inner thighs of Miss Dietrich. *The Blue Angel* (1930). *Filmmuseum Berlin—Marlene Dietrich Collection Berlin.*

it, "Mann was friendly with show-girl Trude Hesterberg, whom he had suggested for the part of Lola."[2] But when Sternberg selected Marlene Dietrich for the starring role instead, Mann apparently complained that his original conception had been compromised because "Miss Dietrich's naked thighs" dominated the picture.

An interesting question arises in relation to this claim; namely, in which film, and with which particular thigh, does Miss Dietrich's nakedness tend to dominate? Although it is well known that *The Blue Angel* was shot simultaneously in German and English with the same principals but with slightly different supporting casts, the various versions have rarely been analyzed in any detail. A closer look at the same scene in the multiple-language versions of this film nevertheless suggests that Dietrich's inner thighs might have something new to reveal to us.

I wish I could say that the idea were my own, but in the spirit of the copy, I must admit that this insight comes from Nataša Ďurovičová, historian of the transitional period in film history from silent to sound.[3] The scene at issue takes place at the Blue Angel cabaret early in the film. Lola Lola sits upon the beer barrel, leaning back, leg raised, and sings "Ich bin von Kopf bis Fuss" ("Falling in Love Again") to Professor Rath, who sits, enamored, in the balcony above. In the German-language version, Lola raises her left leg first, thus revealing her inner thigh. In at least one of the English-language versions, by contrast, she raises her right leg first, and never raises both legs in the air, as in the German version, thereby performing a more demure and less sexually provocative version of the same song.

Obviously, one could attribute this change to the presence of Hollywood's Production Code, written and administered by Will Hays's Motion Picture Producers and Distributors of America (MPPDA). *The Blue Angel* was always destined for release in the United States and, as is well known, the Production Code was created to regulate film expression in an effort to forestall state and federal censorship. As Don Crafton has pointed out, however, the coming of sound posed new problems and "through self censorship, the industry used sound as an excuse to maintain the power to distribute its product without external interference by local censors" (Crafton 17). Again, it is well documented that the coming of sound resulted in demands from exhibitors to make changes to films, which entailed recutting, reshooting, and preparing multiple versions for different world regions and national audiences.[4] The result was hybrid films referred to at the time as "multilinguals" or "foreign-language versions." This is the focus of my essay, in which I attempt to analyze the salient differences between the multiple-language versions of *The Blue Angel* and their imagined national audiences. Such an analysis is especially warranted, given the proliferation of various versions of this film (most recently, a new Kino DVD release, which provides yet another English-language version of *The Blue Angel*, which I discuss in greater detail near the end of the essay).

Even more ambitiously, however, I hope to assess the historical status of this film and determine whether it actually achieved what Erich Pommer, its producer, hoped for and aspired to with this prestige German sound film: namely, the "synthesis of Hollywood and Neubabelsberg."[5] Central to this synthesis, moreover, was the creation and promotion of Marlene Dietrich's star image, particularly as constituted both in and by the multiple-language versions of this film. Indeed, as Elisabeth Bronfen points out in her contribution to this collection, the story of Lola Lola's rise to fame parallels that of Dietrich's own rise to international stardom—a stardom based precisely on the performance of a hybrid identity or, rather, a synthesis of Weimar Berlin and thirties Hollywood.

The Blue Angel and Multiple-Language Versions

The Blue Angel began production on 4 November 1929 and was completed on 22 January 1930. It premiered in Berlin in April 1930 and was withheld for release, in its English-language version, until later in the same year, after the successful promotion of Dietrich as a Hollywood star with the release of *Morocco*. The film was made in part at the request of a world-famous actor. Following the success of *The Last Command* and his Oscar for best actor, German film star Emil Jannings had asked Erich Pommer, who himself had just been recalled from Hollywood to Ufa in 1928, to hire Josef von Sternberg for his next, critically important, German film—his first with sound. Jannings had insisted that this production be made in his own country and language, but wanted von Sternberg to direct. Von Sternberg welcomed Jannings's and Pommer's offer, and came to Berlin in the autumn of 1929. Once there, he enlisted the talents of the relatively unknown and untested Dietrich, who surprisingly overshadowed Jannings in her performance and then was signed by Paramount to a two-picture contract in February of 1930. Dietrich attended the premiere of *The Blue Angel* in Berlin on 1 April, only to sail for New York later that night. The rest, as they say, is history.

But what *kind* of history exactly? *The Blue Angel* occupies a paradoxical and yet significant place in German as well as American film history. It is part of a curious international language landscape and the fascinating trace of the complexity and turbulence brought about by the transition to sound. *The Blue Angel* is, moreover, much more hybrid than other multiple-language versions of the time. In the German and the English versions, we are never quite sure which language a character will speak, whether English or German or the heavily accented English that is taken for American vernacular. *The Blue Angel* was shot simultaneously in German and English at the Ufa studios. Ufa distributed the film in Germany, while Paramount distributed it in the United States. This particular arrangement was the result of long-standing agreements and interchanges between the two companies, notably, the infamous Parufamet Agreement of 1925–26, which enabled Paramount and MGM to enter into an agreement with Ufa to found a joint distribution company.[6] Although this original contract was renegotiated in 1927, with looser terms and restrictions, it served as the basis for this joint venture, which came at a critical time in Ufa's history and in the history of the transition from silent to sound film.[7]

As many scholars have pointed out, the coming of sound sharpened the issues of cultural identity raised by the international trade in motion pictures and led producers, audiences, and governments alike to reassess their relation to the medium. As Ruth Vasey and Richard Maltby have argued, sound standardized the movies in a very material sense, making them less malleable and restricting their cultural adaptability. Hollywood's American identity became audible and forced it to confront the cultural and linguistic diversity of its international audience.

To be sure, intertitles had long served as the principal site of international adaptability. As early as 1927, films were routinely translated into thirty-six languages. Visuals were subject to excision or rearrangement, but titles could be creatively modified to cater to diverse national and cultural groups. Sound technology changed all this, making movies far less adaptable. It was no longer possible, for instance, to rearrange or excise sequences without ruining entire reels. And even recorded music caused problems. Vasey and Maltby point out that Italian and German exhibitors, for example, accustomed to providing their own musical accompaniments, complained that the new sound tracks sounded "too American" for the taste of their audiences.[8]

When sound came to involve "talking," the problem of language specificity and the loss of ambiguity in the treatment of sensitive and especially sexual subjects only compounded these problems. Dubbing was not fully operational, although most major studios experimented with it. The other alternative was more expensive and complex—namely, the production of different talking versions of selected films, each in a different language. Stars could retain their own parts if they were multilingual; otherwise, replacements would be used. By 1930, all the major companies were producing foreign-language versions. The most conspicuous action was taken by Paramount, which in 1930 established a studio at Joinville, outside Paris, specifically for the production of multiple-language versions.

The Blue Angel was made just prior to the establishment of operations at Joinville and was always understood to be an Ufa project. As Thomas Saunders explains, "At the beginning of 1929 Ufa sent a team to the United States to study sound production. On the basis of its findings Ufa decided to proceed at maximum speed to make the switch. The language barrier and patent war notwithstanding, the substantial lag of German development behind Hollywood posed a recognized threat. In addition, American companies began to hire German talent in an attempt to circumvent the language barrier. While the sound revolution brought the repatriation of Conrad Veidt and Emil Jannings, both of whom figured prominently in pioneering German talkies . . . it also revived suspicions that Hollywood would launch another recruitment drive and plunder the German industry" (Saunders 228).

As mentioned earlier, Pommer's strategy with *The Blue Angel* was somewhat different from Saunders's scenario of competition and mutual suspicion. In contrast to the general trend of the time, where German actors and directors were recruited to work in Hollywood, in this case, an eminent Hollywood director took up a German producer's request to come to Berlin to direct the world's most popular leading man in his first sound film. Furthermore, like Pommer, Sternberg gambled that he could make a film that was neither German nor American, but rather one that would be the synthesis of Hollywood and "Neubabelsberg." The German cinema would draw upon the talents of an acclaimed Hollywood director as well as its own internationally famous leading man. Returning to its roots (in German literature as well as its lengthy, sophisticated stage tradition) and reaching out to Hollywood, Ufa would create multiple-language versions that would garner success worldwide.

The Blue Angel and Film History

With this in mind, it is interesting to take up the question of the place of *The Blue Angel* in history—a question of long-standing concern in the vast literature on this film. Some commentators regard any reference to the film's historical realism as utterly misguided. As John Baxter explains, not only was this 1930 film based on a 1905 novella, but from the very "first shot of twisted roofs and crooked smokestacks, one is aware of a nineteenth-century ambiance rather than a twentieth-century one. There are no cars in *The Blue Angel*, no radios or cinemas, and the lamps that hang in almost every shot are gas-burning. Except for a short sequence showing Rath peeling leaves from a calendar that begins at 1923 and ends on 1929, the film is exclusively an image of the Europe in which Sternberg grew up" (Baxter, *Cinema* 70).

In a frequently cited analysis, Siegfried Kracauer takes issue with this kind of assessment, and claims in his retrospective reading of Weimar cinema in *From Caligari to Hitler* that *The Blue Angel* remains a document very much reflective of its time.[9] "*The Blue Angel* poses anew the problem of German immaturity," Kracauer famously wrote, "and moreover elaborates its consequences as manifested in the conduct of the boys and of the artists, who like the professor are middle-class offspring." "It is as if the film implied a warning," Kracauer concludes, "for these screen figures anticipate what will happen in real life a few years later. The boys are born Hitler youths" (Kracauer 218). Commentators from Andrew Sarris to Gertrud Koch (not to mention von Sternberg himself)[10] have challenged Kracauer's sociological reading of the film, insisting that *The Blue Angel* is understood as the product of its director's personal history and vivid imagination. Koch puts the matter succinctly: "*The Blue Angel* is probably the first film in which Sternberg produces a merely illusory reality of place, one whose reality originates wholly in his fantasy" (Koch,

"Between Two Worlds" 65). It is not a German film, writes Koch; it is a von Sternberg film—and one that "foreshadows his later—and more accomplished—artificial and exotic worlds."

In all the scholarly writing on this film, critics constantly split on this issue of sociology versus auteurism, insisting on either its German or its Hollywood origins: *The Blue Angel* is either a reflection of its turbulent times or the product of its Hollywood director's vivid imagination. In this regard, the most compelling commentary on the film is a 1978 article by French critic Michel Bouvier in *Ça Cinéma*, titled "Hollywood on Spree." As Bouvier explains it, "Neither the German team nor its famous director's contributions to this film nor the true nationality of the film really matter." Instead, he argues, what matters is the way in which *The Blue Angel* both embraces and extends the Hollywood as well as the German model, and the way it accomplishes this, above all else, by reflecting upon the status of cinematic representation and the circulation of images.

This is not to say, of course, that either Bouvier—or, indeed, I myself—believe the question of film authorship is unimportant to this film. But rather than pose the issue in psychological or purely individual terms, as most critics tend to do, it is important to recognize the historical significance of Sternberg's status as a U.S. director in Europe at the time of the transition to sound. *The Blue Angel* is in fact among the extremely rare instances of a non-U.S. film produced with the credit byline of a major Hollywood director, thus reversing the usual trend of the times for European directors to work in Hollywood. It is in this sense that *The Blue Angel* benefits most from a full authorial reading, but only within the context of this film's hybrid and transnational status. Indeed, *The Blue Angel* both established and exemplified a procedure distinctly different from Paramount's own Joinville approach to international filmmaking (organized even as *The Blue Angel* was going into release in the mid-spring of 1930). With the presence of its major Hollywood director,[11] not to mention its German producer and international star, *The Blue Angel* was intentionally designed as a "two-originals-no-copy" venture into foreign-language filmmaking.[12] It therefore demanded to be read as an authorial text, and as very different from the typical multiple-language versions of the time, which were thought—even at the peak of their production—to be, by definition, debased by their status as copy.

The success of *The Blue Angel*, finally, had as much to do with the director's affinity for Weimar culture and its cultivation of surface effects as it did with the particular casting of Dietrich in the starring role. Reviewers at the time consistently comment on von Sternberg's emphasis on surface effects and on the externality of film mechanics.[13] Furthermore, as is well known, Dietrich's own background in cabaret and reputation for sexual experimentation undeniably enhanced the reception of the film. But the cultivation of surface effects and the exploration of sexuality were as much an American as a German preoccupation at this time. As one historian writes of 1920s New York (although these remarks resonate with 1920s Berlin as well): "Commentators throughout the 1920s were gripped by the certainty—exhilarating to some, troubling to others—that their society had moved headlong into a sexualized modernity marked by sophistication and complexity. The 1920s saw an increasingly intense public debate over what seemed radically nontraditional sexual behavior: a newly aggressive and public middle-class female sexuality, exemplified by women who streamlined their bodies into sleek instruments of pleasure, embracing styles of dress and expression previously associated only with prostitutes; and new forms of specifically sexual identity—male homosexuality and lesbianism—that blatantly detached sex from procreation, and from traditional notions of masculinity and femininity, and made it into a style of life" (Hamilton 118).

Sexuality as a style of life: this statement suggests Dietrich's persona as well as von Sternberg's aesthetics. Efforts to locate *The Blue Angel* historically, then, must address the multiple locations of which the film is part and which it explores: its place in the history of urban entertainment and the loosening of sexual mores, its place in German history as well as German and American film history, its impact on the careers of its director and stars and producer who worked within an international industry—not to mention the multiple locations of its marketing and distribution. All of this serves to underscore the film's status as a document of *dislocation*, made simultaneously in two languages for distribution in an international market.

The Multiple Film in an Age of Mechanical Reproduction

Even without the existence of two different language versions, *The Blue Angel* would remain a remarkable document about originals and copies and the status of the work of art in an age of mechanical reproduction. An adaptation of a classic novella by the prominent German writer, the film reflects upon the circulation and multiplication of images, and the very status of cinema as a copy without an original.

Many critics have suggested that the film is itself an extensive quotation of other, especially German, films. Jannings's role as Professor Rath is an extended quotation of his previous screen roles, from *The Last Laugh* to *Variety* to *The Last Command*. Several images in the film, moreover, are directly drawn from classical German cinema. The film's opening shot, notes Koch, "consists of an expressionistically chaotic landscape of rooftops and chimneys: a stylistic quotation, placing the film firmly in a film-historical context" ("Between Two Worlds" 69). More than this, the film quotes as much from the other arts as it does from film culture.[14] George Grosz, for example, was a regular visitor to the film set; his *Lustmord* paintings would appear to have inspired the blackboard image of Professor Rath carrying off Lola's leg, although within the fiction, this is ostensibly the work of Rath's students.

Beyond direct quotation, the film explores throughout the status of pictures and postcards and posters that circulate among students, the professor, cabaret audiences, and locales. We in fact first see Lola Lola as poster image, which a cleaning woman washes and then poses next to, in an attempt to emulate the posture of the small town's theatrical star. In the course of the film, moreover, theatricality gives way to distinctly cinematic representation: in our first encounter with Lola Lola, the performer, for instance, both she and the set are dressed in the iconography of cheap vaudeville. She interacts with cabaret performers on stage as well as with members of the audience. In her final performance, by contrast, she is the main performer framed by a group of synchronized, Tiller Girl–type, female dancers. She sings, now in close-up, for a cinematic rather than a theatrical audience and is thereby transformed from theatrical to cinematic icon.

Most important, the postcards and posters that litter this film are symbolically laden objects, reminiscent of Dada and collage and urban art, with a narrative force of their own. They offer the students, and then the professor, a chance to personally engage with Lola's image, in that each gets his very own erotic dance by just blowing on the feather skirt on the postcard. Just as Walter Benjamin argued that availability and easy access to the art image through mass production destroys its aura, so do the replicated picture postcards lack presence in space and time. They lack the ability to lay claim to the significance of the real thing. The illustrations and poster art that cover the windows and cabaret walls arouse and entice the boys and the professor to attend Lola's performances in search of authenticity. In fact, the professor becomes obsessed with positioning himself closer to the original form of the reproduced Lola Lola; but no matter how close he gets, even in marriage, he can never truly possess Lola Lola. The original that he imagined her to be never existed to begin with. Once Rath is transformed from professor to pusher of erotic commodities to vaudeville clown, it becomes clear that Lola Lola, the seductress, lives in a public rather than a private realm.

Most interesting in this regard is the fact that the character Lola Lola is constantly confronted by her own images, whether via the posters that plaster the walls backstage or in the form of the postcards she always carries with her. As I suggested earlier, French critic Michel Bouvier points out that Lola Lola's relationship to her own image does not "generate a narcissism that would demand an ascetic manipulation of the body" (29). Instead, he claims, "it makes the relation between model and image problematic" raising the issue of "which really determines the other?" These remarks recall the cleaning woman who emulates the poster image, and encourages us to consider a more thoughtful investigation of the status of original and copy.

Without a doubt, the existence of multiple-language versions of this same film complicates the notion of copy even further. There are, in fact, at least four versions of *The Blue Angel* still in circulation: a shorter German version, about 90 minutes long, which dates from a 1947 U.S. release and concludes with Lola on stage, rather than with Rath in the classroom; a longer German version, now dubbed "the director's cut," which is 106 minutes long, and which claims to represent the film in its initial German release; and finally, two English-language versions, the first released in 1930 and then reissued on VHS in the 1990s, which is about 90 minutes long, and a second release of this 1930s version in 2001 on DVD, which is 100 minutes long. In a 1994 essay in *Film Comment*, Peter Hogue writes in detail about the differences between the two German versions as well as those between the German and English versions.[15] While the existence of multiple versions of multiple-language films raises all kinds of questions for rethinking the place of *The Blue Angel* in film history, I would like to underscore how these changes profoundly affect our perceptions of Weimar and Hollywood cinema, and especially our perceptions of both Lola Lola and Rath.

Even a cursory analysis of the film's most important song: "Ich bin von Kopf bis Fuss" ("Falling in Love Again") reveals how the English-language versions transform Lola Lola from a creature of sexual instinct to a helpless romantic. The English-language versions, moreover, smooth over and minimize the explicitly sexual, direct, and often surprising instances of what might be considered rude or vulgar or obscene. (Lola Lola can spit into her makeup box and adjust her panties in both language versions, but can only sing with her legs apart, hips in the air, and with direct erotic intent in German.)

The changes to Rath's character in the English-language versions are equally significant, although they ultimately serve to diminish our sympathy for him. For example, in one of the English versions (the VHS version from the 1990s), we never see the professor's gaze at the provocative postcard of Lola Lola and thus are not given a window onto his erotic fantasy. With the scene entirely cut from this version of the film, we can only surmise that he goes to the Blue Angel in search of his students, whom he intends to reprimand, which merely reinforces his melodramatic and one-dimensional portrayal of the tyrannical German pedant. This English version also omits many seemingly peripheral, symbolic, or narratively unessential sequences—notably, the opening sequence with the maid's discovery of Rath's dead bird, which serves as a key motif in the film, linking Rath to Lola Lola (and her very much alive, singing bird) as well as to their marriage and to his cock-crowing and final humiliation on stage.

More than this, however, even when sexually provocative sequences are not omitted, they are often played very differently in the different language versions. In the English-language versions, for instance, the professor is ashamed and uncomfortable about returning Lola Lola's underwear (he cannot bring himself to tell her what is in the package), whereas in the German versions, he admits to taking the garment, and to mistaking it for something that was his. Other examples can be cited: the German versions show us a racially mixed cabaret audience, with prominent black members of the crowd. There are no such racially mixed audiences in the VHS English-language version, again, I would surmise, as a result of the Production Code and the fear of offending white U.S. audiences in the South. This English-language version in fact deletes several key sequences that establish a milieu as well as the characters' relationship to it and to one another. For instance, Lola Lola's relationship with the strongman, Mazeppa, is cut short. And after Rath's jealous attack on Lola Lola, when Kiepert comes to the storeroom to release him from his straitjacket, neither man says anything, which is in marked contrast to the German versions, where Kiepert sadly and compassionately asks Rath if all of this were really worth it for a woman. The German versions make it clear that Rath's crisis and humiliation are as much economic as psychological and sexual. Near the end of the film, Rath burns pages from the calendar that begins in 1923 and ends in 1929. While both versions mark the passage of time through this device, only the German version comments directly on the economic situation, which affects Mazeppa and Lola Lola and the entire cabaret company as well as the peculiar fate of a once-prominent professor.

In addition to the cutting of certain scenes and the revision of others, much erotic content is eliminated or underplayed in the English-language versions. My favorite example is when Rosa Valetti, who plays the magician's wife, sees Rath in Lola Lola's dressing room holding Lola Lola's underwear. In the English-language versions, she merely shakes her finger and remains silent; she thereby functions as a moral observer (waving a tsk-tsk finger at Rath). In the German versions, by contrast, she sees the underwear, looks at him directly with a wry sense of humor, and says, "I don't want to hear any complaints out of you!"

The question of language, of course, is fundamental to all multiple-language films, and in *The Blue Angel*, especially, but not only in the English-language versions, it becomes clear that the film's narrative and dramatic weight is shifted to an English-speaking axis. When Rath first speaks to Lola Lola in German, she responds quizzically, as if she does not understand him, and says, "Sorry, you'll have to talk my language." American vernacular is also added to the English-language versions, most often in connection with Lola Lola, who is made to speak such lines as "Hold your horses!" "Fold up your tent" (for "shut up"), "Patriotic hokum" (in response to the words of a German song), and "Shake a leg." In the English-language versions, moreover, she is an English actress and he is a German high school teacher. In the German versions, she is a bohemian "artiste" (with all its attendant associations), whereas he teaches Shakespeare (a change instituted by Sternberg, since Rath's author in the Mann novel is

Homer). In the English-language versions, Rath remains a one-dimensional tyrant: he forces his students to write the English word "the" two hundred times. In the German version, by contrast, he assigns them an essay topic on Mark Antony, asking them to consider, "What would have happened if Mark Antony hadn't held his oration?"—in other words, if he had not spoken on his own behalf.

Rath's choice of assignment has a particular resonance with his own condition, as he progressively loses his command of language and the authority of his position in the course of the film. For it is not merely the addition of dialogue or American slang, but the painful silences that distinguish the English- from the German-language versions. Without a doubt, this is a vestige of early sound cinema and underscores the hybridity as well as the practical problems of multiple-language versions. As is well documented, Jannings had his own fears of and hesitations with English language.[16] And Dietrich, who spoke very little English at this time—even though her contract specified that the film be shot in two versions—ostensibly required the talents of Berlin's best vocal coach to improve her voice. Friedrich Hollaender created songs that would disguise Dietrich's linguistic deficiencies; most of them are based on two notes, with many words half-spoken rather than sung.

The cumulative effect of these changes is signaled as well by the shift in the name above the title in the opening credits (Jannings is featured in the German-language versions, Dietrich in the 1990 VHS English-language version). But the specific effect in the English-language versions is to diminish our sympathy for Rath and to downplay Lola Lola's eroticism as well as any sexual and emotional complexity of their relationship. Allow me to provide some final thoughts about a key sequence, which illuminates these differences most forcefully.

The sequence involves the public revelation of Rath's infatuation with Lola Lola and takes place in his classroom. In the German versions, the headmaster overhears the rioting in Rath's classroom, runs down the hall, enters the room, and admonishes the students to sit down. He looks at the students' drawings of Rath and Lola Lola on the blackboard. His first comment is, "Not bad." He sides with the students, and then vilifies Lola Lola, to which Rath responds with gallantry and strong words; this is no loose woman, but a woman who will become his wife. The action in this sequence revolves solely around Rath's words: his sudden decision to marry Lola Lola, which seems to surprise even him, establishes him as courageous and principled; he is not just a tyrant or humiliated victim. The headmaster, by contrast, emerges from this encounter as a petty bureaucrat who has no problem with Rath's relationship with Lola Lola, only with his decision to marry her. He then passes the decision about Rath's fate on to higher authorities. In the English versions, the action proceeds differently. In a clear attempt to cut down on English dialogue, the scene is played almost in silence; the headmaster makes no mention of the art work or Lola Lola but merely says, "I'm sorry my friend. You leave me no choice. I must request your resignation." Rath has no words to defend Lola Lola or himself and in fact does not speak at all. The change undoubtedly has to do with the inability of the supporting cast to speak English and also with the demands of Hayes Code censorship. Of course, Rath is dismissed in both versions because he has had sex outside marriage. The German versions, however, attack the phenomenal hypocrisy of a situation in which he can sleep with Lola Lola but cannot, as an upstanding member of the bourgeoisie and *Gymnasiallehrer*, actually marry "a woman like that" and retain his position.

Hollywood versus Berlin

Significantly, Jannings is linked with death from the beginning of the film. Whether he is associated with his dead canary or the fate of the silent clown, whom we only later realize was once Lola Lola's lover, Rath's gradual progress toward the vaudeville stage and loss of language are symbols that point to his inevitable degradation and destruction. To be sure, Jannings's star persona was built on such degradation and humiliation and yet, with *The Blue Angel*, Rath's—or rather, Jannings's—humiliation seems much more poignant and profound. As many critics have noted, the film was supposed to launch Jannings from the silent screen to the sound film and solidify his reputation as international cinema's premiere performer. *The Blue Angel* was released to great critical acclaim in both Germany and the United States but soon became known as the film that inaugurated Dietrich's Hollywood career. In this recounting, Jannings becomes emblematic of German silent cinema more generally: trained in the expressionistic, theatrical tradition, Jannings could not compete with Dietrich's cooler, surface-oriented, cinematic style. As one critic puts it, "As Rath, Jannings gives a tour de force of mannerist acting, easily superior to that of *The Last Laugh* and *Variety*, the themes of which *The Blue Angel* recalls. His style was a dying one . . . but as Lola, Marlene Dietrich began a collaboration with the director that was to result in one of the most original creations in the history of cinema" (Baxter, *Cinema* 70).

This is, of course, a standard interpretation and one not without merit. But it misses what was also lost, or at least what was muted and ultimately transformed, in international film culture at this time. To be sure, Lola Lola, the cabaret singer, returns in *Morocco* as Amy Jolly, the exotic and unknown woman with the mysterious past, fully the product of Paramount's public relations machine. However, this unknowability was adapted to a new and profoundly Hollywood cinematic style: *Morocco* is suggestive, whereas *The Blue Angel* is erotic, although in the case of the English-language versions, sexuality remains understated if nonetheless understood. As John Baxter points out, the mixture was very much to American tastes, and "Paramount signed director and star to contracts for a further three films, at a much higher salary" (81).

The Blue Angel obviously reflects upon the tensions—cultural, aesthetic, economic, social—that so define the hybridity of this period: the tensions between theater and cinema, Europe and America, the Old World and the New, youth and age, high and low culture. In *The Blue Angel*, of course, just as in *The Last Command* or even *The Jazz Singer*, these tensions are in fact given embodiment in the central characters and, in the case of this particular film, in the themes of German versus English, the cabaret versus Shakespeare. I nevertheless submit that *The Blue Angel* is not simply a film about Jannings or the loss of the Old World to the New. In fact, what remains distinctive about *The Blue Angel* is the peculiarity of an international urban culture, defined as much by New York as by Berlin in the 1920s, which Dietrich has since come to embody and personify. In an essay on "Marlene Dietrich and German Nationalism," Gertrud Koch discusses this distinctiveness by describing Dietrich's Lola Lola as "the image iconic of both memory and leaving; the image of a woman as openly sexual and lascivious as she is motherly; an image that died, along with the Weimar Republic, in National Socialism."[17]

This returns us to where we began—to the image of Dietrich's naked thighs. It is significant, I think, that it is this image that has become most emblematic of the film and, indeed, of late Weimar culture more generally. Who can forget the pose of Lola Lola on the beer barrel, right thigh up—the imprimatur of the Berlin culture on the eve of its collapse? Interestingly enough, in both the German- and the English-language versions, we only begin to see English names on the circus posters that grace Lola Lola's dressing room near the end of the film (which has also been identified as the year 1929). *The Blue Angel* was therefore indeed prescient of things to come. For even though the English-language versions are rarely seen today (as they were, in fact, for most of the past century), it is the image of Dietrich's right thigh up, derived from an English-language version, that has long served to advertise the film. The German-language versions, however, with their more provocative display of inner as well as outer thigh, nonetheless remain more obscene, more erotic—and more a trace of the very Weimar culture, itself a copy of an international film and urban culture without an original, which was copied, but never equaled, in the United States, and lost entirely to Germany in the 1930s.

Afterthoughts

The Blue Angel, of course, is not merely a film that was multiply produced. It is also a film that has been variously reedited for multiple release, which requires that we become attentive to the histories of its multiple receptions—in a period spanning from the 1930s until today. A recently released Kino DVD of the film, for example, boasts the inclusion of a new, more complete English-language version of *The Blue Angel*. This latest version is promoted as "definitive"—superior to the English-language version that circulated for almost two decades on VHS (and earlier in the United States, I would assume, on film). To be sure, the new Kino DVD reveals many surprises. For example, in this English-language version, Jannings's name remains above the opening title. The maid still discovers and incinerates the dead bird. Rath still is seen gazing at the postcard of Lola, and the shot of the postcard marks the transition to the cabaret, as in the German version. Rath also shyly admits that the underwear is in the parcel he brings to Lola on the second night. Even more significantly, the pan over the racially mixed audience during Rath's introduction from the side balcony is the same as in the German-language versions.

Most important, there is the matter of Dietrich's legs during her singing of "Falling in Love Again" ("Ich bin von Kopf bis Fuss"). In this newer English-language version, she raises her *left* leg and holds the knee for a while; she then crosses her left leg over her right during part of the second version, and then uncrosses it, with the left thigh still exposed. After a cutaway to Rath during the third verse, her legs are crossed again, left over right. Never, however, is her right leg raised and crossed over the left—as it is in the production still, and briefly during the second verse of the German-language version, before she lifts both legs in the air.

It would therefore appear that some of the English-language version scenes were shot in more than one way, for different English-language audiences. Indeed, several of the English-language passages in the Kino DVD clearly are dubbed, and the production notes indicate that some dubbing and reshooting of the English version was undertaken in May 1930, under the direction of Carl Winston, after von Sternberg and Dietrich were gone.

So what are we to make of this most recent version of *The Blue Angel*? Some scholars have suggested that it is critical to establish and reconstruct the original version of this film—and, indeed, of other notable German films (such as *The Joyless Street*). Indeed, some have gone so far as to claim that film historians, such as myself, have "only seen mutilated versions that in no way represent the original, leading them to false conclusions, based on the evidence that only existed in such false versions" (Horak). Given that the focus of my analysis is the very status of *The Blue Angel* as copy, it would seem pointless to establish which version of the film—in either English or German—stands as the "original." This is not to say, of course, that analysis of the multiple versions of this multiple-language film might not shed significant light on different historical contexts of the film's reception. The 1947 German version, for instance, which closes with Dietrich on stage rather than with Rath in his classroom, would seem to respond directly to Dietrich's new status and visibility as radio star and American patriot following World War II. Furthermore, as I suggested earlier, the 1990s English-language version, with its elision of significant scenes, especially the scene of the racially mixed cabaret audience, would appear to be the U.S. release of the film in the 1930s, given what we know about Production Code at this time and its overriding concern (in the case of this film as well as many others) not to offend white audiences in the South. Needless to say, I have no hard evidence at this point to prove this argument, but given the instability of *The Blue Angel* and its multiple-language versions it is impossible to pretend that the Kino DVD restores the work in its supposedly timeless originality. It exists only as yet another copy.

In this regard, I must admit to feeling a bit like Lola Lola, in this case, pursued by scholars who insist on false and original versions and who thus bear an uncanny resemblance to Professor Rath, who searches in vain for the "authentic" woman behind the reproduced Lola Lola. Lola Lola, of course, constantly eludes such desires for fixity. Like the film itself, she is emblematic of multiplicity, image making, and mechanical reproduction. Her very name, like the various language versions of the film of which she is part, is itself a trace of the copy and the double: she is Lola Lola, after all, not Lola—in the singular. She exists, like the film itself, in multiple-language versions, not in the form of an original to be preserved or possessed.

Notes

1. The version of Heinrich Mann's relationship to the finished film that I rely on here was reported by John Baxter (*Cinema* 66). Yet another account of Mann's remark can be found in Weinberg. As Peter Baxter reports it in his article "Miss Dietrich's Naked Thighs," "Heinrich Mann told Emil Jannings that the success of *The Blue Angel* would depend not on his acting genius but 'on the naked thighs of Miss Dietrich'" ("Naked Thighs" 559). Peter Baxter references Weinberg's book in this regard.

2. Peter Baxter writes, "Difficult to fathom are the motives of Mann himself, who, according to Sternberg, not only agreed to the changes [in his novella] but said he wished he had thought of them himself! As this would have changed the entire point of the book, one can only assume that such flexibility had its root in the fact that Mann was friendly with show-girl Trude Hesterberg, whom he had suggested for the part of Lola. Sternberg declined, hence Mann's later waspish remark that 'Miss Dietrich's naked thighs' dominated the film" (Peter Baxter, "Naked Thighs" 566).

3. This essay was written in close collaboration with Nataša Ďurovičová, who has written extensively on foreign-language versions of films. See, for example, her much-cited essay "Translating America." Ďurovičová not only discussed this topic with me and read this essay in draft several times, but also prepared a written response to it, which was read at the Chicago Film Seminar

in October 2001. I have incorporated all of her suggestions for expansion, revision, and refinement. This essay is the result of this truly collaborative scholarly relationship.

4. See, for example, Ďurovičová; and Crafton. See also Maltby and Vasey.

5. Pommer. This article, among many others written by Pommer at the time, is included in English translation in Higson and Maltby.

6. On Parufamet, see Kreimeier; and Saunders.

7. On this issue, see Kreimeier 183.

8. This is a brief summary of Maltby and Vasey's essay.

9. Interestingly, in his 1930 review of the film in *Die Neue Rundschau* (Berlin), Kracauer relates an alternative view of the film: "This film," he writes, "avoids with an assiduity which must have been exhausting, any reference which could move us to include present social conditions. It suppresses the social environment which would force itself upon the naïve spectator of Unrat's catastrophe, it tears the performers out of any social context in which they have gained contemporary significance and places them in a vacuum. Neither Lola nor Unrat has enough air to breathe, which confirms the claim that it is less the reality of their existence that is to be demonstrated, than the existence of reality that is to be veiled." Translated and reprinted in Peter Baxter, *Sternberg* 22.

10. Sarris; Koch, "Between Two Worlds"; von Sternberg.

11. As Sarris puts it, "The film was produced simultaneously in German and English language versions for the maximum benefit of the Paramount-Ufa combine in world markets, and thus with this one excursion to Europe all the ambiguity of Sternberg's origins reappeared as the 'von' in his name was finally vindicated. After *The Blue Angel*, Sternberg would once more be treated in retrospect as a European legend corrupted by Hollywood lucre" (697).

12. I owe this insight to Nataša Ďurovičová.

13. B. G. Bravermann writes in a 1934 issue of *Experimental Cinema*: "In Sternberg we have a director who concentrates on surface effects, who emphasizes the externals of film mechanics in a most inarticulate manner and represents his own delirious fancies as real life" (qtd. in Peter Baxter, *Just Watch* 29).

14. As von Sternberg relates it in his autobiography, *Fun in a Chinese Laundry*: "Every notable in Berlin was on my stage at one time or another. Not only representatives of the press, writers, actors, directors, and even Max Reinhardt were present (his main concern was how a sibilant could be recorded), but sculptors and painters, among them George Grosz, who gave me a book on his work" (143).

15. Hogue; Tom Gunning suggested to me that much of Hogue's analysis is inaccurate.

16. See, for example, the account in Sternberg's autobiography.

17. In this regard, Koch quotes a previously unpublished text by Franz Hessel from the 1920s: "Those dangerous women incarnated by Marlene Dietrich do not give one the feeling that they mean too much harm. As cheery Lola from the Blue Angel, she takes the schoolteacher's ruffled, bearded head in her kind and maternal hands, pats the cheeks of this man so tenderly enchanted by her as though he were a child, looks up at her poor victim with a bridal smile when he makes this supremely unworthy woman his wife, and smiles him his dream of pure happiness" (Koch, "Exorcised" 13).

MARY BETH HARALOVICH

Marlene Dietrich in *Blonde Venus*

Advertising Dietrich in Seven Markets

THE PHRASE "Marlene DIETRICH in *Blonde Venus*"—with the visual emphasis on "Dietrich" and her face in close-up—dominated the American advertising campaign for *Blonde Venus*. A small feminine image also appeared in nearly all of the film ads: a sketch that portrayed Dietrich as a Venus de Milo, linking Dietrich to the concept of a love goddess. In the sketch she wears a revealing gown and her arms are covered with long, black gloves, evoking the missing arms of the Venus statue. The figure's facial features are indistinct, but her soft, blonde hair makes the connection with Dietrich. This blonde Venus stands or leans in a lower corner of the ads for *Blonde Venus*. These three elements—the phrase "Marlene Dietrich in *Blonde Venus*," the close-up visual image of Dietrich's face, and the blonde Venus sketch, appear in all the ads (for a European variation, see figure 1). But in other ways, the *Blonde Venus* ad campaign drew upon the diversity of Dietrich's star persona to position the film in various markets.

While the role of Helen Faraday in the film lends itself to multiple images of women (she is a wife-mother, a nightclub performer, a fallen woman, an adventurer), the ads did not present Dietrich "in character" as Helen. Dietrich's face appeared in three other very different guises in ads for *Blonde Venus*: in glamour photos Dietrich is presented as a movie

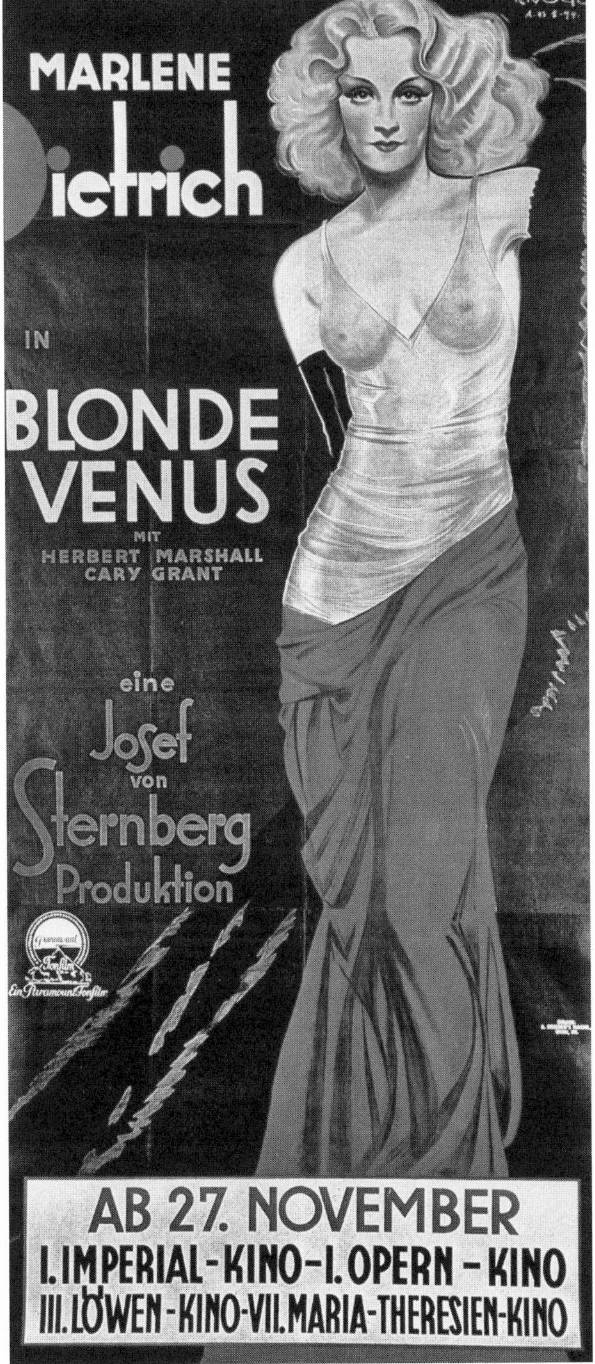

1. This variation of the sketch was designed for the Austrian premiere of the film. The figure in U.S. advertising implies the body, but does not reveal it.

star; in a sketch portrait, her face is vaguely expressionless; and in another sketched portrait, rendered in expressionistic chiaroscuro, she is portrayed as an intense sexual vampire. Although all these advertising images were Dietrich, they were radically different visual identities for the actress. A similar diversity occurred in how film ads presented the storyline of *Blonde Venus*. In some markets, the ads reveled in a hyperbolic exploitation of Helen's relationships with husband Ned and playboy Nick. Some ads offered sympathy for the fallen woman, even as they exploited her. In other markets, the ads sidestepped the storyline entirely, offering Dietrich's face as an object of contemplation instead of situating her as Helen Faraday. Promotion for *Blonde Venus* in newspaper entertainment pages also showcased Dietrich's diversity: as a movie star in glamour photos, as a performer (in her exotic "Hot Voodoo" or other cabaret costumes from the film), and as the fallen Helen Faraday (in a close-up, with hat pulled down over one eye, cigarette dangling from her lips, face hard).

The campaign for *Blonde Venus* indicates that Dietrich's star persona offered exhibitors a variety of ways to connect the film with its potential audiences. This essay explores the diversity of Dietrich's star persona in the promotion of *Blonde Venus* in seven film markets across the United States: two newspapers in America's heartland—middle-class Des Moines, Iowa (*Des Moines Register*), and working-class Cedar Rapids, Iowa (*Cedar Rapids Gazette*); two from the midwestern metropolis of Chicago, the nation's second city—the mainstream press (*Chicago Tribune*) and the African American press (*Chicago Defender*); one newspaper from the southern city of Atlanta (the *Constitution*, whose film advertising was both inventive and luridly exploitative); the home town newspaper of the film industry (*Los Angeles Times*); and the newspaper that was the main east coast site of film criticism (*New York Times*).[1]

Local film advertising demonstrates how exhibitors translated a film for local audiences, drawing on audience expectations and knowledge about stars. Exhibitors would begin with a studio-produced pressbook that provided a range of promotional options (advertising mats, publicity stories and photos, prewritten reviews, product tie-ins, and ballyhoo ideas), from which they could select options that would harmonize with the local market. There was not a single advertising address to audiences across the nation, as the *Blonde Venus* campaign shows. The shape it took suggests both the complexity of Dietrich's star persona and the usefulness of that persona in situating *Blonde Venus* for diverse markets of moviegoers in 1932—audiences of that period would have recognized the many facets of Dietrich's star persona that were used in the *Blonde Venus* campaign.

The purpose of film advertising is to invite the audience to see the film. To do so, advertising typically uses several devices. As I note in my study of Warner Brothers studio film posters (and it is as true of newspaper film advertisements as it is of posters), the key elements are "the title of the film, its stars, character traits and the narrative enigmas in which the characters function" ("Advertising" 52).

With regard to the last of these elements, narrative, Virginia Wright Wexman has described the primary impulse of the Hollywood film as an "obsession with stories of romantic love" between men and women (Wexman 5). The lure of the heterosexual couple has long been recognized as central to film advertising, to the invitation to cinema, and to cinematic pleasure. In most movie ads, story and star expectations conjoin with ideologies of courtship, attraction, and love. Wexman observes that "traditional mainstream filmmaking practice has heavily promoted the ideal of monogamous marriage to a 'suitable' partner" (13). Typically, film ads feature a couple in formation, a man and a woman who are simultaneously drawn together and kept apart. They are presented at a point of narrative tension that can be resolved by seeing the film in the movie theater, where, at the end, the suitable partners will have found each other.

The plot of *Blonde Venus* offered several possibilities for advertising to emphasize the cinema's fascination with the couple. Helen and her future husband Ned (Herbert Marshall) meet in Germany, where Ned watches her swim naked in a lake. Later, living in New York with their child, Helen wears housedresses and does domestic chores. When Ned becomes ill, they need money for his medical care, which is available only in Europe. To earn the money, Helen works as a nightclub performer, the "blonde Venus" of the film's title. She wears exotic costumes, attracts men, meets playboy Nick (Cary Grant), and sends her husband to Europe for treatment. When Ned discovers Helen's relationship with the playboy upon his return to New York, he leaves Helen and takes custody of their son. Helen kidnaps the child, goes on the run, and becomes a fallen woman. Eventually, she returns the child to its father. Helen goes to Paris where she resumes her stage career and her relationship with the playboy. Helen and Nick return to New York, where Helen sees her son and husband. Through the son, the family is reunited.[2]

As is evident from this recounting, Dietrich's Helen engages with two "'suitable' partners": the husband and the playboy. With one man, she is a wife, mother, and homemaker. With the other, she is an adventurer and performer who enjoys her sexuality and provides audiences (diegetic and otherwise) with erotic spectacle. Wexman finds that "*the couple* is a term with many meanings" (Wexman 11), such as domestic companionship, romantic love, and sexual fulfillment. Although potentially in opposition, wifely love and erotic attraction are important both to *Blonde Venus* and to the heterosexual impulses of film advertising. In her book *Wages of Sin*, Lea Jacobs observes that the narrative of *Blonde Venus* uses a productive "division between character and star" (104) that confines Helen's womanly domesticity to the home and reveals her sexuality when she performs on stage. In her analysis of *Blonde Venus*, Jacobs writes, "The sexuality that Helen must hold back, that cannot achieve expression in the domestic space, is displaced to the space of the stage and the image of the star" (104).

This duality of domesticity and sexuality is taken up in the *Blonde Venus* campaign in diverse ways. Dietrich's star persona carried with it an endorsement of sexuality. While this persona may not have been an easy fit with the attributes of wifely love, Dietrich's ability to deliver erotic attraction as well as sympathy for the fallen woman was important to the film's promotion. As if recognizing that a maternal character was a stretch for her star persona, ads cast Dietrich's Helen as a daring role for the actress while ignoring the wife-mother. In some markets, Dietrich-Helen's sexuality appeared too intense for local film advertising. In the absence of clear traits for Helen, the ads relied on the three common elements—the star in the close-up, the film title, and the Dietrich-Venus love goddess sketch—to imply the film's storyline. In the markets that "held back" erotic desire from the film ads, Helen's sexuality was, however, expressed in the film reviews, which detailed Helen's motivations and choices.

Some smaller city newspapers tended to adapt a pressbook prewritten review to the local market. These prewritten reviews summarized the film's story and lauded the performances and production values. In some of these reviews, taglines used in the film ads would also appear in the review. Thus the prewritten review was often an explicit extension of the film's advertising angle. However, local exhibitors and newspapers often combined prewritten reviews with information about local exhibition and their own critical perspectives on the film. Newspapers in major cities tended to have staff film reviewers, whose acerbic prose and critical opinions indicated their independence from the pressbook's euphoric publicity language. Whether taken from the pressbook or written locally, these film reviews were integral to the local newspaper's entertainment section.

The *Blonde Venus* reviews were situated on entertainment pages that showcased Dietrich in diverse ways: in glamour poses, in exotic costumes, and as fallen woman, but not in domestic or maternal situations. The photos and reviews dispel any ambiguity in the film ads and direct the potential audience to the sexual aspects of the film. Some reviews expressed sympathy for Helen's situation and decisions. They refrained from moral judgment and found both Ned and Nick to be suitable partners for Helen. Sympathy for both the sexually active woman and the fallen woman circulated in the local newspaper, suggesting the value for the film of Dietrich's persona as an accomplished actress. Whether prewritten by the studio or locally written, reviews tended to draw on Dietrich's previous film roles. She embodied sexuality and glamour but was also a capable actress who could make the fallen woman an acceptable and sympathetic heroine.

It was not just the on-screen Dietrich that offered an invitation to moral openness about the sexually independent woman; it was also her private-public life. In a discussion of censorship and movie fans, Janet Staiger points out that "audiences were fully aware that movies produced by the major studios in the United States during the classical era were supposed to conform to a set of moral conventions" (Staiger 78). In regard to *Blonde Venus*, Staiger observes, "a semi-autobiographical parallel between the film and Dietrich's life would be obvious to any devoted fan of the movies, of which there were hundreds of thousands in 1932" (83). Staiger argues that fans, because of Dietrich's biographies and alternative *Blonde Venus* accounts, had avenues for reading Helen as "a desiring subject" (88) in love with both Ned and Nick. For filmgoers of 1932 to get the point about *Blonde Venus*, Helen's determination and specific economic circumstances did not need to be exploited or explained in film advertising. It was not necessary for ads to firmly place Dietrich in character as Helen Faraday, because Dietrich's star persona already carried those meanings for audiences.

Although the close-up of her face was one of the key elements that delivered Dietrich's star persona in the *Blonde Venus* campaign, the iconography most associated with Dietrich was her legs. "Oh those frilly knickers! . . . we liked the legs of course. Legs Dietrich," remembers a Mr. Houlston, interviewed in Annette Kuhn's study of 1930s British cinema and culture (Kuhn, *Dreaming* 162). Despite their recognized promotional value, recounted by Peter Baxter in his production history of *Blonde Venus*, the ads for this film do not take the opportunity to fetishize Dietrich's legs explicitly, except through the sketch of the Dietrich-Venus figure. Like her legs, this love goddess figure elicits expectations for "the play of concealment and revelation in the framing and presentation of Dietrich's body" (Kuhn, *Dreaming* 162) in the way she is clothed. In her history of fashion in 1930s Hollywood, Sarah Berry observes that costume design tended toward "reflective fabrics, which emphasizes the surface and tactility of clothing" (49). Although the fabric in the sketch is indistinct, its implied texture and weight suggest transparency, a promise of the visual pleasure of costume design in the film.

The *Blonde Venus* campaign used three very different close-up images of Dietrich's face, each with a different relationship to the viewer-reader and each presenting Dietrich as "a desiring subject" in different ways. In the sketch portrait that appears in one version of the advertisement, Dietrich's face is surrounded by soft, blonde hair like that of the Dietrich-Venus figure (figure 2). Her facial features are vague, and her expression is ambiguous as she looks off into the distance. In its lack of affect and desire, this face could be the maternal Helen, although the ad has no taglines that link Dietrich with the wife-mother aspects of Helen. This vague face recalls Roland Barthes's description of the face of Garbo: "It is not a painted face, but one set in plaster" (Barthes, "Face of Garbo" 536) and the final shot of *Queen Christina* in which Garbo as Christina looks out over the prow of the boat, hair blowing softly in the wind.

Mary Ann Doane has described the impact of a close-up of Garbo: "Behind the perfect, seamless face, the unwavering stare, it is impossible not to project thought, emotion, although the face itself gives no indica-

2. One variation of the advertising image of Dietrich looking off into the distance, her expression passive and ambiguous.

3. In this image from the pressbook, Dietrich looks out at the viewer with the aggressive desire of a sexual vampire.

tion of either" ("Close-up" 104). The advertising for *Blonde Venus* may function in a similar way. The ambiguous and seamless face of Dietrich in this advertisement (which appeared in the Des Moines and Cedar Rapids papers) may invite viewers to imagine Dietrich as a blonde Venus in the film, to project "the desiring subject" that the ad sidesteps. In the version of the ad seen in Atlanta, however, this Dietrich face was used in another way. Lurid and hyperbolic taglines ensured that the reader could find in this face a "desiring subject" and sexual adventurer.

The second face to appear in advertising is an expressionistic rendering of Dietrich's face shown from a slightly high angle (figure 3). Her eyelids and the contours of her cheekbones are in sharp chiaroscuro. A river of dark hair streams upward. Her burning eyes gaze up and out at the viewer. In many ways, this second face is the opposite of the first face. The hair is dark, not blonde. The eyes look directly at the viewer, not off-frame. The face may evoke a horror film (the canted faces and dark-ringed eyes of the brides of Frankenstein and Dracula come to mind) and also the aggressive desire of the sexual vampire. The face in the first image is vague and insubstantial. The face in the second image is present and aggressive. This vampire face dominated the film's advertising in the *Chicago Defender* and appeared only occasionally in Des Moines, Los Angeles, and Atlanta.

The third face of Dietrich in *Blonde Venus* advertising derives from Hollywood glamour photography. Instead of drawings, photos of Dietrich's face were used. Her face is framed by the soft, blonde hair that connects Dietrich with the Venus de Milo sketch. In one of the glamour photos, Dietrich's forearm is visible, adorned with jeweled bracelets. Dietrich looks out directly at the viewer, or diagonally past the frame of the ad and past the viewer. These photographed faces of Dietrich were found in newspaper film advertising in the larger cities (Chicago, New York, Los Angeles). Atlanta, Des Moines, Cedar Rapids, and the Chicago African American press relied on drawings for film advertising, not on photographic reproductions.

Thus, in three very different guises, Dietrich's face dominated the film advertising for *Blonde Venus*. As an object of contemplation and a source of signification, Dietrich's advertising face functions like the close-up in film. In her survey of the of the close-up, Doane makes several observations that can also help us understand the importance of the star's face in film advertising. The film close-up and the advertising face are each "a sign, a text, a surface which demands to be read" (Doane, "Close-up" 94). In the text of *Blonde Venus* advertising, Dietrich's face is expected to carry the meanings of "Dietrich" combined with "*Blonde Venus*." Unlike the close-up in a film, the advertising face is under no compunction to avoid direct address with the spectator. In fact, in many of the ads for *Blonde Venus*, the eyes of Dietrich look out directly at the reader.

Doane writes about nostalgia for the face in silent cinema. The silent film face has parallels with the role that the close-up plays in film advertising: "it is the face that speaks there, and speaks to us (rather than to other characters) so much more eloquently when mute" (Doane, "Close-up" 97). Like the silent film close-up, the mute face of film advertising participates in a narrative, but it is also removed from the "relentless temporality of the narrative's unfolding" (97). Dietrich's face in *Blonde Venus* film advertising is a reminder to the newspaper reader of Dietrich's close-ups in other places. In films, a star's face is bathed in light on the big screen. A star's face may be luminescent on glossy paper in fan magazines or displayed in a fan's scrapbook. Like Dietrich's close-ups in films and in fan magazines, her face in film advertising invites the gaze of the newspaper reader.

The star's face in a newspaper film ad is not situated like the close-up on the big screen in a darkened theater, a moment of time within the unrolling of a film. In fact, the position of the film ad on the newspaper page can produce amazing counterpoints of meaning. The newspaper context of film promotion brings to mind Michel Foucault's notion of "heterotopia," as used by Annette Kuhn to describe movie theaters in her study of British cinema. "One of the principles of the heterotopia . . . is that it 'has the power of juxtaposing in a single real place different spaces and locations that are incompatible with each other'" (Kuhn, *Dreaming* 141). While the film close-up invites contemplation for the duration of the shot, film advertising is situated in the heterotopia of the daily newspaper. A reader might look for what's playing, sweeping the pages for movie stills and announcements. Film ads were surrounded by ads for other products and services. They were embedded in headlines, news stories, and diversions.

The emphasis on her face and the capitalized "DIETRICH" that dominated *Blonde Venus* film advertising in the United States might grab the reader's attention and stop the eyes from roving across the pages of a newspaper. The ads might capture attention, turning a glance into a gaze and thus inviting reader recognition of Dietrich's star persona. Already constructed by her films, von Sternberg, and Paramount, "Dietrich" was a productive and workable strategy for film advertising.

Turning now to the individual markets, we will explore how the *Blonde Venus* campaign engaged Dietrich's star persona. Some themes emerge. First, whether she was presented in glamour photography or as a sexual vampire, Dietrich was not afraid to look out at the reader. Her gaze was not soft, but direct, even aggressive. Second, ads used taglines that assumed moviegoers had experienced Dietrich's past performances. In the absence of any characterization of Helen, ads invited viewers to approach *Blonde Venus* with prior knowledge of Dietrich.

In six of the seven markets (all but the *Chicago Defender*, advertising for the Regal), the campaign for *Blonde Venus* adopted a strategy common to film advertising in the 1930s. Each newspaper introduced the film with small ads prior to its opening ("coming soon" star and title teasers). During the weekend days of the film's run, the promotional campaign was its most intense. Ads for the film were larger, with more information about star and story. The Saturday or Sunday newspaper entertainment section ran a review of the film and publicity photos. After the weekend, as the film's run concluded, the campaign returned to small ads that focused on name of star and title of film. In these small boxes, "DIETRICH" is written twice as large as "*Blonde Venus*."[3] The exception to this campaign strategy was the film's four-day run at the Regal in Chicago. Although *Blonde Venus* did not have a weekend house at the Regal, the *Chicago Defender* ballyhooed the film in its Sunday entertainment section.

Chicago Downtown: Chicago and Oriental

Blonde Venus had a two-week first run in the Chicago Loop. After a week at the Chicago, the Balaban and Katz chain moved the film to the Oriental for a holdover week downtown. The downtown Chicago campaign concentrated on Dietrich's movie star image. In the ads and in the promotional photos, Dietrich appears in glamour poses, leaning out toward the viewer, inviting and capturing the gaze.

In a medium-close shot glamour photo, Dietrich leans into the front of the ad, eyes gazing out softly at the reader. Below her face stands the Dietrich-Venus figure. The text stresses her name, reminds the viewer of her star persona, and offers a single teaser about the story: "DIETRICH, more alluring, more intriguing, than ever in a drama that all the world has waited for breathlessly. . . . She loved two men so well she had to flee from both." The ad is visually interesting, using four different fonts to present "Marlene Dietrich The *Blonde Venus*."[4]

The next day's ad displayed Dietrich in a different medium close-shot glamour photo. Again, she looks out at the viewer. Her right hand rests on the edge of the circular ad, three jeweled bracelets on her wrist. At the bottom of the ad, the Dietrich-Venus figure lounges seductively. The text of the ad repeats the promise of "Dietrich, more alluring, more intriguing than ever" and adds "as an American woman in a drama of American life!"[5]

For the film's first week at the Chicago, the *Tribune*'s Sunday entertainment section publicized *Blonde Venus* with a glamour photo at the top of the page. Dietrich half-sits, half-reclines on a couch, facing out, while Cary Grant leans over the back of the couch, staring at her. "This is a lovely photograph of Marlene, isn't it?" asks the caption.[6]

Chicago Neighborhood: Regal

Blonde Venus played in the Loop for two weeks. A month and a half later, the film screened for four days in one of Chicago's African American neighborhood theaters, the Regal. The *Defender* lead its Sunday entertainment section with the banner headline, "Regal's '*Blonde Venus*' Deserves Six Stars. If others deserved four, then we add two for Dietrich."[7] The entertainment page of this African American newspaper presented Dietrich's star persona in full array: sexual vampire, fallen woman, accomplished actress, and exotic star. While the advertising image converged on the sexual vampire, the *Defender*'s publicity-based review merrily discussed the versatility of her performance and a promotional photo presented Dietrich as the hard-looking fallen woman ("This is one of the many striking scenes the great love drama offers").

In her comprehensive history, *Returning the Gaze: A Genealogy of Black*

Film Criticism, 1909–1949, Anna Everett describes the two poles of black film criticism in the 1930s. There were radical critiques of "the ideology of capitalism codified and reified in mainstream Hollywood films" (10) and accommodationist "criticism and commentary concerned with effecting a progressive reform of Hollywood in matters of race and representation" (180). Although accommodationist in the 1930s, the *Defender*'s Sunday entertainment section ("Stage—Music—Movies") situated the *Blonde Venus* materials in a heterotopic space of stories about white-cast films and black-cast films and performances. Ranged across the top of the page in one issue are the review of *Blonde Venus*; a publicity photo of white actors from *Doctor X* (playing locally at the Metropolitan) under the caption "Mysteries Galore"; a news story on "'The Girl from Chicago' Next Micheaux Film"; the photo of Dietrich as the fallen woman in *Blonde Venus*; and a story on Ethel Waters and the Mills Brothers in a new production in New York, "Dixie to Broadway."[8]

Instead of the glamour photos used in the *Tribune* ads for the downtown theaters, the *Defender* ad presented Dietrich in an extreme and dramatic version of the expressionist chiaroscuro face (see figure 3). Her long, dark hair flows upward to the top of the long rectangular ad. Her eyes burn out at the reader. The Dietrich-Venus figure looks out from the bottom of the ad.[9] The only character traits offered are that Dietrich is playing "in her First American Role!" suggesting that the reader will have knowledge of Dietrich's past roles and films.

Under the byline of Hilda See, the review in the *Defender* begins with a paragraph of opinion on the value of using stars to rate a film, concluding that "pretty Marlene Dietrich always great, but even better in this '*Blonde Venus*' which comes to the Regal theater Sunday, should be given two extra stars." Quoting language that appeared in other published reviews of *Blonde Venus*, See claimed to be delighted to see a film that allows Dietrich to express a range of emotion and depth of character. "It is a new Marlene Dietrich who makes her appearance in '*Blonde Venus*'—warm, loving, humanly-moved, and withal just as glamorously exotic as she ever was." The review connects *Blonde Venus* to Dietrich's other films: "At last she has a chance to give full play to the smoldering emotion, only hinted at in 'Shanghai Express,' 'Dishonored,' 'Morocco,' and 'The Blue Angel.'" The reviewer is happy that *Blonde Venus* "provides her [Dietrich] with a character to portray that is thoroughly human and deeply emotional."

Even though this review is replete with publicity platitudes, its expression of affection for Dietrich occupies the headline position in the *Defender*, days before *Blonde Venus* was to open at the Regal.[10]

New York: Paramount

The *New York Times* ads for *Blonde Venus* focused less on the performance of the actress and more on an indifferent promotion of the film through its star. The ads featured Dietrich's movie star glamour and her cabaret performances in the film. The review, definitely not prewritten, was a lengthy critique. The review and another article discussed, in some detail, production problems on the film.

For the "world premiere" of *Blonde Venus* (a week after its run in downtown Chicago), the ad used a glamour photo of Dietrich's face enclosed in a circle. She engages the reader, looking out with direct address. Overlapping the photo is a sketch of a woman in "hot voodoo" costume, her leg up on a chair. This is the only film ad that exploited the "hot voodoo" routine (performed by Dietrich in the film) in the seven markets in this study. The ad contains no information about the storyline of the film but does list the "on-stage" acts that play with *Blonde Venus* at the Paramount New York and at the Paramount Brooklyn.[11]

On Saturday, 24 September 1932, Mordaunt Hall's review of *Blonde Venus* appeared in the *New York Times* under the headline "Marlene Dietrich and Herbert Marshall in a Film Which Caused a Studio Disagreement." Leading the review was a reminder that *Blonde Venus* was the film "over which B.P. Schulberg, until recently head of Paramount's Hollywood studio, and Josef von Sternberg, the director, clashed last spring." Hall assessed *Blonde Venus* as "muddled, unimaginative and generally hapless" but found it "relieved somewhat by the talent and charm of the German actress and Herbert Marshall's valiant work in a thankless role." Hall recounted the story in detail, including the ending ("the dismal and suspenseless tale of a woman who sinks to selling her favors and finally ends by returning to her husband") and expressed no sympathy for Helen's situation. He found the performers all to be better than their roles: "Mr. Marshall does as well as his lines and the situations permit. Cary Grant is worthy of a much better role . . . little Dickie Moore [playing the son] gives a suggestion of brightness to the unhealthy scenes in which he is sometimes beheld" (A13).

On Sunday, the *Times* entertainment section featured a medium-shot photo of Dietrich in a feathered cabaret costume. Below the picture, Chapin Hall's report from Hollywood leads with three paragraphs that develop the context of Mordaunt Hall's allusion to the production problems of *Blonde Venus*. Chapin Hall recounted the "almost forgotten" studio clash ("Schulberg demanded a certain sympathy in Miss Dietrich's role"), detailed the film's cost ("approaching a million dollars. Some 4,000,000 feet of film was shot to get the 8,000 feet that appears on the screen") and wondered whether the film would be able to succeed financially (X3).

Los Angeles: Paramount

In contrast to the New York coverage, which situated *Blonde Venus* in its financial and production context, the Los Angeles publicity was a multifaceted endeavor worthy of the term "campaign." It focused on Dietrich's star persona, exploited the film's story and Helen's dual roles as mother and scarlet woman, promoted the exhibition venue and production values, made hyperbolic announcements that *Blonde Venus* would be a major screen event, and printed a critical review two days running. The Los Angeles promotion is worth exploring in some detail, as it demonstrates how the film industry presented itself at home and how Dietrich's star persona was thoroughly worked through.

The *Los Angeles Times* promotion began with a publicity photo of Dietrich in close-up with the headline, "'*Blonde Venus*' Arrives Thursday." The caption reads "Marlene Dietrich plays the name role in the next picture at the Paramount Theater. Herbert Marshall appears opposite the star." On the same page is an ad for the Paramount's coming attraction: "Starts Thursday! MAGNIFICENT! DARING! . . . an amazing story made more glamorous by Dietrich the exotic . . . a fallen woman you love . . . understand and forgive!" The visual in the ad is an encircled glamour photo of Dietrich's face looking out over the sketch of the Dietrich-Venus figure. This ad promoted the film through its genre ("fallen woman"), the glamorous and exotic connotations of Dietrich's star persona, and Dietrich's ability to find depth in the fallen woman.[12]

The next day (Wednesday), the publicity campaign promoted the exhibition venue with a large ad for the Paramount, promising "The Biggest Stage Shows! The Greatest Pictures!...THE PARAMOUNT THEATRE RETAINS THE POLICY of giving the best value in entertainment with the BIGGEST STAGE SHOWS and the GREATEST PICTURES in all Los Angeles!" The ad for *Blonde Venus* featured a close-up photo of Dietrich, her face ringed in soft, blonde hair, looking out directly at the viewer. The text anchors the star with both the maternal and sexual traits of the character she plays. The text identifies Helen's desires and gives more information about the story than any other ad in the seven markets. The ad directly addresses the viewer, reminding the viewer of the sympathetic moral understanding that Dietrich brings to Helen.[13]

"DARING . . . Dietrich the wife and mother! The very thought is daring—Dietrich—exotic—glamorous . . . the mother who goes into the pit of hell for her boy! SCARLET . . . No other personality can give such beauty . . . dignity . . . pity-quickening allure to the scarlet letter . . . you love—understand—forgive her. . . . Marlene Dietrich in *Blonde Venus*." The ad lists the performers in the live stage show, which include comics, singers, dancers, and the Greater Paramount Orchestra. This ad plays on the depth that Dietrich's glamorous and exotic star persona could bring to the role of a mother and the "daring" notion that Dietrich would play a maternal role. The ad suggested that it was Dietrich's dignified sexuality that enabled her to generate understanding and sympathy for Helen Faraday.

As the ad campaign continued on Thursday, the day the film opened, a different glamour photo of Dietrich's face looked out in direct address above the sketch of Dietrich-Venus lounging in a seductive pose. The look on this face resembles the expressionist rendering of the face of Dietrich. The headline of the ad screams, "The greatest DIETRICH of them all!" In a box behind her face, "Dietrich the magnificent . . . sweeps aside all former triumphs . . . in amazing story . . . a fallen woman . . . two men claimed her . . . to one she gave her lovely youth . . . for him, she sacrificed her honor. To the other she gave all that he asked."[14] Here, the ad's language evokes Dietrich's previous roles and presents *Blonde Venus* as an even greater challenge and achievement for the actress.

On Saturday and Friday, a review appeared. The Saturday review was reprinted from Friday's late edition. Although the review's headline suggests it is a publicity blurb ("*Blonde Venus* Arrives . . . Marlene Dietrich

Superbly Photographed in Romantic Screen Play at Paramount Theater"), the review did not endorse the film. For reviewer Phillip K. Scheuer, *Blonde Venus* "gets off on the wrong footage, so to speak . . . in trying to be sentimentally realistic as well as glamorously romantic." Although his review did not detail Helen's motivations and choices, he offered a flip summary of the film as a "story of a wife and mother turned streetwalker." He finds it "unpalatable" that Helen takes her son on the run with her. For Scheuer, it strains the imagination to accept Dietrich in U.S. locations ("it is difficult to thrill exotically to the idea of Fraulein Dietrich on the loose in Chattanooga"). On the page with this trenchant review is a small ad for the film. The only image is the sketch of Dietrich-Venus with the tagline: "A new Role . . . Amazing Drama . . . Daring . . . Magnificent . . . a triumph in the career of the star of stars!" The ad's hyperbole and the review rest in proximity and in contradiction.[15]

Atlanta: Paramount

Of all the markets in the study, Atlanta presents the most lurid and hyperbolic film advertising. The local exhibitor promoted the film heavily, changing the ads in the *Constitution* on a daily basis and running *Blonde Venus* ads in the classifieds as well as the entertainment pages. Atlanta's ads featured both the impassive face and the vampire face in the campaign for *Blonde Venus*.

The Thursday "coming attraction" ad for *Blonde Venus* used a sketch of Dietrich's impassive face. "Marlene Dietrich in *Blonde Venus*" is presented in the same visually interesting four fonts used in the *Chicago Tribune*. The Atlanta ad identifies the character's traits and narrative challenge ("She loved two men—one devotedly, the other madly!") and promises that the film has "Dietrich playing an American woman for the first time! A woman who risked everything for what she believed was happiness." At the Paramount in Atlanta, *Blonde Venus* will replace *Back Street*, a film "for every woman who has loved unwisely . . . for every man who has loved too well!"[16]

The next day (Friday), the campaign used the expressionist photo of Dietrich's face and, in the corner of the ad, the sketch of Dietrich-Venus. The text in this ad surrounds the title of the film and Dietrich's face. At the top of the ad, situated in Dietrich's flowing hair: "From the lips of one man to the arms of another!" In a box set next to her head: "EXCLUSIVE! These pictures positively will not be shown in any other Atlanta theatre!" Below the title of the film: "before the first one's kisses had faded from her lips, she longed for the other's embrace . . . because she loved them both, what could she do but flee from love! . . . Singing for the First Time Since 'Morocco!'"[17]

In a clever promotion, the *Constitution* offered "two tickets free with each 3-time want ad paid in advance today." For four days, the paper published an ad for *Blonde Venus* in the classified section, a different ad each day. On Saturday, the ad presented the expressionistic face of Dietrich the vampire, eyes burning at the reader, dark hair rising. The ad's text anchors character ("Glorious Dietrich as an American woman who longs for the love that tortured her!") and audience expectations of Dietrich's star image ("Every Man and Woman will be fascinated by her intensified glamour in her first American role").[18]

On Sunday, the classified section promotion anchored the vague impassive face of the blonde Dietrich with an itinerary of Helen's literal and moral journey: "Hunted by Love! Yet haunted by its dreams as she fled from it! Follow her from a Park Avenue apartment to a second-rate Baltimore hotel. From there to a rooming house in Norfolk and then to a dive in New Orleans . . . until love overtakes her! . . . Her First Role as An American Woman!"[19]

On Monday and Tuesday, the *Blonde Venus* ads in the classified section were situated below the comic strip *Tarzan: The Untamed*. The same ad ran both days. They used Dietrich's impassive face and a large sketch of Dietrich-Venus, this time in a low-cut, form-fitting flowing gown and fur stole draped over one shoulder. The text of these ads reads: "the love that had made her a fugitive . . . that had send [*sic*] her from city to city, eluding police, dreading discovery, sinking lower and lower. . . . What could be the end for this woman?" While the placement of the blonde Venus next to Tarzan connects the two adventurers, the ad does not use "Hot Voodoo" to create links between the African themes of the film and the comic strip. The comic and the film ad are visually assertive on the page and stand out among the classified ads.[20]

The *Constitution*'s Sunday entertainment section, "News of Stage and Screen," edited by Ralph T. Jones, presents a publicity photo of Dietrich ("alluring emotional star") in "hot voodoo" garb, posed next to a large African mask. The photo is one of four publicity shots for films "to be seen on Atlanta screens this week." A review under the title "Dietrich is at the Paramount this week in *Blonde Venus*" first reminds the reader that the Paramount has the exclusive exhibition rights to the film in Atlanta. The review goes on to replicate much of the language of the review in the *Chicago Defender*. The actress is a "new Marlene Dietrich . . . warm, loving, humanly moved, and withal just as glamorously exotic as ever. At last she has the chance to give full play to the smoldering emotions, only hinted at in her former pictures." Like the *Defender*, the Atlanta review presents Dietrich as "a lover of men" who now "concentrates her affections chiefly on a little boy, charmingly lovable little Dickie Moore, while she toys with the affections of two men." The review lauded the support of Marshall and Grant and, in notable contrast to the reviews in Los Angeles and New York, "the inspired genius of Josef von Sternberg."[21]

Des Moines: Des Moines

The *Des Moines Register* ads refrained from textual anchoring of the *Blonde Venus* story and its star. For the film's opening, the ad uses the expressionistic face of Dietrich. "Marlene Dietrich in *Blonde Venus*" is presented in three typefaces, continuing the ad's visual instability. The ad identifies the studio ("another Paramount new season smash hit"), the movie star ("glamorous Dietrich"), the performance ("gloriously triumphant in her first American role") and a suggestion about the story ("a woman—who longed for the love that tortured her!"). Next to the Dietrich-Venus figure in the corner, the ad touts Herbert Marshall and Cary Grant in the cast and invites the audience to "Hear Dietrich sing 'Hot Voodoo'—'Getting What I Want When I Want It' and 'You Little So and So.'" The Des Moines ads attempted to communicate with audiences through signifiers of Dietrich's star persona (the actress is glamorous and performs three songs in the film) and were vague about Helen (the character is emotionally "tortured").[22]

On weekdays, small city newspapers run movie ads with other material. Only on Saturday or Sunday is a full page reserved for local entertainment opportunities. When *Blonde Venus* opened in Des Moines, the expressionistic face of the vampire Dietrich, eyes burning out at the reader, was surrounded by ads for wholesome domestic heartland activities. On one side of the *Blonde Venus* ad was a promotion for the seventh annual Food Show and Cooking School ("free samples and souvenirs for everybody"). On the other side, the Des Moines Hospitality Club promoted a visit to the city, "a splendid outing for the family." While this heterotopic conjunction seems to be a counterpoint of oppositions, the Des Moines paper also featured a tie-in between the Chevrolet dealer and *Blonde Venus*. In the ad for the promotion, the vampire face of Dietrich appears with an invitation to readers: "2 Big Hits! See the Ray Dodge Chevrolet Exhibit . . . on the promenade of the Des Moines Theatre and Marlene DIETRICH in *Blonde Venus*."[23]

On a single page of the Sunday entertainment section, there are three opportunities to engage Dietrich's star persona. There is an ad with the ambiguous Dietrich face ("Glamorous Dietrich Gloriously triumphant in her first American role"), a review of the film and the publicity still of Dietrich as the fallen woman. The review is sparse and lacks the euphoric descriptions of the prewritten reviews. It provides a brief summary of Helen's reasons for being in relationships with two men: she "saves her husband's life by accepting the love of another man" and then "realizes she is actually in love with her benefactor." The review states the crux of Helen's melodramatic dilemma: "her love for her infant son ties her to her husband." About the film's conclusion, the review is vague, suggesting the writer had not seen the film: "the circumstances produces what has been described as a dramatic climax, of the sort excellently suited to the capabilities of both Dietrich and Marshall." The review describes the actors as "invigorating performers" and von Sternberg as "one of the abler directors." This single page in the *Register* contains three *Blonde Venus* items, presenting the reader with the diversity of Dietrich's star persona.[24]

Cedar Rapids: Paramount

Like the ads in the *Des Moines Register*, the *Cedar Rapids Gazette* ads are vague about the story. The opening of the film was announced with the large impassive face of Dietrich and a small sketch of Dietrich-Venus at the bottom of the ad. The words of the ad are routinely hyperbolic, promising (as did the Balaban and Katz chain in Chicago): "Greater Show Season's Greatest Show!" The tagline acclaim for the star and her role, seen in downtown Chicago ads, appears also in Cedar Rapids: "Dietrich, more alluring, more intriguing than ever, as an American woman in a drama of American life!" At the bottom of the ad, next to the Dietrich-Venus, the ad hints at the story: "She loved two men. One devotedly, the other—madly!"[25]

Yet the film's advertising did not promote the drama of Helen's struggle. The ads during the Cedar Rapids run of *Blonde Venus* were dominated visually by either the ambiguous face of Dietrich or the angular chiaroscuro. The taglines offered mundane hyperbole about screen entertainment ("Another Smashing Program . . . Today the Paramount Theatre rises to new heights of entertainment glory!") or focused on expectations for a Dietrich performance ("Here's Superb Entertainment!! DIETRICH, more alluring, more intriguing than ever in the drama that all the world has waited for breathlessly!").[26]

Unlike other ads in this study, the Cedar Rapids ads presented an invitation to the star, to the director, and to the film's production values ("Marlene DIETRICH in Joseph von Sternberg's Paramount Thunderbolt" or "Marlene Dietrich in Josef Von Sternberg's Dramatic Paramount Smash"). Indeed, the Cedar Rapids screening appears to be something of an event. Just as big-city film ads presented the roster for the stage shows that played with films, the Cedar Rapids ads itemized the short subject films on the bill with *Blonde Venus*: Tom Mix and his wife at their California estate, Gary Cooper and his pet chimpanzee, Fifi Dorsay and Benny Rubin in a bit of French Palestine, a Betty Boop cartoon, royal Samoans, and scenes of the first World Series games.[27]

In the early 1930s, Cedar Rapids appeared to have an enthusiastic film exhibitor who took the opportunity to ballyhoo a film. A promotional story appeared in the *Gazette* announcing the film ("*Blonde Venus* is Next at Paramount"): "If Venus de Milo were alive today, and looking for a job in the movies—she'd have to be content with classification in the 'stout women' roster! The casting director would probably tell her: 'Sorry, but you're not the type.' And on her way out she probably would cast envious eyes in the direction of Marlene Dietrich, her 1932 successor and Paramount's glamorous *Blonde Venus* in the picture of that title which is the next big attraction at the Paramount theater starting Saturday. Fashions change in beauty as well as in clothes. The charmer of yesterday is the 'extra size' of tomorrow. Venus would find the lissome Marlene Dietrich particularly intriguing."

After this treatise on historical changes in feminine beauty, the story goes on to repeat taglines that appear in the film's advertising: "her first role as an American woman in a drama of American life . . . a woman who loved two men, one devotedly and other madly." The story concludes with praise for "a strong supporting cast," a mention of von Sternberg's "discovery of Dietrich" and their films together, and a list of the "additional stars [that] are included in the program augmenting the feature attraction." The *Gazette* thus anticipates the film's run in Cedar Rapids with a cleverly written story promoting the film.[28]

The Sunday edition of the newspaper printed a large glamour photo of Dietrich in "Hot Voodoo" attire, one leg up on the seat of a chair. The photo is located next to a review of *Blonde Venus* with the headline "Critic Says *Blonde Venus* One of the Best." Ascribed to "N.D.," the review begins with praise for the "artistry of the production [that] surpasses even the superb acting of the alluring Miss Dietrich." One-third of the review details the first scenes of *Blonde Venus*, the swimming party in the Black Forest where Helen and Ned meet. About the rest of the storyline, the review explains "there is only one chance" for the wife to save the husband's life and is nearly explicit about Helen's sexual work. "The wife returns to the stage, but the money she sends abroad is not earned by dancing." N.D. finds "at last there is a happy ending" when "again the playboy enters her life." The *Cedar Rapids Gazette* appreciates that Helen can be part of two couples (one with a child) and that she has a companionable relationship with the playboy. This review uses none of the language found in the Chicago and Atlanta prewritten reviews, suggesting that Cedar Rapids had, in N.D., a local film reviewer.[29]

The publicity for *Blonde Venus* suggests the complexity of Dietrich's star persona. The film ads used several radically different images of Dietrich—glamour photos, aggressive vampire, expressionless object of contemplation, the Dietrich-Venus figure. On newspaper entertainment pages, Dietrich appeared as a movie star, a cabaret performer, or a fallen woman, but not as a wife-mother. Prewritten reviews expressed affection for Dietrich, appreciation of her acting, and sympathy for Helen Faraday. Newspapers with staff reviewers criticized the film's story. Each of the seven markets organized Dietrich's star persona in a different way. About film stars, Wexman remarks, they "intensify the sexual charge inherent in the act of watching films, promoting a culture of romantic attraction that connects the rituals of love with an ideal of physical beauty" (Wexman 17). Dietrich's star persona does the same for film advertising: she produces the "sexual charge" inherent in situating *Blonde Venus* for local audiences.

Notes

1. The following is a chronology of the run of *Blonde Venus* in the seven markets described in this essay: Chicago Loop, at the Chicago (six days, Friday through Wednesday, 15–28 September); New York, at the Paramount (seven days, Friday through Thursday, 23–29 September); Des Moines, at the Des Moines (seven days, Friday through Thursday, 23–29 September); Atlanta, at the Paramount (seven days, Saturday through Friday, 23–30 September); Chicago Loop, at the Oriental (seven days, Thursday through Wednesday, 29 September–5 October); Cedar Rapids, at the Paramount (five days, Saturday through Thursday, 1–5 October); Los Angeles, at the Paramount (seven days, Thursday through Wednesday, 6–12 October).

Some exhibition patterns emerge from this chronology. The dates suggest that the print was "bicycled" from Des Moines to Cedar Rapids. Films in Cedar Rapids and in Chicago's neighborhood theater (Regal) had shorter runs and faster turnover of screen entertainment, every three or four days. A Paramount studio film, *Blonde Venus* screened at Paramount theaters in New York, Atlanta, Cedar Rapids, and Los Angeles, but not at the Paramount theater in Des Moines. In that city, the Paramount was showing *Doctor X* ("the Strangest Love Story Ever Told!") with Lee Tracy, Fay Wray, and Lionel Atwill.

One expects clearance of some weeks between a film's first run in the city center and its subsequent run in neighborhoods. *Blonde Venus* played at the Regal one month after its downtown Chicago run. The distribution schedule did not favor the major coastal cities. The film opened in Chicago a week before it opened in New York. It concluded its first runs in Chicago, New York, Atlanta, Des Moines, and Cedar Rapids before it opened in Los Angeles. It ran one week in Los Angeles and New York, but three weeks in downtown Chicago theaters.

2. For more on the story of *Blonde Venus*, see Lea Jacobs's detailed discussion of the script and censorship process (86–105).

3. See, for example, ads in *New York Times*, 26 September 1932, 18; 27 September 1932, 24; 28 September 1932, 22; 29 September 1932, 17.

4. Ad, *Chicago Daily Tribune*, 22 September 1932, 20.

5. Ad, *Chicago Daily Tribune*, 23 September 1932, 21.

6. Publicity still, *Chicago Sunday Tribune*, 25 September 1932, 7:1.

7. Review, *Chicago Defender*, 5 November 1932, 10.

8. *Chicago Defender*, 5 November 1932, Stage—Music—Film section, 10.

9. Ad, *Chicago Defender*, 5 November 1932, 10.

10. Review, *Chicago Defender*, 5 November 1932, 10.

11. Ads, *New York Times*, 23 September 1932, A23; 25 September 1932, 4X.

12. Publicity still and ad, *Los Angeles Times*, 4 October 1932, 9.

13. Ad, *Los Angeles Times*, 5 October 1932, 11.

14. Ad, *Los Angeles Times*, 6 October 1932, 9.

15. Philip K. Scheuer, review; and ad, *Los Angeles Times*, 8 October 1932, II 7.

16. Ads for *Blonde Venus* and *Back Street, Constitution*, 22 September 1932, 19.

17. Ad, *Constitution*, 23 September 1932, 8.

18. Ad, *Constitution*, 24 September 1932, 18.

19. Ad, *Constitution*, 25 September 1932, Classified Ads section, 1.

20. Ads, *Constitution*, 26 September 1932, 13; 27 September 1932, 16.

21. Publicity still and review, *Constitution*, 25 September 1932, S18.

22. Ad, *Des Moines Register*, 22 September 1932: A3.

23. Food Show ad and Des Moines Hospitality Club ad, *Des Moines Register*, 22 September 1932, A3; *Blonde Venus* and Chevrolet tie-in, *Des Moines Register*, 23 September 1932, 4.

24. Publicity still and review, *Des Moines Register*, 25 September 1932, X5.

25. Ad, *Cedar Rapids Gazette*, 30 September 1932, 12.

26. Ad, *Cedar Rapids Gazette*, 1 October 1932, 4.

27. Ad, *Cedar Rapids Gazette*, 1 October 1932, 4.

28. Review, *Cedar Rapids Gazette*, 30 September 1932, 12.

29. Publicity still; N.D., review, *Cedar Rapids Gazette*, 2 October 1932, 2, 5.

ERICA CARTER

Marlene Dietrich

The Prodigal Daughter

ON 28 MARCH 1933, Joseph Goebbels gave his first speech as Reich propaganda minister to film industry representatives. Addressing what he dubbed the artistic failings of late Weimar cinema—its low-life themes, its social realism, its distance from popular taste—Goebbels drew international comparisons, most famously with Eisenstein's *Battleship Potemkin* (which he called "unparalleled as film art"), but also with Edmund Goulding's 1927 Anna Karenina portrait, *Love*, in which Greta Garbo played the title role. Of her performance, Goebbels said the following: "Garbo has proved that there is such a thing as a special art of film. This film is no surrogate for theater or stage performance. There precisely *is* an art that belongs to film alone."[1] Goebbels's claim, then, is that it is among other things stars and the quality of their performance that give film its distinctive artistic quality. Especially significant is what Goebbels deems the absence of star quality among German screen actors of the period; instead, he names as his model of stardom Greta Garbo, a European idol long since lost to Hollywood cinema.

This equation of stardom with Hollywood has a long tradition in German star discourse. The very term "star" is an Anglicism in German; and even the most recent film-critical studies often share a vision of Hollywood as the dominant model for German stardom.[2] Two key assumptions underpin this perception. Hollywood is claimed, first, to have held undisputed sway in European film markets since the late 1910s, and thus to represent the dominant economic model for mainstream cinema in general, and star systems in particular. The second assumption is a cultural one, and relates to Hollywood's presumed status as the primary film-cultural paradigm around which European national cinemas have articulated the meanings and values of stardom. Goebbels's comments on Garbo are a case in point; for she figures here as the epitome of a Hollywood stardom that 1930s German film could not yet emulate.

Yet there are reasons to relativize this vision of an unchallenged Hollywood hegemony. Economically, certainly, Hollywood's penetration of German film markets has rarely been matched by exports in the opposite direction; indeed, as Geoffrey Nowell-Smith has observed, film exports to Hollywood from Europe in general remained negligible throughout the twentieth century. Even economically however, there are grounds to assume what Nowell-Smith terms a "dual," not a one-way relation. As he notes, Hollywood's rise to European market dominance was periodically interrupted through the twentieth century: by the coming of sound, for instance, and the concomitant surge in demand for indigenous language productions; or by state-orchestrated protectionism—import quotas and stringent censorship that, in Germany, began as early as World War I and extended with increasing severity through the Third Reich (Nowell-Smith 1–3). Recent reception histories of the period from Weimar to the 1990s, moreover, show how audience demand has provided a further counterweight to Hollywood dominance. Joseph Garncarz uses trade press statistics on the top ten films from 1925 onward to estimate for the Weimar period that German films accounted for over 75 percent of box office revenue from top films, as opposed to just over 15 percent for Hollywood titles. A similar picture emerges for the 1950s, when German films among the top ten attracted over four times the box office revenue of their Hollywood competitors ("Hollywood in Germany" 172).

Garncarz's work is illuminating, too, for its challenge to notions of Hollywood star models as universally dominant. His studies of Weimar stars echo previous scholarship on early cinema in demonstrating both the persistent popularity of such home-grown talent as Charles Willi Kayser or Claire Rommer, and the rooting of that popularity in national cultural traditions ("Warum kennen" 67). What distinguished Weimar's "nationally distinctive star system," argues Garncarz, was both the artisanal economic model on which it depended (until well into the 1940s, stars worked predominantly as freelancers, rather than, as in Hollywood, under long-term contract to a single studio),[3] and its organization around nationally specific cultural values and taste codes. As Garncarz notes, Weimar stars' differentiation from Hollywood was realized "by a discourse on art (not) private lives"; hence the paucity of press coverage, in this period and later, of stars' intimate personal lives, as well as the emphasis on their actorly prowess, their status as artists of genius, and their attachment to theater as the "culturally dominant medium."[4]

The work of Garncarz and others suggests that in studying German stardom, we should abandon binary models of one national cinema's subservience to Hollywood, and conceive that relation instead as a two-way process of translation between culturally specific representational modes, values, and norms—a process that shifts in different historical moments and locations. Our focus here is on the early years of the Third Reich: a period of special interest in the history of German cinema's negotiation with stardom Hollywood-style. That Hollywood remained for the greater part of the 1930s not only Germany's chief rival on the domestic market but also the most coherent example of a cinema whose success Germany wished to duplicate is evidenced by import and distribution data from the period. Although foreign imports fell after the Nazi takeover, Hollywood films retained a significant presence in Germany throughout the 1930s. In 1933, they made up over two-thirds of foreign film imports (sixty-five of a total of ninety-two films imported that year) (*Film-Kurier*, January 1934). Even by 1936, the proportion remained at around 50 percent, although import controls had by this stage reduced total imports to around seventy of the two hundred films required annually to fill exhibitors' programs.[5]

Hollywood's continued success on German markets produced what Markus Spieker terms a characteristic "dualism" in responses from party ideologues and the German industry. Goebbels's desire for an American-style "media modernity" was balanced, Spieker suggests, against the anti-Americanism he inherited from cultural nationalism under Weimar and earlier. That ambivalence was mirrored by an industry that admired Hollywood's technical brilliance, while excoriating its shallowness and low artistic ambition (Spieker 45). The star system in particular provoked ambiguous responses from both industry and regime. On the one hand, their awareness of stars' role in drawing audiences is evident in numerous interventions by the Propaganda Ministry into casting decisions, or in the privileges accorded to stars (high salaries, invitations to social events with prominent Nazis, etc.).[6] That stardom was problematic, however, for both industry and state is evidenced by the ambivalence surrounding stars in film commentary of the 1930s. The cinema owners' trade paper, *Film-Kurier*, commented in early 1933 that it was merely a "love of beauty and glamour" that produced audience adulation of major stars ("Ein Wort"). By 1935, it was by contrast polemicizing against the "monstrosity" of stardom, or, in a 1937 piece, bemoaning the detrimental effects of "star mania" on "individuals and artists of a serious nature."[7]

Film-Kurier's comments draw in part on that conception of the artist-star identified above as a long-standing feature of star discourse in Germany. Their vehemence derives, however, from circumstances particular to National Socialism. The Nazi takeover was followed by rapid moves toward state control of film through *Gleichschaltung* (coordination), increased censorship, and eventual nationalization. Film was seen here, then, as a vehicle for the state-orchestrated assertion of a racist cultural nationalism that was only incipient in German cinema before 1933. Nazi cinema's simultaneous aspiration to European market dominance, however, necessitated a commitment to internationalism associated heretofore primarily with Hollywood directors, film styles, and stars.

Later in this essay, I explore the ramifications of that tussle between national and international ideologies, values, and cultural forms through a discussion of the German reception of Marlene Dietrich after 1933. Reception discourse around Dietrich focused, as we shall see, in part on her capacity to embody attributes perceived in larger debates around stardom as specifically German. It is, then, initially to those debates that I now briefly turn, before exploring in more detail the case of Dietrich, and her paradoxical status both as an embodiment of the national values the domestic industry sought to assert, and as an (ultimately unassimilable) source of trouble within discourses of the star as emblem of nation.

Stars, Character, and Personality

German star discourse, as noted above, has often eschewed the preoccupation with private lives that provides the backbone of Hollywood star-audience relations. Under National Socialism, the public display of private intimacies was especially frowned upon, since it fostered an individualism considered antipathetic to fascism's collectivist ideals. That collective ethos was further buttressed by Nazi cinema's commitment to an ensemble aesthetic that was already pervasive before 1933 in German popular film. As the illustrated weekly *Filmwelt* observed in 1937, "It is not the star who is the most important figure, but the film and the totality of its artistic significance. . . . It is a crime against art for the star to use his power to undermine the integrity of the total work of art" (25 March 1937). Such anti-individualism was embedded, moreover, in the aesthetic structure of Third Reich narrative cinema. Writers on Third Reich film have often claimed that it aped Hollywood's narrative conventions; and indeed, much German genre film deployed the narrative strategies of classical Hollywood style: universal narrative motivation, the concealment of the film text's fabricated nature, and the management of time and space to support narrative causality (Bordwell).

German film style departed from Hollywood, however, in at least one important sense. David Bordwell writes of classical Hollywood film that it accords centrality to character construction, since it is on the psychological plausibility of characters that narrative development depends (12–18). In Third Reich film, by contrast, psychological depth is regularly abandoned in favor of the fabrication of ideal types: the soldier hero, the self-sacrificial mother, the masculine model of racial health. Recurrent features of visual and narrative organization contribute to that location of types, not characters, as the aesthetic centre of Third Reich film. German narrative film of the 1930s and 1940s is notable, for instance, for its preference for static camera and long take. The dominant shot is the medium close-up; in dialogue sequences, the two-shot and the long take prevail over close-ups and point-of-view editing. It is, moreover, not only this characteristically cautious use of camera and montage that mute character interaction and development. The heavy reliance on dialogue as a means of subjective expression—as opposed, for example, to mise-en-scène elements (lighting, decor, gesture, etc.)—situate Third Reich style in a literary-based realist tradition that eschews emotional ambivalence in favor of the supposed clarity of the spoken word.

A number of visual and narrative features in 1930s and 1940s German cinema suppress, then, the psychological depth that is integral to character development in Hollywood realism. Indeed, this rejection of character was made explicit in numerous disquisitions on film acting under National Socialism. The actor-director Paul Wegener, for instance, commented in a 1934 speech that film roles must be "shaped by the actor from the depths of his human essence." The creative process, Wegener continued, gained shape "not on the basis of . . . pre-given stylistic principles. Instead, it grows from the mystical depths . . . of that personality that slumbers at the complex subjective core of genuine talent" (*Film-Kurier*, "Paul Wegener," 22 December 1934).

The romantic conception of "personality" as a subjective core that finds unmediated expression in film art surfaced repeatedly in 1930s film theory. The term differed from Hollywood ideas of character in a number of aspects. Most important was its rooting not in bourgeois humanist ideas of character as the product of personal experience and development (the classic vehicle for that humanist vision being the bildungsroman). Instead, Third Reich film borrowed from race theory a vision of personality as a sociobiological essence identifiable by physical type. As the Reichsfilmintendant and director of the anti-Semitic documentary *Der ewige Jude* (*The Eternal Jew*, 1940), Fritz Hippler, wrote in his *Betrachtungen zum Filmschaffen* (*Considerations on Film Art*, 1942), "That there is a correspondence between character and external appearance is evident not only from modern psychological research; it is also part of ancient and deeply rooted folk wisdom" (91). This *völkisch* vision had various implications for the representation of character in German film. The division of human beings in Nazi race theory into physical and racial types made it the filmmaker's task to reflect that "natural" appearance on film. Film commentators in any case made much of the status of the photographic image as a physical trace of human reality; thus for Hippler, film was "more fundamentally rooted in its material origins than any other category of art" (6). This notion of an organic unity between the film image and its referent in turn produced a distrust of stylization or visual excess—melodramatic acting style, expressionist lighting, extravagant costume—since these were conceived as forms of masquerade that obscured the essence of racial type. Witness Hippler again on film acting and costume: "What is . . . primarily at stake in film is not so much the art of acting style, but rather the representation of personal types. . . . The *nouveau riche* or the metropolitan individual . . . wears masks, even when going about his everyday business. Since he has a sense of being constantly under observation, he never shows his true face, but strikes poses [that] may even appear genuine, despite his use of masquerade" (82).

Here, the association of actorly stylization with metropolitan modernity is the source of its denigration. Elsewhere, the masquerade is linked to other forms of social and racial deviation: with Jewishness, for example, or with female licentiousness. Most interesting for our purposes, however, is the identification by Nazi film commentators of stylistic excess as a key feature of Hollywood stardom: a feature, moreover, that they find distasteful because it infringes the norms of a racially defined national film aesthetic.

Why Dietrich?

In February 1934, Joseph Goebbels revisited a favorite theme. "If German film is one day to conquer the world, then it must appear again as *German* film; it must put into representation our specific essence, our qualities, our character, our virtue—and if you wish, our weaknesses too."[8] Goebbels's caveat ("and . . . our weaknesses too") acknowledges the tension between his imperialist wish for a revitalized German film industry that will displace Hollywood in its ability to "conquer the world," and the völkisch-nationalist aspiration for films expressive of German essence. Until mid-decade, moreover, the key figure on the international stage combined the qualities of Germanness with the world stature that Goebbels demanded. That figure was Marlene Dietrich, and her success as a German star in Hollywood make her an illuminating figure for any study of 1930s Germany's negotiation of Hollywood stardom.

Karsten Witte has noted how Third Reich cinema cultivated a new generation of stars, each partially modeled on a Hollywood alter ego—Adolf Wohlbrück on Clark Gable, Lilian Harvey on Claudette Colbert, Marika Rökk on Eleanor Powell, Zarah Leander on Dietrich and Garbo. In a dynamic of incorporation and disavowal that was characteristic of Third Reich film's "Germanicized Americanism," each of these figures adopted symbolic elements of the star image of their Hollywood other, while at the same time repudiating those features that transgressed German aesthetic and ideological codes (112). Take, for instance, the case of the Swedish-born diva Zarah Leander. Recruited in 1937 by the Ufa studios explicitly as a German replacement for her two émigré counterparts, Garbo and Dietrich, Leander was promoted as Germany's foremost international star. She enjoyed glittering successes in a string of musicals and melodramas, ending her Third Reich career only when contractual disputes prompted her return to her native Sweden in 1943. Like Garbo and Dietrich, Leander cultivated an aura of gender ambiguity (most prominently in her singing, which spanned a vocal range from masculine baritone to the rich contralto of the opera diva), and of sultry sexual allure (one Berlin newspaper described her on her 1937 arrival in Germany "as intoxicating as rich red wine").[9] At the same time, Leander's ambiguities were managed and contained in her films through the anchoring of her star image in narratives of maternal sacrifice (*La Habanera*, Detlef Sierck, 1937), of sexual renunciation (most memorably in her renouncing of her degenerate English lover, Lord Finsbury [Willy Birgel] in Sierck's *To New Shores* [*Zu neuen Ufern*], 1937), or of national commitment (when she played self-sacrificial lover to a Luftwaffe officer in Rolf Hansen's *The Great Love* [*Die grosse Liebe*], 1941).

Most important, extra-filmic systems of representation that construct the image of stars—gossip column coverage, fan magazines, and so on—downplayed Leander's erotic ambivalences and stressed her quality as a state-sanctioned icon of the nation—the same quality that was also foregrounded in Leander's public appearances with the Nazi elite at premieres, galas, and other public functions. In Dietrich's case, by contrast, the ambiguities both of the star's sexual identity, and of her national affiliations, were actively sustained. Thus, as Peter Baxter has observed, the sexual scandals surrounding Dietrich's private life—her penchant for cross-dressing, her rumored affairs, the libel suit brought against her by von Sternberg's divorced wife Riza Royce—were "all drafted into the image that Paramount and the popular press constructed to fascinate the potential filmgoer" (33). That foregrounding of sexual and gender transgression by the Dietrich publicity machine was reinforced in Dietrich's screen roles by an increasing instability in her symbolic status as icon of a knowable national identity. In her early Hollywood years, Dietrich cultivated a screen persona to which her "Germanness" was integral. In the twelve films Dietrich made between 1930 and 1939, her origins were most explicitly referenced in four early Austro-German roles, as a Viennese prostitute in *Dishonored* (1931), a cabaret artiste in *Blonde Venus* (1932),

Desire (1936). *Filmmuseum Berlin—Marlene Dietrich Collection Berlin.*

a German peasant girl in *Song of Songs* (1933), and a Prussian princess in *The Scarlet Empress* (1934). In other films from this period, signifiers of Dietrich's German ethnicity—her accent, her visual and performance style—were harnessed to less specific representations of European identity; thus in her role as the cabaret singer Amy Jolly in *Morocco* (1930), for example, her national origins are unclear, as they are also in her part as Madeleine, the fallen woman—"Shanghai Lily"—in *Shanghai Express* (1932).

By 1935, the more diffuse Europeanness suggested by these three roles had displaced Dietrich's Germanness entirely, and she began exploring new personas culled from the length and breadth of the European continent. Beginning with her role as the seductress Concha Perez in *The Devil Is a Woman* (1935), she now became, variously, a Parisian jewel thief (*Desire*, 1936), a Russian countess (*Knight without Armour*, 1937), a French convent-school graduate (*The Garden of Allah*, 1936), an English diplomat's wife (*Angel*, 1937), and finally, the barroom queen Frenchie in *Destry Rides Again* (1939).

In the German press, the capacity of this German-yet-international star to transcend the boundaries of nation was, initially, proudly celebrated.[10] Her penchant for boundary transgression was evident not only in her screen roles, but in her actual geographical mobility; thus the gossip columns admired the ease with which she traversed cities and continents, appearing now in Los Angeles, now New York, then Paris, Cannes, London. In film reviews, Dietrich's capacity to embrace the world was underscored with metaphors of spatial expansion; thus in *The Scarlet Empress*, a "chapter of world history" was said to be used to create her role (*Film-Kurier*, "Geänderte Pläne"); in *Desire*, she becomes the "great actress" free to explore "the full range of her talents" (*Film-Kurier*, "Sehnsucht"); and in a *Film-Kurier* feature on fans and stardom, the fervor of Dietrich's fans is explained by her capacity to represent "beauty *unbounded*" (*Film-Kurier*, "Ein Wort").

Dietrich's capacity for world conquest, evident in the trope of geographical mobility that surfaced in narrative constructions of her life as a star, made her, then, an ideologically appropriate figure for German audience identification; for her image addressed precisely those desires for geographical expansion that Goebbels articulates in the quote above. More problematic, however, was the association within Dietrich's star image between her traversing of geographical boundaries, and other forms of border transgression. Dietrich hovered on the border between masculinity, femininity, and a more androgynous identity. Her husky vocal delivery suggested gender transgression, as did the men's suits she wore, perhaps most dazzlingly on-screen in *Morocco* and *Blonde Venus*, but offscreen too, where she became a fashion leader in early 1930s cross-dressing. That her status as bigender fashion icon provoked a degree of alarm in the German press is evidenced by *Film-Kurier*'s 1934 caricature of Dietrich as the emblem of a "new sex of silky-soft gentleman," or *Der Film*'s earlier denunciation of the star's trouser-clad arrival in Paris in 1933, when she was admonished to consider her "responsibility . . . to maintain discretion," and thus to do justice to her status both "as a famous star, and as a German."[11]

Dietrich's flouting of sexual codes was similarly condemned, not across the board (hence the widespread press tolerance for Dietrich's rampant eroticism in *The Scarlet Empress*), but most particularly where it was seen to clash with her status as an internationally renowned emblem of German nation. Thus *Blonde Venus*, although initially passed for German release in 1932, was finally banned by the state censors on the grounds that its "lax conception of marriage and morality offends against the efforts of our contemporary state to rebuild the family."[12] *Song of Songs*, similarly, was banned on the grounds of its misrepresentation of the German nation, and Dietrich in particular was roundly trounced as a "German actress whose preference in America is to play the roles of whores" (*Film-Kurier*, "Oberprüfstelle").

Perhaps the most prominent source of unease among German commentators, however, was the suggestion of racial mixing in Dietrich's screen persona. From *The Blue Angel* on, Dietrich's gender and sexual transgressions were brought into association in her films with an implied slippage across ethnic identities. When Emil Jannings as *Blue Angel*'s Immanuel Rath awakes for the first time in Lola Lola/Dietrich's bedroom, his initial encounter is not with Dietrich, but with the black doll that became, as her daughter Maria Riva later revealed, Dietrich's "good-luck charm" throughout her life, and a regular presence in her films (71). Traditionally, the doll is for girls and women a powerful figure of identification; thus Dietrich's capacity to put herself in the place of the black other is already suggested by the black playmate that is an apparently incidental element of mise-en-scène in *The Blue Angel*. The suggestion here of mobile ethnicity is reinforced in Dietrich's later films. In *Morocco*, Dietrich as Amy Jolly is fascinated by local women who form liaisons with Foreign Legion men, then trail them, even into battle, and remain ever attentive to their needs. Although Dietrich at first scorns such primitive subjection, she herself "goes native" in the final sequence, discarding high-heeled shoes to join the peasant women in their pursuit of soldier lovers across the desert.

In the party and pro-Nazi press, antipathy mounted after 1933 to a Dietrich perceived, at best, as un-German, at worst, as racial degenerate. Thus while the NSDAP (National Socialist German Workers Party) mouthpiece, the *Völkischer Beobachter*, in its review of *The Scarlet Empress*, could still grudgingly acknowledge Dietrich's professionalism, even while scorning her "capitulation" to von Sternberg's "monstrous" leanings toward visual excess (16–17 September 1934), the proregime *Acht Uhr Abendblatt* had moved just two years later (8 May 1936) to a thoroughgoing denunciation of the star on racial grounds. In an article on "the racial face in film," Dietrich, the newspaper thundered, "must be decisively rejected. Her facial profile and the color of her hair and eyes may perhaps exactly resemble those of the Nordic race. Her performances, as well as her behavior during the 'system era' [*Systemzeit*] and her particularly intimate intercourse with the Jews [Sternberg!] have nothing in common with the Nordic way of life. In her case, it is a matter of relative certainty that her phenotype [*Erscheinungsbild*] is deceptive; for the hybrid nature of the German population produces a situation . . . in which Nordic appearance does not in any sense always allow one to assume the same inner (*seelisch*) characteristics. Nordic appearance may be conjoined with non-Nordic soul, as non-Nordic appearance may equally be combined with Nordic soul" ("Die Meinung").

I discussed earlier the organization of Third Reich star discourse around notions of "personality" that assumed a mimetic relation between external appearance and racial type. *Acht Uhr Abendblatt*'s comments on Dietrich demonstrate clearly how her star image as constructed in her Hollywood titles was seen by the ideologues of the Nazi racial state to infringe the racial norms around which the discourse of star personality circulated.

But to read German responses to Dietrich's image in purely ideological terms would be to miss what those responses reveal of the specifically cinematic issue of Hollywood stardom and its problematic reception in

Germany. While Dietrich coverage in the party and pro-Nazi press certainly foregrounded ideological issues, the emphasis in film review sections of the regional dailies, or in the trade press, was more centrally on Dietrich's fulfillment (or otherwise) of the *aesthetic* norms of German star representation. A feature of film commentary in the review pages of the post-1933 daily press, for instance, was its emphasis on what were presented as the predominantly aesthetic issues confronting Third Reich film. The "Aryanization" of the press in 1933 had driven into exile some of the Weimar Republic's most influential film critics—Siegfried Kracauer, of course, alongside such figures as Rudolf Arnheim and E. A. Dupont. By November 1936, when the Propaganda Ministry finally prohibited film criticism *tout court* on grounds of its Jewish distortion, the film press landscape had already been irrevocably transformed when Kracauer and others ceded place to a new generation of individuals committed to what the Nazi state would henceforth dub "film commentary" (*Filmbetrachtung*).

The 1936 RMVP directive named film commentary as a journalistic mode that operated "in the spirit of National Socialism" and sustained "a proper attitude" to film art.[13] The directive's emphasis on film commentary's aesthetic project fueled an already lively debate on the relation of press film coverage to Josef Goebbels's larger project for a National Socialist film art. Stung perhaps by "scholarly" critiques of press commentary's alleged inattention to the aesthetic (one 1937 doctoral dissertation, for instance, excoriated "professional film commentators" for operating with "a concept of film art deriving from unclarified interpretations of opinions absorbed through superficial readings whose validity is automatically accepted"),[14] editors of the national and regional broadsheets wrote or commissioned numerous features on such issues as "Film Content and Audience Taste," "Does Film Need the Literary Author [*Dichter*]?" "Film and Literature—a Consideration of the Role of Film," or "The Experience of the Image."[15]

In the debates on "personality" around which film-aesthetic commentary on stars revolved, star personality was seen as best expressed through a visual style that repressed the star system's capacity for a foregrounding of artifice and masquerade. This emphasis on preserving the ideological certitudes of "personality" through a repudiation of semantic ambivalence and visual excess is clearly visible in press coverage of

Dietrich—specifically, in coverage of the three Hollywood titles featuring Dietrich that achieved release in Nazi Germany, *The Scarlet Empress* (von Sternberg, 1934), *The Devil Is a Woman* (von Sternberg, 1935), and *Desire* (Borzage, 1936). Across commentary on those three films, three recurrent tropes are visible. The first involved a repudiation of Dietrich's capacity for masquerade. Constraints on the masquerade, second, were imposed in part through the privileging in reception discourses of linear narrative over visual spectacle (particularly in coverage of *Desire*). Third and finally, Dietrich's image was managed through the rescripting of her personal life as a story of return to home and father/mother Germany: a story that returned Dietrich also to a symbolic place as an icon not of Hollywood, but of the German nation.

From Masquerade to Narrative: *The Devil Is a Woman* and *Desire*

I have suggested that Third Reich film aesthetics circulated around a romantic conception of personality as expressive of inner essence. By contrast, the Hollywood star system can be characterized as modernist in its foregrounding of the split between the star's private and public personae: a split therefore between the self and its image, identity and representation. Unsurprisingly therefore, it was in those films that emphasized Dietrich's status as image that she met with the greatest hostility from German critics. *The Devil Is a Woman* (1935) is a case in point. The film was in any case politically dubious in the Third Reich context, since its plot circulated around a Spanish republican (Cesar Romero), who wins the heart of Dietrich as the seductress, Concha Perez. *The Devil*'s modernist propensities were evident, too, in its bizarrely disjointed scripting by John Dos Passos—a figure already suspect in Germany for his leftist politics and literary experimentalism. But it was the film's visual style that attracted the greatest opprobrium. Like many of von Sternberg's films, *The Devil* was reviled for its "emptiness" and "lack of meaning." This was a film in which visual signifiers were released from their 'real' referents; thus Dietrich's image was split, fragmented, rendered unrecognizable as it became "two (kilo)meters of lipstick-laden lips on screen, amongst a sea of garlands and massed balloons." But the image was not only frac-

The Devil Is a Woman (1935). *Filmmuseum Berlin—Marlene Dietrich Collection Berlin.*

tured, released from what Linda Schulte-Sasse has termed the "illusion of wholeness" that was pivotal to Third Reich representations of "personality" as the fulcrum of star identity. Dietrich is divorced too from the "soul" that should infuse her; she is the "shadow of a costumed vamp" in a film with a "corpse-like absence of soul."[16]

Echoing Hippler's condemnation of modern acting style as masquerade, reviews of *The Devil*, then, deplore Dietrich's departure from her essence as an emblem of German identity. Coverage of *Desire*, by contrast, reveals a Dietrich still worthy of redemption. *Film-Kurier* enthuses: "No longer is Dietrich the centre of some techno-aesthetic experiment à la Sternberg. Here, she plays a role that . . . has a genuine beginning and end, a meaning and a content—a comedy role whose possibilities are recognized and exploited so convincingly that it is toward her above all that applause at the end of the film is directed."[17]

In *Desire*, then, Dietrich's image is seen as rescued from the ambivalences characteristic of the masquerade, and anchored instead in narrative development. In many ways, too, the review was accurate. Borzage (as *Film-Kurier* also notes) abandons von Sternberg's disruptive use of unmotivated star close-up in *The Devil*; similarly, Dietrich's capacity for masquerade, drawn upon in von Sternberg's films to heighten the ambiguity of her image, is both narratively motivated, and negatively valued. Dietrich in *Desire* plays a jewel thief, the success of whose mission (she steals a priceless pearl necklace) depends on her capacity for disguise. That redemption is possible only when the masquerade is relinquished is emphasized in the film's dénouement, when Dietrich dons a demure A-line skirt and workaday jacket to confess her crime to her would-be fiancé, Tom Bradley (Gary Cooper). Earlier in the film, too, the threat of the masquerade—its capacity to destabilize identity—has been deflected by its comedic treatment. In the opening sequences, Dietrich's ability to pull off her crime depends on her disguise as the wife of two men, a psychiatrist and a jeweler. A subsequent scene, in which the two confront each other, each convinced that Dietrich is the other's wife, is not only among the film's funniest; it is also noticeably lengthy—as if it took this long to defuse the threat to symbolic order represented by Dietrich's slippage across identities.

Dietrich the Prodigal Daughter

Film press responses to *The Devil* and *Desire* rehearse, then, both that denunciation of the star-image-as-mask and the desire for stars' integration into aesthetic totalities (the totality of the actorly ensemble, or of well-made narrative) that were characteristic of Third Reich star aesthetics. A third strategy in the regulation of Dietrich's star image surfaced, finally, in press treatment of the continuing uncertainty over Dietrich's future return to Germany.

Dietrich was, of course, but one of a host of film personnel who entered Hollywood in successive waves of Weimar emigration. Her contemporaries, émigrés who tried their luck in Hollywood from the late 1920s on, included such major figures as Emil Jannings; Lil Dagover, the *grande dame* of German expressionism; and Lilian Harvey, the Anglo-German actress who chirruped her way to stardom in the 1930 musical *Die Drei von der Tankstelle* (*The Three from the Filling Station*).

What distinguished Dietrich was her refusal to return. Jannings, despite winning an Academy Award for his performance in von Sternberg's *The Last Command* (1928), came back after only three years (1926–29) to renew his reputation as one of Germany's foremost actors of stage and screen. Dagover's 1932 Hollywood sojourn was still briefer, yielding only one engagement, despite her distinguished history in such films as *Das Kabinett des Dr Caligari* (*The Cabinet of Dr. Caligari*, 1919), or *Der müde Tod* (*Destiny*, 1921). Harvey's come-back was the German remake of Frank Capra's *It Happened One Night*, *Glückskinder* (*Lucky Kids*, 1936), which reestablished her as one of Germany's premiere musical comedy stars (until she fled the country for good in 1939).

The contrast with Dietrich was stark. Although a regular visitor to Europe throughout the 1930s, she never crossed the border to Germany; indeed it was not until 1944–45 that she would return, this time as an American citizen and U.S. army entertainer. Nonetheless, from 1933 on, the film press regularly speculated on Dietrich's return. Until mid-decade at least, the trade journal *Film-Kurier*, for instance, regularly (mis)reported Dietrich's supposedly imminent German visits, beginning with a confident announcement in January 1933 of Dietrich's plans for a February trip ("Paramount"). That those plans were shelved was not finally confirmed until July of the same year, in a report that noted irritably that Dietrich would shortly be visiting Cannes (and could thus, by implication, make a detour to Germany without difficulty) ("Marlenes Pläne"). By July 1934, when Dietrich was reported to have called off a planned Viennese tour, the journal's rancour was evident; thus for the first time, "Marlene" became "Frau Dietrich" in an article that noted with injured irony that "already last year, Frau Dietrich noticeably omitted to grace her German homeland and us unmodern Berliners with her presence" ("Marlene Dietrich").

The piece displays many of the narrative and stylistic features of what was at this stage still a recurrent news story of Dietrich's imminent return. Defending the star against attacks in the German popular press, *Film-Kurier* declares, "Although we never try to obscure . . . the emptiness of her performance, its . . . vapid quality, we (believe that) 'God is glad of the repentant sinner. . . .' And Marlene Dietrich is a beautiful sinner indeed" ("Marlene Dietrich"). The biblical allusion—"God is glad of the repentant sinner"—situates Dietrich as a prodigal daughter whose offenses will be forgiven, if only she comes home. In post-1933 Germany, of course, it was not primarily in Christianity that this prodigal return was ideologically located, but in Nazi myths of ethnic unity. Adolf Hitler's comment in *Mein Kampf* that "people of the same blood should be in the same *Reich*. The German people will have no right to engage in colonial policy until they shall have brought all their children together in one State" was typical of fascist nationalism in its use of a key melodramatic trope—the child's return to the mother—to articulate the racial ideology of *Heim ins Reich* (17). The image of the prodigal daughter, and the narrative of her return, were, moreover, recurrent features of contemporary German film melodrama. Detlef Sierck/Douglas Sirk's early feature *Schlußakkord* (*Final Chord*, 1936) tells the story of an émigré mother who returns to Germany seeking reunion not only with her child, but—through her romance with a prominent conductor—with German cultural tradition. That same year, one of German cinema's then rising stars, Marika Rökk, scored a hit with *Und Du, mein Schatz, fährst mit* (*Come too, my love*) the tale of an operetta-singer-turned-variety-star who abandons an American career in favor of wifely duties in her German home. The formula was perfected in the Zarah Leander vehicle and box-office blockbuster *Heimat* (1938). Based like Dietrich's *Song of Songs* on a novel by Hermann

Sudermann, *Heimat* achieves the resolution that Dietrich's narrative refused; for here, as one contemporary review put it, "Zarah Leander is . . . the great figure of homecoming, a woman who fled . . . her paternal home . . . , then endured the bitterest personal sacrifices before . . . returning to the home she has always loved and never forgotten."[18]

The contrast, both with Dietrich's films and with her biography, is stark. Rarely in her early films does narrative resolution involve homecoming. The final frame of *Morocco*, for instance, shows Dietrich disappearing across the horizon to begin life as a desert vagrant. Similarly, although the dénouement of *Shanghai Express* returns Dietrich to her British lover, there is no suggestion that they will now leave China for less exotic European climes. *Blonde Venus*, too, depicts a vagrant Dietrich: a figure certainly returned finally to her marital home, but denounced nonetheless by German censors for her "whorish" performance, and her "improbable" representation of an ultimate commitment to maternal love (*Film-Kurier*, "Oberprüfstelle").

German commentary on Dietrich defended against what was seen as her films' territorial dispersion of her image by perpetually reasserting the fantasy of her imminent journey home. The fantasy character of Dietrich commentary is most evident in its use of the conventions of film melodrama to cover the life of the star. Contemporary reportage had regular recourse to the great melodramatic motifs: desire (Germany's for Dietrich), transgression (hers, in Hollywood), guilt (Dietrich is a "beautiful sinner"), redemption (achieved by her return home). Those motifs are embedded, too, in the classical narratives of family melodrama: Dietrich is the "child"[19] who has sinned, her German audience a "loyal" public that will "forgive its favorites much; for it takes more than a single error for one who is truly loved to fall out of favor" (*Film-Kurier*, "Fussnoten").

Toward the end of the decade, hopes of Dietrich's return are fading. When the family reunion that is the desired conclusion to her story is finally revealed as unattainable, German press responses are couched in the bitter irony of an Oedipal desire that, once rebuffed, turns to sadism. Thus in December 1937, *Film-Kurier* for the first time satirizes Dietrich, in following vein: "Marlene Dietrich has announced her willingness to make a film for *Tobis* next year, provided that, along with her not inconsiderable fee, she is granted the following conditions: 1) that she receives the title of professor, 2) that no-one answers her back, 3) that her hats be exhibited in Ufa's education department" ("Knapp").

Two years after *Film-Kurier*'s embittered caricature, Dietrich took U.S. citizenship, Germany went to war, and the dream of the star's return was shelved. Yet it did not die, nor indeed did the ambivalence Dietrich elicited in German discourses of nation. In postwar West Germany, the star's wartime absence was widely and perversely interpreted as an attack on German integrity; thus like many returning émigrés, she met pervasive hostility when she visited the country for a 1960 cabaret tour. The smear campaigns that accompanied Dietrich throughout that visit were the final nail in the coffin of her relation to Germany; she returned only in death, to be buried in 1992 in her native Berlin. As Gertrud Koch has observed, moreover, even that return was fraught with difficulty: there were few prominent guests at her funeral, and a planned public ceremony was canceled in view of "vox pop . . . voices . . . that still consider Dietrich a 'traitor'" (Koch, "Exorcised" 11).

Dietrich's status as a political irritant in postwar Germany has been matched by a continuing difficulty in the cinematic assimilation of her image. Josef Vilsmaier's 2000 biopic, *Marlene*, is a case in point. In a manner uncannily akin to 1930s German press representations of the star, the film relies upon a pedestrian narrative realism that suppresses the polysemic sensuality of her image. As one reviewer put it, *Marlene* is little more than an "insipid chronicle of showcase episodes patched together with the glue of . . . embarrassing sentiment" (Karasek 246). Most extraordinarily, Vilsmaier's film, in fabricating as the object of Dietrich's "true love" a German officer involved in the resistance, revives the 1930s fantasy of Dietrich's symbolic belonging to an ethically unsullied German nation. Even after her death, then, it seems that Dietrich's star image lives on as a disruptive element in fantasies of Germany as aesthetic totality and/or integrated nation: a source of trouble that can find a place only within those traditions in German cinema that refuse (unlike Vilsmaier's film) to suppress those ambiguities that are the visual hallmark of stardom Dietrich-style.

Notes

Translations from German into English are by the author.

1. Qtd. in Albrecht 27.

2. Qtd. in Gledhill xiii. Richard Dyer's seminal study, *Stars*, similarly takes

Hollywood as its principal model, as do Helmut Korte and Stephen Lowry, who argue in their book *Der Filmstar*—a work (rightly) greatly indebted to Dyer—that Germany had a Hollywood-style star system at least through the period of Ufa's dominance (259–72). Studies of early cinema often present a less Hollywood-centric view: see, e.g., Hickethier.

3. Garncarz, "Nationally Distinctive Star System." On Third Reich stars, see Winkler-Mayerhöfer; also—specifically on contractual arrangements—Drewniak, esp. 150.

4. Garncarz, "Nationally Distinctive Star System." On stars and the discourse of film art under National Socialism, see Carter.

5. "Liquidiert Amerika seine deutschen Niederlassungen?" *Film-Kurier*, 17 June 1936. U.S. imports were yet more stringently controlled after 1939, in retaliation against alleged anti-German sentiment in numerous films, including Warner Brothers' *Confessions of a Nazi Spy*. Some U.S. films remained in distribution until well into 1940, but by 1941, the import and exhibition ban was total.

6. See Albrecht, chs. 8, 11; also Winkler-Mayerhöfer 91ff.

7. "Das Starunwesen"; "Filmkünstler."

8. Reichminister's address, 9 February 1934, qtd. in Kalbus 102.

9. *Berliner Lokalanzeiger*, 2 September 1937, qtd. in Seiler 43.

10. This and subsequent observations on press coverage of Dietrich in Germany derive from a sample of three trade journals: the exhibitors' organ *Film-Kurier*, the largest trade publication of the period, with an estimated circulation of around 8,500; *Der Film* (circulation 4,500); and *Filmtechnik* (circulation unknown). Of the numerous national and regional dailies carrying regular film supplements, four have been selected to represent a national cross-section: the *Berliner Tageblatt*, *Hamburger Nachrichten*, *Kölnische Zeitung*, and—the only national title—the mass-circulation NSDAP mouthpiece, the *Völkischer Beobachter*. Some coverage is also featured from the *Acht Uhr Abendblatt, Berlin*, which carried occasional articles on Dietrich as a prominent former Berliner. While this by no means represents an exhaustive survey of Dietrich coverage, it includes comments from many of the more prominent opinion-formers on film of the period, and thus provides a reliable snapshot of the dominant tropes and conventions of Dietrich commentary in the early years of the Nazi regime.

11. *Film-Kurier*, "Marlene Dietrich," 4 July 1934; *Der Film*, "Marlene und Renate," 3 June 1933.

12. *Oberprüfstelle* 6759 (4 July 1933), qtd. in Spieker 77.

13. The full text of the directive is available in English in Welch 168–69.

14. Karl August Götz, "Der Film als journalistisches Phänomen," dissertation, Universität Düsseldorf, 1937, qtd. in Wortig 53.

15. Hans-Walter Betz, *Berliner Tageblatt*, 24 October 1937; *National-Zeitung*, 6 April 1939; *Kölnische Zeitung*, 28 February 1937; *Rheinisch-Westfälische Zeitung*, 27 November 1937.

16. Quotations are from *Film-Kurier*, "Die spanische Tänzerin," 29 June 1935, with the exception of the quote from Schulte-Sasse, *Entertaining the Third Reich*, 13.

17. "Sehnsucht." On Dietrich and masquerade, see also Doane.

18. Felix A. Dargel, "'Heimat' im Ufa-Palast," rpt. in Albrecht 32.

19. "What have they done to you, my child?" is the pathetic question that concludes *Film-Kurier*'s review of *The Devil*.

III. "MARLENE HAS SEX BUT NO GENDER"

Filmmuseum Berlin—Marlene Dietrich Collection Berlin.

GAYLYN STUDLAR

Marlene Dietrich and the Erotics of Code-Bound Hollywood

"Whether, as has been somewhere suggested, glamour will cover over a multitude of sins remains to be seen."—JASON S. JOY to Paramount's B. P. Schulberg regarding *Blonde Venus*, 25 May 1932

"Ask Mr. Hammell to let us take a look at this picture. It looks dangerous."—JOSEPH BREEN on Paramount's request for a Production Code Certificate to rerelease *Dishonored*, 25 March 1936

ON 12 MARCH 1930, the Hollywood industry trade magazine *Variety* reported that Paramount Pictures had signed Marlene Dietrich, the German find of Josef von Sternberg, to a six-month contract, because they had assessed her as "a very original type, full of European sex appeal" ("German Girl 'Discovered'" 2). Later that month, the U.S. film industry, through its primary representative, the Motion Picture Producers and Distributors of America, published a "production code" (hereafter referred to as "the Code"), a set of formal guidelines that detailed acceptable ways for the on-screen handling of crime, religion, sex, and violence. Organization president Will H. Hays pledged that his members would abide by both the "general principles" and "particular applications" of the Code, a document coauthored by Daniel Lord, a Jesuit priest, and Martin Quigley, editor of the exhibitors' trade journal *Motion Picture Herald* (Doherty 6).

The operations of the "Hays office" were not intended to function as censorship, but as an industry self-regulation process whose purpose was to avert outside governmental action, mainly from state and local censorship boards. Troublesome moral reform groups also were increasingly vocal in their criticism of Hollywood's depictions of sex and violence, and it was believed by many that Hollywood films presented a dangerous challenge to foundational principles of American society. The Code was Hollywood's response to the expressed civic fear of the power of the cinema to corrupt—especially to corrupt sexually—and therefore, morally. In spite of hostility from some studios and elements in the Protestant religious press (who regarded the code as part of a Catholic publicity campaign), industry executives began regularly sending drafts of scripts to the MPPDA's Studio Relations Committee (SRC), initially headed by Jason S. Joy. In the beginning, abiding by the Code was largely voluntary, with Paramount being among the most cooperative of the majors—at least in submitting to the advisory process (Maltby 49–50). In late 1931, submission of scripts and final film print review became required of MPPDA members.

The virtually simultaneous moment of the institution of the Code with Marlene Dietrich's "going Hollywood" presents us with a little explored convergence. This convergence, and the effects that accrued to it, have significant implications for any assessment of Dietrich's career and of her construction as a "star." In that convergence, we find apparently divergent goals: (1) the need for Paramount Studio to build up a personality/actress whose screen persona was underscored by the presumption that her main value was in signifying sexuality of a specific type, that is, "European sex appeal," and (2) the industry-wide attempt to stave off official outside censorship by carefully controlling the presentation of sexuality (among other things) in its product.

My goal in this essay is to explore how classical Hollywood practice, as influenced by the Code, contributed to the construction of Dietrich's "erotic" screen persona in a period of moral conservatism in U.S. culture. More specifically, I am interested in how Paramount Studio's response to the Code and the latter's changing enforcement (under the Studio Relations Committee and then at the Production Code Administration under Joseph Breen) was instrumental in negotiating Dietrich's value as a sign of sexuality in her U.S. screen roles in the 1930s. I will examine the negotiation of Code self-regulation or "censorship" in Dietrich's films and consider the problems that the narrative and visual signification of eroticism in her screen persona presented to the industry in its attempt to protect the moral well-being of its audience—as well as to Paramount in its attempt to satisfy the Code while enhancing Dietrich's popularity as a star.

In this essay, I am returning to a limited number of texts, but I do not intend to suggest that some unchanging meaning resides in them or that only these texts controlled the public's perception of Dietrich's star persona in the 1930s. Stars are the product of intertextuality. Their reception by audiences is produced by a succession of textual sources as well as by extratextual ones such as advertising and publicity. Following Laura Mulvey, there is no denying that woman functions as the most important signifier of the erotic in Hollywood classical cinema (14–16), but, as Jackie Stacey reminds us, erotic meanings are cultural ones produced by historically constructed spectators (*Star Gazing* 33). Thus, any retrospective assessment of Marlene Dietrich can hardly escape reflecting on the varied knowledge that informs viewers' perception and understanding of what constitutes the pleasures attached to Dietrich's appearance in any given film or as a "star image."

American films under the threat of censorship made for a distinctive period of Hollywood cinema, one in which films bore the mark of how the industry attempted to set limits on the screen articulation of sexuality without sacrificing their products' appeal to a general, that is, broadly defined audience. As a result, it is worth returning to Dietrich's screen femininity and the question of how it came to be realized through industry self-regulation in the 1930s. We cannot ignore how important this regulatory process, in its two distinctive incarnations, was to the representation of Dietrich in her roles, and the part it played in defining and delimiting the star's appeal to movie audiences of the time.

What was this process? Between 1930 and 1934, the MPPDA's Studio Relations Committee was involved from the earliest stages of a film's conception (including the selection of the title and original story treatment), into the reading of successive drafts of the script (in all stages, from original treatment or synopsis to final script). They relied on face-to-face negotiations and discussions as well as ongoing correspondence with key studio personnel to help facilitate the release print's adherence to the Code. In the process leading to their screening of the final film, the SRC also offered the studio advice on what censorship problems the film was likely to encounter from the numerous local and state censorship boards and how trouble from these "political censors" might be avoided with judicious changes. In 1933, Will Hays initiated a major reorganization of Code enforcement.[1] Prompted by unfavorable publicity that gave the impression that the industry had been ineffective in controlling the moral content of Hollywood films (especially after former New York State censor James Wingate assumed leadership of the SRC), Hays's actions ultimately resulted in the creation of the Production Code Administration (PCA), led by Joseph Breen (Jacobs 106–10). Unlike the SRC's collegially toned advisory role, the Breen office took a more adversarial and authoritarian tone in exercising its increased power with a zealous sense of moral mission (Jacobs 114).

Sinful Girls and "The Voice of Love"

In 1930, the year preceding Dietrich's U.S. debut, the Hollywood film industry enjoyed higher box office receipts than in any previous year in its history. In the face of a worldwide economic depression, the successful conversion to talkies was largely responsible for this milestone. Talkies were also thought to contribute to a new filmic "realism," not always perceived as morally uplifting in word or deed. For example, in 1930 and into 1931, the MPPDA's Hays office found itself preoccupied with a number of controversial gangster films with brutal protagonists and graphic violence. But even while this threat to screen "cleanliness" was being dealt with, it was recognized that other types of films presented a different but equally vexing problem to the new Code.

In particular, "women's films," female-centered narratives aimed at female audiences, were implicated in the complex force field of the Code. Heroines enjoying or profiting from sex outside of marriage loomed large in what was at stake in the Code's attempted enforcement of its principles of morality. Those principles included the statement that "the sanctity of the institution of marriage and the home shall be upheld. Pictures shall not infer that low forms of sex relationship are the accepted or common thing" (Doherty 362). Code enforcers were afraid that cinema—of a certain kind—might inspire a change in women's views of their sexual subjectivity. Code coauthor Daniel Lord declared in 1931, that "morals, divorce, free love, unborn children ... 'single and double standards, the relationship of sex to religion, marriage and its effects upon the freedom of woman' no matter how delicate or clean the treatment, these subjects are fundamentally dangerous" (qtd. in Maltby 50). Often taken up in women's films, these subjects were thought to be dangerous because they undermined traditional marriage and the prevailing, gender-divided standards of sexual conduct.

While Joy blamed industry economic woes for the cycle of morally daring pictures, industry trade papers blamed women audiences as being responsible for "sex pictures." A *Variety* headline of 29 December 1931, proclaimed, "SINFUL GIRLS LEAD IN 1931." Reporter Ruth Morris suggested that top actresses were choosing their roles according to a changing public taste that now preferred "glamorous, shameful ladies. ... [Even though] not too long ago, playing an unpunished fallen heroine would have jeopardized the career of a film actress. In 1931 it became her ticket to box office supremacy" (Morris 5). Unlike Daniel Lord, Morris did not appear to worry that women audiences would follow their actress-film heroines down the road to sin; instead, she more benignly suggests that "fanettes" will react to the more "subtle influences that feminine film attendance feeds on," that is, how to wear lipstick or tie a scarf or "spout fashionable backchat" (Morris 37).

Morris's opinions reflect the widely held presumption that female stars provided women audiences with idealized images of sexual attractiveness to emulate, and women were regarded as the primary group that sustained female stars of Hollywood during the 1910s through the 1940s. In a number of genres, such as the romantic comedy, the musical, the melodrama, and its subgenre, the so-called weepie or woman's film, cinematic pleasures were assumed largely to be created for and sustained by female spectators who favored watching women stars (Stacey 110).

In Dietrich, Paramount found a foreign actress to challenge Garbo's popularity with female audiences. The two actresses were linked in the public imagination because of their looks (Northern-Euro-glamour) and their manner (aloof). The rivalry played up in U.S. fan magazines and trade papers reiterated comparisons that had already circulated in the German press (Albert 60; Bach 137). Dietrich was differentiated by her association with German cabaret culture and song performance. American publicity soon encouraged recognition of her as a star of the sound era: "The New Voice of Love!" proclaimed the New York City advertising campaign for *Morocco*.

There was another significant difference: Garbo had come to prominence on the silent Hollywood screen, one that was also pre-Code. Garbo's U.S. film career was built upon a continental-vamp tradition associated with Theda Bara. Starting with *A Fool There Was* (1915), Bara's predatory femme fatale typically used sex to acquire power and wealth and reveled in the destruction of the male (and his family). The vamp figure was sustained by myriad other actresses, home-grown and imported, including Carmel Myers, Nita Naldi, and Pola Negri. Garbo's career reflected the evolution of the type in the late 1920s, an evolution that also impacted the construction of Dietrich's screen persona.

Garbo's portrayal of Felicitas in *Flesh and the Devil* (1926) offered a portrait of destructive female sexuality aligned with the predatory Old World vamp, but the Garbo films moved toward revealing the psychology of the modern woman whose beauty made her the object of male lust. This type did retain some of the qualities of the traditional vamp, including a distinctively languorous eroticism, but she was also marked by her attempt to negotiate her way through the conflict created by old social restraints on women and the possibility of new sexual freedoms. As a consequence, Garbo's silent era heroines typically were flawed, but not always destructive. They were sometimes brought "low" by their desire, as in *The Temptress* (1926), when her character ends up as an alcoholic streetwalker.

Even if their erotic desires did not necessarily bring them happiness in the last reel, Garbo's characters were frequently treated in a way in the 1920s that suggested that the heroine's unconventional search for sexual fulfillment outside of marriage deserved sympathy. Moral judgment encoded into the film's visual system or achieved through a punitive ending did not always unequivocally condemn Garbo's protagonists; nor did it always support the male in his marriage to another, more sexually "virtuous" woman. For example, in her earliest U.S. production, *The Torrent* (1926), Garbo essayed the role of Leonora, a Spanish country girl who possesses a wonderful singing voice. The character anticipates Dietrich's Lily Czepanek in *The Song of Songs*, but resides within a more complex treatment of class relations that suggests a critique of bourgeois sexual values. In *The Torrent*, Leonora is beautiful but poor. Her admirer,

Rafael (Ricardo Cortez), is the son of landed gentry. He abandons her. She becomes a fabulously successful opera star, with many male admirers. Leonora returns to her village; expresses distain for Rafael, but continues to love him. They renew their affair. He promises to go away with her, but he reneges on his promise yet again. Many years later, a prematurely aged Rafael appears at Leonora's dressing room. He wants to go away with her. She sends him back to his wife and children because she recognizes that he is weak and bound to the dictates of his bourgeois family. Garbo's Leonora is a modern woman who freely participates in many sexual affairs, but is capable of one true love and worthy of being loved. She is ultimately more honorable than the man who claims to love her. This type of woman, most often depicted as European, was the star domain of Garbo in the late 1920s. It would also become the blueprint for many of Dietrich's roles in the 1930s.

Rather than being cast as the indifferent destroyer of men (as in *The Blue Angel*), Dietrich was most often cast in Old World melodramas of love, lust, death, and/or redemption that featured her as the aloof, but vulnerable woman disillusioned by sexual experience. In August of 1932, Ruth Biery told readers of *Photoplay* that Hollywood had "created a new woman, a different type of heroine," who was mysterious, glamorous, and possessed of a subtle combination of "both feminine and masculine characteristics"; these "shady dames," she said, were "not vamps in the strictest sense of the word since they are the heroines of the picture" (Biery 28–29). Throughout the 1930s, in both the pre-Breen years and the Breen office period, Dietrich would become expert at the "new vamp," even after the type had outrun its popularity.

In spite of offering "the new vamp," Dietrich's first U.S. production and American debut film, *Morocco* (1931), had few problems with the SRC Code enforcers. Premiering on 14 November 1931, three weeks before U.S. audiences would have an opportunity to view the actress in *The Blue Angel* (1931), *Morocco* became one of the year's biggest moneymakers. Critical reactions to the film were generally lukewarm, but many commentators praised Dietrich, including the reviewer for *Variety*, who speculated about audience reaction to the new female import in gender-specific terms: "Whether the women will like Dietrich will be answered by the women themselves. They likely will from early indications. . . . This is important, in the sense that if the tough ones like 'The Skirt' [a *Variety*

Morocco (1931). *Author's collection.*

columnist] among the women okay Miss Dietrich, what difference what she can do or does, like Garbo?" (*Variety*, "*Morocco*" 21).

Paramount advertised Dietrich in *Morocco* as "the Woman all women want to see." The film's pressbook urged exhibitors to sell the picture as both a love story and an action-adventure flick. Obviously pushed to female audiences, the plot of *Morocco* was not far removed from the "fallen woman" cycle of women's film. However, rather than trace the fall of a respectable woman into sexual degradation, as would later Dietrich films, including *Blonde Venus* (1932), *Song of Songs* (1933), and *The Scarlet Empress* (1934), *Morocco* establishes its heroine as sexually degraded from the story's outset. From the beginning, she is delineated—visually and in dialogue—as an object of sympathy as well as of curiosity.

Amy Jolly (Dietrich) travels alone to Morocco by ship. The vessel is enshrouded in fog. Amy Jolly enters the frame as a slightly shabby figure in black negotiating her way through the passengers on deck. Her gait is unsteady, not from alcohol, but perhaps fatigue. She drops her bag, and a well-dressed man retrieves the contents for her. Then he offers his services with the comment, "I'd be happy to help you." She looks at him (in close-up) then away, with an expression suggesting that she is utterly familiar with men wanting to help her—if she returns the favor in an economy of sexual exchange. "I won't need any help," she says in a monotone. La Bessiere (Adolphe Menjou) then opens his wallet to retrieve his business card, but the scene is visually presented (in full shot) as if he could be a john negotiating with a hooker. She takes the card, straightens up, thanks him (again, without looking at him), and walks away. When she reaches the boat railing, she tears his card into little pieces and contemptuously flicks it overboard. A close-up shot shows La Bessiere looking at her. He inquires of her. The captain speculates that she is "a vaudeville actress. We carry them every day. We call them suicide passengers. One-way tickets. They never return." Following La Bessiere's gaze, we see her again in medium close-up as she leans on the railing to face the sea.

Morocco insinuates through dialogue, visual composition, and performance nuance that the heroine is a sexually experienced woman of the world who is merely one step away from suicide. In this respect, the scene works in concert with the SRC's interpretation of the Code. By suggesting through indirect means that Amy Jolly is sexually experienced and by simultaneously associating that illicit (nonmarital) sexuality with unhappiness, the scene appears to adhere to Jason Joy's view that the Code did not demand the elimination of immorality on the screen. The "unconventional, the unlawful, the immoral" were dramatically necessary, said Joy, because they could show by "immediate contrast the happiness and benefits derived from wholesome, clean and law abiding conduct" (*Little Caesar*, PCA file, Joy to Wingate, 5 February 1931).[2]

After her arrival in Morocco, Amy Jolly's sexual unconventionality is illustrated in her first performance. In one of the most famous scenes in the entire Dietrich canon, she appears cross-dressed in a man's tuxedo and top hat. Gender roles are reversed as she apprises with her gaze a man in her audience—a handsome young private in the Foreign Legion, Tom Brown (Gary Cooper). After finishing a song, she kisses a woman in the audience. The Code specifically forbade homosexuality. With an absence of evidence in the PCA files as they now exist, we can only speculate that perhaps these sophisticated, wordless hints at the transgression of gender and sexual norms were tolerated because they were contextualized as being part of the heroine's "performance." Jason Joy suggests another possible reason when he argued to then New York State chief censor James Wingate that it was dangerous for censors "to stand too close to pictures . . . [for they may have] their perspective destroyed by the close observance of details to such an extent that their judgment regarding the effect of the picture as a whole is seriously impaired" (*Little Caesar*, PCA file, Joy to Wingate, 5 February 1931).

At that point in time, Jason Joy's office was primarily concerned with the "effect of the picture as a whole" in relation to the Code, but it was his job to be prescient in sensing what the public or "political" censors like Wingate—who tended to be overly concerned with "details"—would find objectionable in Hollywood product. Joy's office worried a great deal that local censor boards would react unfavorably to the depiction of Amy Jolly slipping the key to her apartment to the handsome young legionnaire during her opening performance. Referring to this scene, *Variety*'s review asked why the film had to "start out with a heroine and make a bum of her within the first 30 minutes" ("*Morocco*" 21). Many censor boards agreed with this assessment, and deleted a close-up of the key in Tom's hand (*Morocco*, PCA file, Joy to B. P. Schulberg, 2 December 1930, 16 December 1930, 20 February 1931, 30 June 1932).

In addition to working hard to get the studio to change the words to the song, "What Am I Bid for My Apples" (PCA file, Joy to Schulberg, 16 July 1930), the SRC strenuously negotiated to cut a much longer version of the key scene that they found "very suggestive" (*Morocco*, PCA file, Joy to Schulberg, 8 April 1930). The first yellow script draft depicted Amy selling copies of her songs and giving each man in her audience who purchases a song a key that might fit her apartment door. After her performance, all the men line up outside her apartment door to try their keys, but only that of Tom (called "Sam" in early drafts) unlocks the door. In typical fashion, Jason Joy addressed both the story-telling flaws as well as the moral problems inherent in the scene: "It is quite all right to indicate that Amy has known many men intimately but we believe that some other method ought to be evolved to bring Amy and Sam together other than use of the key episode.... [It] is objectionable" (*Morocco*, PCA file, Joy to Schulberg, 8 April 1930).

Paramount listened. In the final film, Tom more discreetly gains access to Amy's apartment, and no sex scene or even the implication of one follows. As repeated so often in Dietrich's films, particularly in *Shanghai Express* and *Song of Songs*, the heroine's signal of sexual availability is not supported by any subsequent action that might demand censorship action. Amy Jolly and legionnaire Tom Brown share a kiss behind a fan, and she then sends him away. Sexual attraction is conveyed in such moments through body language, the breeze of a fan against her face, shimmering soft-focus cinematography that glamorizes the stars, and the power of close-ups and exchanged gazes. As a result, this scene in *Morocco* is exemplary of the sensuality that Code-governed cinema could cultivate around stars like Dietrich—without the necessity of depicting explicit physical sexual encounters.

Amy Jolly follows Tom into the street, and they return together, only to be waylaid by street thugs. Tom is jailed. Later, Tom, like Rafael in *The Torrent*, will agree to run away with the heroine, but changes his mind. La Bessiere steps in, takes care of her, and asks her to marry him. On the night of their engagement party, she learns that Tom may be wounded. Accompanied by La Bessiere, she finds Tom at the edge of the desert with his company, which is preparing to leave. A close-up shows Tom giving Amy a playful salute. Returning Tom's salute, she hesitates, suddenly abandons her high heels in the sand and walks into the desert to join him. Grabbing a recalcitrant goat, she treks alongside a group of native women who follow their men. According to the Code, "the sympathy of the audience" was "never [to] be thrown to the side of crime, wrongdoing, evil or sin" (Doherty 361), but *Morocco* clearly throws its sympathy almost exclusively to Amy Jolly, who rejects conventional marriage and follows—without benefit of matrimony—a penniless, unfaithful legionnaire. The heroine's "shady" past and implied future certainly seem to fit reformists' descriptions of the kind of screen behaviors that were considered to be dangerous deviations from moral norms for women. Yet the ending raised no red flags for the SRC. Amy is neither punished (for her sexuality) nor saved by marriage. Instead, her walk into the desert provides a gesture that speaks to female audiences in familiar terms: in true woman's picture fashion, she is redeemed by love. Her actions reflect a self-determined female desire, self-abnegating as we might now judge it to be.

Eliminating Vice or Eliminating Dietrich?

Dietrich's screen persona as a demimondaine-prostitute, a loose or fallen woman, would become more entrenched with each of her films. She would portray a prostitute-turned-spy in her next film, *Dishonored* (1931); a doctor's fiancée turned prostitute in *Shanghai Express* (1932); a housewife turned prostitute in *Blonde Venus* (1932); a country girl who becomes an artist's model, a baroness, and then a prostitute in *Song of Songs* (1933); a prostitute-courtesan in *The Devil Is a Woman* (1935); and a prostitute transformed into a diplomat's wife in *Angel* (1937).

The opening scene of *Dishonored* succinctly establishes Dietrich as a working prostitute. An intertitle establishes the setting as Vienna in 1915. Rain water pours noisily down a gutter on a dark night. The camera focuses on shapely feminine legs beneath a short skirt trimmed in fur. A woman (Dietrich) is standing under a street lamp in the rain. She taps her foot impatiently. She rolls up a sagging stocking. She turns away from the camera. The camera moves back, and we finally see her face as she looks offscreen. With one hand on her hip, she starts walking toward the foreground. The next shot shows police and people crowding around as the body of a woman is brought out of a building on a stretcher. "They all end up that way!" someone exclaims; another remarks that this is the third

Dishonored (1931). *Author's collection.*

suicide in a year in the apartment house. Dietrich declares that she won't end that way because she's not afraid of life—or death. Her melodramatic outburst draws the interest of an older man. After the crowd disperses, he asks her if they can go somewhere together. She thinks she has a customer. He follows her up the stairs to her room.

A short history of this scene in Hays office correspondence illustrates how the textual construction of Dietrich's transgressive sexuality in *Dishonored* could pass the SRC's review, but would become too explicit in its visual meaning to meet Breen office standards of Code enforcement when Paramount requested a Production Code Certificate to rerelease the film. In the original scrutiny of the film, a nervous Will Hays asked a criminologist to report on the film (*Dishonored*, PCA file, Carleton Simon to Hays, 7 March 1931). To Joe Breen in 1936, the opening shots of *Dishonored* "definitely characterize the heroine as a prostitute," as did the heroine's final request at the end of the film, when, sentenced to death for letting an enemy spy escape, she asks to wear again "any dress I wore when I served my countrymen instead of my country" (*Dishonored*, PCA file, Breen to John Hammell, 27 April 1936).

The opening scene of *Dishonored* illustrates how the question of whether to eliminate vice from motion pictures or merely make it less readable was one of the central problems in the Code's enforcement. The SRC under Joy took the general tack that making vice less readable through "perfectly acceptable and delicately used words and inferences" was an approach that preserved the industry's creative freedom (*Little Caesar*, PCA file, Joy to James Wingate, 5 February 1931). As early as 1927, in language that he would reiterate numerous times over the years, Joy acknowledged the need for Hollywood to develop techniques of expression that would allow multiple readings of films, that is, representations "from which conclusions might be drawn by the sophisticated mind, but which would mean nothing to the unsophisticated and inexperienced" (qtd. in Maltby 40).

In her first six years in Hollywood, Dietrich was directed by top Paramount directors—von Sternberg, Rouben Mamoulian, and Ernst Lubitsch—who had mastered the techniques that allowed sexual inferences to be conveyed through elliptical dialogue, performance nuance in line delivery (including musical lyrics), and wordless elements of mise-en-scène, such as body language, lighting, and costume. This meant that Dietrich's sexuality could be displaced from the level of story and action onto other—more connotative and perhaps less obviously denotative—elements that became crucial if not primary signifiers of eroticism in classical Hollywood cinema under the Code. These presentational strategies contributed to the perception by Code enforcers, reviewers, and audiences, that her films were "sophisticated" in their presentation of erotic content. *Variety* noted in response to *A Devil Is a Woman*: "In many ways Von Sternberg's direction is singularly subtle, his picture being the type that will go over the heads of many" ("*The Devil Is a Woman*," 8 May 1935, clipping, n.p.). Sophisticated direction had the potential to aid Paramount in negotiations with the SRC, as it did in the case of *The Song of Songs*, when Jason Joy could reassure Will Hays that "the fact that Mamoulian is directing would be a further guarantee that it [the script] will be handled properly" ("*Song of Songs*," PCA file, Joy to Hays, 13 March 1933). But good taste and subtlety did not necessarily guarantee the popularity of Dietrich with audiences. By 1935, a critic for the *New York Times* remarked that von Sternberg's work was "misunderstood and disliked by nine-tenths of the normal motion picture public" ("*Devil Is a Woman*," 17).

In spite of Joy's respect for the industry's creative freedom, the advent of the Code presented particular challenges to constructing the screen persona of Dietrich as a "new vamp." A key reason was the association of the type with the "fallen woman" cycle. These films were undergoing increased scrutiny because of the Code enforcers' fears that in creating sympathy for a fallen woman "the double standard shall be seriously affected" (Joy, qtd. in Maltby 54). We know that the 1930s screen representations of femininity changed often in connection with "class A film" production trends favoring one genre or cycle of a subgenre over another. The fallen woman film and the maternal melodrama were in decline; the musical and the screwball comedy were in ascension: these trends were accompanied by the box office rise of often elegant but feisty stars of screwball comedy, such as Carole Lombard, Jean Arthur, and Irene Dunne, as well as of musical stars like Judy Garland, Jeannette McDonald, and Shirley Temple.

However successful the "smart propaganda" was in constructing Dietrich's screen persona as a rival to Garbo, this strategy quickly proved to be out of sync with popular production trends as well as with the new Code (*Variety*, "Morocco"). These changes also affected Garbo. Tino Balio has claimed that Garbo's U.S. box office draw peaked in 1932, leaving her prestige as an actress and her popularity in foreign markets as her chief claim to value at MGM (Balio 149–50). The six von Sternberg–Dietrich films are canonical to film studies, and as a result, we may be tempted to forget that these collaborations were already falling out of favor with audiences by 1932. Thus, Dietrich's box office popularity as a star was both created and made problematic within a relatively short amount of time. In 1933 Ruth Biery already was asking in a very pointed question in *Photoplay*: "Is Dietrich Through?"

While *Morocco* (1930) was a box-office success, *Dishonored*'s (1931) disappointing box office performance prompted Emanuel Cohen of Paramount's New York office to cable West Coast production chief B. P. Schulberg on 7 August 1931: "It is the cold undisputed fact all of this mystery and glamour were not sufficient to give the public complete satisfaction. It is true that *Morocco* went over but with the mystery of this personality in her first picture it had the opportunity of making a much more tremendous success than it enjoyed and establish her on a much larger scale than she enjoys even now." He added that *Dishonored* was "a fairly complete flop," and he wanted "Dietrich to get her man" in her next film, which should have "a better box office result than be solely an artistic triumph" (qtd. in Bach 146–47).

Shanghai Express would give Paramount the box office triumph that Cohen wanted, but it would do little to develop Dietrich's screen persona in any new direction, and its popular success would not be duplicated by another Dietrich vehicle until 1939. Dietrich was again a "shady dame" as "Shanghai Lily." Formerly known as "Madeline," Lily became a "coaster," defined by the film as "a woman who lives by her wits on the Chinese coast." Madeline's "fall" into sexual notoriety occurs offscreen, before the action begins, but we learn that it was the result of her being rejected by her fiancé, Dr. Harvey (Clive Brooks), when he thought (erroneously) that she was unfaithful. Lily and Harvey meet again on the train to Shanghai. Although it is not overtly stated that Lily is a prostitute, her costuming and manner, even her musical tastes, as well as the reactions of other characters, all serve to code her as sexually promiscuous. When Dr. Harvey is held hostage by a Chinese warlord, Lily prays for him through the night, and in the end, they are happily reunited, even though Lily still appears in the swaying black feathers that have marked her visually as a "bad woman" throughout the film.

How could a film be made under the Code with a prostitute as the heroine? Obviously, *Dishonored* already crossed that boundary, but the task was complicated by Cohen's demand that the heroine "get her man" in this film since such an ending would appear to reward immorality. The Code explicitly recognized that "sex and passion exist and consequently must sometimes enter into the story which deals with human beings" but "impure love" was "not be made to seem right and permissible" (Doherty 354–55). Both *Dishonored* and *Shanghai Express* demonstrate the SRC's willingness to approve of the presentation of immorality in a "moral" way, but the recognition that it was impossible for films to depend only on showing "moral, conventional and law abiding people" (*Little Caesar*, PCA file, Joy to James Wingate, January 1931). The SRC general strategy in negotiation was one of controlling rather than forbidding, softening (making "acceptable") vice and unconventionality, not exorcising them (unless judged egregious). Rather than depending on a literal reading of Code detail that took place in the Breen years, Lea Jacobs concludes that under Joy, Code enforcement was much less "systematic" (Jacobs 119). After all, Breen was a man who "annotated each of the sections of the document, interpreting ambiguous clauses and noting how they had been amplified in practice" (Jacobs 114).

In the early 1930s, Dietrich's films came to epitomize a sophisticated cinematic approach to the immoral, the unconventional, and the law-evading that could exist only under the SRC. Without a method of categorizing films to help audiences distinguish between pictures meant for different types of audiences (i.e., children and adolescents vs. mature adults), Joy established a general policy of allowing immorality in pictures as long as it was represented in a morally acceptable way—that is, through techniques that might, in fact, well "go over the heads of many." It is predictable then, that early in the process of Code negotiation over *Shanghai Express*, Lamar Trotti wrote to his boss, Jason Joy: "The fact that Lily is a prostitute, or kept woman, is pretty much stressed. By changing a few lines of dialogue, or a few words, this fact could be made acceptable, for it is of course, essential to the production" (*Shanghai Express*, PCA file, 18 September 1931). A few months latter, Trotti wrote the New York Hays office a memo regarding the rewritten script: "One feels immediately that Harvey is the only man who counts in her life, just as she is the only woman in his. . . . This is an unusually interesting piece of entertainment and the doubtful parts of the story have, in our opinion, been satisfactorily handled" (*Shanghai Express*, PCA file, 1 January 1932). Shanghai Lily is never shown having any interest in any man other than Harvey. Although there is talk of Lily's "unsavory" past, there are no problematic scenes depicting illicit sexuality, such as characterized *Dishonored*'s opening. As a result, much of the negotiations focused, not on the representation of Lily's transgressive sexuality, but on making the film's portrayal of China one that the Chinese government would not find offensive. By the end of the process, the picture was "satisfactory under the code"; however, Joy warned Paramount that he thought three lines would bring the film trouble from local censors; first and foremost among them was: "It took more than one man to change my name to Shanghai Lily" (*Shanghai Express*, PCA file, Joy to Schulberg, 21 January 1932). Paramount did not cut the line as advised. On the contrary, it would be used as a tagline in the advertising campaign for the film. Several state censor boards would object to the line, and to a few others (including one line alluding to a bordello), but these reactions did not prevent the film from becoming a huge box office hit that also garnered four Academy Award nominations.

Paramount selected story materials for Dietrich that often, as in the case of *Blonde Venus*, *Song of Songs*, and *Angel*, presented the studio, from the beginning, with difficulties in satisfying the Code that were equal if not greater than those presented by the suggestive presence of "Shanghai Lily" in *Shanghai Express*. In large part this was because these films dealt directly with the dreaded subject of the fallen woman and/or of adultery. This was certainly the case for *Blonde Venus*, in which Dietrich plays Helen Faraday, who goes from German theatrical personality to wife of a poor American scientist, to small-time songstress, to mistress of a handsome politician, to streetwalker, to Parisian nightclub sensation, and finally, back to being a wife and mother. *Blonde Venus* prompted Lamar Trotti to write to Will H. Hays: "There seems to me a very real and distressing tendency at Paramount to go for the sex-stuff on a heavy scale" (*Blonde Venus*, PCA file, 30 April 1932). Paramount executives joined the SRC in expressing unhappiness with von Sternberg's story idea of the downward trajectory of the sexually fallen woman. Yet prostitution and infidelity remained basic to the story after Schulberg compromised with a very testy von Sternberg (*Blonde Venus*, PCA, Joy to Hays, 12 May 1932).

Placing the film within the generic context of the fallen woman cycle and maternal melodrama, Lea Jacobs has astutely detailed the process of negotiation between Paramount and the Hays office regarding the film. Jacobs argues that Joy reads into the film morally acceptable motivation for Helen's actions to justify adultery that the film actually either undermines or elides (88, 104). The controversy over *Blonde Venus* with the Hays office was taken up in newspapers in September of 1932. In a long letter to Paramount's John Hammell, Joy worried that, as a result, the "censors will be looking rather more critically than usual at this production." To help Paramount in its discussions with local censor boards, Joy offered a detailed account of why the SRC thought the picture satisfactorily adhered to the Code. Primary to arguing for the film's acceptability was *the way* immorality was handled. "Never is she [the heroine] glorified"; he went on to argue that giving up a life of luxury as a kept woman to be with her husband and son "is not the act of an abandoned woman who is finding pleasure and happiness in an unconventional life. It is the action of a mother and of a good woman. . . . These, then, are the fundamental reasons, why, in our opinion, the story is not only in conformance with the Code but really a moral story" (*Blonde Venus*, PCA file, Joy to Hammell, 16 September 1932).

Jacobs argues that "*Blonde Venus* defies the strategy of Joy's reading. . . . [T]he disjuncture between movie and action is pushed to peculiar extremes. . . . Helen's 'good' intentions are made incongruous with the postures she assumes" (Jacobs 95). Joy may be wrong (in not recognizing the contradictions the film establishes in Helen's motivations), but he is also right: Helen is sexual, but contra Laura Mulvey, the woman's sexuality does not make her guilty (Mulvey 21, 23). Instead, *Blonde Venus* assigns guilt to the weak, vengeful husband and, through him, to the repressive patriarchal power that encourages women to use their bodies as their most valuable economic commodity. The SRC's reading of Helen's sexual transgressions and domestic recuperation is entirely consistent with Joy's more generally articulated stance that finding unhappiness in sexual transgression or an unconventional life can be a powerful moral lesson.

"Moral" or not, *Blonde Venus* was unpopular with audiences, and, for Paramount, this required action. Rather than risk another Dietrich–von Sternberg flop, Paramount moved Dietrich into collaboration with another of its directorial stars, Rouben Mamoulian. The selected vehicle, *Song of Songs*, was based on a famous novel and popular stage play twice filmed in the silent era (with Elsie Ferguson in 1918, and then, with Pola

Negri in 1924, as *Lily of the Dust*). Before that, it had been a controversial stage play, criticized for immorality (*Song of Songs*, PCA file, Will Hays to B. P. Schulberg, 2 November 1931). The original story once again raised the specter of the morally objectionable "sex picture": a young woman lives with an artist, is abandoned by him, and then moves from man to man in a vain attempt to find love and some spiritual peace. In response to an early treatment, Fred W. Beetson, executive vice president of the MPPDA, wrote a strong letter of warning to B. P. Schulberg: "We know we do not have to warn you of the elements of danger for the industry and yourself in another picture dealing with a kept-woman. Grave danger lies in seeming to justify or to glorify such women and their lives. . . . To show her [Lily] going from man to man, seeking love, hoping to find happiness in sexual relationships, may be said to definitely to stamp her as a harlot at heart, whatever her alleged attitude may be" (*Song of Songs*, PCA, 22 October 1931).

Paramount listened. The film script that emerged told the story of a naive country girl, Lily Czepanek (Dietrich), who becomes an artist's model and lover (as in Garbo's *Inspiration* [1931]). Wary of marriage and children, the sculptor (Brian Aherne) abandons her to his best client, Baron von Metzbach (Lionel Atwill). The baron marries her, but he is sexually repugnant, even sadistic. Lily is desperately unhappy. The artist pays a visit. Lily revenges herself on him by suggesting that she has taken her tutor as her new lover. This is a ruse, but she and the tutor are caught in a compromising situation. Scandalized, the baron forces her to flee for her life. She is reduced to prostitution. She encounters the artist and they are reconciled.

Deep into the process of negotiating with Paramount, Jason Joy (who had stepped down as head of the SRC) was brought in to consult with the MPPDA. He told Will Hays that *Song of Songs* was the MPPDA's "next big problem" after the notorious *Baby Face* (*Song of Songs*, PCA file, Joy to Hays, 20 May 1932). The problems that concerned the SRC centered primarily on the displacement of sexual action from Lily's body onto art objects. The SRC thought a full-body nude statue representing Lily too explicitly represented the artist's lust (*Song of Songs*, PCA, report of William Wright to James Wingate, 15 May 1933; Wingate to Bostford, 18 May 1933). Lily's fall into prostitution was another problem. Late in the film, Lily consorts with a middle-aged man, obviously her "john." He is extremely disappointed when she changes her mind about accompanying him back to his room. As in *Shanghai Express*, costuming, especially Lily's black-feathered gown and oversized hat, and Dietrich's suggestive facial expressions and vocal inflections during a performance of the Frederic Hollaender song "Jonny" function as shorthand to communicate her promiscuous sexual habits. No wonder that, in spite of the Code, Hollywood's film product continued to be regarded by many social reformists as too "sophisticated" and thus unsuitable for small-town audiences and children. Writing for the *London Times*, Sydney W. Carroll wittily commented on the Dietrich screen persona and the star's role in *Song of Songs*: "Marlene will appear, probably for the first time in her career, as an innocent country girl. Why should she not? It is true this actress has made the vamp queen of the pictures; it is true that every grade of scarlet womanhood has found in her ideal expression; it is true that no more glamorous, seductive, disintegrating personality ever before represented sex upon the films. Such is her range that virginity is not beyond it" (qtd. in Dickens 111).

I will return to the issue of Dietrich's "disintegrating personality," but I want to suggest that critical responses to *Song of Songs* and *Blonde Venus* give us some sense of why Dietrich's U.S.-made films in the period 1931–34 could be regarded as the *essence* of what reform groups were trying to prevent.

In 1934, the newly organized Production Code Administration under the direction of Joseph Breen would begin to enforce the Code in a manner that closed the door on the type of "shady dame" that Dietrich had portrayed so frequently. Their attitude toward two of Dietrich's earlier films is indicative of the broader changes in Code enforcement that were taking place that impacted the erotic content of Hollywood film and Dietrich's presentation. In 1937, Paramount requested a certificate to permit reissue of *Blonde Venus*, just as it had for *Song of Songs* in 1936. In both cases, the Breen office told Paramount that the studio should withdraw its request. While no written commentary on the reasons for the PCA's response to *Song of Songs* survives, the Breen office was very clear why *Blonde Venus* would be rejected out of hand. The film, Breen told Paramount's John Hammell, was "in violation of the Production Code, for the reason that it seems to attempt to justify a wife being unfaithful to her husband, and also entering a life of prostitution. This type of story in our estimation . . . is just the kind of material that has brought about our difficulties" (*Blonde Venus*, PCA file, Breen to Hammell, 8 February 1937).

Dietrich's six-film collaboration with von Sternberg would have its last gasps with *The Scarlet Empress* (1934) and *The Devil Is a Woman* (1935), both critical and financial failures. Production Code files for *The Scarlet Empress* have not survived, but those for *The Devil Is a Woman* reveal that the Breen office thought it could not do much to change the perverse erotic tone and message of this von Sternberg film. In *The Devil Is a Woman*, Dietrich was once again a prostitute in everything but name. In Will Hays's words, the film depicted "successful and progressive prostitution" (*The Devil Is a Woman*, PCA file, "EEB" memo to Breen re. Hays phone call, 16 April 1935). Breen wanted a dose of moral accountancy added to the film. To "make this picture completely acceptable," he told Paramount, "a new ending ought to be shot. . . . [S]ome drastic punishment will have to be meted out to Concha in order clearly and unmistakably to establish the fact that she cannot get off scott-free after years of despicable conduct." He suggested that the blinded Don Pasqual (Lionel Atwill) rise up from his hospital bed and choke Concha to death (*The Devil Is a Woman*, PCA file, Breen to Hammell, 19 April 1935). Paramount did not comply with the suggestion, and generally, the studio took the tack of blaming the film on the previous studio administration that had unwisely let von Sternberg direct Dietrich yet again. Von Sternberg had been fired. What more could the studio do?

The aura of imminent failure surrounding *The Devil Is a Woman* mitigated the Breen office's getting tough and demanding significant changes. In a confidential memo, Hays wrote: "I would not vote to condemn this picture and I don't see how it can possibly be changed to help in any way" (*The Devil Is a Woman*, PCA file, ca. April 1935). An attempt was made to eliminate the most explicit references to sexual exchange, but the film was passed with some confidence that it was a "bad" picture, with an even worse title, that would be seen by only a relatively few paying customers. The PCA was correct: *The Devil Is a Woman* was a critical and box office disaster.

Dietrich's star power had dimmed. David O. Selznick commented to a member of his staff in December of 1935: "I think it is a crying shame that she [Dietrich] has been dragged down as she has been . . . hurt to such a terrible extent that she is no longer even a fairly important box-office star" (Selznick, cable to Kay Brown, 27 December 1935, qtd. in Bach 212). Paramount made one last attempt to revive Dietrich's career. When Ernst Lubitsch's short tenure as head of production at Paramount ended in February 1936, he was asked to supervise the productions of Dietrich and Claudette Colbert; the careers of these two leading ladies were perceived as having taken serious downward turns (Paul 154). The result was that Dietrich was cast in a romantic comedy-drama, *Desire* (1936) in which she appeared as a high-class jewel thief reformed by the love of a Detroit auto executive (played by Gary Cooper). Box office and critical response were both positive. Lubitsch's attempt to lighten and humanize Dietrich's screen persona was a success. Writing in the *New York Times*, Frank Nugent attributed *Desire*'s success to producer Ernst Lubitsch instead of director Frank Borzage: "Ernst Lubitsch . . . has freed Marlene Dietrich from Josef von Sternberg's artistic bondage and has brought her vibrantly alive. . . . [She has been] [p]ermitted to walk, breathe, smile and shrug as a human being instead of a canvas for the Louvre" (Nugent, "*Desire*," *New York Times*, n.p., clipping, AMPAS).[3] *The New York Sun* reviewer enthused: "At last Hollywood has found what to do with Marlene Dietrich; and . . . it has done it superlatively well. Marlene Dietrich is now a comedienne, a human being as well as a great beauty" (untitled clipping, *New York Sun*, n.p., AMPAS).

Nevertheless, the issue of censorship also became a topic of discussion, for *Desire* (1936) was seen by many critics as "putting one over" on the censors. *Time* magazine remarked: "There are two possible reasons why this picture was approved by the Hays organization. The first is that its agents were not sophisticated enough to understand it. The second is that US cinema censors have suddenly become sufficiently enlightened to pass scenes showing a young couple misbehaving together when the picture which includes them has definite esthetic merit" (*Time*, "*Desire*," 47)

The PCA had few worries about *Desire* during the review process. Not one comment was made about the love scene in the film in which Cooper and Dietrich meet in a garden and declare their mutual love. It appeared to meet Code standards: the principle players were standing up, and full clothed. However, Borzage's direction emphasizes close-ups and a breathless desire. *Time* called the film's love scenes "sensationally explicit," at least "in view of the cinema's attitude toward such matters since the Legion of

Decency started to operate in 1934" (47).The fact that Cooper and Dietrich each trundle off to their own separate bed after this sexy scene is given humorous emphasis in the "morning after" scene when Dietrich's fellow thief, Carlos (John Halliday), goes to her room and sees her. He then goes to Cooper's and finds him waking up from a night of equally blissful, if lonely sleep. In typical Code-eliding style, the scenes that follow would suggest through Dietrich and Cooper's intimate physicality and dialogue (to a savvy audience) that more had occurred the previous night than the Breen office would allow to be shown.

Taking the reaction to *Desire* as encouragement, Lubitsch continued to try to lighten and expand Dietrich's persona in her next film, which he directed personally. However, as William Paul has noted, Lubitsch was returning to a brand of sophisticated comedy that had been eclipsed in public interest by the screwball comedy (Paul 116). In addition, Lubitsch was also working with material that presented enormous Code difficulties, for the Breen office took very seriously the Code directions that "adultery as a subject should be avoided. . . . It is *never* a fit subject for *comedy*" (Doherty 353). In response to a synopsis of the play on which *Angel* was based, the Breen office noted in an interoffice memo: "Messrs. Shurlock, Auster and Breen read this synopsis and unanimously agreed that the story therein suggested is definitely in violation of our Code—chiefly because it is a patent condonation [*sic*] of adultery. Part of the story is also played against the background of a Parisian brothel" (*Angel*, PCA file, 5 October 1934).

These elements would remain in the film, but in bowdlerized form. Adultery would be depicted as a dinner date, and the Parisian brothel would become, in the words of Lubitsch, an "afternoon and evening club where smart people . . . congregate to gamble, to meet interesting strangers, and to sample the Parisian diversions arranged by the Grand Duchess" (Lubitsch, qtd. in "A Handbook of General Advance Information on "Angel," in *Angel*, PCA file). Like *Desire*, *Angel* was a romantic comedy, but one that did not succeed, as *Desire* had revealed, in creating a more emotionally accessible and dramatically coherent Dietrich heroine. Dietrich plays Lady Maria Barkley, the wife of a British diplomat. Her husband, Frederick (Herbert Marshall), is so sexually neglectful of her that she flies to Paris and looks up an old friend, a Russian "Grand Duchess" who runs an establishment that the PCA and every reviewer quickly real-

Angel (1937). *Author's collection.*

ized was a bordello. Maria allows the grand duchess, her former employer, to arrange for her to meet a man. Maria spends a night (of dining and discussion) with Tony (Melvyn Douglas), who is smitten with the woman he only knows as "Angel." Later Tony happens to meet Frederick, and they become friends. At Frederick's house, Tony meets Maria, who denies she is "Angel." In the end, Maria sends Tony away and forces her husband to confront the problems in their marriage. They leave the grand duchess's establishment together.

As Paul has noted, *Angel* "garnered the most consistently negative set of reviews of any Lubitsch talkie" (Paul 133). The reviewer in the *New York Herald Tribune* wrote: "The narrative is all about upper-crust adultery and Mr. L. has dodged the censors with a shrewdly elliptical approach" (qtd. in "Roundup of Reviews," *Hollywood Reporter*, 9 November 1937). *Motion Picture Daily* was less sanguine about the results: "Sophisticated is the nice word for *Angel*. . . . In it Marlene Dietrich gives her usual interpretation of the extremely sensitive if not downright sexual, woman" (15 September 1937, n.p., clipping, AMPAS). The *Motion Picture Herald* noted: "The production bears the seal of the PCA, number 3,399 to be specific, from which has been held to violate no section of the rules and regulations other directors go by. It is highly improbable, however, that Herr Lubitsch would recommend making a special appeal to the kiddies to come and see his pictures" ("*Angel*," 25 September 1937, n.p., clipping, AMPAS). *Angel* resoundingly flopped at the box office, Paramount bought out the actress's contract, and released her. In 1938, Dietrich was declared "box-office poison" (Robertson 94).

Box office returns and critical responses to films such as *Angel* demonstrate that the erotic role assigned to Dietrich rarely met the unequivocal approval of audiences in the 1930s. As I have shown, there is substantial evidence that the downward trajectory of Dietrich's career was exacerbated by Paramount's failure to adapt the star's screen persona to emerging production trends, star types, and Code enforcement changes. Her characters were inevitably sexually mobile, promiscuous, and erotically charged. Dietrich's performance style, so admired now, also may have been implicated in her lack of success in the 1930s. As Sydney Carroll's remarks on her "disintegrating personality" in *Song of Songs* suggest, Dietrich's characters seemed to embrace many different personalities—to literally be different women—rather than one woman adjusting to different circumstances and social roles. While Dietrich's multiple masquerades play upon the trope of the sexually promiscuous woman (the mistress, the entertainer/prostitute, the vulgar streetwalker), the theatricality of Dietrich's performance creates an ironic distance from screen stereotypes of sexually transgressive women.

It is likely, then, that the very quality for which Dietrich is so greatly admired by feminists now—her performance style of "masquerade," holding femininity at a distance through a changing and ironically tinged performance of identity—contributed to the problematizing of her screen persona in the 1930s. One might also argue that the peculiar "disintegration" or multiplicity of her transforming characters meant that they lacked the cohesiveness expected of a typical Hollywood character. Dietrich's aloofness from her objectified female subjectivity and the fictional excess and liminality of her characters may have proved difficult for audiences of the 1930s to identify with or accept within the parameters of the conventional screen realism with which they were familiar. Dietrich's screen presence, articulating transgressive modes of triumphant female desire, might have become more threatening than pleasurable.

Indeed, the one thing that we can discern from the films that mark the revival of her career in 1939 is that Dietrich's roles from this later period, with the exception of that in *Flame of New Orleans* (1942), conclusively shut down this multiple-role playing. They also more carefully control when and how her "distanciation" from her femininity is articulated, motivating its appearance within scenes of stage, entertainment, or performance.

Desire and *Angel* attempted to humanize and unify Dietrich's "disintegrating personality" and redefine it generically, but it appears that only by radically altering—and Americanizing—her screen persona could Dietrich return to box office favor with U.S. audiences. This was accomplished through her earthy role as Frenchy, the dance hall hostess–prostitute in the Western comedy-drama, *Destry Rides Again* (1939). Frenchy takes a bullet for the hero (James Stewart) and dies in his arms. Dietrich's irony and distanciation are stabilized. No longer aloof or erotically mysterious, Dietrich's sexuality is made safe within the conventions of comedy and a male-centered genre. Her character's sexuality is an "open book" in this film, but, paradoxically, Dietrich is contained as never before; her erotic threat of multiple masquerades is neutralized through the familiar stereotype of the dance hall hostess. Joe Breen could put down his pencil. The erotic uncertainty of the "Blonde Venus," as Jason Joy had known and defended, was no more.

Notes

1. Most authors refer to the years 1930–34 as "pre-Code," because it was felt that only when the Production Code Administration was created was the Code "rigorously enforced" (Doherty xii). However, this labeling of the SRC years of Code enforcement sustains an inaccurate impression of how the Code was advanced and adhered to during the early 1930s. I believe it is more accurate to refer to 1930–34 as "pre-Breen," the years before 1930 as "pre-Code."

2. Documents in the Motion Pictures Producers Association of America (MPAA) Production Code Administration (PCA) files are held in the Special Collections division of the Margaret Herrick Library, Academy of Motion Picture Arts and Sciences (AMPAS), Fairbanks Study Center, Beverly Hills, Calif. Hereafter cited as PCA files.

3. Margaret Herrick Library, Academy of Motion Picture Arts and Sciences (AMPAS), Fairbanks Study Center, Beverly Hills, Calif. Hereafter cited as AMPAS.

ALICE A. KUZNIAR

"It's Not Often That I Want a Man"

Reading for a Queer Marlene

MARLENE DIETRICH HAS always been an icon for lesbian spectators, her butch look quintessentialized by her signature top hat and tails. The most famous of these "iconic" moments (White, *Uninvited* 47) is the scene from *Morocco* (1930) where Amy Jolly, the tuxedoed nightclub singer, swaggers among the tables and bends down to kiss a woman after asking for her rose. Illustrating the iconicity of this scene, Patricia White, in her book on lesbians in classical Hollywood cinema, reproduces *Morocco*'s image of Dietrich in drag under the caption "The pleasure of the cliché" (46). Other salient moments from Dietrich's life and work have captivated her lesbian fandom. Most notable was her open affair with the screenwriter and actress Mercedes de Acosta, who also bedded Greta Garbo. It was after the making of *Morocco*, Mercedes de Acosta tells us in her autobiography, that she convinced Dietrich, by then her lover, to wear slacks offscreen as well. Dietrich's other cross-dressing parts that intimate butchness are featured in *Dishonored* (1931), *Shanghai Express* (1932), *Blonde Venus* (1932), *The Scarlet Empress* (1934), and *Seven Sinners* (1940). Her sexually and gender-ambiguous role-playing began during her Berlin cabaret career, when she sang in a duet the lesbian cult song "Die beiden Freudinnen," where the girlfriend is referred to tongue-in-cheek as "mein Mann."[1] For the performance Margo Lion and Dietrich pinned a posy of violets, the lesbian flower, to their shoulders (Dietrich, *Ich bin* 75). The twenties also saw Dietrich in a relationship with the openly lesbian Berlin performer Claire Waldorff, about whose influence Curt Bois opined: "What Claire taught Marlene was *backstage*, and it made her *more* sexy and beautiful."[2] Dietrich herself is reported to have said about her same-sex affairs: "When you go to bed with a woman, it is less important. Men are a hassle" (qtd. in Spoto 265).

Both a fantasy production of lesbian fandom as well as a eulogy to it is the found-footage short by Cecilia Barriga, *Meeting of Two Queens/Encuentro entre dos reinas* (1991). It mirrors the fan's strategy to isolate the "iconic" moment by editing and compiling scenes from various Dietrich and Garbo films to make the actresses appear as star-crossed lovers. Mary Desjardins calls this process "poaching" (27) and uses it to refer not solely to the lifting of footage but also to the fan activity of singling out certain key images of Dietrich and Garbo and investing them with affect. However thrilling it is to watch *Meeting of Two Queens* for its layering of stunning images and however gratifying it is to edit out the reverse shots to men and replace them with women, Barriga's film nonetheless reminds one—as does a film like *The Celluloid Closet*—of how fleeting these "iconic" moments actually are—and what an arduous task it is to ferret them out and edit them. Ultimately, it is dissatisfying for lesbian viewers to have to rely on these few "overdetermined" and "fetishized" (White, *Univited* 53, 58) images.[3] Dreams of wish fulfillment have to override dominant, incessantly heterosexual plots. Judith Mayne summarizes: "There is a striking division between the spectacular lesbian uses to which single, isolated images may be applied and the narratives of classical Hollywood films, which seem to deaden any possibilities" ("Lesbian Looks" 103). Clearly, the lesbian fan faces disappointment and limitations when she wants to interpellate herself into Dietrich's films, a handicap that Barriga overcomes by suturing together an alternative narrative. Thus, if *Meeting of Two Queens* finds a solution to the isolated image in the creation of a narrative, one wonders what would happen if one were to examine the plot of a Dietrich film more closely for signifying queerness? Would it be possible to have an *extended* queer reading of a particular Dietrich film? Could one reread the narratives of her films exactly for the possibilities Mayne sees deadened?

Such a reading would entail investigating other patterns of gender and sexual deviance beyond the explicitly lesbian kiss from *Morocco* has to offer. To indicate cursorily how such a reading may develop: if one contextualizes the lesbian interlude from *Morocco* within the sequence to which it belongs, one notes that the gender-bending becomes even more complex. As one fan Internet site puts it, Dietrich makes Gary Cooper her "girlfriend" (www.ivnet.co.at/streif/favsc.htm).[4] Steven Bach writes: "It's not *her* gender she's bending, it's Cooper's. To prove it he puts the flower behind his ear" (133). This brief example indicates how the critic must engage in an oblique search for queerness that would invert heterosexual role-playing. Such a reading would then take into account and theorize the disavowals and contractions that Dietrich's straight performances evoke.

But how far against the grain would one have to read to counter Dietrich's casting as the femme fatal only to men? Could the attempt to locate such a queer film among Dietrich's oeuvre perhaps offer further clues as to why she is attractive not just to lesbian and bisexual women but to gay and bisexual men as well? Or why she inspires gender-switching impersonators? The scholarship that predates the work on lesbian spectatorship, namely, feminist readings of Dietrich's performances, can offer clues as to how to investigate the gender and sexual contradictions that Dietrich embodies. Judith Mayne, for instance, writes that "what [*The Blue Angel*] opens up is another space, another definition of mimicry: the playful, ironic imitation of the conventions of femininity and masculinity" (*Framed* 16). If one can see Dietrich challenging normative gender behavior, as in Mayne's feminist reading, what would it take to see her provocations as queer? When does the parodic performance of femininity veer into queerness? Does it do so automatically? In other words, is every gesture toward heterosexuality suspect of being mocked by Dietrich? Are not all these gestures tinged with exaggeration? Does her excess display of femininity, just as her ironic donning of men's suits, signify a gender dissonance that invokes camp? Moreover, could the exaggeration signify that Dietrich is attempting to pass as straight?

What definitely is gay-inflected are the dynamics of the closet in her films. Josef von Sternberg's 1932 film *Blonde Venus* exemplifies this economy insofar as it centers on moments of telling and not telling with regards to sexuality—of a split between a private and public persona—of a secretive desire that is in danger of being outed. Such diegetic references to revelation and concealment, presumably, would mirror the allegorical reading the gay, lesbian, or bisexual viewer enacts, as he or she sees the film as both the concealment and indirect revelation of a queer desire. The film, in other words, via its dynamics of the closet, guides and encourages the viewer in his/her search for a queer reading. Insofar as the closet demands split impersonations, Dietrich's own bisexuality could have inspired or facilitated her acting out such dual roles.

Concealment involves motifs of self-misrepresentation, the stage, and performance, as well as substitution, barters, and exchanges that do not go off smoothly. This trade can even lead to illicit substitutions involving the same sex, as, for instance, in Billy Wilder's 1948 film *A Foreign Affair*. The readings I propose to offer of both *Blonde Venus* and *A Foreign Affair* track such substitutions and concealments by being attentive precisely to what *is not overtly* there—for what operates "verquer," the German word for "queer" that also means "against the grain." What is unvoiced and ironically invoked in Dietrich's films is the private, illicit passion, one that, for instance, queerly transforms her emasculated male leads into "girlfriends."[5] Working in tandem with such indications of sexually deviant desires is what *is* repeatedly voiced in her films—Dietrich's feigned disinterest in heterosexuality. "Falling in love again" with men, well, she "never wanted to." What becomes crucial in reading Dietrich queerly is how often for her heterosexual attraction is faked, intimating that her actual desires lie elsewhere.

Melodramatic excesses betoken under these circumstances the closet, that is, the need to signify with affect, eye contact, and gestural silence rather than with verbal directness. In the case of Zarah Leander (the actress said to be the Nazis' substitute for the emigrated Dietrich), the pathos of not telling, of the private suffering that the closet entails, struck a chord with Zarah's fandom—both among women in the Third Reich and later among preliberation gays.[6] But with Dietrich, the not telling, especially when combined with her enigmatic flirtatious eyes, offers instead the innuendo of an unlicensed sexuality. Those inviting gazes, as we shall see, rested upon women as well as men in her films. In addition, she avidly solicited the ecstatic gaze of both male and female fans. Thus, although my search for a queer reading that would extend beyond isolated iconic moments is enabled by a response to recent lesbian scholarship on Dietrich and by the rise of queer theory in general in the 1990s, I would not want to exclude that Dietrich herself provoked erotic responses from her female fans. Although I am talking about the contemporary viewer, this viewer is encouraged by the roles—both on-screen and off—that Dietrich herself performed.

Blonde Venus

One could single out two iconic moments for the queer spectator in *Blonde Venus*. They both involve Dietrich's stage persona in the film, that is to say, the sexy, self-confident performer, rather than the devoted mother figure operative in the rest of the movie. The first moment comes when Dietrich opens her second stage act, the singing of "You Little So-and-So," with the provocative line, "It's not often that I want a man." Although the song goes on to intimate that the person she addresses is one of those rare(ly) beguiling men, interpreted iconically—that is isolatedly—the line gestures to Dietrich's bisexuality and, even, preference for women. The second instance would be Dietrich's final stage act, where she wears a white top hat and tails. The camera catches her fondling one of the scantily clad chorus girls. It is the most erotically charged, because sexually unconventional, gesture of the entire film. For the lesbian fan who hangs on such moments, it is gratifying to know that, shortly after the making of *Blonde Venus*, Dietrich started seeing Mercedes de Acosta. Mercedes was on the rebound after Greta Garbo left for Europe, and Dietrich, noticing her sadness, seduced her with shipments of flowers and the meals she cooked (see Acosta 243 and Madsen 67). But are there ways in which *Blonde Venus*, beyond these brief moments, may be seen to signify queerly?

Dietrich's first line in *Blonde Venus* is to tell a man, who later ends up marrying her, to please go away. Ned Faraday proves to be a husband that can provide neither for his wife or son, nor for his own medical costs. Because of his radium sickness that needs expensive treatment abroad, his wife Helen has to become the breadwinner. Unexpectedly, she livens up once she is allowed to return to the stage as a nightclub singer. Her heart is split between her five-year-old Johnny and her work, but definitely does not seem to lie with her stiff husband, to whom, however, she has a strong sense of conjugal duty. Thus the closing scene that brings the nuclear family back together huddled around the child's prison-like crib seems contrived to the point of parody. As cloying heteronormative

Blonde Venus (1932). *Filmmuseum Berlin—Marlene Dietrich Collection Berlin.*

pairing takes over—glued together via the child—the question of where Helen's actual desires lie remains unanswered.

In her first stage act, she appears in a gorilla costume, prompting one woman seated at the bar to ask, "Is that gorilla real"? And, as soon as she doffs the gorilla mask, she dons a huge blonde wig to sing "Hot Voodoo." These allusions to costumes and masking raise the question as to who the real Helen is. Even before her title of Blonde Venus appears on revue marquees, her agent decides to change her name to something more simple and catchy—Helen Jones. This changing of identity evokes the shifting positionality of the bisexual, and this masquerade contrasts with the first glimpse of Helen in the film as an unattached woman swimming naked and relaxed with her fellow actresses. Indeed, throughout the film, Helen's contact with other women are best characterized by an openness and sympathy, as with the black women who support her when she is being chased or with the destitute suicidal woman to whom she gives all her money at the all-women shelter. She is never jealous of her rival Taxi and provocatively asks, almost as if she were propositioning her, if she charges for the first mile. Her candor with women suggests that her relationship with them is not subject to the subterfuge that characterizes all her ties with men: thus, if this latter distantiation leads eventually to an ironizing of heterosexuality, then the same-sex relations can be said to escape such disparagement and hold the promise of a more relaxed intimacy between women.

The issue of disguise versus genuineness involves, of course, the closet. Throughout the film Helen has to guard her private life from becoming public and open, although what this private life is shifts and necessitates new disguises. Initially, she has to hide her identity as a married woman. Then she has to hide her affair with the millionaire Nick Townsend from her husband. Finally, she has to keep her identity secret as she flees from her husband who wants custody of their son. During this episode in her life, Helen tries in vain to create a personal space in the anonymity of the hotel room, and this privacy as well as entrapment are signified by shots through windows, palm branches, and shutters. Her son is instructed to let no one into their room in her absence. Even her hat frequently covers her face. These three private realms are associated successively with three men—her husband Ned, Nick, and the son Johnny.

Because the private sphere shifts, it cannot remain protected. Thus, when Helen first enters her future agent's office, the lettering on his frosted glass door—PRIVATE—is spelled in reverse once she enters the room. Ironically, once she passes through the doorway, she will no longer be able to keep her personal life separate from the public domain: it appears on the stage, on marquees, in missing persons files, and in newspaper photos. What the attempt to guard the shifting private spheres and her identity secret entails is that Helen is forced repeatedly to lead a double life. Of course, she is repeatedly outed. As in the economy of the closet, she is punished for her sexual transgression with Nick. Similarly, in the end, it is a fake seduction that leads to her giving up Johnny. She does so after she has posed as a prostitute to the man shadowing her. Although she reveals her actual identity and thereby blocks his desire and access to her bedroom (where Johnny is instead), she punishes herself for even the mimicry of sexual misconduct by turning Johnny over to his father.

The workings of the closet in this film operate in tandem with von Sternberg's having to censor sequences in which Helen was to engage in prostitution. The Studio Relations Committee did not want to shock audiences with overt references to Helen having slept with Nick for payment or having worked as a down-and-out prostitute to support her son.[7] Helen's own attempts at masquerade thus mirror the evasiveness that characterize such scenes. An unintended consequence of this censorship, however, is that Helen's image as a loyal wife and mother appears overcontrived and the ending a placating gesture to the censors. The viewer is encouraged instead to dwell on and relish the moments of sexual deviance in the film—culminating in her flashy stage performances—and to view her marriage as the result of compulsory heterosexuality. At the end, Helen, like Dietrich in her own marital arrangement with Rudolf Sieber, has to pass as the contented wife, her sham marriage serving as a front for normalcy.

Given the vicissitudes of trying to keep her emotional life private, it is the theater—in her most public persona—where Dietrich seems to be genuinely happy. Like a drag king or queen she is liberated by the stage. There is a gaiety to her revue performances that seems to suggest that for all her exotic costuming—as a gorilla or in the wigs, gowns, and finally white tuxedo—she is not burdened by a mask. She sings of unperturbed, carefree life in the song "I Couldn't Be Annoyed." In her final appearance in Paris, the impresario calls Helen Jones "as cold as the proverbial icicle," while she herself informs the Cary Grant character—equally cool in his seductive ways—that she is not in love with anyone and is happy that way. And why not, at this point, take her at her word? Bill Nichols has written that in this scene "power and control have been transferred to Helen" (*Ideology* 132), for she now has the upper hand with Nick, a superior position underscored by her phallic garb. It is not inadmissible that, in her tuxedo, fame, fortune, self-reliance, and entourage of sexy chorus girls, Helen has indeed finally found gratification, for she has escaped the bonds of heterosexuality.[8] She thus turns down Nick's marriage proposal. On the mirror of her dressing room are written the words, "He travels fastest who travels alone."

The issue here is one of authenticity, despite and even by virtue of the stage persona. In contrasting Helen's mundane role as mother and housekeeper with her first appearance on stage, Lea Jacobs writes: "The 'Hot Voodoo' number provides the return, and with a vengeance, of the image of the star, alluring, glamorous. In a sense, then, it is not Helen but Dietrich who is the Blonde Venus" (102). If Jacobs is correct, then the final number in white tuxedo can also be taken as embodying the star Dietrich—in control and overtly bisexual. What I would like to call "the authenticity effect" is thus enhanced via the accord between the narrative (where Helen achieves financial and sexual independence) and Dietrich's star image.

In contradistinction to this "real" Dietrich is the character who passes as heterosexual. Yet insofar as Dietrich underscores the very act of passing, she is able to ironize heterosexuality. In *Blonde Venus* the passing as straight in the private (as opposed to theatrical) world makes her an unhappy character. But in other incarnations her passing takes various forms of mockery. One can thus differentiate between two forms of masquerade.[9] In the first, Dietrich performs straightness in order to signify conformity and capitulation to heterosexual norms, including a gentle femininity associated with being the obedient, loving housewife. This type of masquerade approximates the one discussed by psychoanalyst Joan Rivière, who contends that an exaggerated femininity is donned in the case of an intellectual woman in order to camouflage her professional "male" qualities and thereby escape reprisals for transgressing her gender-appointed role. Feminist film theorists, such as Mary Ann Doane, refer to Rivière to illustrate how difficult it is for women to distance themselves from a defensive masquerade and to escape the male gaze, which sets the standard prompting her masquerade.[10] But, in the second kind of masquerade, Marlene Dietrich clearly distances herself from her image (on stage) and mocks heterosexuality by faking it. Lending credence to this type of masquerade, Luce Irigaray observes that, "if women are such good mimics, it is because they are not simply reabsorbed into this function" (76). Furthermore, Dietrich encourages us to queer feminist analysis (whether it be Rivière, Doane, or Irigaray), which tends to reinforce gender oppositions. Lacan unsettles the male-female binary when he writes: "in the human being, virile display itself appears as feminine" (85).[11] When Dietrich imitates virile display (as in her swagger and tuxedo), her allure resides in her gender in-betweenism (she is still "femininely" flirtatious with a "masculine" self-assurance). She problematizes the notion that behind the mask is a stable gendered identity, for she can put on masculinity just as easily as femininity and thereby manipulate both images.

In her variegated forms of passing, then, Dietrich can readily subvert heterosexual norms. Repeatedly in her films, she feigns sexual aloofness or, in its reverse correlative, she fakes sexual interest in men (as she does in *Blonde Venus* by passing as a prostitute before the law enforcement officer tracking her). In role after role Dietrich acts as if heterosexuality were a huge bore or charade and that she is searching for something else that her masquerades hide. *The Blue Angel* (1930) initiates this pattern of ironizing heterosexuality by presenting marriage as an opportunity for Lola Lola to humiliate a man under her control. *Desire* (1936) begins by Dietrich posing twice as a rich wife before two men, each of whom takes the other to be her husband. Dietrich uses this occasion not only to make a mockery of the marriage institution but also to escape with a priceless necklace. Likewise, in her favorite film, *The Devil Is a Woman* (1935), she ridicules an older man's attraction to her, repeatedly seducing this officer of the Civil Guard in order to squeeze him for money and to degrade him further. She responds to his demands: "Are you my father? *No.* Are you my husband? *No.* Are you my lover? *No.* Well, I must say, you're content with very little."

More complex still for its self-conscious acting out of heterosexuality is *Witness for the Prosecution* (1958). In this film Dietrich's performance of cold disdain for her husband (Tyrone Power) convinces his defense attorney (Charles Laughton) and the jury of her malicious cunning and thus his innocence. The surprise ending, that she knew of his guilt and that she was only masquerading in order to set him free, seems contrived, even if it is the truth, precisely because her acting was so convincing. These reversals consequently lead one to wonder if what seemed genuine to the spectator paradoxically could not contain a germ of truth. In other words, Dietrich plays the role so remarkably because the *authentic* Marlene (once again, equivalent to the star persona) *is* the icy woman in control of her performance and who, in role after role, despises marriage and a husband. In addition, her long-distance marriage to Rudolf Sieber would seem to confirm that she wished to paint marriage as a performance, done in bad faith, for a public audience-cum-jury. Thus, in the series of reversals, it is *not* the ending to *Witness for the Prosecution* that reveals the truth (as the narrative of the film would have one believe), but the truth must be seen to reside in Dietrich's performance. Ultimately, heterosexuality and, with it, the convention and contract of marriage *are* proven to be a fraud in the film: Christine Vole discovers that the role-playing between husband and wife was actually reversed. Instead of being the devoted, even besotted spouse that he pretended before his defense team, her husband was actually two-timing her with a younger woman. In the end, Dietrich stabs him or, in Laughton's words, she "executes" him for his infidelity.

The Blue Angel, of course, ends where *Blonde Venus* could have—with Dietrich continuing to sing in top hat, brilliantly icy and distant. Yet the artificiality of the ending of *Blonde Venus* nonetheless also scathingly critiques heterosexual norms: husband and wife bond simply because the woman is not allowed to provide for her child as a single mother. Lea Jacobs has noted that "the final reconciliation has a hollow and rather dissonant quality and the expectation of closure is not entirely fulfilled" (94). To repeat, what makes my reading of this ending queer and not solely feminist[12] is my emphasis on the perversity of heterosexuality for Dietrich: she treats all men, even Cary Grant, with blasé semiregard. Even if homosexuality is hardly addressed in *Blonde Venus*, the dynamics of the closet, leading to masquerades onstage and off, suggest a hidden desire, not so much unknown to Dietrich but covered up. She then intimates female homoeroticism covertly via the pants and brief flirtation with the chorus girl.

How crucial this indirectness is cannot be stressed enough. Her songs are addressed to no one in particular, so that each listener can fancy himself or herself, probably erroneously, to be the "you-little-so-and-so" of the song that begins "It's not often that I want a man." Dietrich *never* vocalizes the aim or object of her desires. Instead she cruises (I use that word deliberately with its gay connotations) with her eyes.[13] Dietrich once remarked: "You could say that my act is divided between the woman's part and the man's part. The woman's part is for men and the man's part is for women. It gives tremendous variety to the act and changes the tempo. I have to give them the Marlene they expect in the first part, but I prefer the white tie and tails myself" (qtd. in Spoto 268). Although she initially grants her audience the conventionality it expects, her own preferences lie elsewhere, a proclivity that is bound to disappoint yet also further arouse desire.

Dietrich likewise articulated how she would both meet and fuel the desires of her fandom: "Each man *or woman* should be able to find in the actress the thing he *or she* most desires and still be left with the promise that they will find something new and exciting every time they see her again [my emphasis]" (qtd. in Garber 140). Steven Bach calls this promise "sex with whatever gender one wanted to see or Marlene wanted to project—something for everyone" (74). But perhaps what Marlene offered was not so much varied and abundant as merely a *little* "something for everyone," enough so that they would come back for more. As she herself says, they are "still left with the promise." Rather than cultivate an image of sexual availability and generosity, in other words, Dietrich appears to enact sadistically the Lacanian law of desire.[14] The desire of the Other being inaccessible, her devotees must content themselves with the remnants of the Other, the *objet petit a*—the momentary gaze, the voice, the glimpse of the leg, the mother's milky face, the apparently straight or potentially bisexual Marlene. In other words, sexual obliqueness must be theorized at the core of reading Dietrich.[15]

A Foreign Affair

A Foreign Affair coincidentally also begins with the Dietrich-character telling her male love interest to go away. When he does not, she spits her toothpaste at him. From the beginning until the end, when Marlene is looking for another man with strings to pull for her, she plays the jaded but alluring woman who hooks up with guys solely for economic benefit in the rubble of postwar Berlin. Captain Johnny Pringle (John Lund) has come to her apartment bearing gifts—silk stockings and the mattress he bought by bartering away a birthday cake on the black market. By the time it is eaten, this cake has passed through several hands. It is representative for the other exchanges the film depicts and that Dietrich alludes to in her torch songs as the Lorelei nightclub singer, Erika von Schlütow. Her first song, "Black Market," speaks of this trade, and she promises "I'll show you things you can't get elsewhere," while in a later song she offers to sell "illusions, second-hand." The lyrics characterize her own sanguinity toward heterosexual love, for she knows it to be her best economic asset, but the lyrics equally apply not just to German postwar disillusionment but also to that of the American GIs, who unabashedly buy sex with a candy bar, although with a bit more exuberance. In barter, actual worth is overwritten, as the exchanged object takes on new value. Hence the cake, baked by an Iowa sweetheart to demonstrate her love, holds no sentimental value for its intended recipient, Captain Pringle. It ends up signifying how sexual attraction shifts, so that the real trade is in the women that succeed each other in Pringle's arms. But according to the unpredictability and escalation of the black market, the trade can also go the other way around: what happens if women are attracted to the other women in the exchange?

Into the scenario of illicit trade and candy bar romance walks straight-laced Republican congresswoman Phoebe Frost (Jean Arthur). Come on a mission with other senators to assess the morale of soldiers stationed in Berlin, she soon stumbles onto these forbidden dealings. In fact, fraternizing with the Fräuleins occurs in broad daylight: Miss Frost stares in voyeuristic amazement at the U.S. military lounging on park benches with the German girls, even at the baby carriage adorned with U.S. flags waving as the mother marches it proudly down the street. The zeal of Miss Frost's investigation into this illicit sexuality is motivated by a perverse thrill: she discovers women where she thought she would only be seeing men! The conceit of the film is that this prudish woman is really just a wholesome Iowa girl waiting for true love; however, her induction into sexuality occurs via Dietrich.

That Phoebe is not sexually attracted to the male body can amply be seen in the film. Initially, she behaves frostily, if professionally, to her fellow congressmen and to the military she meets. We later learn, as if a reason needed to be given for her wariness, that she was once betrayed by a southern Democratic congressman trying to woo her vote, not her hand. When she decides to pose as a German Fräulein, the two army men who pick her up thoroughly repulse her. She only feigns eagerness toward their advances. What does catch her interest far more in the bar to which they take her is the *diseuse* Erika von Schlütow. The intensity of this fascination borders on the erotic.

The intrigue of the film picks up as Phoebe doggedly pursues an investigation into Erika's personal life.[16] The irony is that she enlists as help the very officer who is fraternizing with Erika. From Johnny, Phoebe demands to know Schlütow's name and access to her file. She watches old newsreels showing her with Nazi functionaries and even Hitler himself. She then demands to go to her apartment. There she is the one to symbolically pick up the key meant for lover-boy Johnny, and indeed the film progresses to where she gains access to the apartment. Furthermore, when Johnny starts making sexual advances toward her, Phoebe cries out, "Now let's get back to that woman." What makes the intensity of her investigation particularly odd is that she is not after Schlütow but the U.S. military person covering for her and having illicit sex with her. In other words, she wants to get the guy out of the way!

Theories on lesbian spectatorship have addressed the permeability of the distinction between desire and identification. Classically, women identify with a female actress, but this interpellation excludes desire. Not so for lesbian-inflected spectatorship. The female spectator's response "I-want-to-be-that-beautiful-woman-on-the-screen" modulates into "I-want-that-beautiful-woman." This shift can be registered in Phoebe. Ostensibly, Phoebe wants to identify with Erika, in other words, to be in her place as the love interest of Captain Pringle. Hence the film traces her development into Erika: she dons a glittering evening dress traded on the black market, wears excessive lipstick, asks to be taken to the Lorelei, and even sings there. This transformation can even be seen to begin in her earlier passing as a German Fräulein with the two U.S. soldiers who accost her. The mimicry (specifically then of Erika) picks up as the film progresses. The intriguing aspect to the exchange is that it is done at the instigation of Erika: when the women first meet, the nightclub singer mocks Phoebe's asexual looks, so that the congresswoman's subsequent make-

Al Hirschfeld's caricature of *A Foreign Affair*. *© Al Hirschfeld/ Margo Feiden Galleries Ltd., New York.*

over can arguably be done to please Erika, not Johnny. In other words, Phoebe dresses as butch in her business suit until she meets the real top. If Phoebe's sexuality was previously closeted, then it is the lesbian femme that wants to come out.[17]

Erika toys with Phoebe. When Captain Pringle takes Phoebe, as she requests, to the Lorelei, Erika addresses her song "Illusions" directly to her. Erika slowly approaches the table where the couple sit and towers over it, fixing her gaze on Phoebe as she concludes her number. Her image is caught in the mirror behind Phoebe, as if to emphasize the double that Phoebe has become of her but also to demonstrate how Phoebe is entrapped by Erika, whose image now surrounds her. In a remarkable performance, Dietrich continues to focus intensely on Phoebe, who feels flattered by this unwavering gaze, seemingly oblivious to the cruel remarks Dietrich makes about her unexpected transformation. Mesmerized by Erika's attention, Phoebe looks longingly at her. Pringle, sitting between the women, appears to have been forgotten and squirms uncomfortably, perhaps because Erika, with her caustic observations, seems to question his choice in a date. He could equally be disturbed by the intensity of the gazes between the two women. Were the soundtrack to be turned down, the scene could easily be taken as the powerful expression of mutual lesbian desire—as it is, it portrays erotically charged sadomasochism.

When Pringle is called away to duty, Erika ensnares the tipsy girl further—protecting her from the police and bringing her home to her apartment, just as she does with men. (In the conclusion, a huge escort of soldiers accompanies her there.) Phoebe's following of Erika means that she is brought down to the same level: she learns directly about the degraded life for women after the war, rather than having contact solely with the American occupying forces. These, however, always maintain their economic and moral superiority over the Germans, and in the end miscegenation with the former enemy is averted when Pringle and Frost marry. Hence the return to sexual legitimacy (which signifies not only marriage as opposed to illicit affairs but also the avoidance of lesbianism) carries nationalistic overtones. But before the reestablishment of "normalcy" occurs, in Erika's apartment Phoebe sees her fantasy—what she has throughout the film been longing to espy—namely the *Urszene* of Erika with her lover. Into what figure she interpellates herself, I have maintained, is ambiguous. It seems as if she wants to be or supplant Erika as Johnny's lover, but she may also want to be in the place of Johnny in the apartment. Playing on this triangle further, one can speculate that, rather than Phoebe being the unexpected third party when Erika and Johnny rendezvous, Pringle could be the intruder who breaks up the sadomasochistic intimacy between the two women.

To repeat: the main conceit in the film of underground barter calls attention to other exchanges and substitutions. It encourages one to read the film "verquer"—to look for illicit traffic not in but between women. Marlene Dietrich's character calls into question issues of public acceptability and heterosexual normalcy. Granted, this challenge often works to fulfill male fantasies of forbidden affairs, but it also invites feminist recuperation of the femme fatale as strong, ingenious, and resourceful. It may also operate queerly, given the electrical charge that Dietrich brings to scenes with other women—whether it be in the intimacy of the backstage dressing room, in her flirtatious moves on chorus girls, or with the woman she lures to her sleeping quarters. I wanted to suggest that, although key "iconic" moments can titillate the lesbian viewer, they need to be read in terms of a larger allegory of queer sexuality in her films. Dietrich exudes intimations of an other desire, in part closeted and hidden through the very act of masquerading. Yet her sexually deviant voraciousness is also revealed through her predatory glances at women. Not so ambiguous in film after film is her ridicule of heterosexual norms.

An Addendum

The two main operations investigated here in *A Foreign Affair* and *Blonde Venus*, namely the dynamics of substitution and masquerade, pertain to the act of impersonation. Impersonation itself toys with the closet, in the costumes it draws from it, in its camouflaging of identity, as well as in the queer sexuality that the gender inversion evokes. It is no wonder that, if Dietrich is engaged in the processes of mimicry (for instance, in cross-dressing but also in the roles of exaggerated femininity, especially in her Sternbergian incarnations), she would encourage the proliferation of impersonators. With ease they mimic her mimicry.

At the Dartmouth College conference on "Marlene at 100" organized by Mary Desjardins and Gerd Gemünden, participants were treated to an evening of *Black Market Marlene: A Dietrich Cabaret* featuring the impersonator James Beaman. The performance included "Hot Voodoo" and "I Couldn't Be Annoyed" from *Blonde Venus*, "Black Market" and "The Ruins of Berlin" from *A Foreign Affair*, as well as "What Am I Bid for My Apple?" from *Morocco*. Donning not the glittering gowns that Dietrich wore on tour in the 1950s and 1960s and that would most seemingly fit transvestitic exaggeration (as one sees, for example, in the impersonations of the aging Zarah Leander), Beaman chose the more subdued black-tuxedo look from *Morocco*. Consequently, the act was that of a man playing a woman playing a man. The reversals made one question—in a manner similar to how the star image paradoxically embodies authenticity—what constituted the "real" Marlene. Did the impersonator represent Marlene more genuinely dressed as a man? Could sexual preferences also be reversed? Moreover, what was it about the singular makeup of her image that would lend itself to being imitated? The more unique and differentiated Marlene's traits were, the more these were, oddly enough, capable of being copied. Just as Dietrich's voice was marked by her foreign accent, so too were her other characteristics stamped or accented, revealed as acquired rather than natural. For instance, Beaman appropriated Marlene's gestures—the sidelong glances, the fullness of the lips in song, the rolled tongue, the flick of the top hat back and then forward.[18] Corroborating Lutz Koepnick's study (in this volume) of Marlene's postmodern face, Beaman demonstrated how her image was a controlled pastiche.

But not only was the physical appearance presented as a pose, sexual attraction was too. As the faux Marlene sauntered through the audience flirting with men, the gay dimension was evident and lent a queer thrill to the performance, especially when Beaman pulled a student to the stage for the song "The Man's in the Navy" (from *Seven Sinners*), crowning the boy with a sailor's cap. Gender discrepancy (via Beaman's cross-dressing) worked here in tandem with sexual deviance. The reenactment of the lesbian interlude from *Morocco* was less convincing (for one could not imagine away the man behind the impersonation), but neither did the coquetry come off as heterosexual. The gender twists were too complicated to be read straight: a man playing a woman dressed as a man trifling with another woman. The act that was most fascinating, however, involved the use of a doll dressed in the "Hot Voodoo" costume from *Blonde Venus*. While singing, Beaman manipulated the smallish doll to mimic Dietrich's poses, complete with the strutting, stiff legs, and hands on hips. Here was Dietrich revealed truly as composite, reduced to the movements of a puppet.

The male-to-female mimicry revealed the queer tensions latent at the core of Dietrich's persona. Part of the composite of Dietrich's sexuality is a valency directed toward the same-sex, a playing up to the desire in women (just as Beaman brought out the flirtation with other men). Obliqueness electrifies Dietrich's seduction. At the same time, Beaman's careful examination and dissection of his model exposed her own straight flirtatiousness as studied, as if she herself were impersonating the femme fatale.[19] Beaman's imitation corroborates the findings of this present investigation, namely that the Dietrich persona fashions a masquerade that feigns heterosexual attraction and consciously passes as heteronormative. Once implanted on the imitator, Dietrich's gestures, far from natural, demonstrated themselves to be queer instead. Thus when Beaman/Dietrich pass as straight, they do so with a distance to that performance that invites one to read behind the mask for a different kind of passion. There is no need for this passion to dare not speak its name, for the performance says it all.

Notes

1. The song goes: "Ja mein Mann ist ein Mann! / So ein Mann, wie mein Mann! / Wie der Mann von der Frau" (the German plays upon "Mann" signi-

fying both husband and man, which an English translation cannot catch: "Yes, my man is a man! Such a man, like my husband! Like the husband of a wife").

2. Qtd. in Bach (74), who goes on to say: "Marlene confirmed the lesbian initiation in those stories she told on herself to shock Billy Wilder's dinner guests in Hollywood. Claire Waldorff had taught her about a kind of love that not only dared speak its name in Berlin of the twenties, but actually *sang* it" (74). Bach also notes the schoolgirl Marlene's passionate crush first on her French teacher and then on the German actress Henny Porten" (22–23).

3. Studlar also speaks of the fetishistic pleasures, the frozen quality and suspense of the spectacles in Sternberg's films—but in terms of masochism and its infantile fixation. White, Mayne, and Desjardins have skirted the problem of whether lesbian fans of Dietrich would want to identify with this psychoanalytic casting of their spectatorship. Studlar does contemplate the subversiveness of the nonnormative, nonheterosexual pleasure of the masochistic viewer, but does not develop her mention of this spectator being lesbian (*In the Realm* 48).

4. This emasculation is even more true in *Desire* (1936), where Dietrich always has the cool upper hand, whereas Gary Cooper is repeatedly shown as endearingly fumbling and incredulous.

5. Madsen writes: "She would dismiss most of the actors who starred in her films as having 'a peanut where other humans have a brain' " (71).

6. On Zarah Leander's female reception during the Third Reich, see Ascheid. On her later gay reception, see Kuzniar.

7. For instance, she is charged with vagrancy rather than prostitution. For more information on censorship in *Blonde Venus*, see Jacobs.

8. Andrea Weiss links her unnatural, transgressive gender roles with the act of cross-dressing in the white-tuxedo scene: "Because she has been portrayed as an unfit mother, and is now without husband or child, her status as an unnatural woman is confirmed by her cross-dressing" (*Vampires* 292). Weiss also argues that her independence would be appealing to lesbian viewers.

9. There is a third form of masquerade: in the act "Hot Voodoo," where dark-skinned is signified as sexually exotic, Dietrich's sexual mobility is signified as performing "blackness." As a gorilla she is led in on a chain (suggesting slavery and the necessity to tame her wildness) surrounded by dancing chorus girls with white legs and blackface. She is framed by shots to black men who are not permitted to look at her with sexual interest but who instead serve (as bartender) and entertain (as orchestra conductor) the white male audience. Helen goes native as the hot-blooded African queen: "Hot Voodoo—black as mud / Hot Voodoo—in my blood." Lea Jacobs observes that Marlene is "at the center of a symbolic constellation which links female sexuality, animals, and blacks" (100). Despite her association with blackness, animality, and even can-

nibalism ("I want to start dancing in cannibal style"), Helen is set apart racially via her blondeness, marked by her gigantic wig and, of course, her *nom de théâtre*. Mary Ann Doane thus convincingly argues that blackness functions "as an erotic accessory to whiteness" ("Dark Continents: Epistemologies of Racial and Sexual Difference in Psychoanalysis and the Cinema," *Femmes Fatales* 215). See also the response by Patrice Petro (*Aftershocks*). The difference between Helen's racial and sexual masquerade is that the racial performance is not stigmatized and punished in the narrative the way her sexual role playing is, probably because "blackness" is not taken seriously.

10. See Doane's essays "Film and the Masquerade: Theorizing the Female Spectator" and "Masquerade Reconsidered: Further Thoughts on the Female Spectator" in *Femmes Fatales*.

11. Contrast with Doane, who claims that Lacan reifies femininity by reducing it to a mask, "sustained by its accoutrements, decorative veils, and inessential gestures" ("Masquerade Reconsidered" in *Femmes Fatales* 34).

12. For feminist readings see Kaplan, *Women and Film* 49–59; Nichols, *Ideology*; and Robin Wood, "Venus."

13. Cf. Studlar on this active looking (*In the Realm* 48).

14. This sadism corresponds to the "masochistic play of pursuit and disappointment" (*In the Realm* 35) that Studlar finds in von Sternberg's films.

15. My reading of obliqueness is thus consonant and supportive of Studlar's assessment of the masochist's pleasure in masquerade, performance, excess, interruption, and delayed gratification.

16. The plot of *A Foreign Affair* bears resemblance to Hitchcock's *Stage Fright* (1949), where a plain-looking woman (Jane Wyman) displays an obsession with Dietrich in the role of a mysterious criminal actress. Wyman's character Doris, posing as a maid, gains access to her home and backstage dressing room, where all the revelations occur. Dietrich keeps asking for her maid and voices how much she likes her. In the end, Dietrich, previously the icy mistress, generously offers, in a gesture of friendship and solidarity, to give her a lift home. It is at this point that Doris betrays her. The film thus shows Dietrich warming to the dykish woman tracking her (her earlier maid, Nellie Goode [Kay Walsh], looked decidedly mannish).

17. Jean Arthur was purported to be lesbian (see Spoto 105 and Mann xxi–xxii).

18. Bach writes about this gesture from *Morocco*: "To demonstrate her nonchalance she flicks her top hat back with a finger, then flips it forward in an ironic gesture of self-coronation" (133).

19. Joseph Garncarz's essay to this volume suggests that her model was Garbo.

MARK WILLIAMS

Get/Away

Structure and Desire in *Rancho Notorious*

Rancho Notorious, the 1952 "psychological Western" starring Marlene Dietrich and directed by Fritz Lang, has received at best mixed reviews in the popular and academic scholarship on Dietrich. Among her biographers, for example, there is near consensus that, especially as Dietrich's last star vehicle, *Rancho Notorious* may represent the single least interesting role and film in the star's career. For Alexander Walker, it is "only an echo of *Destry Rides Again*" (115). Maria Riva, Dietrich's daughter, calls it "lackluster" (623). Donald Spoto calls it a "disastrous" film, not only because of its poor box office returns but also for its lack of aesthetic appeal, referring to the film as tedious, disappointing, and "monumentally ungripping" (233–34). Steven Bach is less tersely dismissive, noting that the film began a cycle of Westerns starring major female stars, but also characterizing the film as a failed sequel to *Destry*. He especially emphasizes the film's evident "cheapness" of production, and labels Lotte Eisner's defense of the film's look as "auteurist nonsense" (353–58). David Shipman, in contrast, opines that Dietrich's "last good part was out West again as a saloon singer in Fritz Lang's masterly *Rancho Notorious* ([19]52)" (172).

It is not my intention to argue for or against these evaluations—to attempt to resurrect the reputation of a maligned masterpiece, for example.[1] But I do feel that *Rancho Notorious* deserves further critical attention, especially regarding what might be termed its configuration of Dietrich. To put a best-case spin on the evaluations noted above, I think they

Marlene Dietrich and Fritz Lang as friends in the 1930s. *Filmmuseum Berlin—Marlene Dietrich Collection Berlin.*

quite rightly suggest that *Rancho Notorious* is not a classically "successful" film. What I hope to suggest is an alternative context or set of contexts by which to consider this nonclassical status.[2] Marlene Dietrich and her films have attracted an extraordinary range of critical approaches and emphases, as many or more than perhaps any other star or filmmaker. My intention is to respect the complexity of this previous work and also to gesture toward broader historical understandings of *Rancho Notorious*, specifically regarding the relationships between Dietrich and key tropes of representation in classical Hollywood.

To that end, I will discuss the film via a different Dietrich-centric focus than is being used for many of the other essays in this anthology. In the service of working toward a concertedly trans-methodological approach—a traversal of the methods of star studies, auteur studies, genre studies, and feminist close-textual analysis—I want to consider *Rancho Notorious* as the pivot text or axis that anchors a constellation of linked texts: a trilogy of distinct but related film triads. These triads are: first, three Westerns that star Dietrich (*Destry Rides Again* [1939], *The Spoilers*

[1942], and *Rancho Notorious*); second, three Westerns directed by Lang (*The Return of Frank James* [1940], *Western Union* [1941], and *Rancho Notorious*); and third, three 1950s supra-Westerns that star major Hollywood actresses in independent productions (*Rancho Notorious*, *Johnny Guitar* [1954], and *Forty Guns* [1957]). To render a full discussion of all these films is of course beyond what can be achieved in an essay of this length, so I apologize in advance for what may seem at times a truncated consideration of each text. Consider this then as a working paper, gesturing toward the kind of detailed analysis that its methods and designs suggest and imply.

Supra-Westerns

The first triad of films to be considered is in many ways foundational to the contextualizations that my analysis is calling for and working to realize. The term "supra-Western" is coined here in reference to André Bazin's concept of the "super-Western," which he introduced to describe a set of postclassical films of the 1950s that evidenced an anxious self-consciousness about the genre and its conventions (e.g., *Shane*). What I hope to suggest by the term "supra-Western" is a different take on postclassical genre aesthetics of the period, involving new subject matter and aesthetic pressures (especially for these texts via the casting of major female stars) that stretch and make apparent generic boundaries that otherwise might seem impermeable. This distinction is best understood via a careful parsing of the generic delineations undertaken by Bazin.

For Bazin, the emergence of the "super-Western" suggested a discomfort within Hollywood regarding the production of mere genre films, or in any case mere Westerns, since super-Westerns appear to seek justification for themselves by providing supplements from outside the genre. These practices were intended to "enrich" the intellectual profile, erotic appeal, or social significance of the (Western) film in question, and for Bazin represented decadence within the genre. This trend had been met, however, by the rise of more laudable "modern" Westerns, characterized in part by significantly modest budgets, and hence closer to what Bazin calls the "commercial nucleus" of the genre (e.g., *The Gunfighter* and *Rio Grande*).

Bazin's dichotomy between super- and modern Westerns should not be understood to suggest a simplistic class-based "authenticity" for the modern films, by which their smaller budget is presumed to ensure traditional generic boundaries, afford an aesthetic prophylactic to innovation, and so on. (This would contradict much of the critical interest in low-budget and B-films, which seeks out precisely the ways in which this level of production afforded not only creative latitude born of necessity but also aesthetic tendencies typically contentious to classical tropes of "realism.") On the contrary, Bazin argues that the budgetary constraints of increasingly independent production in the 1950s created a new zone of production, somewhere between literal B-levels and the level of highly expensive spectaculars that major studios were embracing, the latter of which in part led to "super-Westerns." The low-to-mid-range level of production had afforded the development of the "modern" Western, involving both veteran directors of the genre and newly emergent directors (e.g., Anthony Mann) who, rather than demonstrating shame for the Western, wrought a newly "novelistic" mode of the genre.

Central to this novelistic mode is what Bazin calls a capacity for " 'feeling,' 'sensibility,' 'lyricism.' " It is in the context of these qualities that he discusses *Johnny Guitar*, a film that demonstrates for Bazin both a lack of naïveté about the genre and a resistance to the preciousness and cynicism he ascribes to the super-Western. Director Nicholas Ray has fun with the genre but is not condescending to his film: "We have proof," Bazin writes, "that it is still possible to be sincere." For Bazin, Ray is able to comment on the limits of the Western in ways that are more subtle and personal than the genre's mythology would appear to allow, and, at least as significant, contributes to "the undying fame of Joan Crawford." Bazin, it should be noted, had not yet seen *Rancho Notorious* when he wrote this essay, but he was aware of the film and anticipated that it would also evidence much of the more novelistic aesthetic he defined as central to the modern Western.

Bazin's discussion contributes significantly to a historicized understanding of these films, and introduces important themes regarding their relationship to issues of gender and genre. But there is also a key disjuncture between the paradigm that Bazin was forming in his reading for novelistic tendencies, and the readings of audiences today, who I think typically privilege as outrageous the vast aesthetic discrepancy between a film like *Johnny Guitar* (or *Rancho Notorious* or *Forty Guns*) and a "mature" Western like *Rio Grande*, despite the latter film's marked attention to issues of female subjectivity. Today these star vehicle films, which I refer to as supra-Westerns, are routinely considered in relation to a camp aesthetic (which may interfere with the consideration that they are ultimately "sincere," though I agree with Bazin that they are). The extraordinary and unprecedented textual dynamics that these films display, apparently as the direct result of casting strong female stars of the classical Hollywood era as leads (but also the initiatives of their auteur directors) make them self-conscious about the genre at another level entirely than other "mature" Westerns.

Via techniques such as extreme contrasts of color in set design and costume, evident play in editing constructions, and use of point of view and narrative tropes that alternately precipitate and expand classical storytelling, these films approximate the kind of aesthetic refiguration that has been identified in certain Hollywood melodramas of the same period.[3] Something about the gendered mythology of the Western had to give, and the results cut a path through most every expressive dimension of the medium. But as with melodrama, these aesthetic pressures and fissures did not serve to dismantle or make interchangeable generic distinctions. Certainly these films can be seen to have had a concerted effect on the history of the Western, despite their paltry box office performances at the time. I would argue that our notion of the very iconography of the genre has shifted since the 1950s to include not only the grandeur of the Monument Valley and vast plains covered with bison, and so on, but also indelible images from the supra-Westerns: Vienna's black gunslinger outfit in *Johnny Guitar*; her stunning white dress as she plays the piano before a vivid red backdrop; the thundering architectonics of Jessica Drummond's initial appearance in *Forty Guns*, as the eponymous gunmen precede her on horseback, configured across the landscape like the whip she is famous for carrying. But this iconographic spectacle is accompanied by if not precisely contained by another spatial register consistent to all three films. The "other space" configured as significant to the identity of each of the female protagonists in these films is rendered as a site for refuge and power, a space that is both distant and mysterious. If at some level these spaces render an "explanation" of where these formidable women may have been dwelling, roughly absent from the genre all these years, they also match well the romantic, adventurous underpinnings and iconography of the genre.

Rancho Notorious, then, should be understood within this context of intervention and innovation—Truffaut's terms to describe *Johnny Guitar* were "hallucinatory" and "delerious"[4]—a kind of experimental film, rather than, for example, merely a failed sequel to *Destry*. It is important to stress that the supra-Westerns are not unproblematic in their depictions and negotiations of gender and sexual difference. Indeed, *Johnny Guitar*, which has received the lion's share of critical attention among these films,[5] is often found at the center of ongoing feminist debates about the genre, especially regarding the depiction of Emma Small (Mercedes McCambridge), Vienna's rather literal "arch"-rival who is killed by Vienna in a climactic shoot-out. Emma's apparent hysteria, both political and emotional, has been criticized in relation to both her coding as a lesbian and her plot function as Ray's surrogate figure for McCarthyism. In *Forty Guns*, Drummond/Stanwyck's ultimate pliancy in being shot by her lawman romantic interest at the conclusion to the climactic duel can be seen to render her previous strength and self-sufficiency as a charade, sufficient to the moment when she can instead be mastered and wounded. (The first script draft called for her to be shot and killed, which the studio would not allow.) For seasoned readers of Hollywood gender politics, the delirious quality of these figurations can readily qualify the attempts at gendered recuperation evident in the resolutions of these films. But the ultimate demise of such strong women characters is certainly significant to considering the ideological tensions that these films both represent and are conditioned by.

Lang and the Western

The capacity for experimentation and nonclassical aesthetics evidenced in the supra-Westerns can be readily positioned as complementary to the aesthetic dynamics of Fritz Lang's Westerns. *The Return of Frank James* and *Western Union* both demonstrate brands of reflexivity and deconstruction that are atypical to the genre. As Lotte Eisner suggests, these films indicate a progression of such tendencies that might be said to culminate in *Rancho Notorious* (Eisner 208, 301).

The Return of Frank James was Lang's entree to the genre, a revenge narrative sequel to 20th Century Fox's very successful *Jesse James*, directed by Henry King the year before. The contrast between these two films identifies significant tropes of Lang's reflexive address toward the genre. The Lang film, his first in color, is literally darker, to the point of brooding. At times the image is so chiaroscuro as to be nearly illegible, such that one can only imagine the discussions between Lang and the Technicolor advisors. More significant, the film indicates a marked tendency for what Gerd Gemünden refers to as "staged authenticity," a key trope of exile cinema: it regularly introduces and foregrounds a notion of the "performance" of its historical depictions. During his pursuit of the Ford brothers, who were responsible for his brother's murder, Frank James attends a stage play depicting Jesse's death, which stars the Fords themselves in falsely heroic roles.[6] Later in the film, Frank's trial and also his subsequent showdown with the Fords are rendered as events attended by "audiences" of townspeople, who are appropriately boisterous or passive as the drama demands. Bob Ford makes a dramatic late entrance to court, indicating to Frank that he is now attending Frank's public piece of theater.

More thorough in its self-conscious aesthetics is *Western Union*. Though not quite Brechtian, it nevertheless succeeds in structurally troubling the genre, to produce a disquieting aftertaste. It is not surprising that Lang would be intrigued by the subject matter: a story about one of the founding technologies of modernity—the telegraph—and its introduction to the West.[7] But if the premise might indicate a classic generic tension between machine and nature, the film's unconventional three-strand narrative can be seen to produce a deconstructive pulling at the seams of the genre.

Central to the narrative is a romantic triangle of classical Western "types": Vance Shaw, a scout for the telegraph company, and Richard Blake, a newly arrived surveyor from back east, vie for the affections of Sue, the sister of their boss, Ed Creighton, who is Western Union chief engineer. Sue works in the "modern" media as a telegraph operator, and so serves as the Western genre's version of the New Woman. (This is also true in the case of *The Return of Frank James*: the female romantic interest is striving to achieve her goal of working as a newspaper journalist.)

Other conventions of the genre are played in explicitly disturbing counterpoint to one another, especially regarding a series of scenes that depict Native Americans. (Lang, it has been noted, had a long-standing interest in the American West, and in fact was reportedly given the job to direct *The Return of Frank James* based on his broad knowledge of Native Americans.)[8] The conventional cinematic dyad of "respect" and murderous animosity toward the First Nations is displayed as if in a self-reflexive series.

For example, while Vern, the scout, can converse with the Indians, and works as their mediator, Richard is plainly blood-thirsty about Indians, and is seen to deceitfully kill one native. Later, in concert with Creighton, their boss, the men act as representatives of the company by cruelly inflicting an electronic surge on a number of Native American men, in order to demonstrate the power of the "singing wire." It is a genuinely painful scene to watch, which gravely undermines the homosocial camaraderie it soon produces among the company men: it is revealed that each of them was "comically" prepared to gun down the natives had their technoplay misfired. More deliberately reflexive is the subsequent revelation of a ruse within the diegesis: the dread of Indian violence (central to many Westerns, and to the white characters in this film) has been parlayed by Anglo raiders, who terrorize the telegraph company for commercial gain while dressed in redface. They attack the company's camps, and then sell the company's own horses back to them.

The third strand of the narrative is soon revealed: Vern, the scout, is himself a former outlaw, and also the estranged brother of Jack, the leader of the faux-Indian raiders, who asks Vern to join up with the outlaws. The depiction of Jack is significant, in that he prides himself without compunction on his ability to exploit the sentiments of long-term conflicts, in order to actualize profits from both sides (e.g., he toasts the Confederacy and the Civil War as providing such an opportunity). As the literal source of the Indian masquerade in the film, which incites fear about First Nation peoples and then profits from these fears, he is something like a surrogate for the Hollywood film industry itself, especially as regards the very genre of this film.

In the climax to the film, following the tenets of the Production Code, those who have been seen to be linked to outlawry meet their demise: both Vern and his brother, Jack, are killed in a shoot-out. But this resolution therefore determines that the casually and brutally racist easterner, Richard, will be unencumbered in his designs to merge with both a founding industry of modernity and the New Woman it has escorted west. This represents a curiously unsettling Western Union.

The spirit of deconstruction evident in these two Westerns is also present in *Rancho Notorious*, but the dramatic and thematic core is shifted toward what Bazin called "feeling and sensibility." In order to better apprehend the dynamics of the experimental status of *Rancho Notorious*, it is useful to survey the other, non-supra-Westerns in which Dietrich appeared.

The Unwritten Law: Freedom and Desire

Bazin's observation about the emergent significance of "feeling and sensibility" in the mature Western warrants further attention, especially in its relationship to more contemporary feminist considerations of the codes and strictures of the Western genre. Pam Cook has delineated the standard stereotypes of women in the genre (mother, schoolteacher, prostitute, saloon girl, Indian squaw, etc.), emphasizing the contradictory role that "woman" serves in the genre: she can be peripheral or more central, but the woman in Westerns is typically rendered as part of a master binary that will be configured to ultimately reestablish sexual boundaries. She assumes a role that is domestic, maternal, or otherwise supplemental and complementary to the protagonist male, as he negotiates his adventurousness. There are of course inherent tensions, ambivalences, and contradictions to these dynamics and functions, which contribute to the capacity for complexity in the genre.

Perhaps more important to the analysis of the Dietrich Westerns is the relation between Bazin's observations and Laura Mulvey's essay "Afterthoughts on 'Visual Pleasure and the Narrative Cinema' inspired by *Duel in the Sun*." Mulvey investigates issues of gendered subjectivity and point of view regarding women as both spectators and as characters within films. The standard masculinist narrative delineates the success of the hero according to the eventual resolution or achievement of success regarding twin narrative threads: vocation and marriage. In the case of the Western, even these threads can be split, such that narrative resolution is conditioned by a tension between "marriage" or social integration, and its complimentary opposite "not marriage," such as when the hero gains in stature by remaining alone.

The difference between these resolutions represents for Mulvey a difference in how these narratives position women in relation to regressive male subjectivity. This brand or aspect of subjectivity is posited as a staple of the Western genre, which is saturated in the latter resolution ("not marriage") via phallocentrism related to narcissism: "resistance to social demands and responsibilities, above all those of marriage and the family, the sphere represented by women." (Such a narrative emphasis is most germane in the present analysis to *The Spoilers*, as will be discussed below.)

But the focus of Mulvey's essay is female subjectivity. She addresses the pleasures that can exist for the woman spectator via ambivalent and oscillating positions of identification regarding a film's (male) hero, particularly the typical active or masculine hero, and especially in relation to this character's access to qualities of freedom, mobility, and control within the diegesis. For women, Mulvey suggests, such trans-sex identification, especially regarding textual configurations of desire wrought within patriarchal culture, is "a *habit* that very easily becomes *second Nature*" (Mulvey, "Afterthoughts" 33). These dynamics of identification allow the woman spectator to "rediscover that lost aspect of her sexual identity," though this position is itself restless and unstable, also subject to oscillation and mutability.

In the second half of her essay, Mulvey considers the ramifications for spectatorship when the text itself introduces a woman as central to the story, especially in the case of the Western genre (34–37). One key result is a shift in emphasis toward "interiority," away from the landscape of action and so toward what she refers to as a more melodramatic register. But it also reopens the text toward the erotic, making sexuality potentially overt, not sublimated, and less containable by the generic convention of "marriage." *The Spoilers*, *Destry Rides Again*, and *Rancho Notorious* appear to demonstrate three very different realizations of this premise.

The Spoilers I will mention quickly as an example of the more phallocentric Western that Mulvey describes. Starring John Wayne as much or more than Dietrich, it is centered on his character's negotiation of the mise-en-scène of desire. After the narrative premise of Alaskan claim-jumping is introduced, including some risqué dialogue regarding the gold commissioner's designs on the sexual "territory" of Cherry Malotte (Dietrich), the plot centers on Glennister's (Wayne) return to town and Cherry's desire for him. He arrives with a possible new romantic interest, and the bulk of the rest of the film concerns his losing and regaining the mine he co-owns, confronting a corrupt legal system, and losing and regaining Cherry: he will traverse the public sphere and her domestic sphere on his terms.

Especially important is the plot's literalization of what I will call, borrowing from Derrida, the law before the Law: the configuration of a corrupt judge and Gold Commission that works to exploit the local economy before the "legitimate" legal apparatus arrives. Their presence gives Glennister a free reign to act out his regressive (white) male subjectivity in the alleged service of preparing the way for the authentic law to appear. This "reign" takes on significantly racialized aspects, including a shockingly casual donning of blackface in several scenes. Glennister's actions ultimately include stealing a locomotive, which he crashes into the barricade outside his mine, an act of phallicly overdetermined absurdity that clearly approaches the genre's capacity for the "delirious."

Dietrich figures more prominently in the other two films of this trio, and they reflect very different dynamics of what Mulvey called "interiority." This interiority has many narrative implications, including what might be characterized as a surfeit complexity of narrative. *Destry Rides Again* is a carnival of narrative discourse: it begins in medias res, with the unruliness of Bottleneck, and soon features Destry's (James Stewart) many folksy stories, in addition to the chicanery and mystery within the crime plot, and assorted other business among its bevy of character actors.

For this and other reasons, *Destry Rides Again* is more complicated as an object of study than it might appear to be. As many have pointed out, it was a key film for Dietrich, jump-starting her sluggish career and altering her overall persona toward greater accessibility for the U.S. audience especially.[9] Yet it is a deeply problematic and contradictory film regarding the depiction of her character and women characters in general, especially in that it affords such evident pleasure for the audience even as it adheres so stridently, with such fidelity, to the perversity of the Hollywood Production Code "law" regarding the sexual double standard. Has there ever been a film more ingratiating in its invitation to condemn a woman for being sexual? Once again, the narrative circulates around a premise that introduces a law before the Law: Frenchy (Dietrich) has participated and thrived in the corrupt world of Bottleneck before Destry arrives as the "return" of legitimate law. For this she is prone to be punished under the Production Code. But she is especially punished because she is a "painted lady," and as such, she excites Destry.

A key scene that delineates the film's stake in the sexual double standard and its binary configuration of generic stereotypes for women occurs concurrently with the discovery of a key narrative transgression, when Destry fools Frenchy into admitting the fate of the missing sheriff he has been hired to replace. Subsequent to their barroom brawl, Destry calls on Frenchy at her home, and inquires about rumors regarding her reputation. After settling down with a cup of coffee, he quickly angers Frenchy by mentioning her alleged role in crooked poker games, and especially by implying that he might be endangered should he turn his back on her. She is obviously flustered, and Destry deploys this state of excitement to learn the truth about the former sheriff. But he is not finished with their exchange, and clearly enjoys their close proximity when he says, "I don't think you're half as bad as you make out to be." After giving her a slow look up and down, he tells her, "I'll bet you've got kind of a lovely face under all that paint." He wipes his fingers free of some of her makeup, and adds, "Why don't you wipe it off someday and have a good look. Figure out how you can live up to it." She ponders this thought, and her interior monologue is provided by her maid, who remarks about the considerable "personality" that Destry has evidenced. Frenchy's subsequent gaze into the mirror, when she wipes off her lipstick with the back of her hand, is followed by a dissolve to a graphically matched mirror shot, in which Miss Tindle, the "appropriate" love object for Destry, finishes adjusting her own makeup. In this case, we are informed, she is employing a new chamois skin to remove the shine from her nose.

This scene condenses the bad girl/good girl dichotomy that the narrative trajectory will follow: Frenchy, whose makeup designates someone false and corrupt (a prostitute), must endure the "truth" of her sexual disguise and experience self-loathing at the very moment Destry is being recognized as a proper love object; Miss Tindle (the chaste Eastern miss) is her equal and opposite "rival" for a heteronormative resolution, introducing cosmetics that remove even a small sign of calling attention to

Destry Rides Again (1939). *Filmmuseum Berlin—Marlene Dietrich Collection Berlin.*

oneself. The use of the mirror for both characters indicates the cliché of narcissistic "closeness" to their own image, and resultant lack of self-knowledge, akin to Riviere's notion of "masquerade." Especially since this is Dietrich, and subsequent in her career to the von Sternberg films which, as Gay Studlar argues, reworked just these kinds of specular issues away from the sexism that underlies scopophilic models, such a critique of the means and capacity to "produce" one's own look and cater it for appeal seems especially confining and condemnatory. It serves precisely that function regarding the film's resolution.

Frenchy plays a crucial role in sparking the women to take collective action against the violence and lawlessness of Bottleneck. But her own concerns are strictly personal at that moment of social revolt, focused on the endangerment of Destry as her love object. She takes the bullet meant for him, and again wipes the lipstick off her mouth to embrace him one last time before she expires. It is literally the kiss of death, but she had been condemned to its sentence since the moment Destry first became sexually interested in her. (Narratively, his desire is configured in conjunction with Frenchy's performance of the song "See What the Boys in the Back Room Will Have," which figures and foreshadows her death.) Her memory seems to haunt the conclusion of the film, when some boys in the street are singing another of her signature songs, "Little Joe." This has been read as a final confirmation of her power in the narrative, a reading that is indicative of the strong desire by many to read against the grain of the film's narrative recuperation. But the song also can be read as the sign of Destry's "petit objet a," the available trigger for his regressive male subjectivity, by which to maintain a position of power within the community but outside of marriage. Indeed, we see him respond to the song by engaging Miss Tindle in yet another folksy story, once again deferring the expectation of romantic union as the credits roll.

Get/Away

Rancho Notorious features the tropes of narrative complexity and genre experimentation that the above discussion might be seen to predict. (Indeed, the film is difficult to describe in declarative prose.) The diegesis begins, for example, with the typical conclusion of many classical films: a close-up on a passionate heterosexual kiss (by protagonist Vern and his fiancée, Beth), which we learn is filled with the promise of impending marriage and the future this implies. But this projected scenario is quickly destroyed by a brutal rape and murder, the first of many sudden narrative reversals. This foundational reversal is the consequence of wanton (masculinist) avarice.

As two rough-hewn men are riding out of town, they stop to observe Beth waving goodbye to Vern in front of the general store and assayer's office where she works. Recognizing that she will be alone, the two ride back to the store, their plan immediately understood and motivated by an evident availability. As one man (referred to by his partner as Whitey) waits outside, the other man (we will learn his name is Kinch) enters the store and demands to see the contents of the assayer's safe.

The mise-en-scène begins to suggest the menace to come, as Beth kneels before the safe, slightly shadowed by the pattern of the wire mesh that separates the back office. Kinch moves closer, his shadow passing over her. She looks up at him as she dials the combination to the safe. He is framed in a kind of two-shot, his face registering anticipation on screen left, his open hand on screen right, fingers threaded into the wire mesh. With the safe open, her hesitant gaze up at him is met by the movement of his hand as he wets his lips. She braces herself, but the film cuts far away to a vantage point looking at the storefront from the sidewalk across the street: a young boy is playing. The boy's actions are interrupted by Beth's distant cry, which is soon followed by a more sustained scream and then a gunshot. Kinch rushes out to his partner on the street, and they race out of town.

In this way, the narrative trajectory becomes set. The normative tropes of civilization are established suddenly, in medias res, then casually but lethally violated via sexualized greed. Vern's revenge quest is begun, in the mode of a mature and adult version of male regressive subjectivity: purposeful, single-minded, and project-oriented. The film assays his journey across varied landscapes and seasons, from Wyoming to the Mexican border, emphasizing his isolation and drive.

This trajectory is soon underscored—many would say undermined—by the reflexivity of the narrative, especially via the somewhat experimental use of a theme song to convey key narrative information and exposition. From the initiation of the project, Lang and screenwriter Daniel Tarradash had conceived a film that utilized the convention of a narrative song (the much-derided "Ballad of Chuck-a-Luck") as a key element. Regardless of the perceived "quality" of the song (or perhaps consequent to it), the ballad is intentionally foregrounded so as to produce an evident paratext regarding narrative and thematic elements ordinarily "embedded" into the Western genre. The resultant tone of arguably Brechtian reflexivity contributes to the overall experimental aesthetic that makes the film so odd, and so potentially delirious.

Robin Wood has discussed various aspects of a Brechtian reading of the film, noting that the ballad chorus ("Hate, Murder, and Revenge") has been regarded as a kind of signature motto for Lang's work. Wood goes on to suggest that the association of the revenge theme to that of "the gamblers wheel" affords the film a distilled ideological position regarding patriarchal capitalist culture:[10] the depiction of "the revenge hero's moral decline" culminates with Vern's increasingly manipulative behavior in the name of morality, especially "in his treatment of women." (The first sign of this corrupt behavior is his encounter with Whitey, when Vern lethally withholds water from the dying man in order to extract information in support of his revenge quest.) For Wood, the film's Brechtian and modernist elements are deployed in an "awkward and uneasy" fashion, but nevertheless contribute to much of the film's interest.

A close reading of several aspects of the film's nonclassical aesthetics can clarify and qualify these assertions. Many of the aesthetic codes of the film relate directly to the depiction of Vern and the issues of control that underlie his tortured subjectivity.[11] But these codes can be seen to vie for attention with those demanded by Dietrich, both as star and character. As the film proceeds, Vern's revenge story, augmented by the narrative condensations of the theme song, is regularly interrupted and sent on a series of evident tangents as if in battle for control with the backstory of Altar Keane (Dietrich).

For Stephen Jenkins, these flashbacks are significant because "they permit the depiction of the woman as unproblematic object of desire, in contrast to the film's present, through the stereotype of the 'fiery,' 'wilful' saloon girl" (48). Certainly this seems to be true regarding most of the male characters' recountings of Altar's legend: she represents a fetishized, sexualized ideal regarding their own past sexuality.[12] But her depiction is far less "unproblematic" for Baldy (William Frawley), whose attitude is colored by the large amount of money he lost to Altar the very night he had fired her. He loses this money due to the deployment of Baldy's own rigged chuck-a-luck gambling wheel, via the intervention of Frenchy Fairmont (Mel Ferrer). (Frenchy knows how to rig the game, and does so for Altar's sake under the protection of his expertise with a gun.)

This overdetermination of "chance" and fortune establishes a romantic and gendered ethics related to but also distinct from Vern's quest: Frenchy acts outside the Law in order to square the unfair treatment that Altar has received. Their relationship, too, involves a negotiation of the past, which is consolidated during an extraordinary long-take walk down the street (2:15 minutes). This shot exists in particular tension with the constructedness of edited looks that characterizes the relation between narration and Vern's subjectivity. Frenchy and Altar's life together is forged in this scene, which features a series of dialogue exchanges about their respective, storied reputations. Their present circumstances intrude as ironic, quotidian counterpoint (e.g., the encounter with a mud puddle), as Altar imagines for a moment what idealized future her winnings might afford. Frenchy enacts his "investment" in their future by standing guard outside her door that night, a sign of his commitment to the melding of his fantasy history of Altar with his present projections about her. The money from these events eventually pays for a future: the ranch that she will secretly name Chuck-a-Luck—a displaced version of Beth's projected future home with Vern: the Lost Cloud Ranch—which further complicates the thematics of chance, escape, space, and subjectivity/desire.

On the basis of the information from Baldy, Vern eventually locates Frenchy, and arranges for Frenchy to escort him to Chuck-a-Luck, where he meets Altar and begins a kind of masochistic relation to his own desires regarding her. (She immediately recognizes Vern's scopophilic drive: "Uses his eyes, too, doesn't he?") A romantic triangle emerges between Vern, Altar, and Frenchy, which effectively completes the narrative pivot away from the centrality of Vern's subjectivity alone. This emerges in both temporal and spatial registers. Issues related to time, which had been implicit to the flashback interruptions noted above, become increasingly explicit subjects for discussion and thematic resonance related to these characters and also Dietrich as screen persona.

Vern strategically manages to involve both Frenchy and Altar in considerations of their past, including the subjective weight of each of their reputations. This is especially marked in the case of Altar, both because of the rules of Chuck-a-Luck (no questions allowed regarding past events), and because it is Dietrich speaking the lines. "Every year is a threat to a woman," she suggests, collapsing the danger her character senses regarding her continued control over Chuck-a-Luck, and what we now know Dietrich herself was experiencing over the control of her image during the production of the film. (This latter point will be addressed in more detail below.) She is aware of Frenchy's anxiety about his age as well, telling him the night before her birthday, "And don't ask me how old I'll be tomorrow, or I'll ask you." Later, Frenchy responds to the threat that Vern presents to their relationship when he suggests to Altar, "Time holds us together. And time's stronger than rope." But this sentiment is mitigated by Altar's wishful assertion to Vern that "I wish you'd go away and come back ten years ago." (She ultimately changes her mind, and tells him to leave.)

Visually, the key scene that establishes Vern's masochistic relation to his desires for Altar/Dietrich is her performance of the song "Get Away, Young Man," which functions to ground Altar/Dietrich as centrally important rather than ancillary to the film's narrative core. The rich combination of a thematically pertinent song, and a significantly performative rendering of it, provides a flexible context for the repurposing of narrative that occurs during the song.[13] The configuration of varied, contestatory narrative trajectories collide and collapse into a melodramatically rich, extended "moment," only to immediately defer all of these trajectories by producing the demand for escape, for precisely a literal getaway. A delineation of the song lyrics and the actions that occur during Altar/Dietrich's performance of them suggests this dynamic interplay (see table).

Altar finishes the song with a series of gestures that flirtatiously contradict the command to "get away." She draws close to Frenchy, then moves back as she waves for him to follow, tugging the scarf as if to draw him closer, then flicking it quickly toward him and away during the song's final punch line ("Get away . . . if you can!"). All the men converge to congratulate her performance as Vern charges forward to confront Altar about the brooch, but the narrative again features a sudden reversal and change of action on demand: the lookout announces that a posse is approaching Chuck-a-Luck, so that all the outlaws must immediately disperse to another camp.

Part of what I find interesting about this scene is its narrative overdetermination of the melodramatic moment: its configuration of such a "moment" as fundamentally "interior" but also contending with and even competing with adjacent "interiorities." For Vern, this competition occurs within his own subjectivity, regarding his interest and delight with Altar, his suspicion of Wilson and the other men, and the revelation of an object (the brooch) that consolidates his regression toward this interiority. This is in stark contrast to Altar herself, whose performance creates a playful counterpoint to the lyrics, opening meaning away from the literalism that Vern pursues as ethical rationale.

Altar's performance fleetingly concretizes the kind of balancing acts she has already demonstrated as key to her maintaining an equilibrium within the lawless nonplace of Chuck-a-Luck. Her authority is guaranteed by what might be regarded as movement between the symbolic registers that the ranch and its clientele seem to demand. For example, the film points out (especially through Vern's comments) that her clothing

A young man is reckless and ready A young man is handsome and vain He's young and intense But hasn't the sense To come in out of the rain	Altar's play with her fan punctuates her performance of the song throughout, often gesturing to suggest arousal.
Get away, get away, Get away, young man, get away	She comically pushes "away" the middle-aged preacher, who is noticeably not a "young man." All laugh, even Vern, who smiles for the first time in the scene.
A young man is full of adventure And eager to do what he can He may be a joy But don't send a boy To do the work of a man	Altar entices Wilson, the womanizer, then moves away from him to throw her scarf around the neck of Frenchy. She continues to sing to Frenchy.
(CHORUS)	
A young man will come when you call him And leave when you tell him to go But someday he'll guess A woman means yes Whenever a woman says no	Close-up of Vern; line echoes earlier dialogue. Altar removes her scarf, revealing the brooch on her bodice, which Vern recognizes is the same brooch torn from Beth's dress by her murderer.
(CHORUS)	
A woman is only a creature Of notions and dimples and lies So learn if you can This lesson young man And don't run away if she cries	A flurry of cross-cutting ensues, centered between Vern's anguished acts of looking: at Altar, the brooch, Frenchy, Wilson, and ultimately every man in the room.
(CHORUS, with final line: "Get away, get away . . . if you can!")	

at the ranch stands in direct contrast to her attire in the flashbacks, involving a kind of oscillation between hard-work attire (pants and flannel shirts) and glamour.[14] Such an oscillation serves as a marker of the supra-Western heroines' iconicity,[15] and in this instance relates to the ranch rule that, while residing there, everyone must work to maintain the ranch. Altar is clearly not above this regulation, though she also insists that she is the boss of Chuck-a-Luck—a claim that easily threatens many of the men. Her authority therefore necessitates additional methods to maintain equilibrium, involving both sexuality and wit grounded in anticipatory psychological insight. When a gunman resists her standard 10 percent premium on bonds that he may not be able to cash, she insists, deferring his anger with the promise that he will have a chance to win it back at poker that night. When he then tries to cheat her at the subsequent poker game, she defuses the potential for violence by producing his beloved musical stopwatch, which she has stolen, and trades him for the money in the pot.

The song "Get Away" condenses the erotic role significant to her maintenance of Chuck-a-Luck: her sexualized presence among all these male outlaws is a quality she both relies on to some extent but also defers toward a future never to be realized. Her ironic performance of the song, and especially her concluding flicking of the scarf to both reindicate the space of desire and then evaporate it, produces the potential for an entirely different sense of the "interior" moment: a moment of interruption, placelessness, a freedom of sorts from the ground of the symbolic, via the oscillation between "get" (goal-defined drive, progress, acquisition, claim) and "away" (not necessarily an opposite direction, but potentially an abnegation of directionality itself; not the resolution of the goal but potentially the evacuation of the goal; drive's "other"; a kind of death). The sudden demand for escape produced by the immediate appearance of the lookout serves as an external corollary to this trope, especially regarding Vern's newly recharged subjective regression.

One can contrast this configuration with, for example, *The Searchers* (dir. John Ford, 1956), which features a theme song that emphasizes the motif of "ride away." Here, the gap between pursuit (ride) and withdrawal from community (walk away) effectively "produces" community as the space between. *Rancho Notorious* is more "interior," and its thematic constructions are more temporal in nature. To be sure, Chuck-a-Luck is a

Rancho Notorious (1952). *Filmmuseum Berlin—Marlene Dietrich Collection Berlin.*

liminal place, outside the recognition of the law and at the border of the state. The divide of get/away, then, can be seen to be located first as a configuration of space: Chuck-a-Luck is maintained by collecting a percentage surcharge from criminal acts—"get"—and functions quite precisely as a haven from the responsibilities and rules of society—"away"—its chief rule being that no questions may be asked of anyone. But get/away is ultimately revealed as a trope of subjectivity itself. Part of what the film's experimental or nonclassical qualities afford is an address to this latter register of thematics, and a curious ambivalence within this trope. What becomes apparent via close analysis is a doubling or coincident appearance: what we might refer to as masculinist exiled Weimar subjectivity in relation to the codes of queerness.

Rancho Notorious has been a camp favorite for many years, and likely for more than its studio-bound Technicolor aesthetics alone. At one obvious level, if this film does bear a direct relationship to *Destry*, the character named Frenchy—played by Dietrich in the earlier film—is now portrayed by Mel Ferrer. But the film can also be seen to render its version of regressive male subjectivity in productively campy terms. Vern's obsessive search is figured, and often appears to the other characters, as distinctly peculiar behavior, and is readily otherwise read as queer. He intently surveys the face of every man he meets (such that his many scrutinizing close-ups during "The Ballad of Chuck-a-Luck" might be construed as a cruising scenario). He manufactures his own arrest in order to spend the night in jail with Frenchy. Kinch suggests to Wilson, the womanizer who Vern initially suspects among the group at Chuck-a-Luck, "He was sure lookin' strange at you last night, all through supper," adding later: "He looks straight through a man." The pairing of Vern and Frenchy that concludes the film has been read beyond homosocial terms. This may be reinforced by a queer reading of Frenchy's line to Altar as they admiringly watch Vern break a particularly difficult stallion: "I might have liked that kind of riding say ten or twelve years ago."

This reconfigures Vern's marked anxiousness during the "Get Away" song as well, in terms that range across various sexual configurations. Especially as regards the image and sound relations in the editing, the song eventually appears to be directly about Vern, whose youth and attendant behavior toward Altar are threats to Frenchy. (After the first of Vern's acts of supplication, when he gets Altar a drink at the poker table, she says, "You're always right there when you're needed, aren't you?" This line is nearly duplicated in the song.) Instead of being concerned about the brooch alone, is he jealous of Altar's claim on Frenchy, or the obverse; of the other men, watching the desire on Frenchy's face or the desire on Altar's face, each of which he wants to claim; or is he jealous of their very looking at Frenchy, or Altar, or anyone other than Vern himself?

From this point, Vern engages in a more elaborate schema of investigation, an intensified project that begins almost immediately when he drops away from the escaping men to return to Altar's aid, providing a key alibi in her encounter with the law. This is the opposite behavior, for example, from Wayne in *The Spoilers*: Vern is attendant and solicitous of her needs, resourceful and admiring, even as the audience "understands" this to be at some level a ploy. He is interested in gleaning information—to overcome the great taboo against questions at Chuck-a-Luck—and his eventual success in breaking down Altar's resolve of discretion is what fulfills his revenge quest and also dooms Altar.

It is significant that he vents his moralistic condemnation of Altar at the very moment he obliterates the mise en scène of "get/away" desire. Having coaxed her to reappear in the same gown (which still features the brooch), he negates her capacity for oscillation and symbolic slippage, in the name of literalizing again the haunting image that originally triggered his regression into vengeful obsession. Vern accuses Altar of murder, pulling her forward and insisting that she "see" his outraged and dead fiancé on the floor in front of them. Altar is shocked to the point of despair in her realization of Vern's accusation, but also that of her unwitting betrayal of the ranch code of silence about the past, and especially the evident lie at the heart of her romantic attachments to Vern.

The "triangle" Vern-Altar-Frenchy is resultantly open to a variety of interpretations. Vern is masquerading in order to fulfill his desire for revenge, but is evidently blind to his other, more erotic desires that are enabled by and intrinsic to his masquerade. But are these desires for Altar, or for Frenchy, or for both, or are they perhaps finally manifested in jealousy for the intensity of the Altar-Frenchy relationship?

At the "straight" level of the text, these issues can be posited as questions regarding Dietrich and Altar, vis-à-vis modernity. If the anxiety about male subjectivity within modernity was regularly configured in relation to the related phenomenon of the New Woman, there appears to be a recognizable trace of such anxiety in Lang's Westerns. In the first two, the New Woman is allied with mass media—the newspaper and the telegraph—that represent early deployments of the means to collapse time and space via modern technology. In *Rancho Notorious*, this image of the New Woman—crucially determined by the casting of Dietrich, and perhaps the Weimar and post-Weimar baggage that both she and Lang represented to each other—becomes not only an image but the source for a return gaze, a key register by which to confirm and put into play Lang's version of male subjective anxiety and its desire. But as was true in *Destry*, it is a model of the gaze based on scopophilia—the desire for control that Vern's gaze so consistently registers.[16]

The final image of Altar in the film, Dietrich's final close-up in a starring role, seems to confirm this scopophilic hierarchy. After the gunplay inspired by Vern's betrayal of Altar's affection (in the pursuit of his revenge) we are presented with Vern's realization that his obsessive looks and duplicitous masquerades have doomed Altar, a realization of what Eisner calls "the vanity of violence." Altar is configured as despairingly incapable of continuing the return of Vern's gaze. Her visage is now a death mask, blind and unseeing, even as her eyes remain hauntingly open. I am suggesting that this may represent as well the final salvo of the Langian discourse on Dietrich.

Although I am typically resistant to overtly biographical renderings of textual analyses, it seems possible that the famous interpersonal hostilities reported between Lang and Dietrich on the set of *Rancho Notorious* literally "figure" (perhaps prefigure) the aesthetics and mise-en-scène of the film.[17] Lang is quoted to have told her on-set "I am Lang, not von Sternberg!" Lang claimed to want to give Dietrich a "new screen image," acknowledging her age. He has been quoted as being shocked that Dietrich instead showed up on set looking younger and younger. The two allegedly did not speak by the end of shooting. Dietrich biographers especially have subsequently criticized Dietrich in their claim that she undermined the character of Altar in attending to her vanity regarding her appearance (Spoto 233), a spurious claim in light of her nuanced performance and in any case merely contributing to the double bind in which Dietrich increasingly found herself.

The project of enforcing a displacement of the von Sternbergian scopic regime and discourse by that of the Langian scopic regime and discourse, especially vis-à-vis the crucial image of Dietrich and its configuration within the economy of textual desire, attempts to perform as authentic the presumed superiority of the Langian discourse. The more masochistic figuration of Dietrich is written over by a more Freudian one, at the "moment" of the rise of the supra-Western and the decline of classical Hollywood cinema. This would be unavoidably linked to another key "moment": the disruption of an economy of desire between Lang and Dietrich that had existed for years—a disruption of his desire for her and desire to control her, and her blanket refusal of him—now rerendered via his diminished desire in recognition that this potent figure of desire had herself actually aged.

In this way, *Rancho Notorious* might be seen to be central to the formulation of a long-term vicious cycle that we now recognize to be increasingly central to Dietrich's career from this point forward: her compulsion to perform a regime of public concerts while appearing to retain her youthful countenance, and defy the aging process via a full-body mask. Indeed, it was during the press tour for *Rancho Notorious* that Dietrich recognized and began to devise the formats for her personal appearances and concerts. During a legendary appearance for the film's premiere in Chicago, Dietrich (with the significant help of her daughter, Maria Riva, whose training in "live" television proved crucial) produced her first rave miniconcert, complete with a quick change of her costume.[18]

In a curious way, as discussed above, the film can also be seen to "out" itself, in a manner we would likely presume to be unconscious or unintentional. But if the film's depiction of Dietrich reveals both evident and close-textual brands of misogyny, it seems to me that the film also ultimately outs itself as homophobic: the possibility or potential for homosexual desire is figured, but in a fashion that is, like Freud's discussion of homosexuality for example, ultimately pathological (e.g., chronically, even dangerously, narcissistic and antisocial; caught in a loop of sexual loathing, rather than mobile and transgressive). In other words, despite the film's delirious aesthetics, its particular rendering of both feminine and queer sexuality constitutes *Rancho Notorious*'s law before the Law.

Notes

1. Some critics have valorized the film, to be sure, especially in the name of Lang. Dave Kehr in "*Rancho Notorious*" in *The Chicago Reader* calls the film "a perversely stylized western by Fritz Lang (1952), his last and best." See http://onfilm.chicagoreader.com/. Most positive critiques similarly claim the film to be "personal" or "psychological," assigning its aesthetics to auteur experimentation.

2. Robin Wood's essay "*Rancho Notorious*" also constructs an analysis in relation to other key films (principally *The Big Heat*, and briefly *Destry Rides Again*), which suggests a matrix of genre, star, and auteur considerations. Wood's essay was not available to me before the Dietrich conference at which the first draft of my essay was delivered. It has been a happy surprise and also a challenge to revise the present essay with respect to Wood's analysis.

3. The most famous essay introducing this concept about 1950s melodramas is Thomas Elsaesser's "Tales of Sound and Fury," which has been anthologized in Gledhill (*Home* 43–69).

4. Truffaut, "Nicholas Ray" and "A Wonderful Certainty."

5. See, for example, Cook; and Peterson.

6. In an essay on Lang that discusses both *The Return of Frank James* and *Rancho Notorious*, Stephen Jenkins suggests that this theatrical episode is part of Lang's distinctive usage of various kinds of "flashbacks," which for Jenkins tend to "specifically question the status of filmic images as unproblematic, objective representations of truth." In this case, what is depicted is the process of recreating a version of the past, and a version that is marked as fantasy (46).

7. I am referencing here Tom Gunning's excellent recent book on Lang, which configures the director expressly in terms of "a complex and profound meditation on the cinema as a means of representing modern experience." Gunning, it should be noted however, dismisses the Lang Westerns as "conformist."

8. Daniel Taradash, screenwriter for *Rancho Notorious*, noted that Lang's personal library was especially extensive as regards the history of the American West: "Fritz was a man who really knew the American west. I found out, since I worked often at his house, that he had a remarkable Western library. Any research that I needed, I got from his library" ("Oral History with Daniel Taradash," interview by Barbara Hall in 2001, Oral History Program, Margaret Herrick Library, Academy of Motion Picture Arts and Sciences (AMPAS), Fairbanks Study Center, Beverly Hills, Calif.). Thanks to Barbara Hall for alerting me to this document.

9. See Britton for an interesting analysis of *Destry* with regard to the negotiation of star persona and genre (esp. 145–49).

10. Wood; see also Koepnick for an extended contextualization and analysis of the Brechtian aspects of "The Ballad of Chuck-a-Luck" (*Dark Mirror*, esp. 219–26). Koepnick's consideration of *Rancho Notorious* is inspired by his study of the imaging of pianos in the film.

11. As Cook notes, "Partly because of distancing techniques used in image, sound, and narrative, this is one of a few westerns in which the overriding male perspective is brought into question: Altar is explicitly seen as a victim of Vern's need to project on to an external image his own violent, destructive urges" (297).

12. Dietrich's apparent defiance of time, which was an important sticking point in her on-set quarrels with Lang, was remarked upon in certain reviews of the film, which evidence a great investment in this capacity and often "claimed" it in the name of other times and other places. Two examples exist in uncredited 1952 newspaper reviews from Great Britain. One review suggests that "her beauty and personality bridge the decades and afford to those on the bleak side of the divide a glimpse of what things were like before the bombs began to fall on Warsaw." Another, dismissive review of the film (which refers to it as "Gun shots by Strauss"), opines: "Yet no amount of banality can dim the glow that is Dietrich's. She defies the demands of authenticity and credibility. She pronounces 'Wyoming' as if it were a suburb of Vienna. She makes an elegant art of chewing gum and she converts in her guttural tones the most jingling cowboy ballad into something by Offenbach" (*Rancho Notorious* clipping file, British Film Institute, National Library, London).

13. For Wood, this scene epitomizes the presentational, Brechtian aesthetics of the film. It evokes "the simultaneous experiencing of pleasure and awareness of it, so that its premises and sources are called into question" (90).

14. Jenkins suggests that her oscillation in attire produces Altar as a "problematised" object of desire for Vern, since she assumes "female and male roles, functions and dress." This leads to Jenkins's claim that "Haskell's quest can be read as having a repressed homosexual aim which will be fulfilled at the film's conclusion" (49). I will suggest a slightly different reading of homosexual desire across the film text, less dependent upon the question of Altar's attire.

15. This oscillation exists at the level of secondary identification, unlike that ascribed to female spectators by Mulvey in her essay referred to above. Nevertheless, it raises issues pertinent to further consideration of the supra-Westerns as regards the study of genre and gender theory in Film Studies. Another site for speculation regarding costumes and gendered oscillation is raised by the promotional materials for the film. It is worth noting that the costumes that

Altar/Dietrich wears in the flashback sequences of the film were promoted as authentic in design, especially true to the colors of the period. They reportedly cost $30,000, among them a gown "made up in 'Parma Violet' a shade that had a great vogue in the 1860's and was revived for a time in 1905." The promotional campaign also discussed these costumes as "breath-takingly lovely ensembles which contrast sharply with the heroine's latter-day garb of breeches and shirt in which she works around the rancho of the title" (pressbook for *Rancho Notorious*, *Rancho Notorious* clipping file, Margaret Herrick Library, AMPAS).

16. See Jenkins for an insightful discussion of the desire of Vern's gaze (47–48).

17. See Bach; McGilligan; and Aurich et al. This last source quotes Dietrich as labeling Lang a member of "Sadist Incorporated" regarding the production, and further quotes (from a document in the Filmmuseum Berlin, Marlene Dietrich Collection), "The teutonic Arrogance which he was feeding on was repulsive to me. Only my professional dedication saved me from the complete DESERTATION [*sic*] of my contractual duties" (400). See also Higham and Greenberg, 104–27; the comments by Lang on pp. 118–20 are especially pertinent.

18. See Riva; and Bach. Among the songs she performed was "Get Away, Young Man."

6 August 1945

Mami, my angel —

It was so wonderful to hear your voice and to know that you are allright. I sent you a letter with Colonel Stephens and photographs of myself and Liesel. Did you ever get it? I am sending some more in case you didn't. — Maria is taller than I and very beautiful. She is a great actress. All the

Filmmuseum Berlin—Marlene Dietrich Collection Berlin.

AMELIE HASTIE

The Order of Knowledge and Experience

Marlene Dietrich's ABC

THE ALPHABET gives us access to language and thus to communication. It functions mnemonically as well as visually; it provides us with a system to organize knowledge so that it can be recalled. In this way, the alphabet enables the preservation of history and of knowledge itself—allowing, of course, for the ways in which language and knowledge are also always in the process of transformation.

Alphabet

Marlene Dietrich's ABC, although a work innately structured by categories (that is, of course, the letters of the alphabet and words that spring from them), is itself difficult to categorize. At the most basic level, it is an alphabetical listing of words, names, and situations that Dietrich defines, reflects on, and in regard to which she offers advice. It is therefore indeed a reference book, an encyclopedia, a how-to manual. But it is also a memoir, a philosophical treatise, and a quotation book. On the one hand, its definition is in part lodged in the very premises—and promises—of the alphabet itself. Like other archetypal ABC books—dictionaries and encyclopedias—it is a compendium of knowledge organized alphabetically. However, unlike most of these books, it is written by one author, and the knowledge therein is based upon her own lived experience—and,

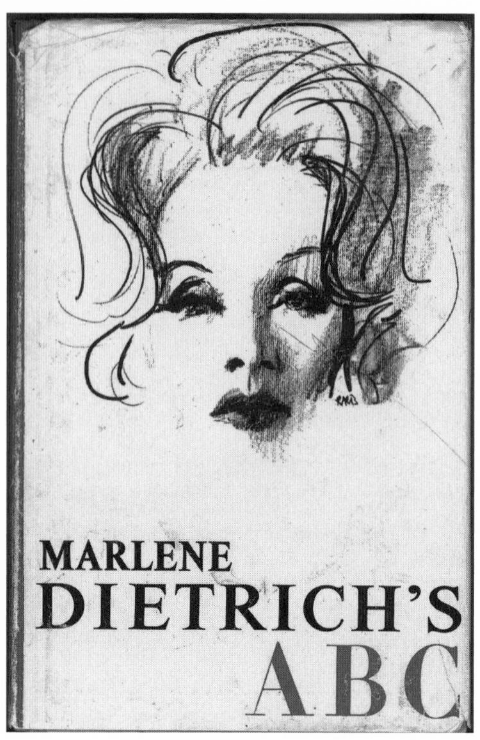

Marlene Dietrich's ABC
by Marlene Dietrich
(Doubleday, 1961)

in a sense, her readers' experiences (or expectations) of her. For instance, a stream of entries under the letter "S" include Stationery Store, Steak, Sternberg (Josef von), Stravinsky, and Stupidity.

Marking the "S" through such vivid entries, Dietrich's volume is also like classic ABC primers, those children's books that are designed for the act of memorization by teaching the alphabet through individual words and pictures. These books, themselves dictionaries and encyclopedias of sorts, are also compendiums of knowledge, and as such they structure and generate knowledge for their readers as well. Yet the key difference between these texts and Dietrich's own is that her work does not necessarily incite memorization (although this can be an effect of it); rather, it is based on the author's memory itself (of von Sternberg, of a stationery store she visited in Haddonfield, of her experience with music and with personality "defects"). Dietrich's work thus follows the alphabet—"the key to any study or branch of knowledge; the first rudiments" (*Oxford English Dictionary*)—as a way to logically organize something that is abstract or seemingly without logical order itself, using knowledge based on memory and lived experience.

As a ruminative volume that covers a range of topics and ideas ordered by the alphabet, her work is also akin to the texts of two of her contemporaries (she was born within ten years of each of them): Walter Benjamin's *Arcades Projects* and Roland Barthes's *A Lover's Discourse*. In *A Lover's Discourse* Barthes describes concepts and emotional states—absence, *comprendre* (to understand), *fou* (mad)—in alphabetical order and through constellations of narratives drawn from a myriad of sources (literature, philosophy, psychoanalysis, conversations, experience). Benjamin's *Arcades* uses the alphabet as an overarching structural device, but the concepts he describes do not conform to the letters as in the case of a conventional encyclopedia or a work like Dietrich's or Barthes's. His "convolutes" (literally, bundles) contain ruminations on history and historical objects that constitute "the rags, the refuse" of culture (460). His project is indicative of Benjamin's role as a collector: it comprises a series of reveries and reflections he has composed and drawn from a wide array of sources. Dietrich, too, collects citations and proposes ruminations; although rarely as extensive as a single entry by Benjamin or Barthes, her work does constitute a similar practice as these theorists of culture and history. In fact, her entry on "Quotations" might very well also describe both Benjamin's and Barthes's projects: "I love them because it is a joy to find thoughts one might have, beautifully expressed with much more authority by someone recognizedly wiser than oneself" (137). Given these likenesses, conglomerations, and even refusals, what exactly does Dietrich's work express through its alphabetical organization? What authority does it reveal even with such modest claims to the contrary? What, in essence, is this funny book?

Based on the ABC form, Dietrich's work is itself a "primer" on language, nation, and everyday living. Most of all, it is a primer on Dietrich herself. As such it reveals her range of knowledge that extends beyond the expertise of stardom and even domesticity—two arenas with which she was often associated. Indeed, although her individual entries are not as copious as those found in *A Lover's Discourse* or *The Arcades Project*, if we read across the whole book, even the shorter entries expand, particularly through the relations created between them. (Hence, as with Benjamin's intention for his book, we can read Dietrich's work through the practice of montage.) Undeniably, *Marlene Dietrich's ABC* has not been credited with the same intellectual capital as these works of Barthes or Benjamin, and it would doubtless be foolish to suggest that it should (particularly because of its inevitable tie to capitalism, rather then its critique of it). However, considering that it follows similar patterns, we might at least recognize it as demonstrating similar elements of such theoretical paradigms and historiographical practices. At least it might offer its readers the opportunity to contemplate the production and assemblage of knowledge in any work of this kind.

autoBiography

To understand—is that not to divide the image, to undo the *I*, proud organ of misapprehension?—ROLAND BARTHES, *A Lover's Discourse*

Hollywood costume designer Edith Head begins her own autobiographical how-to manual, *The Dress Doctor* (published just three years after the first edition of Dietrich's book) with a story about Dietrich. She describes fitting her for *Witness for the Prosecution*. As she tells it, fitting Dietrich is a collaborative affair—and has been every time she has worked with her. Two details especially stand out in this anecdote: first, Head describes Dietrich as one who is knowledgeable, and second, yet relatedly, she depicts the star in the terms with which she has often been represented: as one who easily (I might even say seamlessly) moves between the spheres of glamour and domesticity. Head declares: "Fashion is a language. Some know it, some learn it, some never will—like an instinct. . . . But Dietrich was born knowing, and when we work together, it is less doctor and patient than two specialists in consultation with the character in mind" (12). As part of this collaboration, it is apparently Dietrich's role to bring both her expertise and nourishment for the other workers. Head thus describes the contents of the "fantastic piece of French luggage" that Dietrich brings along with her: "Out of it comes a Thermos of coffee . . . , books, scripts, an extra pair of shoes, and one of her famous tortes, a seven-layer cake she learned to make in Vienna" (12). Dietrich, Head remarks later, "is no perennial orchid, drinking champagne in bed." Rather, "this is an energetic woman with the common touch. She likes cooking, she likes sewing, she likes children and grandchildren, she likes people. In her French lingerie and a mannish hat, she has just stopped to show us pictures of her grandchildren, her daughter, her son-in-law" (15). All of these anecdotes paint Dietrich as both "knowing" about fashion and domestic matters. This combined knowledge is particularly drawn in relief when Head recounts their discussion over how to dress Dietrich for the flashback sequence in Wilder's film, that is, when she must be a "hausfrau." Says Head, "'The producer and director are worried, Marlene; they want you to look like a hausfrau. The question is, what does a hausfrau look like? Homesy? Ginghamy? Provincial? Dowdy?'" And Dietrich responds, "'Why don't they ask me? . . . I *was* one! . . . I was not dowdy'" (13).

These little sketches that begin Head's book exhibit the mobility commonly associated with Dietrich—she merges masculine and feminine fashions, for instance—and, moreover, they represent Dietrich as she often represented herself, as one who is fluent in both the world of glamour and the world of domesticity. These "worlds" themselves might seem to be two opposing poles of femininity—especially as enunciated between the "movie star" and the "housewife." Dietrich's work and her persona, however, show the inherent intersections between these feminine camps. Such intersections are made particularly keen through acts of repetitive labor: keeping house, making up. Both are ephemeral, both require constant repetition or maintenance to presume or pretend a kind of continuity. And in Dietrich's case, both are kinds of knowledge that women are trained in (although, as Head would have it, Dietrich herself was simply born "knowing"). These fields of knowledge and labor, often sketched as incompatible yet ever drawn as almost one for Dietrich in her biographical and autobiographical discourse, are also, then, arenas in which Dietrich trains her readers. Indeed, these fields of knowledge and practice are neatly joined in the opening of her entry on "Schnitzel": "If you can flirt your butcher out of real pink baby veal you can make schnitzels" (148); she follows with a lengthy description of how to make schnitzel properly, from buying veal to preparing it, from cooking it to serving it.

Such tensions between modes of femininity characterize Dietrich's autobiographical discourse; in fact these tensions around knowledge are made more evident by Dietrich's balance between revealing and refusing information, however implicitly. As a text, Dietrich's volume defies generic boundaries, in much the same way Dietrich herself defied boundaries—sexual, certainly, but also national and even, in a sense, ontological. Given the enigmatic nature of the volume, it thus appears to comment on the enigmatic nature of the star—however "real" she pretends to be. It becomes a text that reiterates and then extends her filmic output, but also remarks both on how we conceive of film as an art and industrial form and on the very nature of stardom, each of which are an admixture of the ephemeral and the perpetual, the fleeting and the permanent. These same qualities might also describe the autobiographical: a form that offers a *feeling* of transience or at least intangibility (we can never fully grasp the life before us—this may indeed be why we are reading about it) and durability at once (this life once lived cannot really be altered, although maybe its telling can be "corrected"). Indeed, there is something both appealing and fitting about the form of Dietrich's book, of the creation of arbitrary categories for definition and reflection about her life and what she knows. But this, as I suggested above, is the very paradox of the book: as much as the work appears to define and illuminate, it is essentially structured by caprice, however "logically" arranged via the alphabet, and leaves out as much as it sets down. (Just look at one page of the volume and you can easily see what I mean: between each entry is a blank space, testifying to the *want* that Dietrich ever carefully crafts. We are always left, in other words, wanting more.)

Interestingly, this is also the form that Dietrich ultimately produces for her memoir as well. Given that she originally intended the volume as an autobiography, this move is not surprising. Dietrich biographer Steven Bach notes that the ABC book had its origins in an article Dietrich published "under [Dietrich's] byline" in *Ladies' Home Journal* called "How to Be Loved." Based on this piece—"*Hausfrau* advice about whipping up scrambled eggs and champignons at the end of a long day to keep husband or lover lively enough to tear away the velvet hostess gown she also recommended and cut some mustard"—Doubleday offered Dietrich a contract for an autobiography called *Beauty Is an Illusion* (365). Rather than producing a full-scale memoir at this time, Dietrich ultimately published *Marlene Dietrich's ABC* with Doubleday in 1961. Her memoir, *Marlene*, was published almost three decades later in 1987 in German and translated two years later for its Grove Press publication in the United States.

Although structured somewhat more like a conventional memoir, this last volume also is characterized both by its terseness and by categorization. Many of the chapters are subdivided into categories that are mainly names of various celebrities with whom Dietrich was involved or associated (Orson Welles, Ernest Hemingway, Burt Bacharach, and so on), but some chapters also include other headings consistent with the ABC book. Thus the chapter entitled "Hollywood" includes the following sections: "'Glamour Styles,'" "Actors' Styles," and "Jealousy." These sections are as much ruminations on concepts as they are autobiographical; the first section begins thus: "No lexicographer has yet succeeded in exactly defining the word *glamour*. It just cropped up one day, but nobody can explain it or trace its etymology. I have often been asked about the meaning of this word and have always had to throw up my hands" (104). This description neatly illustrates the connections between the two autobiographical volumes: both are dependent upon gaps and fissures, and both demonstrate Dietrich's interest in defining and displaying knowledge. In this particular case Dietrich reveals herself as knowing (she claims to know about the lexicography of "glamour," even in that it is unknowable itself) and as unknowing (when asked to define the word, she throws up her hands). This picture of herself neatly coincides with the image of her as knowable and unknowable; indeed, such an example obviously points to the ways in which Dietrich constructed this persona for herself as a star.

Cultural Capital

> That anamnestic intoxication in which the flâneur goes about the city not only feeds on the sensory data taking shape before his eyes but often possesses itself of abstract knowledge—indeed, of dead facts—as something experienced and lived through. This felt knowledge travels from one person to another, especially by word of mouth. But in the course of the nineteenth century, it was also deposited in an immense literature.
> —WALTER BENJAMIN, *Arcades Project*

The male flâneur, according to Walter Benjamin, is defined in his relation to the city. His knowledge is based upon his experiences while traveling through the city, especially in the marketplace, as well as his experiences as a reader. Indeed, many of Benjamin's own "studies" of the flâneur are based on his own travels through literature (Baudelaire, Dickens, and Victor Hugo are among the writers in whose work he dwells). The flâneur is at once known for his "idleness"—as a "demonstration against the division of labor" (*Arcades Project*, 427)—and as one who scrupulously observes the marketplace. Although he moves through this space of capitalism, in a sense the flâneur trades in a sphere of cultural capital rather than in the world of labor's capital. Yet because his movement is in part predicated on the marketplace—he is defined in large part by his relation to it, however seemingly "idle"—his cultural capital, as the term suggests, is never far removed from an economy based on the division of labor. Anne Friedberg, while she notes that the flâneur Baudelaire (and then Benjamin) describes is "a (male) painter or a (male) poet . . . whose mobility through the urban landscape allowed him access to the public sphere of the streets and to the domestic realms of the home" (29), also proposes that we might also recognize a female flâneur—a "flâneuse"—who was active in the cultural capital of nineteenth century as well. Recognizing her existence as a paradox of consumer culture, Friedberg claims that "the flâneuse appeared in the public spaces—department stores—made possible by the new configurations of consumer culture" (36). Consumer culture affords women in the nineteenth century a newly "mobilized gaze"; this is later the gaze of cinema.

Like Benjamin's flâneur or Friedberg's flâneuse, Marlene Dietrich gathers knowledge and "makes 'studies.'" These studies have as much to do with her movement and experience in time as they do in space. While her studies are based in part on wandering through a variety of national, economic, and cultural arenas—Hollywood, Paris, Berlin; labor in the film industry, labor in the home—Dietrich's gathering of knowledge is more of an "internal" study. But of course this is the space that the city ultimately takes, according to Benjamin. This internal study, with its reaches into various industrial sites, capitalizes on her image as a star—and one that was produced in the sphere of capitalism itself. Yet as her dual image shows, this is an image of a star based on her own knowledge and expertise in the public realm of celebrity and in the "private" space of the home.

In this way, Dietrich is at once linked to Benjamin's flâneur (and to Benjamin himself as one who is producing "studies" in his *Arcades Project*) and to traditional advice manual authors of the nineteenth century. The first women to write advice manuals in the nineteenth century, such as Lydia Maria Child and Catharine Beecher, marked the home as a field of cultural capital. That is, they staged the home as a cultural and economic sphere in the content of their writings and in the literal circulation of their ideas between the home and the marketplace. As Kathleen McHugh notes, "Child's housekeeper is not a consumer, although her household economy coexists with a nascent market economy" (20). Her book, *The Frugal Housewife* (later retitled *The American Frugal Housewife*), however, implicitly made her housekeeper a consumer, as six thousand copies of the book were sold in its first year (1829), and it remained in print until 1850 after going through thirty-three editions (Karcher 98). Moreover, her manual also emphasized the ways in which women are undeniably a part of the market economy. Writes McHugh: "As Child herself articulates it, domestic gender/knowledge constitutes the necessary complement to a market economy, an essential counterpart that can compensate for or ameliorate the market's destabilizing, undemocratic, or hierarchical effects" (27). McHugh also implicitly compares Child to the flâneur: "She thereby signifies herself as a collector, not the author or owner, of her information" (30). Other women advisors of this period could be paralleled more explicitly with Benjamin's flâneur. In her study of Fanny Fern and Jennie June, women who wrote about shopping and consumer culture in the 1800s, Elana Crane declares that these figures "highlight the visibility of women's experiences in urban life." As she continues, "Their own experiences as flaneuses gave them an authority for their commentaries, and it was this experience and authority that lent them the expertise to become writers about urban space" (484).

Significantly, Fern, June, and Child were also novelists. Thus, one of the ways that women's advice traveled in the nineteenth-century United States was via fiction (in their works and in the works of many others). Sarah Leavitt underscores this connection: "Writers of sentimental fiction explored moral integrity through broad, often epic, plot lines involving dozens of characters. The popularity of fiction for women gave domestic advisors an audience that would understand their work" (12). As Leavitt further notes, "The close connection with novels gave domestic-advice manuals a familiar literary form" (12), although in the mid-century the manuals took on a form that also distinguished them from the novel. Even as the forms themselves might have been distinct from one another, their readers were often the same; moreover, the link between fiction and the practical vision of reality in the advice manual was already established. In a sense, Dietrich's work continues this tradition, born as it is out of the junction between the movies and her domestic life (or lives). Indeed, McHugh—as does Leavitt after her—suggests a structural and narrative link between the advice manual and melodramatic films of the silent and early classical period in particular. As I will elaborate later, Dietrich's work also shares an affinity with the structure of film, although my emphasis is less on the narrative structure and more on its temporal form. Either way, Dietrich's advice manual is dependent upon her association with the movies—the most transparent form of "cultural capital" in which she participated.

As Crane also suggests, a by-product of one's labor within the field of cultural capital is authority. Dietrich's own authority necessarily crosses boundaries of different fields of labor, as I have noted. Importantly, she ruminates on this very notion; under the heading "Authority," she writes: "Necessary to possess when in a position of leadership, may it be in a home, office, etc., or governing towns, states, and countries. Requirements for authority: knowledge not only of the general matters, but also of the problems confronting all departments working toward the same end. Nothing undermines authority faster than a gap in the familiarity with every facet of the particular subject at hand. Any man assuming authority in a cooperative undertaking must be able to judge achievements and contributions regarding elements legitimately interfering with the results. Most people in a position of authority who *are* equipped with knowledge, understanding, tolerance, dedication and love for their fellowmen, are respected and loved" (24).

This entry is, in many ways, descriptive of Dietrich's own self-portrait in the *ABC*. Her knowledge, of course, comes from a range of experiences. And from this knowledge—and authority—gained from experience, Dietrich offers advice. In this way, her proffering of advice is akin to an autobiographical composition: an authority of self-representation, an authoring of her own life, which in turn circulates among its readers. Through the knowledge she shares with us, we get to know Dietrich herself. As might be expected, given Edith Head's account, Dietrich's book thus includes several entries under the broad category of "Cooking" (with subcategories below), and she also gives advice on dressing and fashion. Across these entries she paints herself—through the knowledge and advice she shares—as a practical woman, knowing about fashion but against trendiness (thus she champions "elegance" over "fashion" in the infinite cross-referencing that the entries invite—which is also a championing of timelessless over the ephemeral; in this way, she shares some of Benjamin's apprehensions about fashion). Although a glamorous star who did not have to dress on a budget, she also offers advice to women readers on this topic. Thus, under "Dress (On a budget)," she recommends: "Don't say you can't afford a dress made of expensive materials. Save up for it.... And while you're saving for that good black dress, on your next date wear a black sweater and skirt. Nothing wrong with that as long as you don't ruin the elegance of the outfit by overemphasis of the bosom" (55).[1] In general, though, while her most practical advice is largely limited to these fields, her "authority" is not.

That is, while fashion and domestic life are conspicuous fields throughout Dietrich's volume, they are further conjoined to others in the story of Dietrich's life, as told in the *ABC* book. Unsurprisingly, for instance, Dietrich also depicts her life in film, although from sometimes oblique angles. The volume includes many references to other film stars (such as Mae West, Anna Magnani, and Cary Grant), directors (Welles and Hitchcock among them), and a number of entries on (usually male) laborers who work behind the scenes on film productions, such as "electricians," "film cutter," "makeup man," and "property man" (sadly, there is no entry for "costume designer" or Edith Head, although she addresses this occupation in her memoir). She often describes their work through a combination of metaphor and practical terms. Of the "makeup man," she begins: "The relationship between the makeup man and the film actor is that of accomplices in crime" (105). "Electricians" receive a slightly more pedestrian yet deeply appreciative entry, as Dietrich notes: "They are the backbone of the studio. Great individualists, craftsmen with an extra eye for detecting phoniness.... This holds true for every nationality. One can work in a film studio anywhere and be home. See PROPERTY MAN" (58). And if we turn to "Property Man," we read a portrait of a traveling magician, a "lovable" man who has "a twinkle in his kind eyes" and who keeps his goods in a box: "Besides the objects demanded by the script it can produce a vast array of articles that have no relation whatsoever to the film in the making," Dietrich writes (134). This remark might also appear to apply to Dietrich's volumes—the "articles" included in it also often have seemingly little relation to "film."

Dietrich's entry on "electricians" is significant not just because it contributes to her autobiography as one who worked in the film industry (yet who enjoyed a knowledge that seems beyond the stereotypical star), but also because of the reference to nationality embedded in it. These workers are the same in every "nation," she claims, so that when one works in a film studio, one can feel at home. And with this description Dietrich creates further intersections: here between the two definitions of domestic life also forged in advice manuals of the nineteenth century (the familial space and the national one).

Throughout the book, Dietrich points to her own shifts in nationality and national allegiance. Surprisingly, given her change in citizenship from German to American, this sometimes comes in the form of a denigration of U.S. culture and—perhaps not surprisingly—praise for German culture, apart from and emphatically against Nazi Germany. Her highest compliments, though, are often reserved for France—an everyday France but one which, in spite of its ordinary being, Dietrich can still depict as glamorous or at least ineffable (of France, she says: "I learned the language when I was four years old. I loved the country long before I saw it and the people long before I met them. I am very happy with that love which bears no trace of logic or sanity" [67]). At the center of most of these depictions of nation and nationality we can see two things: first, Dietrich's complex national or "domestic" identity, embodied in an expanse of memories and a range of "homely" tastes, and, second, the presence of World War II throughout and hence its impact on her life and her self-representation. Even a simple entry on "Taxi Drivers" turns to the war: "They and I reminisce shortly on short rides, long on long rides, but there is no ride without reminiscing. We also sing when a song belongs to a particular kind of reminiscing we are doing. Most taxi drivers I have met were once GIs. The conversation starts like this: 'Last time I saw you . . .' See AMERICAN SOLDIER" (160). And when we turn to "American Soldier" we get a very different tenor in her portrait: "Lonely men fighting on foreign soil. In the European theatre of war they did not even have an idea to uphold their moral hearts. They fought because they had been told to and had their eyes shot out and their brains, their bodies torn, their flesh burnt. They accepted pain and mutilation as if they fought and fell defending their own soil. That made them the bravest of all" (14–15).

The visceral nature of this image itself carries with it a kind of authority. Dietrich's memories of the war, her firsthand knowledge of it, and her very real affective relation to it might make her a kind of flâneuse of history, but they also suggest that she moved in fields that are not only dominated by the capital of consumerism.

Dietrich and Decipherment

> DIETRICH: In the German language: the name for a key that opens all locks. Not a magic key. A very real object, necessitating great skill in the making.—MARLENE DIETRICH, *Marlene Dietrich's ABC*

> *Cacher*/to hide: The task of the verbal signs will be to silence, to mask, to deceive: I shall never account, *verbally*, for the excesses of my sentiment. Having said nothing of the ravages of this anxiety, I can always, once it has passed, reassure myself that no one has guessed anything. The power of language: with my language I can do everything: even and especially *say nothing*.
> —ROLAND BARTHES, *A Lover's Discourse*

Through all of her portraits of other people—both the specific and the generalized—emerges, of course, a portrait of Dietrich's own life. But this is a portrait that is formed by allusion and even absence. In its refusal to offer a full-blown depiction of and by the star, it may be even more "truthful" than the typical memoir—as it offers us an image of one both known through contradiction and ultimately unknowable in full. How, then, might we decipher what "Dietrich" is? How do we read her, literally? That is, is there a key to read her alphabet book?

Dietrich inscribes a form of reading in her volume, which in turn can become a way of knowing her, however limited a form our knowledge might take. The process of reading the book produces is evident in two elements of its form. First, our reading is constructed through the very size of the entries: the individual entries are usually quite brief, encompassing just a few lines, or even just one line. This structure in part links Dietrich's book to other traditional forms of both reference texts and how-to manuals. Describing *The American Frugal Housewife*, for instance, Kathleen McHugh states that its "combination of the list and the prescription" make it akin to "a familiar domestic text, the cookbook." As she writes, "These organizational formats, copied from discursive sources in the home and then used to represent its overall economy, shape the

DIARY

Diaries of famous writers surely have been written with some part of the brain contemplating publication.

DIETRICH

In the German language: the name for a key that opens all locks. Not a magic key. A very real object, necessitating great skill in the making.

DILL

The best herb I know. Obligatory for: fish, shellfish, mushrooms, cucumbers, sour cream, buttermilk soup, lettuce, dill sauce. If you like dill as much as I do, try it on fried potatoes. It doesn't sound right, but it is.

DISHWASHING

A woman can stand at the sink, damp under the spray of her dishwashing, the steam in her hair. She, like Phoenix out of the ashes, can emerge and be utterly desirable afterward. She has magic powers. The man has not. Anyway, not when he is being domesticated. A man at the sink, a woman's apron tied high around his waist, is the most miserable sight on earth. No woman should make her man wash dishes.

She did not find him at a kitchen sink when he first caught her fancy—or, if she did, he was the plumber.

DISREGARD

With a good deal of disregard for oneself, life is a good deal easier borne.

53

An entry from *Marlene Dietrich's ABC* (Doubleday, 1961)

vision of housekeeping that emerges. They constitute its grammar" (28). While Dietrich's work, too, is shaped like a cookbook (it also includes recipes throughout, as "definitions" of various terms), the "grammar" constituted by this brevity also means that the book is largely structured by desire. As I suggest above, the short entries invariably leave the reader wanting more.

Our desire is in part fulfilled through another element of the design of the book: its relatively frequent cross-referencing, as between "Taxi Drivers" and "American Soldier," "Dress (On a budget)" and "Brassiere," or between "Osteopathy," "Charlatan," and "Quack." Under "Osteopathy" she writes: "The dogma of this science is the most logical of all. The A.M.A. considers osteopathy to be a cult (1961 Convention Report). *See* CHARLATAN" (125). "Charlatan" reads: "The name given by medical men to any medical man who uses means to treat illnesses not yet used by the medical men and judged by them according to standards sanctioned by the A.S.A. *See* QUACK" (42). And there we read: "Not everyone called a quack is a quack—except quacks and ducks" (136). The tracing she offers here through cross-referencing at once confirms her original definition through a tautology and questions it. With entries like these, Dietrich also guides her readers to follow a nonalphabetical course. The practice of reading that this book invites ultimately offers some commentary on the author/star herself as well as on the form of knowledge that she produces about herself and for her readers.

Given that this is an "encyclopedia" of sorts, one could read it by looking up particular terms to see what Dietrich has to say about them; but that practice would be frustrating in the end, as her choices for entries do not follow a clear logic and one could not predict what one would find therein. Alternatively, because this is an ABC book, one could read it alphabetically. But while this might be a way to begin, the reader would most likely eventually start following Dietrich's suggestions for cross-referencing and then—as we probably all do with reference books of whatever kind—begin to read across pages, flipping through to discover the unpredictability (or perhaps the predictability, once you start reading) of her various entries. We might discover, for instance, the direction that Dietrich takes us from "Bizbuz" ("A Hebrew word meaning 'waste,' which I have added to my vocabulary because it sounds more humorous and not as accusing as 'waste'" [36]) to "waste" ("I hate it with a passion" [177]) to "English" ("A beautiful language and a rich language, yet most of us neglect the beauty and use only a fraction of the riches. Even worse, we pedal through life on our small vocabulary, detouring thought in roundabout words. See WASTE" [59]) and thus back to "waste." These cross-references produce an even more fabulous paradox than the one which begins with "osteopath"; decrying the scant use of the English language—and offering a Hebrew word in exchange for an English one—Dietrich actually sends us on our own "roundabout" tour of words, which creates a potentially endless circuit between two words alone ("English" and "waste"). At the same time, Dietrich makes other connections to these terms: "Kisses" ("Don't waste them. But don't count them" [95]) also leads to "waste" which leads, back again, to "English." Even as she counsels against such "counting" (of kissing) or sparse use (of language, and of kisses, by implication), though, this text is in part a highly economic one. Throughout the volume, as these entries attest, Dietrich describes an economy of household labor and living, as well as economies of feeling and self-representation.

But each of these things—however economical—are also rich in the implicit connections that Dietrich and her reader constantly make. In a sense, the practice of cross-referencing is actually embedded in every entry in some form, for most entries refer to multiple parts of Dietrich's life. For instance, while "Taxi Drivers" explicitly directs us to "American Soldier," it gestures well beyond "Taxi Drivers" in other ways: as she offers a portrait of her performing a song with the driver in that entry, she presents at least an implicit reference (and gives new meaning) to her famous cabaret acts. Yet, as the above series on "waste" shows, not every entry ends up directing us to Dietrich the performer—although of course she is always in the process of performing *knowledge* in this work. It is this performance of knowledge that is undeniably at the heart of the volume. As I have said, this knowledge is itself a form of autobiography and is evident of Dietrich's "authority" (or, of course, authorship). Her very autobiography is, indeed, written through this authority. And further, in her advice to her reader is embodied her knowledge and authority gained from experience. As the historical subjects that we study, Dietrich both confounds and enables our understanding of her. Through the reading practices directed or allowed by this volume—through the invited cross-references and the suggested imitation—we end up producing a reading of her through her. Like von Sternberg, Bacharach, Schell, Head, or others who worked with her, we as scholars also become collaborators with her. Of course this does not mean (I hope) that we reproduce the errors of historical fact (or fiction) lodged in her work, but that we recognize the substance of this woman's authority over her image in history.

Through an engagement with history—that is, as readers with our own fields of knowledge—we might also cross-reference between Dietrich's book and works by other authors, producing further implicit collaborations in the process. Her claims about the origins of glamour in her memoirs, for instance, lead me to the *Oxford English Dictionary* to test her assertions. There I see that she is partially right: "glamour," in use since the early eighteenth century, originally meant "magic, enchantment, spell; esp. in the phrase *to cast the glamour over one*." The word first appears in the more contemporary sense—the one to which Dietrich refers—in the United States in the 1930s, according to the *OED*; this colloquial definition—"Charm; attractiveness; physical allure, esp. feminine beauty"—thus appears to come out of nowhere, but it is obviously linked to the term's original meaning.

Certainly it would be absurd to constantly cross-reference Dietrich's "definitions" with those found in the *OED*; hers are speculative and affective, based as they are on her own memories and experiences. However, in a scholarly approach to her work—mining the manual for the sake of our own understanding—we inevitably also connect her ideas to those of others (Child, Beecher, Benjamin, Barthes). I might therefore see her as like Walter Benjamin, a collector and bundler of knowledge about modern life. She is also similar to Child and Beecher in her production of knowledge about the home in relation to other economic spheres and in the very organization of this knowledge.

And we might go further still in our comparisons, our collaborations, our cross-referencing strategies. For instance, I might move between Dietrich's descriptions of terms and those by other authors of the very same words. Both she and Roland Barthes, for instance, contemplate "tenderness." Dietrich's entry reads as follows: "Tenderness is greater proof of love than the most passionate of vows. *See* CON AMORE."[2]

In his own reference book, *A Lover's Discourse*, Roland Barthes begins his rumination on *tendresse* (tenderness) as follows: "There is not only need for tenderness, there is also need to be tender for the other: we shut ourselves up in a mutual kindness, we mother each other reciprocally; we return to the root of all relations, where need and desire join. The tender gesture says: ask me anything that can put your body to sleep, but also do not forget that I desire you—a little, lightly, without trying to seize anything right away" (224). These entries each mark the ways that both volumes are exegeses on affect. Dietrich offers her definition as a possible form of advice as well as a proclamation to her reader; the implied "you" of her work, on the other hand, is that person who is also led to follow this same definition of tenderness. The "you" of Barthes's volume is seemingly quite different; while the reader might first be inscribed in the "we" of his description, that reader becomes another "you," the one to whom Barthes speaks, the one whom Barthes desires. In a sense, then, his entry also offers a model for the reader to follow in relation to the terms he describes, such as tenderness. As well, desire itself is related to the structure of both Dietrich's and Barthes's works. Through this act of cross-referencing we can see how both Dietrich and Barthes are compilers of knowledge, speaking to a reader interpellated as a desiring subject—desirous of knowledge, desirous of the author herself or himself. Through this cross-referencing and subsequent comparison, we can display Dietrich as a producer of cultural knowledge and Barthes as a compiler of practical advice. Dietrich becomes also a critic; Barthes becomes also a star.

Ephemerality

> The motion picture camera seems to be partial to the least permanent components of our environment. . . . "The cinema," says Aragon . . . "has taught us more about man in a few years than centuries of painting have taught: fugitive expression, attitudes scarcely credible yet real, charm and hideousness."—SIEGFRIED KRACAUER, *Theory of Film*

> The housekeeper must . . . make an art out of gathering together all that would otherwise be lost. Her material resources, the basis of her economy, consist of fragments, throwaways, things that would be wasted without her intervention. Housekeeping carefully, artfully prevents waste by preserving what would be discarded and reusing it. —KATHLEEN MCHUGH, *American Domesticity*

> *To make a Frock.* The best way for a novice is, to get a dress fitted (not sewed) at the best manufacturer. Then take out a sleeve and rip it to pieces, and cut out a pattern. Then take out half of the waist . . . and cut out a pattern of the back and fore body. . . . In cutting the patterns, iron the pieces, smooth, let the paper be stiff, and then, with a pin, prick holes in the paper. . . . Then, with a pen and ink, draw lines from each pinhole. . . . Then baste the parts together again. . . . When this is done, a lady of common ingenuity can cut and fit a dress, by the patterns thus obtained.—CATHARINE BEECHER, *Treatise on Domestic Economy*

Reading Dietrich through practices of desire is in part a way of knowing her. The cross-referencing strategies that she produces themselves simultaneously incite desire for more and structure our knowledge from and of her. Important, too, through this practice of cross-referencing we are always in the midst of reading across entries, rather than sustaining an examination of one thing. In many ways, this strategy is definitive of our reading of the volume as a whole.

Given its very nature—as offering tantalizing information and rumination and ever producing a desire for more—this book also has a design of ephemerality. We have fleeting glimpses of the star's life—often elaborated through cross-referencing or just cross-reading, but still fleeting nonetheless. In a sense, this design is like those other forms and practices that defined Dietrich: glamour and domesticity, surely, as I noted earlier, and film. As many early theorists of film have proclaimed, film's essence is to capture the ephemerality of movement. For instance, for Siegfried Kracauer this meant that film could capture "things normally unseen," and for Maya Deren this meant that film could capture and then transform time itself. In many ways *Marlene Dietrich's ABC* could not be called a "cinematic" text: it is not highly visual itself and it barely sustains attention on any given subject (with the exception, most notably, of "Married Love" and the numerous entries on cooking). But it is linked to film form in its ability to capture and display the ephemeral. The cross-referencing that the book directs, in fact, produces both an ephemeral process of reading and its capture at once.[3] At the same time, the function of this text, like film, is also to provide a sense of timelessness through suggested reproduction and imitation.

Such acts of reproduction and imitation are underscored in the book's form as an ABC manual. We learn our ABCs through imitation; our memory of the alphabet is formed by habitual repetition. Like other writers and artists, Dietrich imitates this form in order to organize her knowledge and the portrait she designs of herself. Indeed, we might also turn to visual examples that utilize the same tool to organize knowledge (and to display its limits): Martha Rosler's video *Semiotics of the Kitchen* and Su Friedrich's film *Sink or Swim*. Rosler's video catalogues kitchen tools in alphabetical order: Apron,[4] Bowl, Chopper. She imitates the use of these various instruments, often violently, always out of context (for instance, she violently "uses" a knife to slice the air). *Semiotics of the Kitchen* playfully critiques the limits of semiotic discourse—in part through linking it to a feminized space of work. Friedrich organizes her film alphabetically in reverse (Zygote, Y-Chromosome, X-Chromosome, and so on, although increasingly less clinical) in order to narrate an autobiographical story. The partitioning of verbal and visual fragments—and the frequent sense that the visual and the verbal are not matched—implicitly point to the limits of autobiographical discourse, tied as it is to the ephemeral nature of memory. In Friedrich's work, the ephemeral nature of memory is inscribed in the ephemeral form of film.

Film and video capture movement and in so doing seize the ephemeral, the transient, the "refuse." As Kracauer writes, "Many objects remain unnoticed simply because it never occurs to us to look their way. Most people turn their backs on garbage cans, the dirt underfoot, the waste they leave behind. Films have no such inhibitions; on the contrary, what we ordinarily prefer to ignore proves attractive to them precisely because of this common regret" (*Theory of Film* 54). As Rosler and Friedrich show, the refuse of our social experience is often lodged in women's lives. While we cannot capture these experiences in total, we can gesture toward them, analyzing how we see them as well as displaying their definitively fleeting presence. Benjamin's work is such an attempt, particularly as it imitates film form. He delineates *The Arcades* as follows: "Method of this project: literary montage. I needn't *say* anything. Merely show. I shall purloin no valuables, appropriate no ingenious formulations. But the rags, the refuse—these I will not inventory but allow, in the only way possible, to come into their own: by making use of them" (460). Given renewed value to those things we normally discard, Benjamin's strategy of recycling is like that of the frugal housewife, the hausfrau, the filmmaker.

In her own strategy of flânerie, the compilation of knowledge gained from observation, and the ordering of knowledge through the il/logical organization of the alphabet, Dietrich produces a mobile form of reading. Through the very imitation of the ABC book (whether an encyclopedia, a how-to manual, or a children's primer), she implicitly points to the limits of language and experience, or the limits of language to define our experience. Therefore the mobile practice that Dietrich's book invites—itself also designed, in part, after film—enables and confounds our understanding of her, making us her collaborators, allowing us to embody her through the knowledge she shares.

Notes

1. The entry also notes: "Here are some basic rules: Don't ever follow the latest trend, because in a short time you will look ridiculous. Don't buy green, red or any other flamboyant-colour dress. A small wardrobe must consist of outfits that you can wear again and again. Therefore, black, navy blue, and grey are your colours. Don't buy separates. Don't believe the sales talk that you can have five dresses for the price of one. And don't buy cheap materials, no matter how attractive the dress looks to you. . . . If you have one good suit, preferably grey (navy gets shiny), two black dresses, a black wool skirt, a couple of black and grey sweaters, you'll be well dressed most of the year until summer, when you'll wear simple cotton dresses. Another suggestion, don't send your clothes to the cleaner's all the time. Spot-clean and press them yourself. It is worth it because they last longer. . . . *See* BRASSIERE" (55).

2. "Con Amore" reads: "With love. Used as direction in music: Tenderly. *See* TENDERNESS" (46).

3. It also might be likened to the film *Marlene*, by Schell, in that we hear Dietrich's voice but she refuses to actually appear.

4. Dietrich defines "Apron" as follows: "I love aprons. The large white ones with the broad bands and large square pockets. Before 'The Lighthouse for the Blind' had them for sale, I used to buy nurses' aprons, the old-fashioned kind with all-around gathers. Pockets in a clinging apron don't mean much. A woman in an apron invites hugging. The apron of a woman flung over a kitchen chair is a wonderful still life. And the pockets of that apron, harboring sticky unwrapped candies, crumpled bits of paper, newspaper ads hastily torn out, pennies and nickels and a ribbon stuck to a band-aid, a baby's sock and a bottle cap, should be food for poets who are so easily tempted to linger on the treasures in a little boy's pants pocket" (17).

MARY R. DESJARDINS

Dietrich Dearest

Family Memoir and the Fantasy of Origins

WHEN MARLENE DIETRICH DIED in May 1992 at the age of ninety, she was far from forgotten, although she had been a "recluse" in her Paris apartment for the last twelve years of her life. Before that voluntary seclusion, she had been in the public eye for over fifty years in a long film, radio, recording, and concert career. Her retirement in the 1970s coincided with a period of both great critical and nostalgic investment in Hollywood film, and Dietrich's cinematic collaborations with director Josef von Sternberg were of interest in those contexts. Rediscovery of the work of Hollywood's great glamour photographers, which also began in the 1970s and continues today, has ensured that Dietrich's image continues to circulate on postcards, posters, and in coffee table books. The ubiquity of her image has been for many a powerful reminder of the pleasures of Hollywood cinema. The cool, distant image that Dietrich had crafted with von Sternberg, which was captured in so many of the photographs that have recirculated since the 1970s, have more or less erased other images that had some authority in earlier periods, such as the fan magazine articles in the 1930s constructing her as a maternal figure, or *Life* magazine photos and articles in the 1950s detailing her passion for grandmotherhood. But within several months after her death, impressively comprehensive biographies of her appeared that described a complicated relationship between her and daughter, actress Maria Riva, suggesting that the continuing circulation of Dietrich's image might have a different valence for her family than for fans and critics (Bach; Bret; Riva; Spoto). A few pages before the end of *Marlene Dietrich*, Riva's memoir of her mother, which was one of the biographies published shortly after Dietrich's death, the author reflects on the afterlife of the famous, and how the circulation of their images seems to "haunt" their children: "Our ghosts can never be laid to rest. They wander through countless laudatory tomes, photographic images, television screens, giant movie screens, their forms magnified a hundredfold—they breathe eternally! Alive forever. This continuous resurrection, this immortality constantly reconfirmed, is a haunting that invades our daily lives as when they lived. There is no escaping them, dead or alive. . . . Fancy card shops are one of [Dietrich's] favorite places—there she sits in long racks, in multiple choice. . . . Another poltergeist specialty is her voice, moaning through 'La vie en rose.' It captures you in elevators, pursues you through supermarkets, airports, department stores, ricochets off tiles in fancy ladies' rooms, follows you through hotel lobbies in countries you wouldn't believe. . . . Never is there a day completely free of Marlene Dietrich. What is it like, to have a mother no one knows? Must be nice" (780).

In her foreword to her mother's "found" autobiography, Lucie Arnaz, the daughter of Lucille Ball and Desi Arnaz, writes something similar, if in a less eloquent manner: "Oddly, in some ways, after all these years, life goes on as if they were still here; simply off somewhere, on location perhaps, and unable to get to the phone. If you go by the daily requests for their services, they'd both be happy to know . . . that they're almost busier now than they were when they were alive! On any given day, we field dozens of requests for film clips, memorial awards, memorabilia for charities, documentaries, television specials, movie deals, and countless licenses to merchandize rights" (Ball ix). One of the things Riva does not mention, but the quote from Arnaz makes clear, is that the children of the famous usually own the famed one's estate, so that much of the circulation of the haunting commodified star image is fretted over and controlled by, and its recycling is economically beneficial to, those children. Riva and her family have been among the most generous star estate owners—generous not only to academic researchers and conference organizers who need to use Dietrich's image with little economic expenditure, but also in their philosophy about how a star image relates to the culture that contributed to its stardom. Peter Riva, Maria's son, has licensed the digital rights to

Dietrich's image to a 3D computer generation company, so that she may appear, in digitized form, in future visual media projects. He claims that the estate does not want to control the way artists use her image—in fact, the estate philosophy is that the Dietrich legend should continue to be the part of the ongoing creation of culture (phone interview with Peter Riva, July 2001).

Those who control star estates rarely convey their philosophy to the public in an explicit manner, even though that philosophy, supported by legal ownership, shapes or delimits the horizon of meanings that present and future audiences may make from the star image. But children of stars, whether owners or controllers of legal estates or not, do often convey their feelings about their parent's image and life to the public in very explicit ways through the publication of the family memoir. In fact, many stars of the classical Hollywood period are known to the public now less through their films than through memoirs that promise to tell all about the person behind the image. Although Marlene Dietrich is still known to at least some parts of the public through her films and recordings, one reason why it is important to analyze child-of-the-star memoirs, including this daughter's memoir, is that they are crucial components in the ongoing construction of star personas that continue to convey historical meaning despite having outlived the flesh-and-blood person who carried or lived "beneath," as it were, the sign of that star name. Few of these memoirs provide a satisfying analysis of the famed parent's subjectivity as star "laborer"—that is, worker in a rationalized, corporate environment that produces "star signs." However, most reveal significant clues for a fuller understanding of how the Hollywood studios exploited even their most valuable employees and participated in the construction of impossible family ideals through star mythologies. Perhaps their most important achievement is in how they reveal star making as an enunciation that is publicly—and perhaps collectively—performed, not only by studio publicists and star laborer, but also by those who have family ties to the star and the fans who consume their biographical narratives. Riva's exhaustive—and exhausting—memoir revels in the irony that it details the *private* life of her family to expose how both star and daughter understood Dietrich's stardom as collectively made (contributions by von Sternberg, Bacharach, Rudy Sieber, Riva, Dietrich herself, among others) and *publicly* shared and identified (movie fans, lovers, concert audiences).

There are some important distinctions to be made between the biography—authorized or unauthorized—written by the professional biographer and the memoir written by the children of stars. Star biographies, of course, have been central to the construction of the star image for a long time, at least since the 1910s, the period Richard deCordova has identified as marking the transition among different kinds of discourses about film players. DeCordova argues that the conceptualization of film stardom itself was the effect of an expansion of knowledge about film performers, from actors known only in terms of their status as enunciators of an aesthetics of acting, to picture personalities known in relation to the roles they played, to finally, the star, who is known through writing that "reveals what she or he is 'really like' behind the screen." The actor is transformed into the star when he or she is "assigned a personality, a love life, and perhaps even a political persuasion." deCordova suggests that by the mid-1910s, this figure was given "a rather detailed, and typically 'realistic,' human identity" (21). In other words, biographies, which told the public and private life of the film player, constituted him or her as a star. Stars are not only imaged, but narrated.

Since stars were crucial to the product differentiation strategies of the studio system from the 1920s to the 1950s, star biographies were crucial, too, as constant reconstitutions of the star. In this way, star biographies of the studio era were complicit with what William Epstein has identified as the role of biography in eighteenth- and nineteenth-century Anglo-American capitalist culture: as a way to plot a trajectory for the individual that would help negotiate patriarchal culture's administration of the body into the machinery of capitalist production (147). Many of the articles in fan magazines during the studio era were basically short star biographies, and many other media outlets relied on the heavily edited, even fabricated, biographies that were disseminated by studio publicity departments. Although they existed early on in the history of stardom, professional book-length biographies and ghost-written or assisted autobiographies became more numerous and popular as the studio system waned in the 1950s and 1960s, and as many stars of the classical era were either retiring from their careers or dying.

Memoirs written by children of stars began to be published at this time. Both Diana Barrymore, daughter of John Barrymore, and Edward G. Robinson Jr., son of Edward G. Sr., published autobiographies in the late

1950s, after much of their notorious behavior had already been documented by the scandal magazines that emerged in the early part of that decade. But, it was not until the late 1970s that the child-of-the-star memoir became a huge publishing phenomenon. Brooke Hayward, daughter of film star Margaret Sullavan and agent-producer Leland Hayward, wrote *Haywire*, a memoir about her and her siblings' troubled lives growing up as children of Hollywood figures, and it was published to great critical acclaim in 1977. However, it was Christina Crawford's *Mommie Dearest*, her 1978 memoir detailing the abuse she suffered at the hands of her adoptive mother, star Joan Crawford, that started a twenty-year trend in memoir writing, which includes (daughter of Lana Turner) Cheryl Crane's *Detour*, (daughter of Bette Davis) B. D. Hyman's *My Mother's Keeper*, (daughter of Loretta Young) Judy Lewis's *Uncommon Knowledge*, (son of Humphrey Bogart and Lauren Bacall) Stephan Bogart's *In Search of My Father*, (daughter of Judy Garland) Lorna Luft's *Me and My Shadows*, Lucie and Desi Arnaz Jr.'s television and CD-ROM documentaries about their parents, and Maria Riva's *Marlene Dietrich*. Not all these productions deal with child abuse, but they are all tales of survivors of a family environment negatively influenced by the Hollywood star system that created destructive myths about their parents and was responsible for taking them away from crucial moments in their children's lives.

Many biographies written by professional biographers and star autobiographies (e.g., Esther Williams's autobiography) also focus on the power dynamics within the star subject's marriage and parenting. But one of the crucial differences between these forms and the child-of-the-star-authored narratives is the latter's blurring of the lines between biography and autobiography—the memoir is both record of their parent's life and (sometimes of their career) and their reminiscences of how they as children of the stars experienced a shared life with the parent. This hybrid status does not make the memoir necessarily more accurate (or inaccurate, for that matter) than the biography or autobiography, but it does give it at least the appearance of having a different relation to truth. Another way of saying this is that to the extent that biographies, autobiographies, and child-of-the-star memoirs are complicit with aspects of star discourse that started in the 1910s, they all play with concealment and revelation that promises to tell the ultimate, ulterior—most private—truth, and they all potentially awaken the investigatory urges of the reader. But it is the child-of-the-star memoir (and sometimes the star's own autobiography) that evidences the most personal, urgent investment in the family romance because its author has the most at stake in the betrayal of family secrets. This fact can also lead to it being a suspect form—why has the child chosen to betray family secrets? It must be revenge or exploitation for profit are common critical responses. As Mary Beth Haralovich reminds us in her essay on the critical responses to the book and film versions of *Mommie Dearest*, Christina Crawford's motives in writing the memoir and the accuracy of her perceptions were heavily debated at the time of its publication. While many have since pointed out how survivors, especially female survivors of abuse, are often not believed, it is possible that Crawford's motives were suspect to some because her account was, in fact, too credible.[1] Its place in the history of survivor literature, as well as in the history of the child-of-the-star memoir, suggests that, accurate or not, it tapped into some of the primary pleasures and disturbances that the form can take—our ongoing fascination with the family romance as a primary way of investigating identity and explaining origins of the self, and that parents and institutions are not always benevolent witnesses or helpers in the child's maturation to adulthood. These memoirs attest to the fact that the family romance is a narrative of both longing and dread. For that reason, the reader of the child-of-the-star memoir is asked to sympathize with the author's desire to break free from a parent whose own life is so enmeshed in a publicly accepted mythology that the child can neither have the parent nor an identity separate from her.

Maria Riva's reflection on the haunting effect of the circulation of her mother's image and voice, which I quoted earlier, is, then, not only revelatory of the author's beliefs about fame, or of how the child-of-the-star experiences that fame of the parent differently from the general audience. Her choice of words suggest a paranoid fear of a continuous presence. The sudden appearance of Dietrich's voice follows her in the monstrously mischievous way of a poltergeist, even into the bathroom. Curiously, this complaint about being followed into the bathroom is most often voiced by mothers about their small children. Riva's paranoid—although not unbelievable—meditation comes in the last few pages of her book, while she is in the midst of describing how she cared for her increasingly frail, increasingly infantile ninety-year-old mother. It confirms what the reader has known through most of the book: we are in the midst of a family romance, in which origins, boundaries, and endings of the self are of great concern.

For the rest of this essay, I would like to examine Riva's memoir in the context of the family romance and the generic forms it takes in the child-of-the-star-authored memoir. I will conclude with some observations about how Riva's memoir avoids some of the typical conundrums of the genre through the ways it values mother Dietrich's awareness of her own powers of self-mythologization. The family romance is a concept that Freud used to designate the repetitive interrogation of origins that is manifested in the fantasies of the subject in stages of developing a notion of the self. As Marianne Hirsch argues, the family romance describes the experience of familial structures as discursive—it consists of the stories "we tell ourselves about the social and psychological reality of the family" (10). The family romance provides settings and positionalities of desire in imaginary scenarios of wish fulfillment. For example, the fantasy of imagining oneself to be an orphan or bastard child whose parents are really nobility is a way of imaginatively reconstituting the family and replacing one's parents with superior figures. This is why Hirsch can argue that it is a notion that can "accommodate the discrepancies between social reality and fantasy construction, which are basic to the experience and institution of the family" (11). This basic fantasy construction is embedded in contemporary stories about mothers and daughters, in which the daughter seeks a disidentification with the mother in order to individuate and avoid the mother's fate (what does it mean to avoid the mother's fate when your mother is a star?). This is the daughter's recognition of the social reality of the ("ordinary") mother in patriarchal culture—she is both powerless as a woman in patriarchal culture, but because that culture also never questions the place of the mother as the primary caregiver, all too powerful. But the daughter may also participate in the fantasy shared by male children as well—the fantasy of the remerging "with the other who was once part of the self" (Williams 12).

If child-of-the-star-authored memoirs are compatible with the family romance fantasy in which the child imaginatively replaces the "real" parent or parents with superior one(s), they also appear to provide an ironic twist on it. By social understandings of status in capitalist culture, the star is a "superior" being. Riva says: "I always knew my mother was special. Why had nothing to do with it—she just was—like winter was cold and summer warm. She commanded the emotions one felt for her. In the park, I often saw little girls hug their mothers, take their hand—touch them spontaneously. One just didn't do that with mine. It wasn't that she would have pulled away or been angry if I had. One just didn't dare, until she indicated that you could. My mother was like royalty. When she spoke, people listened. When she moved, people watched. At the age of three, I knew quite definitely that I did not have a mother, that I belonged to a queen" (56).

The child is often allowed to participate in this creation in the role of princess or prince. For instance, in almost every book mentioned, the author reminisces about the lavish parties thrown for them or other star children. (This includes the dystopic vision of these birthday parties: some of the stars, most notoriously Joan Crawford, felt ambivalent about the royal status—or took its noblesse oblige very seriously—and made their children give away their presents to orphanages.) Traces of the royal bond shared by star and child are seen in the studio- or fan-magazine-initiated photos of them together, which not only fulfill the studio system's need to put stars in acceptable family contexts, but which allow the child to share in the parent's star aura. Riva is acutely aware of these positionings. Her discussion of the way Paramount Studio found that it could not only compare Dietrich to MGM's Garbo through a constructed aura of "mystery," but contrast her as well through her role as mother, is one of the few instances in which Riva suggests that the studio system, rather than Dietrich and Sternberg, were responsible for important aspects of Dietrich's star persona (Riva 111–12).

If the star parent is already a superior figure, what does the child-of-the-star author fantasize about? As the first quote I used from Riva's book suggests, to have a "mother no one knows . . . must be nice." Riva dedicates her memoir to the Rivas (husband, sons, grandchildren) and to Tami, who was her mother's friend from her days in the theater and her father's long-time mistress. A few paragraphs after Riva has first described her mother as royalty, she writes, "Tami never pretended, never lied, never faked, never deceived. . . . During my entire youth, Tami was the one person I loved the most" (57). This fantasy of the loving, more traditionally maternal woman as the "real" mother, opposed to the less approachable, although biological, star mother, is not present in every one of these memoirs, but the opposition that Riva sets up between Tami and Dietrich as mother figures is not unique. In *Detour*, Lana Turner's daughter, Cheryl Crane, chooses her grandmother as the "real" mother as opposed to the pretentious, self-involved, rarely present Lana; B. D. Hyman in *My Mother's Keeper* contrasts the controlling, domineering mother Bette Davis with Davis's submissive, homebody sister, Bobbie.

These oppositions between mother figures reveal that the family romance fantasy is appropriable for, if not fundamentally about, sexist positionings of the mother—"Is any biological mother good enough?" prompts the fantasy. The child-of-the-star memoirs trace the troubled relation between daughters and their mothers who have a public persona that is constituted out of a commodified image. Whether imposed on or created by them, the star mother must continually maintain this persona and sometimes—at least to the daughter—believe in it too deeply. For that reason, the daughter usually identifies the persona as destructive, and the commodified image as more important to the mother than her own daughter. Cheryl Crane, about a year after she has accidentally killed the abusive boyfriend of her mother, Lana Turner, sees *Imitation of Life*, in which Lana plays an actress-mother who neglects her daughter. Turner's vocal inflections and facial expressions in the film so remind Crane of how her mother has behaved in arguments with her that she wonders if her mother is not always acting. For Crane, it is as if her mother were stealing from their private interactions to feed the commodified image of Lana Turner, star-actress (307–9).

Riva's memoir suggests a more complex, contradictory, and ambivalent relation to the tensions that structure a star mother's performative identity—that is, the acting in real life versus acting in film or stage opposition. According to Riva, she was brought up with the phrase, "in life." This meant "anything that is real, as opposed to anything that is 'movie star' work associated and, therefore, unreal" (170). Dietrich, for example, knew the difference between what her body was expected to look like for films and what it did in fact look like. She and Maria's father, Rudi Sieber knew and accepted how they were expected to appear in public as husband and wife and parents was distinguishable from what they had agreed on in private as an open marriage. Riva's memoir details the extent to which a star's work was in part making and then exploiting those distinctions. One of the remarkable aspects of Riva's writing is the way she constructs her shifting perspective on Dietrich's negotiations of "in life" and "movie star work," a construction noticeably absent from most child-of-the-star-authored memoirs. When writing about the period in which she was a child, Riva describes her mother's negotiations of "in life" and "movie star work" with some awe and pleasure. In the course of the memoir, which corresponds to the period in which Riva is reaching adolescence and thus more capable of understanding the sexual arrangements in her family's dynamic, her narrative voice becomes more critical of Dietrich's particular way of negotiating "in life" and "movie star work" because it negatively affected Riva's beloved Tami. Sieber's mistress Tami was apparently hidden away in sanitariums so she could get abortions that would hide the scandal of Dietrich's open marriage, and then plied with amphetamines to manage the subsequent depression. According to the memoir, Dietrich's status as the superior being and star is only achieved through a deception that hurts others. The reader can then understand the meaning of Riva's previous beatification of Tami as the one who never lied, never faked, never deceived. The social reality of a star system that works by duplicity complies with the family romance fantasy of finding a better mother. Riva believes she found one, and Tami earns her place alongside the author's husband and children in the book's dedication, as apparently Dietrich as mother earns her absence there.

But the memoir's take on Dietrich's participation in the opposition between acting in real life and acting on film does not involve only condemnation. It presents the possibility of another perspective on Dietrich's "movie star" work in its detailing of the star's creation and appreciation of her own legendary image. For several of the most important years of Dietrich's career at Paramount, Riva was allowed in the dressing room and on the set with her mother. Here, the author would experience what would later be among her happiest childhood memories, when pleasure could be gained from how her mother's participation in her own star making could command the attention of other professionals and still allow her to work with them. In this way, she could take multiple positions in the spectrum of the daughter's family romance fantasy—her mother was both ordinary and extraordinary, part of the crowd and unique: "This, my very first day of the beginning of shooting a film, remains a kaleidoscope of firsts that would become an integral part of my life. . . . Make-Up Department all garish light. . . . Hair-Dressing, equally lit, equally exposing the normalcy of flat-haired goddesses and some slightly balding gods, the sweet, sticky smell of setting lotion and hair glue replacing the linseed oil of greasepaint, the perfume of coffee and Danish. My mother becoming one of the crowd, an astounding revelation to me, who believed she was unique, the only one of her kind. Watching as she pushed skilled hands away, took over the task of doing her own face, drawing a fine line of lighter shade than her base, down the center of her nose, dipping the rounded end of a thin hairpin into white greasepaint, lining the inside of her lower eyelid. Looking at her in the big bulb-festooned mirror, seeing that suddenly straightened nose, those now oversized eyes, and coming all the way back to my original concept: that yes . . . she was, after all, truly unique" (124–25).

If other stars' children were taken rarely on the set (Cheryl Crane didn't even get to see her mother's movies), often sent away to school (Christina Crawford would be left for months at a time at a boarding school only forty-five minutes from her mother's home), Riva was a privileged star child whose mother not only wanted her with her, but seemed to relish sharing her justifiable pride in her successes in creating the object that would be known as "Marlene Dietrich," star. If Riva would later resent the way her mother's continuous desire to have her involved in aspects of her career competed with the needs of her own growing family, the reader can see it was because of Riva's childhood exposure to her mother's "movie work," her training to remember all aspects of the process that goes into the material creation of the film star image, that she later became a successful actress on early live television and eventually could write a memoir of staggering detail. It is Dietrich's discipline that Riva admires most, and even after she has battled with her mother for years to attend to her dangerous health situation, she cannot help paying tribute to her mother's ability to perform magnificently even when in terrible pain. Of her 25 March 1973 concert in Montreal, Riva writes: "For the first time in years sober, she strode on stage, her swan's coat a huge marshmallow wave rolling behind her, and like the phoenix, the symbol of resurrection she so adored, she rose triumphant and gave a performance that, in my opinion, she never had nor could equal. No one who was privileged to witness her triumph that night in Montreal would have believed that under that lithe incandescent form oozed an open wound, swathed in wet gauze and thick bandages. For a full hour, she stood unwavering, immobile, sang encore after encore, bowed her famous low bow, finally begged her audience to stop, left the stage, and walked firmly to her dressing room. We had to strip her dress off in order to change the bandages. She had a second show to do" (731).

Riva's memoir was savaged in *The New York Review of Books* for what the reviewer called its "vindictive, sanctimonious" tone. When Riva describes her rape by a lesbian governess and suggests that Dietrich may have perhaps wished for a lesbian seduction of her daughter so that she would never marry and leave her side, the reviewer does not see the author's experience as tragic or her beliefs about her mother as understandably paranoid, but instead states that "child abuse is a fashionable complaint" (Annan 7–8). Gabriele Annan, the reviewer, seems to miss some of the ways "abuse" functions in the child-of-the-star memoir. Riva's belief that her mother was to blame for her sexual exploitation by others is typical of survivors of abuse, and it serves to validate, on the one hand, that stars are so disconnected from their children that they are perhaps even worse than ordinary parents in assessing the vulnerability of their children. But abuse tales in child of the star memoirs, whether the parent is the actual perpetrator or ignorantly (or intentionally, as Riva claims Dietrich was) looking the other way, are also the most extreme evidence of the author's need to distance herself from her mother, a need which dominates the second half of this memoir and is the necessary component of any family romance of lengthy duration. This leads not to unjustifiable vindictiveness, but to a juxtaposition of Riva's temporary spiral into alcoholic degradation with her mother's triumph's on the stage entertaining the troops in World War II. In this way the memoir suggests that the maternal melodrama in which mothers mourn their lost children—according to Linda Williams the genre best expressing the fantasy of origins—can be reversed, where only *the child* in the mother-child dyad realizes both the necessity of separation and the loss it entails (10–12). Riva's inner life and her suffering, which she must experience alone, constitute a trajectory of self-identity to rival Dietrich's ascent to stardom and legendary status.

Nancy Miller argues that "a parent's history is a life narrative against which the memorialist ceaselessly shapes and reshapes the past and tries to live in the present" (5). It is a way to return home as "the author, not the authored" (94). Riva's memoir—and its "abuse tale" component (whether the abuse of Riva, of Tami, or Dietrich's self-abuse of her body to keep the "legend" alive) then, can be seen as a way for Riva to counter her positioning as a character in her mother's narrative. In shaping and reshaping the story she shares with her mother in the past, she can prove her individuation and provide a narrative not only counter to her mother's, but also to that of media-constructed fame, which helped contribute to what Riva sees as the "fear of tumbling man-made gods." What appears as vindictive—and which it might be in part—is by this point a trait of the genre, a kind of pro–social activism, and a testament that literary authority, like stardom, is most fascinating to audiences when invention and reinvention is performed as equal parts scandalous revelation and ambiguous motivation.

Most star children's memoirs effectively destroy the aspects of the Hollywood star sign that were meant to signify an appealing wholesomeness, ordinariness, or glamorousness of the star persona, and to that extent, work against what Epstein argues is biography's complicity in smoothly ensuring the subject's insertion into the machinery of capitalist production. But in writing their books, star children also confirm that their parents are worthy of sustained fascination, and, for that reason, they find that book reviewers are less interested in their skills as memorialists than in the significance of the star parent. In other words, as far as the public is concerned, in the memorialist's bid to author rather than be authored, they are again positioned—and seen as pathetically complicit in this positioning—as secondary characters in the parent's story.

To some extent, Riva, *New York Review of Books* review notwithstanding, is able to preempt or mitigate this critical paradox. She positions herself as an authority on the construction of the Dietrich star image (having the dressing room credentials to claim this), relishes her role in debunking the ideological work of the star image, but in simultaneously demonstrating an appreciation of the value of her mother's disciplined commitment to it, is able to elevate herself as having an authoritative, connoiseurial persona that is capable of escaping or stepping outside an exclusively parent-child dynamic. This is demonstrated in the memoir's ongoing commentary on which of her mother's performances were most effective, on how much her mother worked to create a unique image, and on how disciplined she was to recreate that image exactly over and over. As an actress in live television dramas in the 1950s, Riva learned how to play a variety of roles, earning the right to be distinguished from her mother, movie star, but this never causes her to devalue her mother's own gift. At one point, she reveals a sincere wish that her mother had pursued film directing because she had such an eye for what made a scene play well and how to edit it. Although never free from mother-daughter tensions, which grew as Dietrich's problems with alcohol grew, Riva took on the job of choosing much of her mother's performance material in the concert years, which required insights into what made the Dietrich persona popular. Unlike the child-of-the-star authors who have barely seen their parents' work, much less understood its contribution to their personas, Riva is able, with critical judgment, to participate in the process of her mother's star construction and recount that process in a biographical narrative of both their lives.

The power reversals and distinction between the two women was first validated, albeit ambivalently, in a *Life* magazine cover story on Riva and Dietrich in 1952 in which the mother-daughter closeness is both asserted and denied, anticipating the complex text and subtexts of Riva's own memoir, and complicating the later criticisms of Riva as vindictive and self-satisfied when mother and daughter roles become reversed in Dietrich's later years (Sargeant). The *Life* cover features a Milton Greene photograph of Riva and Dietrich appearing as "mirror images" of one another. On the top half of the right side of the cover is a photo of Riva, blonde hair styled in the fashion Dietrich was known for at the time (parted to one side, shoulder-length curled hair), dressed in black, lying or leaning forward on a table, arms straddling its length, face toward the camera. The caption beneath this image says "Dietrich's daughter, Maria," and just below this, on the top left of the bottom image, is written, "And Marlene herself." On the right side of the bottom half of the cover is a photo of Dietrich, "Marlene herself," also dressed in black, arms outstretched, lying face up, but not looking at Maria. The effect of the composite photographic image and its anchoring caption is of a slightly off-centered reflection. In the article, which is really focused on Dietrich, Riva is described as different from her mother in negative and positive ways—a series of photos document Riva's "weight problem" in contrast to her svelte mother who "never diets," but Riva is also considered to have serious ambitions for acting and theatrical direction, in contrast to the "glamorous" Dietrich (88–89). Already at this point, Riva is described as Dietrich's indispensable judge on performance material and career choices. Some reviewers after Die-

Photos of Dietrich and Riva used for *Life* magazine's cover story, August 18, 1952. Dietrich image © 2005 Milton H. Greene Archives, Inc. www.archivesmhg.com. Riva image © 2005 Milton H. Greene Archives, Inc. www.archives mhg.com.

trich's death suggested that Riva had "an investment in her mother having suffered aging trauma [in the last years of her life], for it was (arguably) only at that point that Maria could begin to reverse the power imbalance she had thus far had to endure all her life up to then."[2] But the *Life* magazine story attests that this reversal had started much earlier, that it was assented to by both women, and that Riva is ambivalent about its value, rather than eagerly anticipating its possibilities for revenge. She is quoted in the article as saying, with a reflective attitude, "Sometimes . . . it seems as if I were the mother, and Mommy the child" (Sargeant 102). If Dietrich was not conscious before this story of the way her daughter read the power reversals in their relationship, she certainly was after its publication. This suggests that her continuing solicitation of Riva's help after the publication of these kinds of articles was some sort of assenting acknowledgment of the shifting power dynamics that now characterized the mother-daughter dyad, and of Dietrich's belief that the maintenance of her star persona was a shared enunciation.

The quotation that started this essay suggests that Riva's memory work is testimony to the need for acts of individuation to be performed over and over. The writing and publishing of the family memoir is testimony to the child-of-the-star's need for such acts to be *publicly* performed, much to the distaste of some cultural critics and book reviewers. That these books are often bestsellers, however, points to the public's acceptance of this performative need—after all, the star's public, her fans most particularly, themselves experience the blurred boundary between being and desiring the star body and identity. And like the child-of-the-star memoir author, sometimes they want to reject the power of the star identity. According to Annette Kuhn, memory work always extends beyond personal action and the individual meaning. "[Memories] spread into an extended network of meanings that bring together the personal with the familial, the cultural, the economic, the social, and the historical." Ideally, public acts of memory work make "it possible to explore connections between 'public' historical events, structures of feelings, family dramas, relations of class, national identity and gender, and 'personal' memory . . . [with] the web of interconnections that binds them together" made visible (Kuhn, *Family Secrets* 4). The child-of-the-star's memoir, because it shares personal memories of the life of the publicly known and idolized figure, is one site where the visibility of these interconnections could be made most visible. Perhaps few of these memoirs are able to adequately reveal, much less analyze, the interconnections of the personal and the social, even as their popularity attest to existence of such interconnections and the public's desire to understand them. In her memoir, however, Riva is torn between a longing for a mother-daughter relationship of mutual recognition and an admiration for her mother's disciplined crafting of her own self-mythologization. In the process of expressing this tension, Riva is at least able to make vividly visible the implications of star production on the everyday lives of the star and her family. This is accomplished through a thoroughly detailed chronicle of not only the struggles and complicities between media industry and star, but also those between mothers and their daughters, and the star and her public. Even when they fail, these child-of-the-star memoirs are remembrances we should try to understand, and not only because memory work is never done for the many of us still in thrall to the family romance. There is nothing to be gained from a demystification of stars that would disavow the strong cathexes that bind us to them, for, like Riva followed by the ghost of her mother's face and voice every time she ventures in public, we too are haunted by star images that circulate in our culture, offering us often ambivalent fantasies of affective identification and self-recognition. Maybe Dietrich "lives" because her star mythology—as much constructed by posthumous biography and memoir as by her past films, performances, and promotions—exemplifies this most powerfully.

Notes

1. Over the years since the publication of *Mommie Dearest* in 1978, Christina Crawford's account of her abuse at the hand of her mother has come to be accepted. Slowly, people who knew Joan Crawford and witnessed some aspects of her unreasonably strict behavior began to publicly admit that they had wondered for years whether the Crawford children were in some way physically or emotionally abused by her. The documentary about Joan Crawford that was aired on Turner Classic Movies Channel in summer 2002 takes Christina's story as truth, and does so in a taken-for-granted manner that would make any viewer wonder why Christina was not believed at the time of the initial revelations. Christina herself is interviewed in the documentary and, as in her book (although few readers seemed to sense this at the time), she takes a mature and

understanding—even forgiving—perspective on her mother's behavior even though she was the prime victim of it.

2. Kaplan, "Trauma and Aging" 177. Kaplan's argument about Riva's attitude toward Dietrich is not referring to Riva's comments about her mother in the memoir, but instead in the on-camera interviews in the documentary *Shadow and Light* (dir. Chris Hunt, 1993). Although Kaplan does express some sympathy for Riva growing up in an unusual family arrangement, she mainly focuses on Riva's harsh commentary on her mother. My reservations about the criticisms directed at Riva's motives by Annan and Kaplan do not mean that I do not also see the presence of resentment, anger, and even bitterness in Riva's words in the documentaries and in the memoir. I am trying to suggest that the emotions expressed are complex, that the power reversals between mother and daughter were constantly shifting and ambivalently experienced, and that this memoir stands out among child-of-the-star memories in its ability to assess the star parent's work and image.

ERIC RENTSCHLER

An Icon between the Fronts

Vilsmaier's Recast *Marlene*

IN HIS 1983 documentary portrait *Marlene*, the director Maximilian Schell asked Marlene Dietrich about her return to Berlin during her famous German concert tour of 1960. It was awful, she replied, "people went and put bombs in the theater." They stood on the street with signs that said "Marlene go home." "They didn't want me. They were angry with me. . . . They claimed, 'She left us. She didn't want us.' They loved me and hated me at the same time." She did, however, speak fondly of a meeting with Willy Brandt and also recalled a conciliatory voice that emerged amidst all the outrage. "And then there was this woman, a real Berliner, and she said to me, 'Well, can't we be friends again?' " (Na, wollen wir uns wieder vertragen?). Let us, the old woman proposed, put aside the bad memories and the different histories that divide us and recognize what we have in common: a city, a homeland, a culture. To be sure, Marlene is quick to add, few Germans shared these sentiments: "There were a lot of others who wouldn't forgive me." Marlene Dietrich's place in Germany and her relationship with Germans were contested then and remained embattled even well after her death in 1992. Joseph Vilsmaier followed Schell with another biopic, also entitled *Marlene* (2000), which repeats the old Berliner's question almost forty years later and responds to it in ways that reveal much about the conflicting historical energies catalyzed by this prominent icon.

Katja Flint as Marlene in Joseph Vilsmaier's biopic *Marlene*

A Body Too Much

For us to accept a portrayal of a well-known historical figure, Jean-Luc Comolli once noted, the film actor must perform so convincingly that spectators, at least to a sufficient degree, can stifle their memories. Famous personages, after all, "have a past, they have a history before the film began"; indeed, they have been dealt with by historians, perhaps even by other scriptwriters and directors (Comolli 43). In *Marlene*, Joseph Vilsmaier cast the young actress Katja Flint[1] as the legendary diva Dietrich.[2] The director faced a considerable creative challenge, given the profusion of images and stories, "the already mediated and abbreviated versions" of a legendary career (Custen 179). A historical figure who appears in a historical film, Comolli points out, possesses at least two bodies. In the case of Marlene, we might say, one abides in preexisting images and recollections of the star, the other in the actress who stands in for her. These two bodies compete with each other and that means potentially a body too much. For this reason historical films "usually try to ensure that the actor's body is forgotten, to cancel it, to keep it hidden, at least, beneath the supposedly known and intendedly pre-eminent body of the historical character to be represented." The filmmaker counts on spectators with limited recollections and hopes that a relatively credible resemblance will suffice (Comolli 49).

Joseph Vilsmaier's *Marlene* constituted one of the most expensive postwar German film productions, costing almost 18 millions marks, with extravagant sets by Oscar winner Rolf Zehetbauer, costume design by Ute Hofinger (who had worked on *Comedian Harmonists*), a script based on the bestselling biography by Dietrich's daughter (Maria Riva), and elaborate commercial tie-ins. The director invested much time and great ambition. Vilsmaier, writes the film's press agent (the former movie critic of *Tip*, Alfred Holighaus), is a man of good will, with a strong respect for both the immensity and the gravity of this undertaking. He "is a craftsman of emotionality. He transforms written scripts into authentic feelings. Anything he puts his hands on is stirred, not shaken. For that reason he does not shy away from political controversy. And it may well be that one or other historical scene [in *Marlene*] will not stand up to closer political analysis; no matter, it will in any event not seem false or untruthful. And that counts for something in a medium that shapes feelings and is shaped by feelings" (Holighaus, "Normal ist" 158). Just how authentic or moving this film's display of feelings actually turned out to be remains a question that I will return to later. *Marlene* depicts historical scenes, certainly, and these scenes ordered as a narrative constitute a history lesson, one that will stand up to analysis, even if that analysis might lead us to conclusions that go beyond the director's claim to authenticity and his high regard for feelings. Just how much truth or untruth is at issue here remains to be seen. Taking my cue from Simon Frith, I will examine not only how truthfully the film recounts Marlene's biography, but also "how it sets up the idea of 'truth' in the first place" and for what reasons and with what consequences (Frith 137).

Box Office Poison

The director Vilsmaier had enjoyed critical accolades, box office success, and a degree of international attention with *Stalingrad* (1993), an epic war film recounting the tragedy of German soldiers on the Soviet front. His *Comedian Harmonists* (1997) told a tale of a popular German singing group that gained international renown during the Weimar Republic only to be driven apart by the subsequent course of German history. In his lavish narrative feature *Marlene*, Vilsmaier turned to the biography of Germany's greatest film star (after Hitler) of the twentieth century.[3] The story begins in 1975 with fireworks bursting over the sky of Manhattan and the star's triumphant farewell performance in Carnegie Hall, before flashing back through a procession of tableaux from 1929 to 1945: the discovery of the actress by Josef von Sternberg, her big breakthrough with the premiere of *Der blaue Engel*, her arrival in Hollywood and her subsequent path to international stardom, the continual tension between personal ambition and domestic responsibility as wife and mother, a secret love amidst a series of romantic partners, fluctuations in her career, her enlistment in the war effort, and her return to Germany after the Allied victory.

Immodest and hyberbolic announcements preceded the film's opening. Press releases promised an unknown Marlene, a glimpse behind the scenes at the real person and the truth behind the mask. But in the end the production did not fulfill the great expectations raised by the advance billing. Vilsmaier's makeover of the famous actress failed to convince or compel German viewers. Despite the director's sincere desire to rouse feelings, popular audiences were neither stirred nor shaken. Rarely, in fact, has a domestic production been so roundly and viciously panned by the nation's critics, individuals who are not exactly reluctant when it comes to expressing their displeasure with German features, especially ones that involve large amounts of public funding.[4] In an outraged editorial, Alfred Holighaus attacked journalists for transforming the film's noble ambitions into "the greatest fall from grace" in the recent history of Germany cinema (Holighaus, "Die Kritiker"). Above all, three major concerns fueled press responses.

The film, claimed reviewers, failed miserably in its attempts to capture Marlene's magic and fascination. For all the effort put into makeup, costume design, and lighting, and even though Katja Flint had mastered Dietrich's vacant look with a perfect Valium gaze, said Rainer Fellman, the actress on-screen remained limpid and lifeless. The director takes great pains to show us the construction of a face and the making of a star, maintained H. G. Pflaum in the *Süddeutsche Zeitung*, but Vilsmaier never manages to probe beneath the surface. There is a protracted sequence in which von Sternberg molds and makes over his star with lighting, makeup, and camera; the only thing he does not do himself, commented Pflaum, is to extract her wisdom teeth. For Pflaum, the film is most persuasive at its beginning and end: here Marlene appears as a pure icon, without commentary, powdered and silent; but, he asserts, the minute Flint begins to sing she becomes a karaoke diva. Even if she at times uncannily resembles Dietrich, Flint never succeeded in sounding like a Berliner.

Marlene lacked a trajectory and a telos, according to the critics; its narrative, they complained, had a hectic and episodic structure; the mise-en-scène was wooden and one-dimensional; dialogues more often than not sounded trite or flat. The film is, to be sure, very busy. The pyrotechnic opening sequence, with its elaborate fireworks, displays the considerable production values—quite literally, showing the money. These opening minutes exhibit glamour and allure with glitzy choreography, grand-scale décor, and extravagant set and costume design. The section programmatically sets the stage for the film's unrelenting celebration of surfaces and also intimates its decided discrepancy between production cost and aesthetic sensibility. Its story line is constantly on the move, at times even harried. We begin in Carnegie Hall then flash back to the past in the kitchen of a Berlin apartment; then the film races from place to place, from 1929 to 1945. There are numerous fluid traveling shots, though that does not mean that the story has a clear sense of direction. Repeatedly, scenes seem to move with great velocity toward a dramatic payoff only to yield a feeble conclusion. Vilsmaier, in Peter Körte's judgment, "has described himself as a person 'who does not constantly second-guess himself intellectually.'" Be that as it may, says Körte, one look at a classical Hollywood biopic and its care for plot structure might have made for a more user-friendly experience ("Fernsehens Schwester").

The movie, argued Georg Sesslen and a host of other critics, played like a harlequin romance in its transformation of a life and a career into a grandiose kitsch spectacle. Marlene adores men, women, her husband and her child, and Berlin and Germany. Above all, she is obsessed with a (fictional) Prussian officer, Carl Seydlitz, who becomes the love of her life. They meet, cutely, on the streets of Berlin, trade barbs in a bohemian night club, ride horses through the green countryside (with lyrical touches straight out of Veit Harlan), share romantic interludes (including a nude sex scene on an Austrian hillside) before a dramatic final wartime encounter behind the lines in the Ardennes[5] where Carl in the meanwhile has joined the French resistance. (So that there is no doubt about his change of allegiance, he is seen wearing a Basque beret.) Focusing their dismay in particular on this contrivance, German critics complained bitterly about the liberties that *Marlene* took with history.

The Great Love

The dream lover was, unlike the film's heroine, not a body too much, but rather a bold addition, a fictional figure without a historical referent. In some regards, Carl looks like a German stand-in for Jean Gabin, a romantic partner who actually did participate in the French resistance, the great passion of Marlene's life, whom she in the end could not have.[6] The figure likewise reflects the actress's high regard for soldiers (especially officers)[7] as well as her own anti-Nazi initiative as a selfless performer for the Allied troops and the United Service Organizations (USO). Despite her shift of citizenship and her commitment to the American war effort, it was well known that Dietrich remained at heart the product of a rigorous Prussian upbringing, a controlled person whose foremost virtues were loyalty, work, duty, and discipline. "Changing your nationality," she once said, "is not an easy step to take, even when you despise the beliefs and actions your country has taken. Whatever you tell yourself to the contrary, denying what you were brought up to cherish makes you feel disloyal. The love and respect for the country that is taking you in has nothing to do with it" (*Marlene Dietrich's ABC* 120). If Marlene embodies a better Germany, so too does the fictional Carl, who will die a resistance hero. I am "no Nazi," he tells Marlene. "I am a German officer. And I was one long before Hitler became the Reich Chancellor." He is a Prussian soldier and a man of cultivation. Indeed, he is a veritable *Zitatenschatz* (treasure trove of quotes), conversant with the poetic canon from Hölderlin to Heine, and able to recite long passages at a moment's notice from authors as diverse as Erich Kästner or Ferdinand Freiligrath. This high-low merger between a *Bildungsbürger* (educated citizen) and a movie star represents the screenplay's greatest indulgence; the anti-Nazi exile-activist and the anti-Hitler resistance fighter become a good German dream team, the revisionist's ultimate fantasy couple.

Katja Flint as Marlene with her "Zitatenschatz" (Heino Ferch). From *Marlene*, directed by Joseph Vilsmaier.

Particularly during her encounters with Carl, Marlene confronts strong and conflicted feelings.[8] Were it not for him, suggests the scenario, she could easily pursue her career in Hollywood and not be so heavily burdened by her love of Germany, specifically the better Germany and the noble Prussian heritage embodied by her soulmate. He alone, avers Marlene, allows her to escape a life of playacting and become authentic, to feel comfortable and safe, "accepted as the person she really is." "When you're with me," Carl assures her, "you don't need to act. The actress Marlene Dietrich is of no interest to me." Here we see a performer portray a more contained Marlene, who has the opportunity to become what the film would have us believe is her true self, a person who is direct and loath to pretense. She becomes, in effect, the opposite of Frank Wedekind's narcissistic Lulu and von Sternberg's indifferent Lola Lola.[9] When she speaks with Carl, she ceases to think at all.

The narrative distinguishes between Carl, who allows Marlene to be herself, and von Sternberg, who transforms her into something larger than life. The director introduces her to a world of luxury; he guides her through a lavishly furnished house, in which she finds the script to *Morocco*. He tells her she is too fat and that she needs to exercise. He works over her eyelids and hair, applies just the right amount of makeup, sculpts her figure with light, teaches her how to pose and how to speak. The choice between von Sternberg and Carl becomes an overdetermined one between artifice and authenticity, between Hollywood illusionism and Prussian substance. This construction, to be sure, echoes in curious ways the rhetoric of Nazi pamphleteers who contrasted the calculated falsehood of images made by Jews with the honest German respect for real and truthful representations.[10]

Clearly, Vilsmaier's construction of a Marlene who wishes to cease acting and become real is at striking odds with the studied lack of fixity and the highly self-conscious performativity that constitute the central aspects of her persona.[11] Here, as James Naremore observes, "visible artifice becomes the sign of authenticity" for "a star who *acted* stardom" (Naremore 131, 132). Dietrich's image negotiated seemingly contrary properties: cruel woman and devoted lover, sexual being and maternal presence, Hollywood luminary and Prussian hausfrau, exotic beauty and American patriot, object of a fetishistic gaze and yet an agent with an active look. She was a cross-dresser, romantic partner of both men and women, playful and inexorable, ironic and earnest, striking and yet ever elusive.

Dietrich strategically choreographed the on- and off-screen dimensions of her public presence. In performing for the USO, for instance, she nimbly mobilized "her association with illicit sexuality, Germany, cross-dressing, and spectacle," demonstrating, submits Andrea Slane, how this arsenal could both represent Nazism and work against it (231). Indeed, the image of a nightclub singer who is also a Nazi is essential to her roles in *Foreign Affair* and *Witness for the Prosecution* where the exemplary "icon of seduction" (Bronfen 170)[12] becomes associated with the seduction of the Nazis themselves. Put differently, she functions as a Hollywood double agent, at once "as an icon of fascism *and* an antidote to it" (Slane 218). Onstage before the troops, she stepped out in a U.S. Army officer's uniform before changing into elegant slippers and a sequined dress, thus deploying her two most famous styles, "her penchant for menswear and fabulous evening gowns and her history as a Weimar-era German performer." In the end, Slane submits, "it is the fabulous sequined gown that anchors her femininity, her obvious love for men that mitigates her occasional lesbian affairs, and her rousing American patriotism that dispels any negative aura around her German origins." Seen from this perspective, the mobilized Marlene served to make ambiguity safe for Allied democracy (Slane 231–32). By introducing the dream lover and showing us a previously unseen Marlene, Vilsmaier sought to divest the Hollywood celebrity of both her illicit allure and her stark ambiguity and make a woman widely perceived as a turncoat acceptable for a German audience.

Extreme Makeover

"I am not," proclaimed Josef von Sternberg, "an archeologist who finds some buried bones with a pelvis that indicates a female. I am a teacher who took a beautiful woman, instructed her, presented her carefully, edited her charms, disguised her imperfections and led her to crystallize a pictorial aphrodisiac. She was a perfect medium, who with intelligence absorbed my direction, and despite her own misgivings responded to my conception of a female archetype" (*Blue Angel* 260). Vilsmaier, many decades later, likewise sought to shape Dietrich into his own medium. He took a star sign that had lent itself to many different meanings and appealed to a diversity of viewerships as well as having been historically problematic for German audiences. Marlene, he believed, needed to appear more determinate and less resistant if his film was to be commercially viable. How, though, was one to make over the transgressive international star sign of history into an affirmative national symbol of reconciliation that she had never been? To be sure, this dilemma was hardly novel; managing the unruly performer had caused insuperable difficulties for Goebbels and his minions. After her move to Hollywood and well into the 1930s, Dietrich possessed a large and growing appeal for German audiences. *Scarlet Empress*, *The Devil Is a Woman*, and *Desire* all ran for at least four weeks in the Reich's cinemas. Indeed, the world premiere of *Desire* took place in Berlin, even though it was no secret that its producer, Ernst Lubitsch, was Jewish (*Variety*, "Dietrich Pictures"). Goebbels's representatives wooed her with great care, believing that she offered a unique and much desired blend of German distinctiveness and international flair. Goebbels, as minister of propaganda, would order the press to desist from all negative comments about Dietrich. Even as late as November 1937, he harbored the belief that "she stands steadfast to Germany" and will return within the near future (see Spieker 233–35).

Managing Dietrich also proved to be a serious problem for Nazi pundits. As Erica Carter argues, Marlene's penchant for artifice and masquerade was held to be out of keeping with the Reich's anti-individual and ensemble production aesthetic (73). Commentators blamed Josef von Sternberg for abducting the star and distorting her appearance. In doing so, they readily took recourse to anti-Semitic constructions of Jews as master manipulators of the image. Von Sternberg, claimed Ewald von Demandowsky, "has led Marlene Dietrich down the path that, in keeping with Hollywood notions, will create the world champion of seductive depravity."[13] German reviewers consistently sought to neutralize her excessive performativity by stressing its larger aesthetic function within narrative economies. Likewise, they countered the international circulation of her image by cultivating the fantasy that she soon would be returning to Berlin.

Katja Flint as Marlene playing the singing saw. From *Marlene*, directed by Joseph Vilsmaier.

Vilsmaier, likewise, worked over an unruly image. With great zeal, *Marlene* shows us the construction of a face and the fabrication of a persona. We see von Sternberg literally making the star and remaking the woman so that she might appear acceptable for Hollywood cameras and American audiences. Vilsmaier, however, aimed to go beyond surface values. He wanted to imbue the figure with depth and emotion, presenting Marlene as a person dominated by her love for and obligation to others. The film acknowledges that she had many romantic partners, even that she was bisexual, but it tones down the promiscuity and emphasizes her maternal instincts and domestic aptitudes. Vilsmaier's Marlene is not so much vampish as what critics deemed trustworthy and well-behaved. The actress Katja Flint expressed her surprise at how resolutely Vilsmaier insisted on underplaying Marlene's erotic dimension (Lössl). The director, for instance, cut out shots in which the diva takes off her clothes and joins GIs in the shower. He also deleted a protracted and explicit bed scene with Marlene and Mercedes de Acosta.[14]

The film also carefully purges signs of Dietrich's controversial postwar status in the Federal Republic of Germany. We only get a brief written reference in the closing credits, but no visual evidence, no shot of her return to Berlin in 1960 with the bomb scares, smear campaigns, and angry protesters. Goebbels, eager to lure back German stars to the Reich, had issued directives prohibiting negative words about Dietrich. Vilsmaier, in his own way eager to bring Marlene back home, sought to control past damage by editing it out of his narrative and providing prospects of a more comforting and conciliatory relationship with the country of her birth. Marlene loves a resistance fighter; but instead of Jean Gabin and the French resistance, she adores a Prussian officer who in the course of the war champions the partisans. We hear few overt expressions of her well-known disdain for fascist Germany—and none of her anti-Nazi comments are political. What she dislikes most about Hitler's Reich, the narrative stresses, is the fact that its critics badmouth her films (which, as we know, is at best only a partial truth). The historical Dietrich rejected the Nazis' offer to become the "queen of Ufa" (Universum Film) and instead greeted German Jewish emigrants in Hollywood with open arms. The vituperative welcome that she received upon her return to Berlin happened because people still considered her a traitor to her country, "a star who had pledged allegiance to the Stars and Stripes and come back to Germany in an American uniform" (Koch, "Exorcised" 11).

A recent German documentary produced by Guido Knopp[15] (and screened in the United States on the History Channel) at one point shows Marlene, the sole female in the image, literally bathing in a wave of American soldiers, recalling the evil Maria of *Metropolis* and her lascivious embrace of male masses. The voiceover narrator insinuates, in a rhetorical question, that Marlene not only enjoyed, but also enthusiastically returned the amorous attention of many GIs—thus building on (both visually and by innuendo) the popular German notion of a love affair between a performer and a national audience that had been betrayed and in the end, to quote Helmut Karasek's confirming phrase, was to remain forever unreconciled. And it is this haunting image and this troubled relationship that Vilsmaier's Marlene works so hard to revise and refurbish. In the compensatory fiction of a great love, the Prussian soulmate and resistance fighter becomes the ultimate object of her affections, militating against popular German images of Marlene as a consort for the Allies. So that Marlene might be reclaimed for Germany, her foreign affair with America and its GIs is relativized and redirected. Vilsmaier revives the star's myth and infuses it with new meanings, prosthetically enhancing the image of the icon by airbrushing the troubled memories that attend it.

To Forgive and Forget

In Schell's *Marlene*, we recall, the actress described how an old Berliner woman came up to her during the postwar German tour and asked, "Na, wollen wir uns jetzt wieder vertragen?" Let us look at Vilsmaier's scenario and the manner in which it restates that question.

It is October 1944 and Marlene is performing for American troops in the Ardennes. She jokes around with some GIs and then requests to see the wounded German prisoners.[16] A pan follows her point of view as she beholds signs of pain and suffering; her gaze indicates both distress and sorrow. Walking forward, she scrutinizes the invalids. One of them calls out her name; she is surprised. "You recognize me." "*Blue Angel*," responds the perhaps twenty-year-old.[17] She strolls over to him, kneels, and takes his hand. "Na, dann wollen wir uns wieder vertragen, was?" she asks, "Well, now let's be friends again, OK?" Hans, she learns, is from Berlin, "just like me" (which she says in the local dialect). The war is coming to an end, she assures him, and, anyway, he's much too young for this nonsense. "No one asked me," he replies. She strokes his forehead tenderly; countershots alternate between increasingly closeup views of the dying soldier and the angel-nurse-mother Marlene. After he expires, her hands close his eyes and another sustained closeup registers her anguish.

With its solemn piano music background, this tableau commingles kitsch and death. It also provides a surprising, indeed stunning role reversal. Marlene is now the one who takes the initiative and proposes that she and the bleeding German youth get along again. She makes the conciliatory gesture, as if she, the conqueror and the survivor, had wronged the wounded party. The reiteration of the famous turn of phrase fosters a tableau of reconciliation between warring partners, both of whom come from Berlin. In its fantasy restatement, Marlene is recast in a pieta and a national allegory. The prodigal daughter becomes the nurturing mother who offers the wounded son of Germany solace in his moment of need. She asks Hans where he comes from ("Wo kommst du her?"), a commonplace, to be sure, but a phrase that recalls a well-known scene in *Triumph of the Will.* As in Riefenstahl's Labor Service Rally, a figure musters the troops in order to heal a wounded Germany, just as we see Hitler's redemptive gaze put together the separate pieces of a fragmented nation.

In Vilsmaier's metamorphosis, the outspoken enemy of Hitler and champion of the Allies transmutes into, when all is said and done, a German patriot. The narrative seeks to neutralize more disturbing images of the Dietrich who insisted all Germans were guilty for the war, the Dietrich who returned to Berlin in the uniform of an American officer, much less the Dietrich who visited Bergen-Belsen with Allied troops and felt intense horror and chagrin at the cruelty and crimes of a nation. Marlene appears in this revisionist scenario as the contrite party, as if she were somehow guilty for innocent ("No one asked me") German suffering. The offer of reconciliation is made to a seemingly randomly chosen German soldier, who just happens to be from Berlin, who (implausibly, given his age and Nazi film censorship) recalls having seen *Der blaue Engel.* In asking for normalized relations, Marlene in effect is asking to be forgiven. She at once assumes the role of the conqueror and yet renounces the claims of the victor, sympathizing with and taking responsibility for the other party, indeed becoming once again a part of that party.[18]

Coming Home

Upon its release, *Marlene* realized its protagonist's worst nightmare: box office poison (*Kassengift*). That the film failed is a matter of fact; why it failed warrants three final reflections.

First, the Marlene fashioned by Vilsmaier was an overliteral and, precisely for that reason, an utterly unconvincing simulation. To see Dietrich's unique and legendary pictorial beauty replicated by a relatively unknown actress and shackled in a contrived narrative of a tragic love affair gave rise to a sense of "one body too much." This body too much was a tamed corpus, a stillborn entity, defetishized and domesticated for the German market, divested of its vibrancy, robbed of Marlene's very essence, namely, her powers of mystery, ambiguity, and contradiction. In various regards we can understand Vilsmaier's film as a formal antipode to Maximilian Schell's *Marlene*, in which we partake of a voice without a body.[19] Schell signed a contract to make a film with an unruly actress who refused to stand before his camera. Insisting that she had been photographed to death, Dietrich would only agree to speak off-screen. In effect, the problem for Schell was less that of a body too much than one of a body too little. The filmmaker rose to the challenge and transformed this serious constraint into an aesthetic advantage. Faced with the star's own visual proscription, he decided to scrutinize and study a voice and a body of recollections, images, and performances, including the presence of an aged diva "speaking in a baritone that itself seems to scoff at her mezzo-soprano days" (Kauffmann 29), providing a retrospective view of her experiences that is alternately obstinate, humorous, warm, and willful. The ultimate body in question, the film leads us to conclude, remains forever out of reach, auratic and enigmatic, always far away no matter how close it seemed to be, an imaginary signifier that possessed a magic presence and yet never really was all there—in short, an invention of the cinema "und sonst gar nichts."[20]

Second, in trying to repatriate Marlene, Vilsmaier's film focused on her altercations with Hitler's Germany, at the same time curiously reworking, even replicating, the parameters of Nazi attempts to domesticate the wayward star. Indeed, the mission of luminaries from the Ministry of Propaganda whom Vilsmaier shows appealing to Marlene unwittingly mirrors his film's own project. It is not just the body too much that is the problem, but rather the film's own recourse to the rhetoric of the narrative's ostensible adversary. The film's presentation of von Sternberg at times recalls anti-Semitic paradigms in which the Jew is the master of the image, the highwayman who abducts a healthy German woman, leads her astray, and renders her homeless. Carl, the educated Prussian officer, is portrayed as the more appropriate object choice. The ultimate tragedy that the narrative presents is that of an interrupted great love between Marlene and a better Germany. The closing sequence spirits us back to Carnegie Hall where we see the aging diva start to sing the Lola Lola song, "Ich bin von Kopf bis Fuss auf Liebe eingestellt," only to stop. This is utter nonsense, she protests, in effect negating this role and the memories of Weimar nightlife and lascivious display that attend it. Instead, she decides to sing something for a fallen soldier (thirty years later, Carl is still on her mind) and proceeds to do a German rendering of "Where Have All the Flowers Gone?" The parting gesture is very much in keeping with a film that has desexualized the icon of erotic transgression and transformed her into the unrequited lover of a soldier and a nation. In keeping with this logic, the final sequence translates Pete Seeger's pacificist folk song into a German war memorial. What we are left with is less a celebration of a great diva than a performance of her unrelenting work of mourning.

Third, Vilsmaiaer wanted to reclaim Dietrich's star sign, to refurbish her myth in the form of a popular feature. Like the German emissaries who during the film visit Marlene in Salzburg, the director sought to bring the Hollywood star if not *Heim ins Reich* then back to Germany, to recast her as a national icon, as the centerpiece in a German film with the allure of a Hollywood blockbuster. Ironically, it has proven far less difficult for a unified Germany to rehabilitate Ufa[21] and even to honor Leni Riefenstahl. When Dietrich died in 1992, the prospect of a final resting place in the city of her birth prompted renewed controversy. For many she abided as a symbol of German self-hatred and, for that reason, a source of bitter feelings, for her life offered incontrovertible proof "that there were indeed Germans capable of mustering the courage to object to Hitler's totalitarian regime" (Bronfen 172). By the end of the 1990s, however, after many heated debates, the éclat had subsided and post-Wall Germany seemed by and large to have reconciled itself with Marlene. The star's vast estate of photographs, letters, documents, costumes, and props was brought back to Germany and is now on display in the Filmmuseum Berlin. There is a

Marlene-Dietrich-Platz near Potsdamer Platz as well as a bistro named Dietrich's and a bar called Marlene.[22] The figure that the New Berlin embraced was an international star, not just a prodigal German daughter, in keeping with the unified nation's desire to commemorate a better German past.[23] Perhaps we might view this development positively, not as a cynical and belated gesture of reconciliation, but rather as an act of what Andreas Huyssen terms "productive remembering." If contemporary German (but not only German) commemoration culture produces and confronts a surfeit of memory, he submits, it is crucial that people "make the effort to distinguish usable pasts from disposable pasts. Discrimination and productive remembering are called for, and mass culture and the virtual media are not inherently irreconcilable with that purpose" (Huyssen 28). Vilsmaier's attempt at a redemptive reclamation was in this regard both miscalculated and belated. By the year 2000 Marlene had already been brought home and accepted by the New Germany, to a great degree on her own terms. In this sense, the film fought a battle that had already been won—and it did so with a rhetorical arsenal that was untimely and misguided, out of the past and off the mark.

Notes

The translations in this essay are my own unless otherwise stated.

1. See Blum and Blum 128: "At least since Dominik Graf's *Die Sieger* (*The Invincibles*), Katja Flint has become an important presence in the German film landscape."

2. *Marlene*, 1999, directed by Joseph Vilsmaier; produced by TPI Trebitsch Produktion International (Hamburg) and Perathon Film (Munich) in cooperation with the ZDF (Mainz), with additional backing from FilmFernsehFonds Bayern, Filmförderungsanstalt, Filmboard Berlin-Brandenburg, Filmstiftung NRW, and FilmFörderung Hamburg; producers Katharina M. Trebitsch, Jutta Lieck-Klenke, Joseph Vilsmaier; script by Christian Pfannenschmidt, based on Maria Riva's biography, *Marlene Dietrich*; cinematography by Joseph Vilsmaier; set design by Rolf Zehetbauer; editing by Barbara Hennings; costume design by Ute Hofinger, Lisy Christl, and Brian Rennie; makeup by Ruth Philip, Heiner Niehues, Gerlinde Kunz, and Gerd Nemetz; music by Harald Kloser.

Principal cast: Katja Flint (Marlene Dietrich), Herbert Knaup (Rudolf Sieber), Hans-Werner Meyer (Josef von Sternberg), Heino Ferch (Carl Seiditz), Christiane Paul (Tamara Matul), Josefina Vilsmaier (Maria as a child), Theresa

Vilsmaier (Maria as an older child), Janina Vilsmaier (Maria as a teenager), Ute Cremer (Maria Riva), Armin Rohde (Emil Jannings), Cosma Shiva Hagen (Resi), Heiner Lauterbach (Erich Pommer), Monica Bleibtreu (Widow von Losch, Marlene's mother), Katharina Müller-Elmau (Margo Lion), Suzanne von Borsody (Charlotte Seidlitz), Oliver Elias (Jossi Winter), Mike Wimbly (Harry), Götz Otto (Gary Cooper), Gloria Gray (Mae West), Michel Francoeur (Maurice Chevalier), Basia Baumann (Mercedes de Acosta), Ben Becker (Ernst Linke), Jürgen Schornagel (Friedrich Mollner), Otto Sander (stage manager), Heinrich Schafmeister (pianist).

Marlene was filmed from 31 August to 10 November 1999 at a cost of 17.8 million marks. The original length was 3,420 meters (128 minutes) of 35mm color film. It was given general release in Germany on 9 March 2000.

3. Vilsmaier had also planned to release a director's cut of 160 minutes for Dietrich's hundredth birthday, but this did not happen (*Filmboard News* 4 [2000]).

4. Commentators described the film as the worst blunder in recent memory by the German film subsidy system. At a panel discussion in the Filmmuseum Potsdam on 9 September 2000, Vilsmaier complained vehemently about the mistreatment of *Marlene* by the German press. "I have memorized the names of the film's five harshest critics and as long as I'm around, I'll do everything within my powers to make their lives hell."

5. Cf. the entry "Ardennes" in *Marlene Dietrich's ABC* 18. Among her memories, it is not a fond one. "I acquired my worst war wounds there. I froze my hands and feet during the winter of 1944."

6. Marlene's relationship with Gabin, claims biographer Steven Bach, was stormy and "unique. It combined an outlet for her mothering instincts with the high romantic excitement of a volatile sexy man . . . who would tell her what to do, whether she actually did it or not. No one doubted she was madly in love with him" (317–18).

7. Cf. the entry "Army" in *Marlene Dietrich's ABC* 19–20.

8. Marlene's uncertainty of place is foregrounded in an early scene where the couple dance to the song, "Ich weiss nicht, zu wem ich gehöre" (I Don't Know to Whom I Belong).

9. Cf. Slane 219–21.

10. See Neumann, Belling, and Betz.

11. Dietrich, however, repeatedly portrayed characters who express a desire to be known for their authentic selves. In *Destry Rides Again*, she plays the bar girl Frenchie who confides to Destry that he is the one who knows who she really is. The bad woman aligns herself with her legitimate (but impossible) lover and the right cause. Here, as ever, she is a woman between the fronts.

12. The phrase is taken from Bronfen 170.

13. See Ewald von Demandowsky's review of *The Devil Is a Woman*, "Die spanische Tänzerin," which appeared in *Völkischer Beobachter*, 30 June 1935 (qtd. in Spieker 138). He notes: "A person of healthy sensibilities would be tempted to make certain that such a woman receive a thorough dunking in the River Spree."

14. In various interviews and discussions after the film's disastrous reception, Vilsmaier maintained that he had been put under legal pressure by Maria Riva to delete any scenes that suggested sexual license or excess on the part of Marlene.

15. *Marlene Dietrich: Die Gegnerin*, a 45-minute portrait, appeared in the series *Hitlers Frauen* (2001). See also the accompanying book by Guido Knopp.

16. Frank Noack points out that Marlene had spoken to Leo Lerman, a journalist for *Vogue*, about an encounter in 1944 with wounded members of the Wehrmacht (34). Whether this meeting actually transpired remains, however, uncertain.

17. *The Blue Angel* had not been screened in Germany since 1933, so it is unlikely that this young Berliner recognizes her from the film.

18. This tableau is in keeping with Vilsmaier's penchant for retrospective tales of reconciliation. Consider, for instance, the Soviet soldier and the Prussian officer who end up in a bedroom during the final scenes of *Stalingrad*. Vilsmaier's camera frames them in a composition with a studious symmetry. What the image suggests is a relationship of equivalence; both parties, the visual and aural track insist, have been abused by Hitler Germany. The constellation equates a woman, a Soviet soldier who has been made into a consort for the SS, with a noble German officer, son of a Prussian family, who has been mistreated by the Nazi order. The two will become comrades and ultimately march into death together. The revisionist rhetoric of Vilsmaier's retro project is, of course, quite familiar: above all, in the way that the myth of the German victim goes hand in hand with a gesture of rapprochement. In this display of spurious harmonizing, the victim is seen to recognize the moral as well as technical nobility of the victimizer. *Stalingrad* acknowledges German violence, even misdeeds by the military, but makes a point of redeeming a better German army and a noble military tradition by making them into victims of the Nazis. This is a well-known cinematic legacy that extends from *Des Teufels General* and *Die Brücke* to *Das Boot*, a rhetoric that has become far less credible in light of the historian's debate from the mid-1980s. Indeed, the rhetoric of the scene (and the film as a whole) might be said to enact the revisionist interventions of Ernst Nolte.

19. The opening sequence in fact foregrounds this aesthetics of reduction

by showing a closeup of a reel of tape unwinding on a recording machine from which Marlene's reproduced voice emanates.

20. In David Thomson's assessment, Schell's documentary "is a magisterial maintaining of the legend, to such an extent that she managed not to appear. She was radio, and in charge" (238).

21. See my essay "Springtime for Ufa."

22. See Wiebrecht 146. A restaurant in the Gotenstrasse near her Schöneberg birthplace is called Der Blaue Engel. It displays pictures of the star and features a menu with dishes prepared according to Marlene's original recipes.

23. David Riva's documentary portrait, *Marlene Dietrich—Her Own Song*, might be best understood as a response to and a refutation of Vilsmaier's problematic initiative. The production of 2001 documents the biography of his grandmother and in the process discloses the irresolvable tension between the star's German past and her international career. The portrait is, no doubt, in crucial regards touched up. Dietrich's family members, the moving forces behind the production, studiously stifle the more transgressive aspects of Marlene's star sign.

JUDITH MAYNE

"Life Goes On without Me"

Marlene Dietrich, Old Age, and the Archive

WHEN DID MARLENE DIETRICH become an old woman? At what point in her career did she begin to show the signs of (old) age? Since aging is a process and not a fixed event, these are impossible questions to answer with any precision. But the specter of aging—of denying it and negotiating with it, of examining it and turning away from it—is dramatically foregrounded in Dietrich's career and in the proliferation of commentaries, texts, and spectacles that career has inspired. During her period of seclusion (the years between 1978, when she made her last professional appearance, and 1992, when she died), and especially since her death, Dietrich's visibility as an icon has been inextricably tied to her image as an aging star. Perhaps the most obvious example of the obsession with Dietrich's age is Maximilian Schell's 1984 film *Marlene*. Dietrich's reluctant collaboration with Schell and his documentary becomes the occasion not only for an overview of Dietrich's career from its beginnings to its end, but also and especially for a cruel yet very engaging exploration of the aging icon's attempt to assert control. Schell's film may be the most spectacular attempt to juxtapose Dietrich's legendary (and youthful) screen persona with the presumed realities of old age, but virtually every account of Dietrich's life of the last two decades—from the televised documentary *Shadows and Light* (directed by Chris Hunt, 1996) to Maria Riva's exposé of the supposed truth behind her mother's glamorous persona, and including virtually every biography or memoir about Dietrich—is preoccupied

Just a Gigolo (1979). *Author's collection.*

with demonstrating, exposing, and lingering upon the effects of age on Dietrich.[1]

To be sure, the fascination with Dietrich's age is not unexpected. The very nature of female stardom means that aging is a potentially terrifying fact of life, greeted with responses ranging from gleeful mockery if the female star attempts to thwart the vicissitudes of age, to staid if often suspicious admiration if she seems to "accept" (whatever that might mean) the inevitability of old age. One only has to think of the simultaneous humiliation and triumph (and often more of the former than the latter) associated with aging for many great Hollywood actresses, from Bette Davis to Joan Crawford, to appreciate the extent to which female stardom relies upon both a denial of and an encounter with the process of aging.

Like Davis and Crawford, and despite her long period of seclusion, Dietrich aged visibly in the public eye. Dietrich was known to be very wary of any acknowledgment of age; indeed, the concealment of her real age was one of the many ruses of her career (she routinely shaved several years off her age by claiming to have been born several years later than 1901, her actual year of birth). At the same time, the ways in which Dietrich performed her age suggest a woman who worked the "age angle" quite successfully. Despite the fact that Dietrich was still appearing on stage when she was in her seventies, she is routinely described as a woman intent on denying her age. This is one of the central paradoxes of Dietrich's status as an aging icon: she embodies both visible old age and its denial.

Perhaps the paradox of Dietrich's old age is merely an extension of how Dietrich has functioned as a paradigm of virtually every argument that has been made about the specificity of the cinema. Dietrich has always been an important figure in film theory, and particularly in feminist film theory and criticism. Dietrich has been used to make larger claims about the cinema and gender, most classically in the casting of Dietrich as the embodiment of the woman-as-object-of-the-look in Laura Mulvey's account ("Visual Pleasure"), as well as in Gaylyn Studlar's alternative theorization of the cinema and masochism (*Realm of Pleasure*). While it is not my purpose here to rehearse all of the criticisms that have been made of 1970s and 1980s feminist film theory, it is interesting to note that Dietrich figures just as forcefully in those critiques as she did in the foundational work that preceded them. Dietrich was proposed, in feminist psychoanalytic accounts of the cinema, as the model of the fetishization of the woman, the representation of (male) lack and fear of castration, the woman rendered desirable yet inaccessible through her demeanor and especially through framing and costumes, from veils to feathers. Yet she also emerged as a point of resistance to those claims of heteronormativity and passivity—Dietrich returned the look, mocked the male gaze, offered herself as the embodiment of plural desires. Thus Dietrich has served to theorize both the paradigmatic workings of the cinema in patriarchal terms, and exceptions, excesses, and resistances to such definitions.

Classical feminist film theory has been criticized for its inattention to matters of race, and Dietrich—in particular, the Dietrich of *Blonde Venus*—has served as a reminder of the extent to which gender and race are intersecting categories in the classical cinema (Gubar 221–23; Petro 136–56; Snead 69–75). Feminist film theory also has been criticized for its elision of lesbian pleasures in the cinema, and Dietrich, once again, has been a central figure for an understanding of how the presumed heteronormativity of classical cinema is far less fixed or monolithic than is usually assumed to be the case (Desjardins; Weiss 30–35, 42–48; White, *Univited* 49–57). Indeed, that Dietrich's first American film, *Morocco*

(1930), features, very early in the film, her star turn as a cabaret singer in top hat and tails who kisses a female member of the audience, suggests that lesbian desire was foundational in Dietrich's appeal.

Dietrich remains an icon in these more recent explorations, but one shaped by different explanatory narratives—of lesbian history, say, or of the production of whiteness. Such a range of possibilities contained within the Dietrich persona may well be the perfect embodiment of the contradictory qualities of stardom identified, in Richard Dyer's groundbreaking work, as essential to the dynamics of the performer/spectator relationship. Yet in the contradictory claims of female stardom embodied in Dietrich—heterosexual and lesbian desire, whiteness and its limitations, passivity and agency, objectification and resistance—age is rarely identified as central to her iconic status. Of course this may have less to do with Dietrich and more to do with the fact that, with some notable exceptions, the aging female star has not received extensive theoretical or critical attention.[2] I want to suggest that in the case of Dietrich, the very nature of "age work"—her management of the inevitable process of aging and its effects on her spectators—is central both to the star's iconic status and to the ways in which her legendary status is appropriated and understood.

A consideration of the Dietrich persona in relationship to aging, as well as her attendant age work, engages not only with Dietrich's film persona, but also and especially with how, during a period in her life when film roles were more and more difficult to come by, Dietrich began a successful career as a recording artist and in particular as a stage performer. As numerous biographies and documentaries about Dietrich have reported, Dietrich's cinematic possibilities were declining in the 1950s. She appeared as the ringmaster at a circus benefit in Madison Square Garden in 1953 (in an outfit strikingly reminiscent of Lola Lola in *The Blue Angel*), which led to an offer to appear at the Sahara Hotel in Las Vegas. Dietrich premiered at the Sahara in December 1953, and as Steven Bach puts it, she "overnight became the most desirable nightclub attraction in the world" (371). Dietrich continued to appear in films, often times in cameo roles (as in *Around the World in 80 Days* [1956] and *The Monte Carlo Story* [1956]), and occasionally in roles that were remarkable (*Witness for the Prosecution* [1957] and *Judgment at Nuremberg* [1961]), and sometimes both at once (*Touch of Evil* [1958]). But Dietrich's greatest success during these years came in her one-woman show, which she perfected and performed for over twenty years, until 1976.

Stories of Dietrich's stage career include details of her alcoholism, her nagging perfectionism, and her failing health. The most exhaustive source for these tales of imperfect age is the exposé by Dietrich's daughter, Maria Riva. Riva's account of her mother's complex, narcissistic life may well be informed by the inevitable tensions between mother and daughter, but Riva's description of the aging Dietrich mirrors the culturally entrenched notion that age must be a degrading, humiliating process. Riva thus describes Dietrich's state of mind, at age seventy-three, facing surgery: "This woman, who reconstructed her aging body to suit an illusion of youth, who concealed the crepe-flesh of her hanging thighs in a thousand ways, who hid her thinning, wispy hair beneath golden wigs, who folded sagging breasts into gossamer harnesses, ever re-recreating the Venus the world wanted and expected Dietrich to be . . . was about to be laid bare" (735).

The "laying bare" is more than a surgical procedure, for it quite obviously describes the scope of Riva's own book. While Riva's description of her mother's "reconstruction" is meant to provoke horror and perhaps pity at the spectacle of the Blue Angel clinging so desperately to her youth, the specter of Dietrich "clinging" to her youth may well be just as efficient a projection as Dietrich's own costuming and makeup. Attempting to preserve an iconic illusion is not the same as fooling oneself into thinking one is forever young. It is perhaps difficult to separate the cultural assumption that aging is a shameful, pathetic process from the specifics of Dietrich's own battles and encounters with old age, yet Riva's account of Dietrich's aging consistently juxtaposes the beautiful image with the harsh reality. For instance, Riva writes about the wound on her mother's leg that would not heal, here in the context of a show in Montreal: "No one who was privileged to witness her triumph that night in Montreal would have believed that under that lithe incandescent form oozed an open wound, swathed in wet gauze and thick bandages" (731).

The oozing wound in Riva's account trumps Dietrich's magnificent performance, but nonetheless the two domains, the physical degradation and the shimmering spectacle, are juxtaposed. Indeed, accounts of Dietrich's stage performances document the sheer magic that she created. As Bach writes: "It is unlikely anyone who saw Dietrich on stage ever forgot it—or ever will—because she unfailingly confounded expectation. She always delivered the legend, but always more" (438). Ironically, perhaps, for a stage act that relied so heavily on the performance of songs associated with Dietrich's most famous film roles, the show only exists in recollections and reviews, or in very imperfect recordings of it.

The relative lack of documentation of Dietrich's stage performances presents a research challenge. One can find sound recordings by Dietrich fairly easily, but video or filmed recordings of her stage shows are rare. In other words, the observation of Marlene Dietrich as an aging woman on stage is based largely on ephemeral evidence and anecdotal tales. In archival terms, Dietrich's stage shows cannot be subjected to the same kind of analysis as her cinematic roles. This does not mean, of course, that they cannot be analyzed at all, but rather that Dietrich's stage performances, while building upon her cinematic status, are also qualitatively different. There is something ephemeral about Dietrich's stage performances; no matter how many film or video records of the events might exist, they can never approximate fully the experience of being there. One cannot help but wonder if Dietrich planned it that way, if she was not cagily aware of this ephemeral quality as both limitation and possibility. Portions of different renditions of her stage show can be seen in documentaries on Dietrich, and a television recording of a 1972 London performance, shown on U.S. television in 1973 as *I Wish You Love*, is available on video as *An Evening with Marlene Dietrich*. The taped concert is not widely considered to be a success. As Steven Bach puts it, "Television is a technician's medium, not a performer's, and Marlene was denied the control that made her concerts models of professionalism—witty, majestic, moving" (428). If *I Wish You Love* is a poor substitute for the real thing, then the real thing must have been something, for even in this "technician's medium" Dietrich delivers everything that the rhapsodic descriptions of her stage presence lead one to expect.

To be sure, her face is taut, her eyelids are heavy, her hair is obviously a wig, and her dress seems to have a life of its own. But Dietrich manipulates her body like so many props, and stares you down while doing so. There is a defiance in her performance, not a denial of age but rather a visible display of it, quite suggestive of what Kathleen Woodward describes as the defiant posture of the "aging body in masquerade" (148). Dietrich flirts and teases; she looks tired and bored. She sings as if she really wants to please this particular audience but at the same time as if she couldn't care less; she recites the songs as if by rote, yet at the same time seems to take pleasure in the trip down memory lane that the songs evoke. Dietrich's hair—or rather her wig—is big, and she wears one of her famous shimmering skin-tight dresses in which she appears both contained and ethereal. She wears a huge white fur coat that frames her body yet could easily overpower her at any second. (When Dietrich sheds the coat in the second half of the performance, she seems less imperious.) Her jewelry, in particular the diamond necklace she wears, sparkles. She is flirtatious and cunning, imperious and poignant. Dietrich evokes the Marlene Dietrich of decades past, the desiring woman who seems simultaneously to be detached and distant.

Dietrich's performance has a narrative, for she introduces her songs by describing the development of her film career, with all of the erasures and changes that have become part of the Dietrich legend. She calls herself a "student in a theater school" in Berlin (not a cabaret performer or a film actress) when she was discovered by Josef von Sternberg. After a rendition of "You're the Cream in My Coffee," which she describes as the song she sang for Josef von Sternberg in her audition for *The Blue Angel* (which she describes, erroneously, as her first film), Dietrich looks slyly at the audience, with the huge coat seemingly about to fall off her slightly thrown-back shoulders, and says, "As you all know, I got the part." Applause follows, and Dietrich looks at her audience both gratefully and with the world-weary gaze of one who knows applause is sure to come at that particular moment. She adds: "It's surely not because I sang that song so well." She pauses again and waits for the requisite chuckles, both for her sexual innuendo and for her acknowledgment that she is not a terrific vocalist. When she sings the most famous songs from *The Blue Angel*, she moves in and out of impersonations of her film performances of the songs, from the hips thrust forward ("Lola") to sultry and seductive detachment ("Falling in Love Again"). Throughout the performance, Dietrich evokes her famous past. Yet the concert is not only about nostalgia. For throughout her performance, Dietrich's role is that of a narrator, a mistress of ceremonies, looking back but also looking "out," as it were, that is, offering the spectacle of a woman watching herself perform.

Dietrich's stage persona is evocative of the detached, ironic smirk associated with so many of her film roles. Yet the combination of the stage (mediated, in my reading of it, through the television screen) and Dietrich's age gives the stage persona a different quality. Dietrich is not only a narrator, but also and particularly an archivist. In her most famous film roles, Dietrich occupies the role of an actress watching herself perform, but in her performance of old age, Dietrich rearranges the pieces of her career into a whole—a not always particularly coherent whole. As an archivist, Dietrich evokes a persona that is shaped by distinct songs that can summon up a career, even if it is a career that is filtered through a particular lens. As an archivist, Dietrich recollects, but there is a decided resistance to nostalgia; it is, rather, the arrangement and rearrangement of bits and pieces of her career, now, in the present tense of the stage, that matters.

One of the best-known and most influential readings of Dietrich in relationship to detachment and irony is found in Silvia Bovenschen's groundbreaking 1977 essay "Is There a Female Aesthetic?" which formulated many of the notions of female agency and artistic practice that have remained central to feminist criticism. Bovenschen used Dietrich, as she appeared on stage in the 1970s, as a sign of the agency of the actress "citing" her film career. Two aspects of female creativity are of particular interest to Bovenschen: First, the ways in which acting, whether on stage or on screen, is one of the few artistic endeavors historically available to women, and second, the way the "preaesthetic" realm—home crafts, letter writing, decoration of the body—provides means of access to artistic expression. Bovenschen's discussion of Dietrich appears in the context of how, in the first category, "instances of female resistance and uniqueness . . . have always been contained in the artistic product" (127). Noting the effect throughout Dietrich's performance of both absolute control and ironic commentary, Bovenschen says: "Her face is older now, but even this change seems not so much the result of the biological aging process; it seems much more something artificially arranged, a sort of displacement intended to signify historical distance. And her body is just as artificial, absolutely smooth as though encased in some unfamiliar fabric—we are watching a woman demonstrate the representation of a woman's body" (129). Bovenschen introduces her discussion of Dietrich by noting that at the time of the stage performance, numerous feminists were critical of how Dietrich's age work—the face lifts, the wigs—presents an artificial image of woman. Because Dietrich's body is her art and her performance,

Bovenschen dismisses the desire to bring the actual construction of the body onto the stage: "All this has little to do with the actual woman whose real name most people have forgotten. Who knows how she looks in the dressing room afterwards; who knows how we will look at her age. That is another world" (129).

Because Bovenschen is concerned with female aesthetic production, the dressing room and the projection of the spectator's own aging process may well be "another world." In other words, Bovenschen traces the very conditions of possibility of female artistic agency, and questions about Dietrich's age work may well function to marginalize her own status as creator. Bovenschen is concerned primarily with authorship, not spectatorship. But both perspectives, that of the author and that of the spectator, are implicated in Dietrich's ability to work her persona so successfully on stage; this, too, is central to her role as an archivist, for she attends not only to the objects of her own past but also to the effects they produce. The fascination with Dietrich, the glamorous woman, has another side, the fascination with both the aging body and the work required to present it on stage. Bovenschen's point may be less to dismiss the backstage dynamics of performance, and more to insist that however "present" Dietrich was on stage, she was citing, transforming, and perpetuating a screen persona. In other words, the stage performance both promises and shuts down the possibility of immediacy, of direct connection between star and audience.[3]

Curiously, Bovenschen's analysis of Dietrich seems both to require the aging persona (in order to "gaze down from the stage not once but twice, once as an image and once as an artist" [130]), and to repress it (the "other world" of the dressing room and the future). Perhaps this ground-breaking essay on reading against the grain has its own blind spot, in as much as the "age work" performed by Dietrich is summoned as an aesthetic distance, an ironic commentary, that erases its own physicality in order to underscore illusion and artifice. In insisting that the old Dietrich performs a distanced commentary on her own film career, the aging Dietrich persona, as a complex process of negotiation and labor, is ghosted. While such a move might be necessary in order to underscore Dietrich's function as a creative artist, such ghosting, by leaving aside the question of age, affirms, even if passively, the most stereotyped view of aging as inevitable humiliation and defeat.

If Marlene Dietrich successfully cited her film career in her stage show, documentary renditions follow a somewhat similar structure of reminiscence, juxtaposing the young Dietrich with the old. E. Ann Kaplan analyzes the ways in which Dietrich's age is addressed in the televised documentary *Shadows and Light*, particularly insofar as the relationship between Maria Riva and Dietrich is concerned ("Trauma and Aging"). Riva in the film is a marked counterpoint to Dietrich, for Riva appears to have aged "naturally" to the extent that her skin is wrinkled, and thus is very much unlike the pulled and taut face we see in footage of her aging mother in the film. While Riva is meant to be a narrative voice of truth in the film, Kaplan notes that it is obvious that Maria "has an investment in her mother having suffered aging trauma, for it was (arguably) only at that point that Maria could begin to reverse the power imbalance she had thus far had to endure all her life up to then" (177). Kaplan acknowledges that there is a complex play of ambivalent identifications in the film, and she notes that the film presents Dietrich as "devastated by the split between dramatic aging on the outside and the inner desire for continuing beauty and professional involvement" (179). But Kaplan quickly assumes that despite Maria's own investment in that particular image of Dietrich, the portrait of the aging actress presented by the film is an accurate portrayal of Dietrich herself: "Once aging was outside of her control, and her body could not be patched up, then she wanted to preserve her public and perfect image by not allowing anyone to see her as she now was, and thus imposed a prison sentence on herself" (179). It is as if the spectacle of humiliation associated with aging is so compelling that it serves as its own justification.

Implicitly present in virtually all of the explorations of the aging Dietrich persona is the "desperate aging actress" motif, best known perhaps in Gloria Swanson's turn in Billy Wilder's *Sunset Boulevard* (that film has served as a kind of touchstone, not only of the aging actress but also of the aging woman in American culture [Banner; Fischer, "*Sunset Boulevard*"]). Indeed, some great actresses come to mind, for whom aging presented uncomfortable realities and spectacles of humiliation—Bette Davis, and Joan Crawford in addition to Gloria Swanson. Davis, Crawford, and Swanson all starred in films about performance that dramatize the very process of female aging—*All About Eve* (1950), *What Ever Happened to Baby Jane?* (1962), and *Sunset Boulevard* (1950). Jodi Brooks, describing these films as marking a reflection on the cinematic past as well as a mourning of the actresses' former selves, observes: "The fascination of these films is primarily in the ways in which each of these characters resists being positioned as a figure of loss, a resistance which, not surprisingly, by and large fails, given their limited options" (234).

Surely the notion of a "resistance to being positioned as a figure of loss" applies to Marlene Dietrich. But Dietrich figured her own age differently. If we can point to specific individual films that articulate the drama of the aging of the female actress in the case of Davis or Swanson or Crawford, this is not necessarily the case with Dietrich. For the process of aging was built into so many of Dietrich's films that it is difficult to isolate one, or two, as dramas of her resistance to age. *Stage Fright* (1950) reads in part as showdown between an "older" and a "younger" woman in terms of their allure, but in both cases the opposition between the younger American and the older European recasts the opposition into one of experience versus innocence. In *Rancho Notorious* (1952) and *Witness for the Prosecution* (1957), Dietrich elaborately stages allusions to her own earlier roles, as Frenchy (in *Destry Rides Again* [1939]) and Lola Lola (in *The Blue Angel* [1930]) respectively. While these instances are fascinating as indications of the complexity of the Dietrich persona, they do not drive the films in question as centrally as the "actress" plots of other films do.

Indeed, one of the particularities of Dietrich's image in relationship to the specter of aging is that aging has always been a part of her persona. In Dietrich's films with von Sternberg, there is always a shady past or a mysterious secret to which the on-screen Dietrich seems to respond, as if she were a jaded narrator reflecting back on a distant past. Werner Sudendorf observes that "in Sternberg's films, death is never far from the figures embodied by Marlene Dietrich; death is almost an incidental accessory that does not affect her and which she can nonchalantly ignore" (147). While the presence of death does not necessarily mean the presence of aging, in Dietrich's case the famous nonchalance, the irony, the detachment, do suggest that this young, beautiful star is narrating her own decline. Thus the apparent irony of the application of lipstick while facing the death squad in *Dishonored* (1931) is not only a willful distance from the tragedy of a beautiful woman's death, but also a suggestion that the artifice of beauty calls up its opposite.

If Dietrich's stage presence was intimately connected to her film persona, it relied on a reverse process of narration from what we see in her earlier Hollywood film roles, and that process is central to Dietrich's role as archivist. Dietrich flaunts the aging body and mocks the gestures of retrospection, as if to suggest not so much that her career has come full circle, but that the spectacle of aging has been implicit in that career all along. The stage performances are not, however, the final chapter in Dietrich's career. Her final professional appearance was in the 1978 film *Just a Gigolo*. Dietrich's role occupies only a few minutes of screen time. As in her stage performances, she still performs the citation of her own career, and of her own process of aging. Here, however, the stakes are quite different.

The film traces the adventures of a World War I veteran played by David Bowie, who returns to Berlin and discovers the sexual and political turmoil of the 1920s. That the film is set in 1920s Berlin only adds to the sense of an actress quoting her own career. Dietrich took the role of a madam—a "commander-in-chief of a regiment of gigolos"—that was initially designed for Trevor Howard (Bach 448). One of the many curiosities about the film, however, is that independently of Dietrich as a substitute for another actor, the film reads as compendium of allusions to her persona. Some of these—like the use of the song "I Kiss Your Hand Madame" (from the 1929 German film starring Dietrich)—were added after the fact to increase the association with Dietrich. Bowie's character is paired with a risqué cabaret singer with a husky voice who is recruited for Hollywood stardom, and her breakthrough appearance includes a production number with chorines dressed in white tuxedos and top hats. The cabaret singer's manager is a female impersonator, who seems to imitate other impersonators of Dietrich. Bowie himself, famous for his androgynous good looks and bisexual appeal, seems to be mirrored in Dietrich's gigolo, who hires him (this despite the fact that their scenes together are conspicuously "apart"; Dietrich's scenes were shot in Paris independently of the rest of the film).

Dietrich seems elsewhere in the film, yet her presence exudes the powerful feel of the star looking back on her past, casting a detached eye on her surroundings. "Come here" are the first words she speaks, after a carefully composed close-up reveals a veiled head turning to face her gigolo. Yet the artificiality of the scene increases the sense that Dietrich is addressing her audience outside of the film. At the same time, Dietrich seems to be surveying an archive of her own past. While my description of the film suggests a seamless flow from Dietrich's stage performances, the differences are just as striking, for Dietrich in *Just a Gigolo* appears frail. If she was playing with, negotiating, and mocking age in her stage performances, there is no question that here, on-screen, Dietrich is an old woman. Frailty notwithstanding, she still exudes a powerful archival presence, and she is still breathtaking.

Given that *Just a Gigolo* is Dietrich's final appearance in public, it is not surprising that the film figures prominently in the various accounts of Dietrich's legacy, whether in stills of Dietrich's two scenes in the film or her rendition of the song "Just a Gigolo" (her final scene). Indeed, the song is so eerily evocative of Dietrich's own aging persona that virtually every commentator on the film has noted how oddly appropriate it is that Dietrich's final moments on screen should include references to a youth that has gone away, and, perhaps most hauntingly, to the knowledge that "life goes on without me" ("When the end comes I know / they'll say just a gigolo. / Life goes on without me"). The particular way in which *Just a Gigolo* is evoked, however, speaks to the complicated ways in which the Dietrich persona functions in relationship to old age. In Donald Spoto's 1992 biography of Dietrich, *Blue Angel*, the making of *Just a Gigolo* frames the text. We are introduced to Dietrich as she prepares for filming, a "wizened old lady" (Spoto 1) transformed, via make-up and costume, into the Baroness von Semering for the two-day shoot. Given Dietrich's ill health and her own professed dislike for the song "Just a Gigolo," it was unclear how successfully she would be able to perform her song number. Noting the appropriate poignancy of the lyrics, Spoto describes Dietrich's moving and flawless rendition. "Nothing she had done on stage or screen over a period of sixty years could have prepared witnesses that day (or viewers of *Just a Gigolo* since then) for her astonishing rendition of this simple confessional song" (2). All of the observers on the set were moved, some to tears (3). Spoto's framing of his biography with the story of the making of *Just a Gigolo* also functions to cite Dietrich's own stage mystique; as Bach tells us that those who attended her shows will never forget the experience, so Dietrich's final film elicits a sense of wonder by those who witnessed her participation.

Spoto's reverential tone has its apparent opposite in Schell's *Marlene*, in which *Just a Gigolo* also occupies a significant place. Early in the film, an unidentified old woman (Lucy Fischer refers to her as "a stand-in for the elusive Dietrich" ["*Marlene*" 202]) is a somewhat confused spectator to the preparations of filming and editing that are taking place as a part of the film we are watching (her relationship to the film is never explained). She asks questions about Dietrich, and when she asks how old Dietrich is now, an assistant hands her a still of Dietrich in *Just a Gigolo*, telling her that this was her last film role. Since Dietrich refused to show her face on camera in Schell's documentary, her last film role, which is also her last recorded appearance, obviously has significance. Schell shows many film clips in the documentary, and the final clip is Dietrich's last cinematic appearance, the scene in *Just a Gigolo* when she sings the title song. The image is frozen, and Schell finally succeeds in forcing an emotional response from Dietrich when the two recite together a poem about death and forgiveness (Dietrich says that her mother loved the poem). The closer the camera comes, the grainier and more unreadable the still image becomes, which is, of course, the process demonstrated within the film over and over again. As a marker of Dietrich's age, *Just a Gigolo* gives Schell the opportunity to present the aging Dietrich, or more specifically, to provide a visual accompaniment to the voice of Dietrich that we hear with Schell. As Lucy Fischer describes the scene, evoking the title of Molly Haskell's classic volume on the representation of women in film, Schell has moved "from a posture of Reverence to Rape" ("*Marlene*" 206).

Just a Gigolo is not only significant in Schell's film as the final screen appearance of the icon. At one point, in a discussion of the academy awards, a very brief clip of Dietrich in *Just a Gigolo* appears, and she speaks; but a single word appears to come from her mouth—"quatsch," the term repeated by Dietrich throughout Schell's film to describe anything she doesn't like. Much later in the film, Schell has finally gotten Dietrich to agree, reluctantly, to comment on *The Scarlet Empress* (1934). Intercut with these images of Dietrich is the elderly Dietrich of *Just A Gigolo*, as if the elderly Dietrich is watching and observing her younger self. Dietrich achieved this effect throughout her career, yet Schell appropriates the practice in order to reify a rigid contrast between the "young" and the "old" Dietrich. Both Spoto and Schell are archivists of Dietrich's legacy, and despite the differing uses to which *Just a Gigolo* is put in their texts, the effect is to displace Dietrich's own agency—her own considerable skills as an archivist of her career—onto the spectators who observe her with awe (Spoto) or with annoyance (Schell).

Quite a different approach is offered in James Beaman's performance *Black Market Marlene*. Beaman is a Dietrich impersonator who has created two shows on Dietrich (the second, more recent show is *Marlene! Live at the Café de Paris*), both of which have been successful in New York. Beaman presented *Black Market Marlene* at the 2001 Dartmouth College Conference on Marlene Dietrich. Beaman is a remarkable performer, not only because his impersonations of Dietrich are so evocative and precise. Beaman seems to sidle up to the Dietrich legend, taking on the role of the archivist without appropriating Dietrich's own unique ability to look back on her career. *Black Market Marlene* is a concert of Dietrich's film songs. Beaman is dressed in a tuxedo, suggesting both the early years of Dietrich's career (in *Morocco* and *Blonde Venus*), as well as her stage performances (where she also wore a tuxedo for some numbers). Indeed, Beaman's performance has a strong affinity with Dietrich's own stage performances, in the sense that he provides an overview of her film career. He plays with members of his audience in a fashion that both evokes Dietrich's film persona and comments on it. Beaman has said of his style of performance: "I wanted to do Marlene as she was in her film cabaret performances. In almost every case, she's never separated from the audience. She was always in and around the audience, touching them, teasing them, working with them, moving through them" (Caruso). Hence, Beaman does a lovely rendition of "Quand l'amour meurt," from *Morocco*, and kisses a female member of the audience; he flirts with various male audience members during other numbers. His gender impersonation is not simply an inversion of roles, but rather an engagement with the complexity of identifications offered by Dietrich's performances.

Beaman sings "Just a Gigolo" in a way that also evokes the complexity of identifications offered by Dietrich's relationship to old age. As if to suggest the singularity of the song—it was indeed performed in a bar in *Just a Gigolo*, but the only spectator is David Bowie, edited in later—Beaman moves to one side of the performance space, underscoring the particular significance of the song. His face is nearly invisible during the performance, for his head is covered with a veil. The veil, of course, was one of Dietrich's props, in her earliest films as well as in *Just a Gigolo*. Beaman dons the veil to evoke, simultaneously, a costume and a shroud, a sign of the appeal of both youth and old age. "Just a Gigolo" does not provide the conclusion to *Black Market Marlen*e, suggesting that the interweaving of different "ages" of Dietrich is central to his performance.

Throughout her career, Dietrich was acutely aware of the archive, of its narratives of time and decline. Bach, describing Dietrich's work with Richard Griffith of the Museum of Modern Art in 1959 for a retrospective of her films, says of Dietrich that "she was always the most assiduous curator of her career" (391) and notes that she attempted to control not only the past but the future. No one—not even Dietrich—may be able to control the past and the future, but it does seem altogether fitting that there is an official Marlene Dietrich archive in Berlin, a repository for letters, costumes, and various objects. Yet the Dietrich archive has a wider sense as well, including all of the ways in which Dietrich is documented and remembered.

The term "archive" suggests preservation, but also the passion of stored memories. The Dietrich archive is a vast network of objects and fragments, of shrines and tributes (in cyberspace and in weathered boxes), of texts and images, of performances and parodies. The Dietrich archive is not only a collection of objects and memories; it is also the perspective of the archivist, whether Dietrich herself, or those who remember her in various ways. If Dietrich's old age is central to her archival role, I am not suggesting that we simply reverse the standard formula, whereby Dietrich's old age would be triumphant and positive rather than shameful and pathetic; such a move contradicts the very spirit of an archive, tracing as it does numerous narratives simultaneously. Seeing Dietrich herself as an archivist suggests, rather, that the sight of the aging female body is central to the Dietrich persona as it was crafted by Dietrich herself and by her many fans and admirers. Aging may well be painful and embarrassing; it is also (to state the obvious) inevitable. A recognition of age and aging involves sadness, mourning, and regret, but Dietrich's own complex relationship to aging brings another necessary perspective into the mix. That perspective is the archival vantage point that old age offers, a look that encompasses both the inevitability of decline and the opportunity to look back.

Notes

1. The preoccupation with Dietrich's age is apparent even in those works that have a specific story to tell about the Dietrich legend. The most recent documentary on Dietrich, *Marlene Dietrich: Her Own Song* (dir. David Riva, 2001),

is devoted to an investigation of and reflection upon Dietrich's participation in the World War II effort. The film is a very moving testimony to Dietrich's courage and devotion, yet it opens with Dietrich, on stage, stumbling through the lyrics of "Lili Marleen." Eventually this evocation of Dietrich as an old woman is explained in relationship to the war, but initially the scene suggests that this film will rely on the presumed degradation of Dietrich in old age.

2. For recent feminist explorations of the relationship between aging and female stars, see Basting; Brooks; Kaplan ("Trauma and Aging"); Fischer ("*Sunset Boulevard*" and "*Marlene*"); Woodward.

3. Pam Gems's play *Marlene*, set in Paris during one of Dietrich's stage shows in the 1970s, and starring Sîan Phillips in a remarkable performance as Dietrich, is structured by the tension between the dressing room and the stage. The performance of some of Dietrich's most famous songs is alternated with dressing-room scenes in which Dietrich's fears and insecurities are exposed.

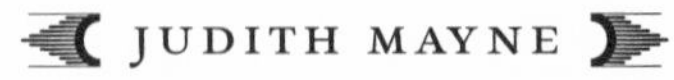

JUDITH MAYNE

Homage, Impersonation, and Magic

An Interview with James Beaman

ONE OF THE HIGHLIGHTS of the 2001 Dartmouth Conference on Marlene Dietrich was the appearance of James Beaman in his cabaret show *Black Market Marlene*. Based in New York City, where he has been performing since the early nineties, Beaman is an exceptional actor and impersonator. In *Black Market Marlene*, Beaman appears in the tuxedo and top hat made famous by Dietrich, and he performs songs sung by Dietrich in her films, from "Falling in Love Again" (from the film that made her an international star, *The Blue Angel* [1929]) to "Just a Gigolo" (which Dietrich sings in her final performance, cinematic or otherwise, in the 1978 film *Just a Gigolo*). *Black Market Marlene* was presented at a campus tavern. Between the students who arrived on the scene, unaware that a drag performance was to take place, and the layout of the bar itself, it was difficult to imagine a cabaret atmosphere. But as soon as Beaman entered the room, the place was transformed and the audience was transported.

Beaman is a classically trained actor, and received a BFA from Boston University's School of Theatre Arts. Prior to *Black Market Marlene*, Beaman did a one-man show impersonating Lauren Bacall, *Bacall: By Herself*. In addition to *Black Market Marlene*, Beaman is the creator and star of another Marlene Dietrich performance, in which he reenacts her opening night performance at the Café de Paris in 1954. Beaman's work on Bacall and Dietrich has been highly acclaimed: he has received the *Back*

James Beaman as Marlene Dietrich. *Photo by Stephen Mosher.*

Stage Bistro award, and he has been nominated four times for the MACC (Manhattan Association of Cabarets and Clubs) Award for Outstanding Impersonation/Characterization. Roy Sander, writing about *Black Market Marlene*, observed: "On very rare occasions—a few times a decade perhaps—a show comes along that is so extraordinary that statements of excellence don't tell the full story. *Black Market Marlene* provides such a transcendent experience." James Beaman may be best known for his Marlene performances, but he has played a wide range of roles in plays from *The Maids* to *Vampire Lesbians of Sodom*. In a recent endeavor, *Crazy World* (which he also directs), Beaman teams up with vocalist Goldie Dver in a celebration of the songs of Oscar- and Grammy-winning composer Leslie Bricusse.

This interview with James Beaman was conducted via email in July and September 2002.

Q: Your physical transformation into Marlene Dietrich is astonishing. Yet I think what is even more striking is how you manage to imitate Marlene, pay homage to her, and comment upon her legacy, all at the same time. So let's start with an obvious question: What led you to Marlene Dietrich?

A: Marlene was a part of my upbringing. . . . She is one of my mother's favorite performers (next to Edith Piaf), and I was surrounded by images of her, and her albums, growing up. But it was my dad who suggested I try Dietrich after he saw me as Lauren Bacall. He thought I could not only look like her but that I could capture an essence of her as an actor that no one else has. I also felt that as an actor doing a female impersonation, I would like to try someone who had a sort of inner stillness and confident economy in her persona and present her as realistically as I could. All the goofs and parodies of Marlene, in my opinion, have been done, and done brilliantly (Madeline Kahn in *Blazing Saddles*, for one), but no one had tried to go within and capture the true radiance of Marlene's presence. That was a challenge I wanted to attempt.

Q: As you just mentioned, prior to the creation of your Marlene Dietrich performances, you did a show based on Lauren Bacall. These two women certainly have distinctive styles, yet they seem so different in so many ways. What, if any, is the connection for you between these women?

A: Bacall was a lark, in a way. I discovered in college that I could do Bacall's voice uncannily well, and I would often imitate her coffee commercials to crack people up! A director friend heard me doing it once in the early nineties and suggested that I try "doing" her. I resisted for a while, because I was afraid of the stigma that a drag performance might place on me as an actor, but she was such fun to do I went ahead and created a cabaret act around the impersonation. There is little that Bacall and Dietrich have in common, except a "whiskey tenor" voice and a style that only a Hollywood diva of the Golden Age could possess. . . . Marlene is much more subtle, and Bacall is, as Noel Coward referred to her, a "noisy, darling broad." Bacall for me is more comedy, Dietrich more drama, and both are satisfying in their ways.

Q: You just mentioned the possible stigma that a drag performance could impose on you. You've said that you were once warned that once you did drag, you would only be offered parts as gay men or drag queens. Was the warning justified?

A: The warning was somewhat justified. . . . I certainly wasn't being called in for leading man roles. However, the benefit of having done successful drag performance won me opportunities to play some great drag roles—Solange in Genet's *The Maids*, the lead in *Vampire Lesbians of Sodom*, the role of Tom/Phyllis/Leslie in *Sylvia*, and most recently I did *Fully Committed*, a one-man show in which I became forty different characters of both genders. Incidentally, I was offered this role when the producer saw my performance in *Black Market Marlene*. So it has certainly been an asset in some ways. I think to a great extent I have had my own feelings of limitation about the drag work, which is why I set it aside for now. I came to realize that I was still a young, attractive man and I was playing middle-aged women! I just want to have as much creative freedom and opportunity to work and stretch my abilities as possible.

Q: Do you see yourself as part of a certain tradition of female impersonation? Whose work has inspired you?

A: I see my impersonations more in the tradition of great transformational actors like Lon Chaney, Alec Guiness, Laurence Olivier, whose performances always included stagecraft like costuming, makeup, and physical work to transform them into the characters they played. . . . I love theatrical artifice and disguise. As for female impersonation, I guess my influences were seeing and meeting the late Randy Allen, who was an actor who did a brilliant old Bette Davis in *P.S. Bette Davis*. For him it was never about drag or dressing up as a woman—but rather capturing the character's true essence. I was also inspired by Jimmy James's fabulous Marilyn Monroe impersonation, which was truly uncanny and had dimension and a believable feminine sexuality that was stunning. I also have admired Jim Bailey's Judy Garland, which is very real and very good.

Q: Your physical transformation into Marlene is quite spectacular. Your choice of costume is quite interesting: by wearing the black tuxedo, you are evoking both the "early" Marlene (of *Morocco*) and the "later" Marlene (of her stage performances in the sixties). You look very young to me, yet in your performance you have an uncanny ability to suggest very different moments in Dietrich's career. I was quite impressed by how you evoke a range of different periods of Dietrich's life; it is almost as if you are the young Dietrich of the 1930s as well as the older Dietrich of the seventies.

A: I am gratified that you picked up on the nuances of *Black Market Marlene*. I wanted in that show to explore gender and the power that clothes have in our culture—a power that Marlene manipulated brilliantly throughout her career. We deceive ourselves into believing that clothes "make the man." As a female impersonator, that is part and parcel of the job. I wanted the audience to be confused in a way—a man, playing a woman playing a man—until they simply accepted the reality of the person they were watching and forgot that I was a man in drag. I also thought it would be fun to try and do a believable female while dressed in men's clothes.

The show incorporates nearly every song Marlene did dressed in men's clothes. There were only certain songs, her "men's songs," as she called them, in which she would perform in the tux, her signature look. So to explore all these songs, I had to capture also the essence of who Marlene was at the various times in her long career that she did those songs. My focus in this show was to try and bring out Marlene's younger persona, which has a vivacity, animation, and charm that people forget she had—they tend to think of her as an ice queen and she wasn't. She had a wonderful sense of humor about herself, particularly when in the "male drag."

Q: Your opening song is "Black Market," which, of course, is also the title of your show. Dietrich biographer Steven Bach describes all of the songs in *A Foreign Affair* as bitterly cynical, with "Black Market" being "the bitterest," a song that "reeks with corruption." Of her performance, Bach says, "Marlene sings it in one of her sequined gowns, her hands uplifted like some ironic Nike strolling through the ruins, a goddess mocking the spoils of victory" (332). Why did you choose this particular song as the title of your cabaret performance?

A: I think that's an interesting take on "Black Market," and I am certainly a fan of Steven Bach's book, which I feel the most balanced and complete of the Dietrich biographies. My personal copy is falling apart, I referred to it so much! I, however, don't find the song bitter or cynical—the lyrics certainly are multilayered and there is a rather ironic Viennese-waltz style to the music; but in the film Marlene's interpretation is playful, seductive, and layered with irony and sex. That song, and her performance of it in that film, inspired the entire *Black Market Marlene* project.

Here is this goddess in a sensational gown, stalking through a bombed-out speakeasy, followed by a makeshift spotlight, as she teases and toys with a room full of drunken GIs. There's darkness, there's elegance, there's girlishness, there's ruefulness and most of all, that self-knowingness that was the magic of Marlene. It was the contradiction that made her unique. Sure, she was gorgeous and glamorous and knew it, but she also was real and vibrant and in touch with reality, she was simultaneously heavenly and earthly. All of these amazing qualities are crystallized in that one performance of that one song—to me, that is the definitive Dietrich film moment. She has arrived at a place of maturity and glamour not even imagined in *Morocco* or *The Blue Angel*. She is performing, very simply, at a piano played by her longtime friend and songwriter Friedrich Hollaender—his performance is equally brilliant in the film. She is surrounded by squalor, informed by the horror of war, at complete ease with the artifice of the set and lights and costume, and full of a completely effortless grace and style and sexuality—for me it is inspiring. I *had* to do that number myself and feel that power! My show opens with the song, and for me it is Marlene inviting the audience to buy her wares, which in the case of my show, are the songs to come.

Q: Could you describe audience responses to your Marlene performances? Since female impersonation has such a large gay fan base, I'm particularly interested in how gay audiences respond to your show.

A: Audience response to the show has run the gamut. Yes, of course, there is a large gay component to the audience—gay men love Marlene's glamour, her strength, and her style, and she is a huge icon for lesbian women. It has been very moving for me to perform for the lesbian audience—when I sing "I've Grown Accustomed to Her Face" as Marlene and see loving couples out front holding hands with tears streaming down their faces, I realize the power Marlene had to help validate these women. But the audience has been much broader for my Marlene work than for the standard "drag" act. I have performed in high-class supper clubs in New York and in cabaret theater in Berlin. I have had student groups, young married couples, older men and women who remember the war and Marlene's presence then. I always have someone in the audience who saw her in concert or met her or worked with her, and they love telling me their stories. In San Francisco, I had an entire table of native Germans who sang along with me on all the familiar Dietrich songs. I have performed for Marlene fanatics and for complete novices.

Q: Marlene Dietrich is one of those rare icons who appeals, with equal intensity, to male and female, gay and lesbian, and heterosexual audiences. Watching your performance, I was struck by the kind of inflection this wide appeal acquires, since you are a man impersonating a woman who herself crossed so many boundaries.

I suspect that the conditions under which I saw your performance (at a bar on the Dartmouth College campus during the Marlene Dietrich conference) were somewhat unusual. Some of the attendees were conference participants, while others were young college students. (Perhaps this kind of [mixed] audience is more common at your shows than I imagine!) In any case, your ability to connect with your audience is quite amazing. You had that cool distance that we associate with Dietrich, but at the same time you engage directly with members of your audience, really drawing them into the performance. You flirt with male and female audience members alike, and it all adds to the overall seduction of your performance.

A: Thank you very much! Marlene had a boldness, a quiet, self-knowing confidence that enabled her to simply command a room and an audience with the power of her presence. As an actor that is an invaluable tool—to simply project your energy into the room and hold everybody in your grip without having to do anything! Marlene had this gift. One of the things that characterized all the performances she did as a singer in her early films was that she was *in* the audience, amongst audience members, flirting, touching, playing with them. I wanted the audience to feel like extras on one of those Paramount sound stages, to be a part of the performance. At first I was concerned that people would resist a man in drag touching them and flirting and being that close. But I learned that if I had the strong belief that I could allow "Marlene" to take over and just move amongst them with that cool, that soft seduction she had, that they would buy into the reality. And they do.

For me as a performer there is a sort of energy that surrounds me when I have performed the show and it is that "magic spell" that allows the audience to go along with me. And yes, at Dartmouth there were Marlene experts and students who had come to the campus hangout not knowing there would be a show—the magic took all of them along for a ride and I love that! Marlene was not an intellectual snob, although she was a brilliant mind and was incredibly well-read and had relationships with some of the great minds of the twentieth century. But she came from Weimar Berlin and a cabaret tradition of the people. She understood the nobility of simple people and especially during the war, the common soldiers that she adored and performed for at great personal peril. She was accessible while at the same time creating this illusion of a goddess. I wanted to capture that contradiction, and it worked!

Q: Why did you make the decision only to sing in the performance? Did you do the same in your Café de Paris performance?

A: The Café de Paris show is an exact recreation of Marlene's 1954 concert. It includes her patter as well. Marlene didn't chat a lot with her audience—it may have been the language barrier or just a desire to put her feelings into songs. She would tell anecdotes about her career and things like that or introduce a song. In *Black Market Marlene* I wanted to tell a story with songs. There is no spoken material except within songs. It is a way of keeping the audience inside the experience and never allowing them to detach from it as can so often happen when a singer steps out and starts speaking. I cover songs from the early thirties all the way up to the early seventies in this show, and I wanted the audience to take the journey through the songs.

Q: One of the most intriguing elements of your performance was the way you presented the "Hot Voodoo" number from *Blonde Venus*. You remained in your tux, as you do throughout your performance, but you used a doll, dressed in a blonde Afro and a costume like Dietrich's in the film, as a prop during your performance. You were almost like a puppet master, as you controlled the doll's movements. I suppose one rationale for the doll is that it allowed you to remain in costume. But I found this number interesting for another reason: the "Hot Voodoo" number in the film is somewhat embarrassing to watch today because of its racism. Certainly, there is a deliberate manipulation of racial and racist stereotypes, but the black women in the chorus line are still exotic backdrops for Dietrich's oxymoronic blonde Afro. Did this kind of reflection enter into your preparation of the number? I found it an ingenious way to both evoke the film and distance its very problematic aspects at the same time.

A: Originally I wanted to try to do a costume change into the gorilla suit and the blond Afro. But it proved to be far too difficult. Also there are some racist overtones to "Hot Voodoo" that posed a problem and I still wanted to do the song . . . so I asked Randy Carfagno (a puppeteer who has worked with Jim Henson) to create a Marlene puppet in her "Hot Voodoo" outfit. What happened with the song is that it became Marlene's little game, playing with the puppet of herself doing a number that she herself must have found silly, and enjoying it with the audience. People love the puppet. In Berlin, it was the encore people requested the most. And Marlene loved dolls—she had a couple that followed her everywhere and are on display in the Marlene Dietrich Collection in Berlin.

Q: One of the most moving aspects of the show was your performance of "Just a Gigolo." As you know, the film *Just a Gigolo* (1978) was Marlene's last professional appearance. She appears for only a few minutes in the film, and her final scene is the singing of "Just a Gigolo." Most critics and observers of Dietrich's career consider the film something of a disaster, despite her moving appearance. When you sing the song, your face is encased in a black veil, suggestive of both the feminine accessory Dietrich wore in many of her early films, and a death shroud. I think it is very tricky to evoke an aging star, since parody is so often the easy way out. You present a performer who is frail, certainly, but who still has a magical presence. Could you describe how you were able to achieve this wonderful evocation of Dietrich as an old woman?

A: I wanted my Marlene in this show to seem like an apparition and part of that was how to make the apparition disappear. "Just a Gigolo" is a very moving and slightly tragic moment in Marlene's career. It marked her last film appearance and was just before she went into seclusion for the rest of her life. In a sense, she "vanished" just after this. She performs the song in the film behind a veil to disguise the fact that she can no longer recreate the famous Marlene image. So I knew that what I wanted to do was to age before the audience and then vanish. The tragedy of Marlene's professional life was her obsession with her goddess image that forced her to go to great lengths to keep that image alive. When she no longer could, she went into hiding. I wanted the audience to feel that sense of loss of youth in a very brief moment, a metaphor for how quickly life and youth can pass us by. So the veil represents many things—age, death, mourning, but also, in the end, the final curtain falling on Marlene. It is a magical and chilling moment for me and the audience. I also chose not to return for a curtain call . . . and never have. Marlene vanishes into the night and it's an effect the audiences really remember.

Q: Given that the songs you performed are from Dietrich's films, I also see in your performance a real love for the movies. In that sense your show reminded me of other stage shows, such as Everett Quinton's *Movieland*, which are love poems to the movies as well as inspired drag performances. Is there a fundamental connection between female impersonation and the love of motion pictures? Are you yourself an avid filmgoer?

A: Of course there is a connection between impersonation and films. As young people, that's how we study the great stars. It is also a very gay phenomenon. Gay kids and gay people in general have a secret life and part of that life is looking for ourselves in our icons, and particularly the old-time movie stars who represented an idealized way of living. They were completely out of the norm yet revered for it—a dream of any outcast in society! Vito Russo's book *The Celluloid Closet*, as well as the film version inspired by it, define eloquently this love of movies for gay people. I have always loved classic films, and as a kid my parents let me stay up whenever a classic was on the late show. They knew I wanted to be an actor and saw it as part of my education. I can quote entire films!! So of course, the great movie divas—Davis, Dietrich, Garland—these are the icons that female impersonators do the most. They combined female allure with masculine power—these contradictions have particular resonance for gay men who find themselves caught between roles in our culture.

Q: Marlene Dietrich is one of the most talked-about, dissected, and parodied figures in show business. What kinds of challenges does the massive amount of material on Dietrich present to you? Do you immerse yourself in Dietrich information? Or try to stay detached from it?

A: The only way to have texture in an impersonation like this is to be as well informed as possible and to immerse completely in the subject. I did exhaustive research and viewing of everything Marlene. Consequently I never needed nor wanted to work in front of a mirror or view video of myself. I was so well saturated with her that I found the impersonation from the inside. One can't get too attached to one's feelings about the subject, because too much reverence makes for a stilted, one-dimensional portrayal. One has to be informed by the attractive and unattractive qualities of the character without judging them.

Q: On the question of parody—many impersonations of Dietrich slide easily into parody, whether intentionally or not. You don't. How do you avoid parody, when you are playing one of the most imitated women in the world?

A: Parodies can be fun, but in my view, they are cheap. They are a caricature, a scribble, a line drawing—reducing the subject to its barest and, usually, most unattractive qualities. In my view there is usually something mean-spirited about parody. To truly play a character like I do Marlene, one has to look for truth. Even if one has some fun with the speech pattern, the familiar gestures, et cetera that make her recognizable and fun for the audience, one still has to come from a place of truth to make the character *real*.

Q: Your love and admiration for Dietrich are apparent in your show. What are specific aspects of Dietrich that you find particularly appealing? Do you have any favorite films? Songs? Stories?

A: I love Marlene and discovered a lot when I studied her for the show. I spent two years poring over every book, film, interview, recording, photo I could find. What I especially love about Marlene is her charm, her self-knowingness, her humor. Her glamour is incredible, her beauty luminous, but it is made interesting (contrary to Garbo, for example) because there is an awareness that Marlene herself feels it is a "put on." That playfulness makes her real, sophisticated, and irresistible.

My favorite film appearance of Marlene is in *A Foreign Affair*—particularly the song "Black Market," her performance of which inspired my entire show. Quintessential Dietrich, in my opinion. Glamorous, gorgeous, flirting with the audience and performing with a sense of ruefulness and danger that are intoxicating. I also love her in *Seven Sinners* and of course, in *Witness for the Prosecution*, one of her greatest acting roles.

My favorite Marlene songs? I love much of her German material and love singing it—particularly "Das Lied ist aus" and "Allein in einer grossen Stadt." Great, sentimental German ballads. I also adore her German-language version of "Surrey with the Fringe on Top," which she turns into a sleigh ride song!

My favorite Marlene story comes from a man who became a fan of mine over the years. He was a dancer in the sixties in Marlene's act in Paris. Marlene often invited the dancers and crew people into her dressing room—she had enormous respect for everyone who did the jobs that supported her show. One night, in her bathrobe, she stopped this man outside her dressing room and enlisted him in a "job" that he would do with her every night after performance. She took him up to the stage, and he helped her go over the stage floor and pick up each and every bead and rhinestone that fell off her dress during the performance. Then she would sit in the dressing room, as he ate scrambled eggs she cooked up for him on a hot plate, and she would personally sew on each bead to her concert dress. That's the Marlene I adore—the trouper, the accessible goddess, the hausfrau in a swan's down coat.

WERNER SUDENDORF

"Is That Me?"

The Marlene Dietrich Collection Berlin

IF YOU MENTION the name Marlene, there is no need to add the surname Dietrich. Likewise with Marilyn, but not with Charlie, Buster, or Greta: Chaplin, Keaton, and Garbo need their last names to be recognized, or at least their nicknames—the Tramp, the Poker Face, the Divine. But there is a fundamental difference between Marlene and Marilyn. Marilyn's star persona was cemented into a stereotype that eventually imprisoned her. Her suicide added a mythical dimension of failure, of a life not completed. Marlene, in contrast, fashioned her own star persona with the help of her director, Josef von Sternberg. When she was twelve years old, Marie Magdalene Dietrich combined her first two names into the new name, Marlene. This name was all but unknown during the Wilhemine era and therefore sounded special and unique. There was no other Marlene.

What characterizes this unique Marlene, what do we associate with the sound of her name? There is the actress who became famous through her roles: Lola Lola, Amy Jolly, Shanghai Lily, Blonde Venus. These are exotic, perhaps also slightly infamous-sounding synonyms for erotic energy, danger, temptation, self-confidence, casualness, seedy dives or luxury clubs, open secrets, and the song of the sirens. Although Marlene Dietrich acted in more than fifty films, we always associate the same films with Marlene: first, of course, *The Blue Angel*, then *Morocco* and *Shanghai Express* and possibly *Blonde Venus* and *Witness for the Prosecution*. Thus it is five films, or maybe eight or ten for more avid cinema goers, that

”Is that me?” *Filmmuseum Berlin—Marlene Dietrich Collection Berlin. Author's collection.*

are present in our memory. In 1932, after *Shanghai Express*, she had become the icon that would turn into a myth. This myth was founded on the ability to survive. She had succeeded in being both Marlene and Shanghai Lily, Marlene and Blonde Venus, Marlene and any other character in her films. As Marlene, she managed to almost disappear into her part but also to surmount it. Her last great films are from the 1950s. Nobody who only knows these late films will ever understand why this woman became so famous. There is one exception, however, *Touch of Evil* by Orson Welles (1958). Marlene Dietrich has a minor role hardly necessary for the storyline, but she endows the film with some of the glamour of Old Hollywood. "Your future is all used up," she tells detective Quinlan, who is asking her to read him the cards. She herself does not live in this past, nor is she a promise for the future—she is mere presence, neither young nor old, neither cold-hearted nor compassionate.

In the 1950s came Marlene, the chanteuse. Just as she never was an extraordinarily talented actress, her voice also lacked range and power. But on stage she performed again as the icon who now appeared, intimately, to her audience. Many of her shows carried her name and stressed her live presence: *Marlene Dietrich—In Person*. Even watching those shows on television, one can immediately see a professional in total command of her audience. She tells her life through songs, and what she learned on the film set, she now uses on the stage. We witness the art of delay, the wait for the resonance of a certain remark whose double entendre was not understood right away but which is emphasized through Marlene's silence and acknowledged by a murmur in the audience. To thousands of people she celebrated the high art of intimation, of performance as seduction. She knew her audience and she knew which tricks to use: sometimes bold, sometimes risqué, but not too much, and sometimes tragic. In the end, there was always the conclusion with the standard song, "Falling in Love Again," as a hymn to eternal youth, which she finished off with a self-deprecating, vulnerable laugh: "I just can't help it."

When she retreated from the stage, her last career began. She became seemingly invisible, a recluse in her apartment who shunned the public. It is safe to assume that when the ailments of old age approached, Marlene carefully staged this career as well. She had made a name for herself, she had been the icon of Hollywood glamour, the dazzle of the international jet set, and now she was truly unique—a mere voice, something beyond both the grave and eternity. That did not mean that she had ever been mild-mannered. On the contrary, whoever dealt with her needed a lot of tolerance. Marlene Dietrich had great professional demands; everything had to be prepared and executed to perfection. She was a German through and through—perhaps the last Prussian—disciplined, headstrong, worldly, trained in music and the arts, tolerant and stubborn, fluent in three languages, but if need be, she could be curt and obstinate. She had defended German ideals against the Nazis. For years, the Germans blamed her for performing for the Allied troops, but now they are proud of her. During the 1950s, many Germans criticized her for not returning to her homeland, thereby also fighting the memories of a past that made them recall their own guilt. Snubbing the world star was some Germans' petty and stubborn way of fending off the big world of which they could not be a part and which they therefore had to reject. And yet, Marlene remained a German legacy, and for many this was the worst part. She was a constant reminder that there was a different and responsible stance toward German history, and that this stance had deeper roots than the German economic miracle and the striving for affluence.

In the past, the Deutsche Kinemathek in Berlin had repeatedly tried to purchase documents by Marlene Dietrich, just as many other archives surely did. She was and remains more than a film and show star; she personifies a chapter of German history. When in 1977 the Deutsche Kinemathek in Berlin organized the first comprehensive Dietrich retrospective, we came closer to Marlene than we would for a long time thereafter. A gentleman who claimed to be an acquaintance of Marlene, and who had actually been one in former years, offered his services as a go-between. And he delivered a request from the star to us: She was looking to borrow a booklet that Manfred Georg had first published about her in the early 1930s. Of course we gave her the booklet, never to see it again. The acquaintance wanted to arrange an interview with Marlene for Wolf Donner, then the director of the Berlin Film Festival. We worked together on a list of questions, and Wolf Donner was escorted to Marlene Dietrich's apartment. There, in front of the door, the journey ended. He had to shove the list under the door, and he received the answers the same way. They must have been the shortest answers ever given in an interview. They consisted only of yes and no. The longest answer was "Yes and no." Years later we had another acquaintance inquire if she still owned contracts, other significant documents, or even costumes. The answer was swift and gruff: no, she owned nothing anymore, least of all costumes. Didn't we know that all costumes were property of the production company? If she had costumes, she would have had to steal them. Were we insinuating that she was a thief? End of communication.

The funeral of Marlene Dietrich in May of 1992 in Berlin was an event accompanied by clumsiness. Marlene's decision to be buried in Berlin surprised everybody, including the Berlin senator of culture. An especially astute administrator proclaimed that Berlin would honor Dietrich with a homage by international artists. The artists were to be flown in from Cannes where they were attending the film festival. But the stars were there to promote their films, and the production companies balked at letting their main attractions leave for Berlin. The homage did not take place.

Berlin had a lot to make up for with Marlene Dietrich. The shameful picketing in front of the Titania Palace in 1961 with "Marlene Go Home" signs, and the many years of slander in the press reflected badly on the new capital, which like the nation it represented, had never cleared its relationship with the world star. When the heirs of Marlene Dietrich offered to sell the contents of her estate, it was the Berlin mayor's office, not the general populace, which was interested in reversing public sentiment about Dietrich. Ullrich Roloff-Momin, then Berlin's senator for culture, did not hesitate a second to put everything in motion to raise the necessary funds for acquisition and preservation. It took exactly one year from the first inspection of the collection in New York to the official handing-over in Berlin, October 1993, a rather short time for a collection of this size. It was paid for with monies from the German lottery and the federal government.

Since 1993, Berlin has owned the Marlene Dietrich Collection. Did this considerable investment pay off? How do scholars benefit from the estate? To what degree is it accessible? What new insights has it produced? And always the same question from the journalists: to what degree has the collection changed the picture we previously had of Marlene Dietrich? To begin with the simplest questions: Since the collection was purchased with federal moneys, it is open to scholars. In the course of five years, an inventory of the majority of the collection has been entered into the computer. All photos have been scanned and are searchable by persons, film titles, and key phrases. The same goes for graphics, textiles, jewelry, props, and three-dimensional objects. The letters, the scripts, and almost all of the written materials can be searched by computer at the Filmmuseum. However, the staff has at times reached its level of resources. Sheet music and scores are included but have not been studied documents. It has not yet been established if all musical records have been published. Similarly, larger parts of the collection, such as the voluminous production materials for Maximilian Schell's interview film *Marlene*, have not yet been archived in detail. The collection thus contains references to existing materials, but not all of them have been catalogued.

It is evident that Marlene Dietrich, and her family, did not start a systematic collection until the fall of 1930, after the success of *Morocco*. Since she always claimed to have had only minor roles in silent films, one would expect that she destroyed everything from her German career prior to

1930, but this is not the case. Thus one finds in the collection an incomplete 16 mm print of *Das Schiff der verlorenen Menschen* (*The Ship of Lost Souls*, 1928), as well as stills from her other German films. Most likely, Dietrich only sporadically collected correspondence and documents of her film work prior to her Hollywood success. A complete set of photographs for a sitting with Irving Chidnoff in April 1930 is a good example of this. Only years later did Chidnoff send her the pictures—Marlene did not save them initially. On the back of several early pictures of her one finds the handwritten note: "Is that me?"

Beginning with her overseas' work for the USO in 1944, the collection becomes very extensive in all areas and remains that way until 1992. Of course there are a wealth of important documents, photos, and scripts from between 1930 and 1944, but not nearly as extensive. The collection also reflects her personal state of mind. While there are many pictures documenting Dietrich's close relationship with Fritz Lang, there are very few after their collaboration on *Rancho Notorious*, which led to their falling-out.

As a German archive, we have of course a strong interest in documents that speak about the efforts of the film industry of the Third Reich to bring Marlene "heim ins Reich." Such documents do exist, but they are not the ones everybody was expecting. Thus the collection remains silent about whether a meeting ever took place with Ribbentrop (the Nazi foreign minister). Even about Marlene Dietrich's contacts with the colony of German émigrés in Hollywood there exists only indirect evidence, which is mostly found in the diaries and materials of her husband, Rudolf Sieber. Sieber wrote down every day whom he had met, with whom he had dined, and, most important, what he had spent. Further details about Marlene's life can be garnered from the collection of Fritz Lang and Max Kolpe, which are also housed in the Filmmuseum Berlin/Stiftung Deutsche Kinemathek.

And how did the collection change the public image of Marlene? This image is of course shaped primarily by her films and possibly a few of her songs, and therefore that image has changed little—if anything, it has been reinforced. The three rooms of the permanent exhibit of the Filmmuseum Berlin devoted to Marlene Dietrich—the part of the collection most visible to the public—underscore the myth, thereby meeting the expectation of the museum goers. The people who come to the museum are eager to take in the glamour of Hollywood films, and we do not disappoint them. Yet those who have worked on cataloguing the collection have indeed been confronted with a different image of Marlene Dietrich. We look into the inner life of a show star, a hard worker, we see what is behind the façade, the true personality, the attitude, the ruses and weaknesses of a woman incessantly working on the perfection of the synthetic character Marlene. This insight does not diminish the respect for the achievement, the admiration for the result that we see on the screen. We understand how the puzzle is put together, but also how many pieces are still missing.

The archivists at the Marlene Dietrich Collection do not evaluate the materials; their task is not the interpretation of the documents and artifacts. But the continuous study of the collection leads to an accumulation of knowledge from which scholars benefit. Thus, for example, Marlene's hints in a letter to Mercedes d'Acosta about terminating friendships with lovers, allusions that are only explained through a letter from fellow émigré actor Hans von Twardowski. Since Marlene and her friends had nicknames for each other, one has to know them to understand the correspondence. During the 1930s, Marlene only used code names when writing to her family in Germany: "Etoile" stood for Josef von Sternberg, "Wald" for Willi Forst.

As of 1931 there exist scrapbooks in which she kept film reviews and reports about the life of the Dietrich family, in German, English, French, Spanish, and other languages. When the production companies stopped doing this for Marlene, she hired clipping services and collected articles until her death in 1992.

Apart from the letters and the press clippings the third big area of the estate are the writings. Here we find versions of her *ABC*, a book too many biographers have ignored (see Amelie Hastie's contribution in this volume). Then there is the original manuscript of her autobiography, which was written in English but never published. The German edition is a translation from the English, the French edition is a translation from the German, and the American copy is a translation from the French. To make things even more complicated, two different versions of her memoirs were published in Germany. *Nehmt nur mein Leben* (*Just Take My Life*) is a translation of the original manuscript; *Ich bin Gott sei Dank Berlinerin* (*I Am, Thank God, a Berliner*) is a retranslation of one of the many

The display of costumes and images in the Marlene Dietrich Collection. *Filmmuseum Berlin—Marlene Dietrich Collection Berlin.*

foreign versions. No matter which edition one quotes, one never quotes the original. That, too, is typical of Marlene.

Of course we are well aware not only that the collection brought a famous name back to Berlin and Germany, but that this collection also needs to be exhibited. Thus there is hardly a month when a piece from the collection is not shown somewhere around the world. We also actively support books, films, and documentations and publish a monthly newsletter that reaches about one thousand people all over the world. The Marlene Dietrich Collection is supported by the Federal Republic of Germany, Maria Riva, and the city of Berlin. The collection relies on commercial revenue but is not dependent on it.

A final reason why the collection is so unique is that Marlene Dietrich confronts us here—with all the things she collected, such as dresses and wardrobes, suitcases and props, and home movies—as a reality, not as a myth, which has a strong irrational component. And yet whenever we assemble pieces from the collection for a new exhibit, this myth is magically recreated. And always new aspects of her persona shine through, just as a kaleidoscope, which always relies on the same elements, creates a new image, and shows different colors with each turn. "Is that me?" Perhaps this question stands for more than a momentary lapse of memory.

Appendix: Marlene Dietrich Collection Berlin

—Over 3,000 textile items from the 1920s to the 1930s, including 50 film and 70 show costumes by, among others, Jean Louis, Travis Banton, Edith Head, and Eddie Schmidt

—1,000 individual items from Dietrich's private wardrobe (including 50 handbags and 150 pairs of gloves), by, among others, Elizabeth Arden, Balenciaga, Balmain, Chanel, Courrèges, Dior, Givenchy, Guerlain, Irene, Knize, Lee, Levis, Schiaparelli, and Ungaro

—400 hats and 440 pairs of shoes, by, among others, Agnès, Aprile, Cavanagh, Lilly Dache, Delman, Edouard, John Frederics, and Massaro

—About 15,000 photographs from 1904 to 1992, including

5,000 film stills and behind-the-scenes pictures

5,000 pictures of show performances

2,000 pictures of public appearances

1,000 private and family pictures

—2,000 original prints by famous photographers such as Cecil Beaton, Mario Bucovich, Irving Chidnoff, Don English, Horst P. Horst, George Hurrell, Armstrong Jones, Ray Jones, Eugene Robert Richee, Edward Steichen, and William Walling

—About 300,000 sheets of written documents, including letters from, Burt Bacharach, Charles Boyer, Yul Brynner, Maurice Chevalier, Noël Coward, Jean Gabin, Douglas Fairbanks Jr., Willi Forst, Ernest Hemingway, Alfred Kerr, Hildegard Knef, Karl Lagerfeld, Lilli Palmer, Alfred Polgar, Nancy and Ronald Reagan, Erich Maria Remarque, Maximilian Schell, Johannes Mario Simmel, Josef von Sternberg, Orson Welles, Billy Wilder, and Carl Zuckmayer

—2,500 sound recordings from the 1930s to the 1980s

—300 posters, drawings, and paintings

—80 pieces of luggage (trunks, suitcases, hat boxes, vanity cases)

Web site: http://www.marlene.com; subscription to the free newsletter from mdcb@filmmuseum-berlin.de

Translation by Gerd Gemünden.

BIBLIOGRAPHY

Abel, Richard, ed. *French Film Theory and Criticism*. Vol. 1. Translated by Hugh Gray. Princeton: Princeton University Press, 1988.

Acht Uhr Abendblatt. "Die Meinung der Andern: Das Gesicht der Rasse im Film." 8 May 1936.

Acosta, Mercedes de. *Here Lies the Heart*. New York: Reynal, 1960.

Alberoni, Franceso. "The Powerless Elite: Theory and Sociologial Research on the Phenomenon of the Stars." In *Sociology of Mass Communication*, edited by Denis McQuail. Harmondsworth, U.K.: Penguin, 1972. 75–98.

Albert, Katharine. "She Threatens Garbo's Throne." *Photoplay* (December 1930): 60.

Albrecht, Gerd. *Die grossen Filmerfolge*. Ebersberg: Edition Achteinhalb, 1985.

———. *Film im Dritten Reich: Eine Dokumentation*. Karlsruhe: Schauburg, 1979.

———. *Nationalsozialistische Filmpolitik: Eine soziologische Untersuchung über die Spielfilme des Dritten Reichs*. Stuttgart: Enke, 1969.

Améry, Jean. "Die Künstlerin Dietrich und die öffentliche Sache." In *Marlene Dietrich: Dokumente, Essays, Filme*. Vol 1. Edited by Werner Sudendorf. Munich: Hanser, 1977. 7–19.

Annan, Gabriele. "Electra from Beverly Hills." Review of *Marlene Dietrich* by Maria Riva. *New York Review of Books*, 8 April 1993, 7–8.

Arbuthnot, Lucie, and Gail Seneca. "Pre-Text and Text in *Gentlemen Prefer Blondes*." In *Issues in Feminist Criticism*, edited by Patricia Erens. Bloomington: Indiana University Press, 1990. 112–25.

Arecco, Sergio. *Marlene Dietrich: I piaceri dipinti*. Recco-Genoa: Le Mani, 2005.

Aros. *Greta Garbo: Ihr Weg von Stockholm bis Hollywood*. Berlin: Scherl, 1932.

———. *Marlene Dietrich: Ein interessantes Künstlerschicksal*. Berlin: Scherl, 1932.

Ascheid, Antje. "A Sierckian Double Image: The Narration of Zarah Leander as a National Socialist Star." *Film Criticism* 23 (1999): 46–73.

Astruc, Alexandre. "The Birth of a New Avant-Garde: La Caméra-Stylo." In

The New Wave, edited by Peter Graham. Garden City: Doubleday, 1968. 17–23.

Aurich, Rolf, Wolfgang Jacobsen, and Cornelius Schnauber, eds. *Fritz Lang: His Life and Work, Photographs and Documents*. Berlin: Jovis, 2001. 397–402.

Bach, Stephen. *Marlene Dietrich: Life and Legend*. New York: William Morrow, 1992.

Bade, Patrick. *Femme Fatale: Images of Evil and Fascinating Women*. New York: Mayflower Books, 1979.

Balio, Tino. *Grand Design: Hollywood as a Modern Business Enterprise, 1930–1939*. Berkeley: University of California Press, 1993.

Ball, Lucille, with Betty Hannah Hoffman. *Love, Lucy*. New York: Boulevard Books, 1996.

Banner, Lois. *In Full Flower: Aging Women, Power, and Sexuality: A History*. New York: Alfred A. Knopf, 1992.

Barthes, Roland. "The Face of Garbo." In *Film Theory and Criticism*, edited by Gerald Mast, Marshall Cohen, and Leo Braudy. 5th ed. New York: Oxford University Press, 1992. 536–38.

———. *A Lover's Discourse: Fragments*. Translated by Richard Howard. New York: Hill and Wang, 1978.

Basting, Anne Davis. *The Stages of Age: Performing Age in Contemporary American Culture*. Ann Arbor: University of Michigan Press, 1998.

Baty, S. Paige. *American Monroe: The Making of a Body Politic*. Berkeley: University of California Press, 1995.

Baxter, John. *The Cinema of Josef von Sternberg*. London: Zwemmer/Barnes, 1971.

Baxter, Peter. *Just Watch: Sternberg, Paramount and America*. London: BFI, 1993.

———. "On the Naked Thighs of Miss Dietrich." In *Movies and Methods*, vol. 2, edited by Bill Nichols. University of California Press, 1985. 557–66.

———, ed. *Sternberg*. London: BFI, 1980.

Bazin, André. "The Evolution of the Western." In *What Is Cinema?* vol. 2, edited by Hugh Gray. Berkeley: University of California Press, 1971. 149–57.

Beecher, Catharine. *Treatise on Domestic Economy*. New York: Schocken Books, 1977.

Belach, Helga, Gero Gandert, and Hans Helmut Prinzler, eds. *Aufruhr der Gefühle: Die Kinowelt des Curtis Bernhardt*. Munich: Bucher, 1982.

Bemmann, Helga. *Marlene Dietrich: Im Frack zum Ruhm*. Leipzig: Kiepenheuer, 2000.

Benjamin, Walter. *The Arcades Project*. Translated by Howard Eiland and Kevin McLaughlin. Cambridge, Mass.: Harvard University Press, 2002.

———. *Illuminations: Essays and Reflections*. Translated by Harry Zohn, edited by Hannah Arendt. New York: Schocken, 1969. 217–52.

Berger, John. *Ways of Seeing*. Harmondsworth, U.K.: Penguin, 1973.

Berliner Illustrierte Zeitung. "Doppelgängerinnen—Angleichung an die Erfolgreichste." 27 October 1929.

———. "Sex-Appeal ist erlernbar." 30 March 1930.

Berliner Tageblatt und Handels-Zeitung. "Die Frau, nach der man sich sehnt." 20 January 1929.

Berry, Sarah. *Screen Style: Fashion and Femininity in 1930s Hollywood*. Minneapolis: University of Minnesota Press, 2000.

Biery, Ruth. "The New 'Shady Dames' of the Screen." *Photoplay*, August 1932, 28–29, 90–91.

Blees, Christian. "Marlene Hörspielstar: Die unbekannte Seite der Dietrich." *Filmgeschichte* 16–17 (June 2002): 123–26.

The Blue Angel: The Novel by Heinrich Mann, the Film by Josef von Sternberg. New York: Ungar, 1979.

Blum, Heiko R., and Katharina Blum. *Gesichter des neuen deutschen Films*. Berlin: Parthas, 1997.

Bordwell, David. "The Classical Hollywood Style." In *The Classical Hollywood Cinema: Film Style and Mode of Production*, edited by David Bordwell, Janet Staiger, and Kristin Thompson. London: Routledge 1985. 1–84.

Bosquet, Alain. *Marlène Dietrich, une amour par téléphone*. Paris: Minos La Différance, 2002.

Bouvier, Michel. "Hollywood on a Spree." *Ça Cinéma* 18 (1978–79): 19–35.

Bovenschen, Silvia. "Is There a Feminine Aesthetic?" *New German Critique* 10 (1977): 111–37.

Bret, David. *Marlene Dietrich—My Friend: An Intimate Biography*. London: Robson Books, 1993.

Bristol Evening World. "Garbo Likes Dietrich." 15 August 1933.

Britton, Andrew. *Katharine Hepburn: Star as Feminist*. New York: Continuum, 1995.

Bronfen, Elisabeth. "Zwei deutsche Stars/Two German Stars." In *Filmmuseum Berlin*, edited by Wolfgang Jacobsen, Hans Helmut Prinzler, and Werner Sudendorf. Berlin: Nicolai, 2000. 169–90.

Brooks, Jodi. "Performing Aging/Performance Crisis (for Norma Desmond, Baby Jane, Margo Channing, Sister George—and Myrtle)." In *Figuring Age: Women, Bodies, Generations*, edited by Kathleen Woodward. Bloomington: Indiana University Press, 1999. 232–47.

Bun, Austin. "Heaven Sent: The Dead Celebrity Who Comes Back to Life." *New York Times, Sunday Magazine*, 11 June 2000, 92.

Burger, Erich. "Vom deutschen Film." *Berliner Tageblatt und Handels-Zeitung*, 20 January 1929, 23.

Cahiers du Cinema Collective. "Josef von Sternberg's *Morocco*." In *Cahiers du*

Cinema, 1969–1972, edited by Nick Browne. Cambridge, Mass.: Harvard University Press, 1990. 174–86.

Carter, Erica. *Dietrich's Ghosts: Stars in Third Reich Film*. London: BFI, 2005.

———. "Marlene Dietrich—The Prodigal Daughter." In *The German Cinema Book*, edited by Tim Bergfelder, Erica Carter, and Deniz Göktürk. London: BFI, 2002. 71–80.

Caruso, Jim. "James Beaman: Black Market Marlene Unveiled." *Cabaret Scenes*, October 1999, http://www.jim-caruso.com/library/9910_cabaretscenes.htm (accessed 6 June 2002).

Chicago Defender. "Regal's *Blonde Venus* Deserves Six Stars: If Others Deserved Four, Then We Add Two for Dietrich." 5 November 1932, Stage—Music—Film section, 10.

Collier's. "Dietrich: The Body and the Soul." 14 May 1954, 25–29.

Comolli, Jean-Luc. "Historical Fiction: A Body Too Much." *Screen* 19, no. 2 (1978): 43.

Condon, Frank. "Greta and Marlene." *Saturday Evening Post*, 30 May 1931, 29.

Constable, Catherine. *Thinking in Images: Film Theory, Feminist Philosophy, and Marlene Dietrich*. London: BFI, 2005.

Cook, Pam. "Women and the Western." In *The Western Reader*, edited by Jim Kitses and Gregg Rickman. New York: Limelight Editions, 1998. 293–300.

Cork, Richard. "'A Murderous Carnival': German Artists in the First World War." In *War, Violence and the Modern Condition*, edited by Bernd Hüpphauf. Berlin: Walter de Gruyter, 1997. 241–76.

Crafton, Donald. *The Talkies: American Cinema's Transition to Sound, 1926–1931*. Berkeley: University of California Press, 1999.

Crane, Cheryl. *Detour: A Hollywood Story*. New York: Avon Books, 1988.

Crane, Elana. "Shopping Sense: Fanny Fern and Jennie June on Consumer Culture in the Nineteenth Century." In *Hop on Pop: The Politics and Pleasures of Popular Culture*, edited by Henry Jenkins, Tara McPherson, and Jane Shattuc. Durham, N.C.: Duke University Press, 2002. 472–86.

Curry, Ramona. *Too Much of a Good Thing: Mae West as Cultural Icon*. Minneapolis: University of Minneapolis Press, 1996.

Custen, George F. *Bio/Pics: How Hollywood Constructed Public History*. New Brunswick, N.J.: Rutgers University Press, 1992.

deCordova, Richard. *Picture Personalities: The Emergence of the Star System in America*. Urbana: University of Illinois Press, 1990.

de Lauretis, Teresa. *The Practice of Love: Lesbian Sexuality and Perverse Desire*. Bloomington: Indiana University Press, 1994.

Desjardins, Mary. "*Meeting Two Queens*: Feminist Film-making, Identity Politics, and the Melodramatic Fantasy." *Film Quarterly* 48, no. 3 (1995): 26–33.

Dickens, Homer. *The Films of Marlene Dietrich*. New York: Cadillac, 1968.

Dietrich, Marlene. *Ich bin, Gott sei Dank, Berlinerin: Memoiren*. Translated by Nicola Volland. Munich: Ullstein, 2000.

———. *Marlene*. Translated by Salvator Attanasio. New York: Grove Press, 1987.

———. *Marlene Dietrich's ABC*. Garden City, N.Y.: Doubleday, 1961.

Doane, Mary Ann. "The Close-Up: Scale and Detail in the Cinema." *Differences: A Journal of Feminist Cultural Studies* 14, no. 3 (fall 2003): 89–111.

———. *Femmes Fatales: Feminism, Film Theory, Psychoanalysis*. New York: Routledge, 1991.

———. "Film and the Masquerade: Theorizing the Female Spectator." *Issues in Feminist Film Criticism* (1982): 41–57.

Doherty, Thomas. *Pre-Code Hollywood: Sex, Immorality, and Insurrection in American Cinema, 1930–1934*. New York: Columbia University Press, 1999.

Dorn, Thea. *Marleni: Preussische Diven blond wie Stahl*. Frankfurt am Main: Verlag der Autoren, 2000.

Drewniak, Boguslav. *Der deutsche Film, 1938–1945*. Düsseldorf: Droste, 1987.

Dunning, John. *On the Air: The Encyclopedia of Old-Time Radio*. New York: Oxford University Press, 1998. 130–31, 673.

———. *Tune in Yesterday: The Ultimate Encyclopedia of Old-Time Radio, 1925–1976*. Englewood Cliffs, N.J.: Prentice-Hall, 1976.

Ďurovičová, Nataša. "Translating America: The Hollywood Multilinguals, 1929–1933." In *Sound Theory/Sound Practice*, edited by Rick Altman. New York: Routledge, 1992. 138–53.

Dyer, Richard. *Stars*. London: BFI, 1979.

Eisner, Lotte H. *Fritz Lang*. New York: Da Capo Press, 1986.

Elsaesser, Thomas. "Ethnicity, Authenticity, and Exile: A Counterfeit Trade? German Filmmakers and Hollywood." In *Home, Exile, Homeland: Film, Media, and the Politics of Place*, edited by Hamid Naficy. New York: Routledge, 1999.

———. "Falling in Love Again (and Again): Marlene Dietrich und die ewig singende Säge." In *Die Wiederkehr des Gleichen*, edited by Jürgen Felix. Marburg: Schueren, 2001. 347–55.

———. "Tales of Sound and Fury: Observations on the Family Melodrama." *Monogram* 4 (1972): 2–15.

Engelstein, Stephanie. "Out on a Limb: Military Medicine, Heinrich von Kleist, and the Disarticulated Body." *German Studies Review* 23, no. 2 (2000): 225–44.

Epstein, William H. *Recognizing Biography*. Philadelphia: University of Pennsylvania Press, 1987.

Erens, Patricia, ed. *Sexual Strategems: The World of Women in Film*. New York: Horizon Press, 1979.

Everett, Anna. *Reinventing the Gaze: A Genealogy of Black Film Criticism, 1909–1949*. Durham, N.C.: Duke University Press, 2001.

Fellman, Rainer. "*Marlene*: Der blaue Engel." *Spiegel*, 7 March 2000. Online edition, www.service.spiegel.de/.

Der Film. "Marlene und Renate." 3 June 1933.

Film-Kurier. "Das Band, das uns verbindet: Tatsachen und Anmerkungen über den ausländischen Film in Deutschland." 1 January 1934.

———. "Filmkünstler im kleinen Kino." 3 March 1935.

———. "Fussnoten: Natürlich zieht Marlene." 3 July 1935.

———. "Geänderte Pläne von Marlene Dietrich." 5 April 1934.

———. "Knapp und witzig." 31 December 1937.

———. "Liquidiert Amerika seine deutschen Niederlassungen?" 17 June 1936.

———. "Marlene Dietrich befindet sich nicht in Wien." 4 July 1934.

———. "Marlenes Pläne: Kein Besuch in Deutschland?" 15 January 1933.

———. "Marlene und die Unaussprechlichen." 4 February 1933.

———. "Oberprüfstelle über Song of Songs." 16 March 1934.

———. "Paramount klagt gegen Marlene." 3 January 1933.

———. "Paul Wegener sprach in der Lessing-Hochschule über die Schauspielkunst." 22 December 1934.

———. Review of *The Devil*. 29 June 1935.

———. "Sehnsucht." 3 April 1936.

———. "Die spanische Tänzerin." 29 June 1935.

———. "Das Starunwesen, seine Folgen und möglichen Gegenmaßnahmen." 1 January 1935.

———. "Ein Wort über die Star-Verehrung." 12 January 1933.

Finler, Joel W. *The Hollywood Story*. London: Octopus, 1988.

Fischer, Lucy. "*Marlene*: Modernity, Mortality, and the Biopic." *Biography* 23, no. 1 (2000): 193–209.

———. "*Sunset Boulevard*: Fading Stars." In *The Other within Us: Feminist Explorations of Women and Aging*, edited by Marilyn Pearsall. Boulder, Colo.: Westview Press, 1997. 163–76.

Fischer, Lucy, and Marsha Landy, eds. *Stars: The Film Reader*. New York: Routledge, 2004.

Flinn, Tom. "Joe, Where Are You? (Marlene Dietrich)." *Velvet Light Trap* 6 (Fall 1972): 17–20.

Freud, Sigmund. *The Standard Edition of the Complete Psychological Works of Sigmund Freud*. Translated by James Strachey. London: Hogarth Press, 1953.

Friedberg, Anne. *Window Shopping: Cinema and the Postmodern*. Berkeley: University of California Press, 1993.

Frith, Simon. "Towards an Aesthetics of Popular Music." In *Music and Society: The Politics of Composition, Performance, and Reception*, edited by Richard

Leppert and Susan McClary. New York: Cambridge University Press, 1987. 133–49.

Fuld, Werner, and Thomas Schneider, eds. *"Sag mir, daß Du mich liebst": Erich Maria Remarque—Marlene Dietrich. Zeugnisse einer Leidenschaft.* Cologne: Kiepenheuer and Witsch, 2001.

Gandert, Gero. *Der Film der Weimarer Republik 1929: Ein Handbuch der zeitgenössischen Kritik.* Berlin: de Gruyter, 1997.

Garber, Marjorie. *Vice Versa: Bisexuality and the Eroticism of Everyday Life.* New York: Simon and Schuster, 1995.

Garncarz, Joseph. "Art and Industry: German Cinema of the 1920s." In *The Silent Cinema Reader*, edited by Lee Grieveson and Peter Krämer. London and New York: Routledge, 2004. 389–400.

———. "Hollywood in Germany: Die Rolle des amerikanischen Films in Deutschland: 1925–1990." In *Der deutsche Film: Aspekte seiner Geschichte von den Anfängen bis zur Gegenwart*, edited by Uli Jung. Trier: Wissenschaftlicher Verlag, 1993. 167–214.

———. "The Nationally Distinctive Star System of the Weimar Republic." Paper delivered at the Popular European Cinema Conference 3, University of Warwick, U.K., March 2000.

———. "Die Schauspielerin wird Star: Ingrid Bergman–eine öffentliche Kunstfigur." In *Die Schauspielerin: Zur Kulturgeschichte der weiblichen Bühnenkunst*, edited by Renate Möhrmann. Frankfurt am Main and Leipzig: Insel, 2000. 368–93.

———. "Top Ten Stars, 1923–1926." In *The BFI Companion to German Cinema*, edited by Thomas Elsaesser and Michael Wedel. London: BFI, 1999. 228.

———. "Warum kennen Filmhistoriker viele Weimarer Topstars nicht mehr?" *montage/av* 6, no. 2 (1997): 64–92.

Gems, Pam. *Marlene.* London: Oberon Books, 1996.

Gemünden, Gerd. *Filmemacher mit Akzent: Billy Wilder in Hollywood.* Vienna: Synema, 2006.

———. *Framed Visions: Popular Culture, Americanization, and the Contemporary German and Austrian Imagination.* Ann Arbor: Michigan University Press, 1998.

Gledhill, Christine, ed. *Home Is Where the Heart Is.* London: BFI, 1987.

———. Introduction to *Stardom: Industry of Desire*, edited by Gerd Albrecht. London: Routledge, 1991. xiii–xx.

Griffith, Richard, ed. *The Talkies: Articles and Illustrations from a Great Fan Magazine, 1928–1940.* New York: Dover, 1971.

Gubar, Susan. *Racechanges: White Skin, Black Face in American Culture.* New York: Oxford University Press, 1997.

Gunning, Tom. *The Films of Fritz Lang: Allegories of Vision and Modernity.* London: BFI, 2000.

Hall, Chapin. "Pictures and Players in Hollywood." *New York Times*, 25 September 1932, X3.

Hall, Mordaunt. Review of *Blonde Venus*. *New York Times*, 24 September 1932, A13.

Hamilton, Mary Beth. *When I'm Bad I'm Better: Mae West, Sex, and American Entertainment*. Berkeley: University of California Press, 1997.

Haralovich, Mary Beth. "Advertising Heterosexuality." *Screen* 23 no. 2 (July–August 1982): 50–60.

———. "Too Much Guilt Is Never Enough for Working Mothers: Joan Crawford, Mildred Pierce, and *Mommie Dearest*." *Velvet Light Trap* 29 (Spring 1992).

Harper, [Mr.]. "After Hours: The Kraut Woman." *Harper's Magazine* (May 1955): 82–83.

Haskell, Molly. *From Reverence to Rape: The Treatment of Women in the Movies*. New York: Holt, Rinehart, Winston, 1974.

Hemingway, Ernest. "A Tribute to Mamma from Papa Hemingway." *Life*, 18 August 1952, 92–93.

Hessel, Franz. *Marlene Dietrich: Ein Porträt*. 1931. Berlin: Arsenal, 1992.

Hickethier, Knut. "Vom Theaterstar zum Filmstar: Merkmale des Starwesens um die Wende vom 19. Zum 20. Jahrhundert." In *Der Star: Geschichte, Rezeption, Bedeutung*, edited by Werner Faulstich and Helmut Korte. Munich: Fink, 1997. 29–47.

Higham, Charles. *Marlene: The Life of Marlene Dietrich*. New York: Norton, 1977.

Higham, Charles, and Joel Greenberg. *The Celluloid Muse: Hollywood Directors Speak*. Chicago: Regnery, 1971.

Higson, Andrew, and Richard Maltby, eds. *"Film Europe" and "Film America": Cinema, Commerce and Cultural Exchange, 1920–1939*. Exeter, U.K.: University of Exeter Press, 1999. 325–96.

Hippler, Fritz. *Betrachtungen zum Filmschaffen*. Berlin: Hesse, 1942.

Hirsch, Marianne. *The Mother-Daughter Plot: Narrative, Psychoanalysis, Feminism*. Bloomington: Indiana University Press, 1989.

Hitler, Adolf. *Mein Kampf*. 1925–26. London: Hutchinson, 1976.

Holighaus, Alfred. "Die Kritiker jammern meckern höhnen." *Tip*, 21 June 2001.

———. "Normal ist, wenn es verrückt ist." In *Marlene: Der Film*, edited by Christiane Pfannenschmidt and Joseph Vilsmaier. Hamburg: Europa, 2000. 154–58.

Horak, Jan-Christopher. "Film History and Film Preservation: Reconstructing the Text of *The Joyless Street* (1925)." Revised and translated version of "Der Fall *Die freudlose Gasse*. eine Rekonstruktion im Münchner Filmmuseum." In *Frühe Filme, späte Folgen. Restaurierung, Rekonstruktion und Neupräsen-*

tation historische Kinematographie, edited by Ursula von Keitz. Marburg: Schüren, 1998.

Hogue, Peter. "True Blue: Josef von Sternberg's *The Blue Angel* and Others." *Film Comment* (1994): 38–43.

Huyssen, Andreas. *Present Pasts: Urban Palimpsests and the Politics of Memory*. Palo Alto, Calif.: Stanford University Press, 2003.

Irigaray, Luce. *The Sex Which Is Not One*. Translated by Catherine Porter. Ithaca: Cornell University Press, 1985.

Jacob, Lars, ed. *Apropos Marlene Dietrich*. Frankfurt am Main: Neue Kritik, 2000.

Jacobs, Lea. *The Wages of Sin: Censorship and the Fallen Woman Film, 1928–1942*. Berkeley: University of California Press, 1997.

Jacobs, Lea, and Richard deCordova. "Spectacle and Narrative Theory." *Quarterly Review of Film Studies* 7, no. 4 (Fall 1982): 293–308.

Jelinek, Elfriede. "Das zweite Gesicht." Obituary. *Die Zeit* (Overseas Edition), 22 May 1991, 19.

Jenkins, Stephen. "Lang: Fear and Desire." In *Fritz Lang: The Image and the Look*, edited by Stephen Jenkins. London: BFI, 1981. 38–124.

Johnston, Claire. "Women's Cinema as Counter-Cinema." In *Sexual Strategems: The World of Women in Film*, edited by Patricia Erens. New York: Horizon Press, 1979. 133–43.

Kalbus, Oskar. *Vom werden deutscher Filmkunst*, vol. 2, *Der Tonfilm*. Altona-Bahrenfeld: Cigaretten-Bilderdienst, 1935.

Kaplan, E. Ann. "Trauma and Aging: Marlene Dietrich, Melanie Klein, and Marguerite Duras." In *Figuring Age: Women, Bodies, Generations*, edited by Kathleen Woodward. Bloomington: Indiana University Press, 1999. 171–94.

———. *Women and Film: Both Sides of the Camera*. New York: Methuen, 1983.

———, ed. *Women in Film Noir*. London: BFI, 1980.

Karasek, Hellmuth. "Der ungeliebte Engel." *Der Spiegel* 25 (2000): 240–52.

Karcher, Carolyn L., ed. *A Lydia Maria Child Reader*. Durham, N.C.: Duke University Press, 1997.

Kauffmann, Stanley. "Long Twilights." *New Republic*, 8 December 1986, 28–29.

Der Kinematograph. "Ich küsse Ihre Hand, Madame." 19 January 1929, 3.

Knopp, Guido. *Hitlers Frauen und Marlene*. Munich: Bertelsmann, 2001.

Koch, Gertrud. "Between Two Worlds: Von Sternberg's *The Blue Angel* (1930)." In *German Film and Literature: Adaptations and Transformations*, edited by Eric Rentschler. New York: Methuen, 1986. 60–72.

———. "Exorcised: Marlene Dietrich and German Nationalism." In *Women and Film: A Sight and Sound Reader*, edited by Pam Cooke and Philip Dodd. Philadelphia, Pa.: Temple University Press, 1993. 10–15.

Koepnick, Lutz. *The Dark Mirror: German Cinema between Hitler and Hollywood*. Berkeley: University of California Press, 2002.

———. "Reframing the Past: Heritage Cinema and Holocaust in the 1990s." *New German Critique* 87 (2002): 47–82.

Korte, Helmut, and Stephen Lowry. *Der Filmstar*. Stuttgart: Metzler, 2000.

Körte, Peter. "Fernsehens Schwester." *Frankfurter Rundschau*, 8 March 2000.

Koszarski, Richard. *An Evening's Entertainment*. Berkeley: University of California Press, 1990.

Kracauer, Siegfried. *From Caligari to Hitler: A Psychological History of the German Film*. Princeton, N.J.: Princeton University Press, 1947.

———. *The Mass Ornament: Weimar Essays*. Edited and translated by Thomas Y. Levin. Cambridge, Mass.: Harvard University Press, 1995.

———. *Theory of Film: The Redemption of Physical Reality*. Princeton, N.J.: Princeton University Press, 1997.

Kreimeier, Klaus. *The Ufa Story: A History of Germany's Greatest Film Company 1918–1945*. Translated by Robert Kimber and Rita Kimber. New York: Hill and Wang, 1996.

Kreuzer, Hermann, and Manuela Runge. *Ein Koffer in Berlin: Marlene Dietrich. Geschichten von Politik und Liebe*. Berlin: Aufbau, 2001.

Kuhn, Annette. *Dreaming of Fred and Ginger: Cinema and Cultural Memory*. New York: New York University Press, 2002.

———. *Family Secrets: Acts of Memory and Imagination*. London: Verso, 1995.

———. *Women's Pictures: Feminism and Cinema*. London: Verso, 1994.

Kuzniar, Alice A. *The Queer German Cinema*. Stanford: Stanford University Press, 2000.

Lacan, Jacques. *Feminine Sexuality: Jacques Lacan and the "Ecole Freudienne."* Edited by Juliet Mitchell and Jacqueline Rose, translated by Jacqueline Rose. New York: Norton, 1982.

———. *The Four Fundamental Concepts of Psychoanalysis*. New York: Norton, 1977.

Leavitt, Sarah A. *From Catharine Beecher to Martha Stewart: A Cultural History of Domestic Advice*. Chapel Hill: University of North Carolina Press, 2002.

Leonard, Jim "Supersaw," and Janet E. Graebner. *Scratch My Back: A Pictorial History of the Musical Saw and How to Play It*. Santa Ana, Calif.: Kaleidoscope Press, 1989.

Lössl, Ulrich. "Katja Flint: Vom Kopf bis Fuss auf Marlene eingestellt." *Der Spiegel*, 6 March 2000, 230–32.

Loubier, Jean-Marc. *Jean Gabin—Marlene Dietrich: Un Rêve Brisé*. Paris: Acropole, 2002.

Madsen, Axel. *The Sewing Circle: Hollywood's Greatest Secret: Female Stars Who Loved Other Women*. New York: Birch Lane Press, 1995.

Maltby, Richard. "The Production Code and the Hays Office." In *Grand Design:*

Hollywood as a Modern Business Enterprise, 1930–1939, edited by Tino Balio. Berkeley: University of California Press, 1993. 37–72.

Maltby, Richard, and Ruth Vasey. "The International Language Problem: European Reactions to Hollywood's Conversion to Sound." In *Hollywood in Europe: Experiences of a Cultural Hegemony*, edited by David W. Ellwood and Rob Kroes. Amsterdam: VU University Press, 1994. 68–93.

Mann, William J. *Behind the Screen: How Gays and Lesbians Shaped Hollywood, 1910–1969*. New York: Viking, 2001.

Manvell, Roger, and Heinrich Fraenkel. *The German Cinema*. New York: Praeger, 1971.

Mao, Douglas, and Rebecca L. Walkowitz, eds. *Bad Modernisms*. Durham, N.C.: Duke University Press, 2006.

Mayne, Judith. *Framed: Lesbians, Feminists, and Media Culture*. Minneapolis: University of Minnesota Press, 2000.

———. "Lesbian Looks: Dorothy Arzner and Female Authorship." In *How Do I Look? Queer Film and Video*, edited by Bad Object-Choices. Seattle: Bay Press, 1991. 103–35.

———. "Marlene Dietrich, *The Blue Angel*, and Female Performance." In *Seduction and Theory: Readings of Gender, Representation, and Rhetoric*, edited by Dianne Hunter. Urbana: University of Illinois Press, 1989. 28–46.

McGilligan, Patrick. *Fritz Lang: The Nature of the Beast*. New York: St. Martin's Press, 1997.

McHugh, Kathleen Anne. *American Domesticity: From How-to Manual to Hollywood Melodrama*. New York: Oxford University Press, 1999.

McLean, Adrienne L. *Being Rita Hayworth: Labor, Identity, and Hollywood Stardom*. New Brunswick, N.J.: Rutgers University Press, 2004.

Miller, Nancy K. *Bequest and Betrayal: Memoirs of a Parent's Death*. New York: Oxford University Press.

Milne, Tom. *Rouben Mamoulian*. Bloomington: Indiana University Press, 1969.

Morris, Ruth. "Sinful Girls Lead in 1931." *Variety*, 29 December 1931, 5, 37.

Moseley, Rachel. *Growing Up with Audrey Hepburn*. Manchester, U.K.: University of Manchester Press, 2002.

Motion Pictures. "Garbo Likes Dietrich." 29 July 1933.

Mulvey, Laura. "Afterthoughts on 'Visual Pleasure and the Narrative Cinema' inspired by *Duel in the Sun*." In *Visual and Other Pleasures*. Bloomington: Indiana University Press, 1989. 29–38.

———. "Visual Pleasure and Narrative Cinema." *Screen* 16, no. 3 (1975): 6–18.

Naremore, James. *Acting in the Cinema*. Berkeley: University of California Press, 1988.

Nauder, Jean Jacques, and Peter Riva. *Marlene Dietrich: Photographs and Memories*. Berlin: Nicolai, 2001.

Neumann, Carl, Curt Belling, and Hans-Walther Betz. *Film-"Kunst," Film-Kohn, Film-Korruption*. Berlin: Scherping, 1937.

New York Times. "Eight Liners Due: Six Will Sail Today." 4 September 1930, 23.

———. "*Three Loves*." 9 September 1929, 35.

New Yorker. "Marlene's Joint." 29 November 1952, 33–34.

Nichols, Bill. *Ideology and the Image*. Bloomington: Indiana University Press, 1981.

———, ed. *Movies and Methods*. Vol. 2. University of California Press, 1985.

Noack, Frank. "Rückkehr der Zeitzeugen." *Filmforum* 30 (2001): 34–37.

Nowell-Smith, Geoffrey. Introduction to *Hollywood and Europe: Economics, Culture, National Identity 1945–95*, edited by Geoffrey Nowell-Smith and Steven Ricci. London: BFI, 1998. 1–3.

Nugent, Frank. "*Desire*." *New York Times*. 13 April 1936, 15.

O'Hara, John. "Appointment with O'Hara." *Collier's*, 10 March 1954, 6.

Paul, William. *Ernst Lubitsch's American Comedy*. New York: Columbia University Press, 1983.

Peterson, Jennifer. "The Competing Tunes of Johnny Guitar: Liberalism, Sexuality, Masquerade." *Cinema Journal* 35, no. 3 (1996): 3–18.

Petro, Patrice. *Aftershocks of the New: Feminism and Film History*. New Brunswick, N.J.: Rutgers University Press, 2002.

Pflaum, H. G. "Melodrama Drama." *Süddeutsche Zeitung*, 8 March 2000, 15.

Photoplay. "Is It Goodbye to Each Other as a Studio Team?" March 1933.

Place, Janey. "Women in Film Noir." In *Women in Film Noir*, edited by E. Ann Kaplan. London: BFI, 1980. 35–67.

Plazy, Gilles. *La véritable Marlène Dietrich*. Paris: Pygmalion, 2001.

Pomerance, Murray, ed. *Enfant Terrible! Jerry Lewis in American Film*. New York: New York University Press, 2002.

Pommer, Erich. "The International Talking Film." In *Universal Filmlexikon*, edited by Frank Arnau. Berlin: Universal Filmlexicon, 1932. 13–16.

Rentschler, Eric. "Springtime for Ufa." *Quarterly Review of Film and Video* 15, no. 2 (1994): 75–87.

Rilke, Rainer Maria. *Ausgewählte Gedichte*. Frankfurt am Main: Insel Verlag, 1932.

Rinke, Moritz. *Der graue Engel: Ein Monolog zu zweit*. Berlin: Fannei and Walz, 1995.

Riva, David, ed. *A Woman at War: Marlene Dietrich Remembered*. Detroit: Wayne State University Press, 2006.

Riva, Maria. *Marlene Dietrich*. New York: Alfred A. Knopf, 1992.

Rivière, Joan. "Womanliness as a Masquerade." 1929. Reprinted in *Formations of Fantasy*, edited by Victor Burgin, James Donald, and Cora Kaplan. London: Methuen, 1986. 35–44.

Robertson, Pamela. *Guilty Pleasures: Feminist Camp from Mae West to Madonna*. Durham, N.C.: Duke University Press, 1996.

Rosen, Marjorie. *Popcorn Venus*. New York: Avon Books, 1973.

Russo, Vito. *The Celluloid Closet: Homosexuality in the Movies*. New York: Harper and Row, 1981.

Salber, Linde. *Marlene Dietrich*. Reinbek: Rowohlt, 2001.

Sanders-Brahms, Helma. *Marlene und Jo: Recherche einer Leidenschaft*. Berlin: Aargon, 2000.

Sander, Roy. Review of *Black Market Marlene*. Quoted in "Letters from Camp Rehoboth," 6 April 2001, http://www.camprehoboth.com/issue04-06-01/marlene.htm.

Sargeant, Winthrop. "Dietrich and Her Magic Myth." *Life*, 18 August 1952, 86–93, 101–2.

Sarris, Andrew. "*The Blue Angel* and *Morocco*." In *Great Film Directors: A Critical Anthology*, edited by Leo Braudy and Morris Dickstein. New York: Oxford University Press, 1980. 697–702

———. *The Films of Josef von Sternberg*. New York: Doubleday, 1966.

Saunders, Thomas J. *Hollywood in Berlin: American Cinema and Weimar Germany*. Berkeley: University of California Press, 1994.

Schulte-Sasse, Linda. *Entertaining the Third Reich: Illusions of Wholeness in Nazi Cinema*. Durham, N.C.: Duke University Press, 1996.

Sedgwick, John. *Popular Filmgoing in 1930s Britain: A Choice of Pleasures*. Exeter, U.K.: University of Exeter Press, 2000.

Seiler, Paul. *Zarah Leander: Ein Kultbuch*. Reinbek: Rowohlt, 1985.

Sennwald, André. "*Devil Is a Woman*." *New York Times*, 4 May 1935, 17.

Shawell, Julia. "Garbo or Dietrich?" *Pictorial Review* (July 1933): 16–17, 65–66.

Shipman, David. "Marlene Dietrich." In *The Great Movie Stars: The Golden Years 1*. Boston: Little, Brown, 1970. 166–73.

Skaerved, Malene Sheppard. *Dietrich*. London: Haus Publishing, 2003.

Slane, Andrea. *A Not So Foreign Affair: Fascism, Sexuality, and the Cultural Rhetoric of American Democracy*. Durham, N.C.: Duke University Press, 2001.

Smith, Paul. *Clint Eastwood: A Cultural Production*. Minneapolis: University of Minnesota Press, 1993.

Snead, James. *White Screens, Black Images: Hollywood from the Dark Side*. New York: Routledge, 1994.

Sobchack, Vivian, ed. *Meta-Morphing: Visual Transformation and the Culture of Quick-Change*. Minneapolis: University of Minnesota Press, 2000.

Spieker, Markus. *Hollywood unterm Hakenkreuz: Der amerikanische Spielfilm im Dritten Reich*. Trier: Wissenschaftlicher Verlag, 1999.

Spoto, Donald. *Blue Angel: The Life of Marlene Dietrich*. New York: Doubleday, 1992.

Stacey, Jackie. "Feminine Fascinations: Forms of Identification in Star-Audience Relations." In *Stardom: Industry of Desire*, edited by Christine Gledhill. London: Routledge, 1991. 141–61.

———. *Star Gazing*. London: Routledge, 1994.

Staiger, Janet. *Perverse Spectators: The Practices of Film Reception*. New York: New York University Press, 2000.

Startt, James D., and William David Sloan. *Historical Methods in Mass Communication*. Hillsdale, N.J.: Lawrence Erlbaum Associates, 1989.

Steinberg, Cobbett. *Reel Facts: The New Movie Book of Records*. New York: Vintage, 1978.

Stern, Guy. *Marlene Dietrich: My Chance Encounters with a Movie Star*. Max Kade Occasional Papers in German-American Studies 8. Cincinnati, Ohio: University of Cincinnati, 2002.

Studlar, Gaylyn. *In the Realm of Pleasure: Von Sternberg, Dietrich, and the Masochistic Aesthetic*. Urbana: University of Illinois Press, 1988.

———. "Masochism, Masquerade, and the Erotic Metamorphoses of Marlene Dietrich." In *Fabrications: Costume and the Female Body*, edited by Jane Gaines and Charlotte Herzog. New York: Routledge, 1990. 229–49.

Süddeutsche Zeitung. "Melodrama Drama." 8 March 2000.

Sudendorf, Werner. *Marlene Dietrich*. Munich: Deutscher Taschenbuch Verlag, 2001.

———. "Marlene Dietrich from Head to Toe." In *Filmmuseum Berlin*, edited by Wolfgang Jacobsen, Hans Helmut Prinzler, and Werner Sudendorf. Berlin: Nicolai, 2000. 131–68.

Tatar, Maria. *Lustmord: Sexual Murders in Weimar Germany*. Princeton, N.J.: Princeton University Press, 1995.

Thomson, David. *The New Biographical Dictionary of Film*. New York: Morrow, 2002.

Time. "*Desire*." 9 March 1936, 47.

———. "Still Champion." 21 January 1952, 40.

Tolischus, Otto. "Dietrich—How She Happened." *Photoplay Magazine*, 19 April 1931, 28–29.

Trask, C. Hooper. "German Film News." *New York Times*, 30 November 1930, X6.

———. "Woman Longed For." *Variety*, 22 May 1929, 24.

Truffaut, François. "Nicholas Ray: Johnny Guitar." In *The Films in My Life*. New York: Simon and Schuster, 1978. 141–43.

———. "A Wonderful Certainty." In *Cahiers du Cinema, the 1950s*, edited by Jim Hillier. Cambridge, Mass.: Harvard University Press, 1985. 101–8.

Tyler, Parker. *Screening the Sexes: Homosexuality and the Movies*. New York: Henry Holt, 1972.

Vanity Fair. "Both Members of the Same Club." March 1931.

Variety. "Dietrich Pictures Bows ahead of New York." 13 March 1936.

———. "Garbo Checking Marlene's Disks." December 3, 1930, 3.

———. "German Girl 'Discovered' Given Par Contract." 12 March 1930, 2.

———. "*Morocco*." 19 November 1930, 21.

Vernissage 2 (2001). Special issue on Marlene Dietrich. Guest editor Ulrike Wiebrecht.

Völkischer Beobachter. Review of *The Scarlet Empress*. 16–17 September 1934.

von Cziffra, Géza. *Kauf dir einen bunten Luftballon*. Bergisch-Gladbach: Gustav Lübbe, 1978.

von Sternberg, Josef. *Fun in a Chinese Laundry*. New York: Collier, 1973.

Walters, Suzanna Danuta. *Material Girls: Making Sense of Feminist Cultural Theory*. Berkeley: University of California Press, 1995.

Weinberg, Herman. *Josef von Sternberg*. New York: E. P. Dutton, 1967.

Weiss, Andrea. "A Queer Feeling When I Look at You: Hollywood Stars and Lesbian Spectatorship in the 1930s." In *Stardom: Industry and Desire*, edited by Christine Gledhill. London: Routledge, 1991. 283–99.

———. *Vampires and Violets: Lesbians in Film*. New York: Penguin Books, 1993.

Welch, David. *The Third Reich: Politics and Propaganda*. London: Routledge, 1993.

Weth, Georg A. *"Ick will wat Feinet": Das Marlene Dietrich Kochbuch*. Berlin: Rüten and Loenning, 2001.

Wetzig-Zalkind, Birgit. *Marlene Dietrich in Berlin: Wege und Orte*. Berlin: Edition Gauglitz, 2005.

Wexman, Virginia Wright. *Creating the Couple: Love, Marriage and Hollywood Performance*. Princeton, N.J.: Princeton University Press, 1993.

White, Patricia. "Black and White: Mercedes d'Acosta's Glorious Enthusiasm." *Camera Obscura* 45 (2001): 227–65.

———. *Uninvited: Classical Hollywood Cinema and Lesbian Representability*. Bloomington: Indiana University Press, 1999.

Wiebrecht, Ulrike. *Blauer Engel aus Berlin: Marlene Dietrich*. Berlin: be.bra, 2001.

Williams, Linda. "Film Bodies: Gender, Genre, and Excess." *Film Quarterly* 44, no. 4 (1991): 2–13.

Winkler-Mayerhöfer, Andrea. *Starkult als Propagandamittel*. Munich: Ölschläger, 1992.

Witte, Karsten. *Lachende Erben, Toller Tag: Filmkomödie im Dritten Reich*. Berlin: Vorwerk 8, 1995.

———. "Visual Pleasure Inhibited: Aspect of the German Revue Film." *New German Critique* 24–25 (1981–82): 238–63.

Wollen, Peter. "Brooks and the Bob." *Sight and Sound* (February 1994): 22–25.

———. "Modern Times: Cinema/Americanism/The Robot." In *Raiding the Ice-*

box: Reflections on Twentieth-Century Culture. Bloomington: Indiana University Press, 1993.

Wood, Ean. *Dietrich: A Biography*. London: Sanctuary, 2002.

Wood, Robin. "*Rancho Notorious*: A Noir Western in Colour." *CineAction!* (Summer 1988): 83–93.

———. "Venus de Marlene." *Film Comment* 14 (1978): 58–63.

Woodward, Kathleen M. *Aging and Its Discontents*. Bloomington: Indiana University Press, 1991.

Wortig, Kurt. *Der Film in der deutschen Tageszeitung*. Frankfurt am Main: Diesterweg, 1940.

Zweig, Stefan. "The Monotonization of the World." 1925. In *The Weimar Republic Sourcebook*, edited by Anton Kaes, Martin Jay, and Edward Dimendberg; translated by Don Reneau. Berkeley: University of California Press, 1994. 397–400.

CONTRIBUTORS

NORA M. ALTER teaches German, film, and media studies at the University of Florida. She is author of *Vietnam Protest Theatre: The Television War on Stage* (1996), *Projecting History: Non-Fiction German Film* (2002), *Chris Marker* (forthcoming 2006) and is coeditor with Lutz Koenick of *Sound Matters: Essays on the Acoustics of Modern German Culture* (2004). She has contributed essays to collections on film, cultural studies, and visual studies. She is currently completing a book on the international essay film.

STEVEN BACH, who studied with Josef von Sternberg, was the head of Worldwide Production for United Artists. He is the author of *Final Cut* (1985), *Dazzler: The Life and Times of Moss Hart* (Knopf), and *Marlene Dietrich: Life and Legend* (Da Capo), which has been translated into many languages. He teaches at Bennington College and in the Film Division of Columbia University. His biography of Leni Riefenstahl is forthcoming from Knopf.

ELISABETH BRONFEN teaches at the University of Zurich. She is the author of *Nur über ihre Leiche: Tod, Weiblichkeit and Ästhetik* (1994), *Death and Representation* (1993), *Home in Hollywood: The Imaginary Geography of Cinema* (2004), as well as numerous articles on gender studies, psychoanalysis, and film and cultural studies.

ERICA CARTER teaches German studies at the University of Warwick. Her books as author and editor include *How German is She?: Postwar West German Reconstruction and the Consuming Woman* (1996), *The German Cinema Book* (2002), *Cultural Remix: Theories of Politics and the Popular* (1995), *and Dietrich's Ghosts* (2005).

MARY R. DESJARDINS is an associate professor of film and television studies at Dartmouth College. She has written widely on stardom, including the essay "Meeting Two Queens," an article about *Confidential* magazine, and an article on Hedda Hopper's role in the star system of postwar Hollywood. She is currently completing a book entitled *Recycled Stars: Hollywood Film Stardom in the Age of Television and Video* (forthcoming from Duke University Press).

JOSEPH GARNCARZ is a privatdozent in film studies at the University of Cologne in Germany. He is the author of *Filmfassungen* (1992) and numerous essays on European film history and is currently working on two books: *On the Origins of Cinema: Variety Theaters and Traveling Shows in Central Europe 1895–1924*, and *German Cinema: A Comprehensive History*.

GERD GEMÜNDEN is the Ted and Helen Geisel Third Century Professor at Dartmouth College. He is the author of *Framed Visions: Popular Culture, Americanization, and the Contemporary German and Austrian Imagination* (1998), *Filmemacher mit Akzent: Billy Wilder in Hollywood* (2006), and coeditor of volumes on Wim Wenders, R. W. Fassbinder, and Douglas Sirk. He is currently completing a book on German exiles in Hollywood.

MARY BETH HARALOVICH teaches film and television history at the University of Arizona, Tucson. She has published on television portrayals of suburban family life (*Magnum, P.I.*) and international spies (*Spy*). She is editor of *Television, History, and American Culture: Feminist Critical Essays* (1999) and a contributor to *Flow*, an on-line journal. The essay in this volume is part of her book-in-progress on local film promotion in the 1930s.

AMELIE HASTIE teaches courses on film and television theory and history at the University of California–Santa Cruz. She has published *Cupboards of Curiosity: Women, Recollection, and Film History* (2006), as well as work in *Afterimage*, *Camera Obscura*, *Cinema Journal*, and *Postscript*, and in anthologies on contemporary television.

LUTZ KOEPNICK teaches German, film, and media studies at Washington University in St. Louis. His books as author include *The Dark Mirror: German Cinema between Hitler and Hollywood* (2002) and *Walter Benjamin and the Aesthetics of Power* (1999). He is coeditor of *Sound Matters: Essays on the Acoustics of German Culture* (2004) and *Caught by Politics: German Exiles and American Visual Culture* (forthcoming).

ALICE A. KUZNIAR teaches German and comparative literature at the University of North Carolina, Chapel Hill. Her books as author and editor include *Delayed Endings: Nonclosure in Novalis and Hoelderlin* (1997), *Outing Goethe and His Age* (1996), *The Queer German Cinema* (2000), and *Melancholia's Dog* (2006). In the area of cinema studies, she has also published on David Lynch and Wim Wenders.

AMY LAWRENCE teaches film and television studies at Dartmouth College. She is the author of *Echo and Narcissus: Women's Voices in Classical Hollywood Cinema* (1991) and *The Films of Peter Greenaway* (1997). She has also written on animation, star issues, and nineteenth-century photography.

JUDITH MAYNE teaches French and women's studies at Ohio State University. She is the author of several books in film studies, including most recently, *Claire Denis* (2005) and *Framed: Lesbians, Feminists, and Media Culture* (2000), which includes an essay on Marlene Dietrich and *The Blue Angel*. She has also written on Fassbinder, Murnau, and other aspects of German cinema.

PATRICE PETRO teaches English and film studies at the University of Wisconsin-Milwaukee, where she is also director of the Center for International Education. She is the author of *Joyless Streets: Women and Melodramatic Representation in Weimar Germany* (1989) and *Aftershocks of the New: Feminism and Film History* (2002), and is coeditor of *Truth Claims: Representation and Human Rights* (2002), *Global Cities: Cinema Architecture and Urbanism in a Digital Age* (2003), and *Global Currents: Media and Technology Now* (2004).

ERIC RENTSCHLER is the Arthur Kingsley Porter Professor of Germanic Languages and Literatures at Harvard University, where he chairs the German Department. He also teaches in the Department of Visual and Environmental Studies and is a member of the Committee on Literature. His books include *West German Film in the Course of Time* (1984) and *The Ministry of Illusion* (1996). He is currently completing two books, *Courses in Time: Film in the Federal Republic of German, 1949–1989* and *The Continuing Allure of Nazi Attractions*.

GAYLYN STUDLAR is Rudolf Arnheim Collegiate Professor of Film Studies at the University of Michigan, Ann Arbor, where she has directed the Program in Film and Video Studies since 1995. She is the author or coeditor of six books, including *In the Realm of Pleasure: Von Sternberg, Dietrich, and the Masochistic Aesthetic* (1988).

WERNER SUDENDORF is the head curator of the Marlene Dietrich Collection at the Filmmuseum Berlin. A contributor to numerous publications on German film history, he has been an authority on Dietrich for many years. He is editor of *Marlene Dietrich: Dokumente, Essays, Filme* (2 vols., 1977) and author of the biography *Marlene Dietrich* (2001). He maintains a website at www.soundslikemarlene.de.

MARK WILLIAMS teaches in the Department of Film and Television Studies at Dartmouth College, which he also chaired from 2000 to 2006. Author of *Remote Possibilities* (forthcoming from Duke University Press), he has published widely on U.S. film and television history. He recently edited an issue of *Quarterly Review of Film and Video* on nonnetwork and regional television histories.

INDEX

GERD GEMÜNDEN
is the Ted and Helen Geisel Third Century Professor at Dartmouth College.

MARY R. DESJARDINS
is an associate professor of film and television studies at Dartmouth College.

Library of Congress Cataloging-in-Publication Data
Dietrich icon / edited by Gerd Gemünden and Mary R. Desjardins.
p. cm.
Includes bibliographical references and index.
ISBN-13: 978-0-8223-3806-2 (cloth : alk. paper)
ISBN-13: 978-0-8223-3819-2 (pbk. : alk. paper)
1. Dietrich, Marlene. I. Gemünden, Gerd
II. Desjardins, Mary R.
PN2658.D5D55 2007
791.4302'8092—dc22 [B] 2006027827